Social Mobility, Social Inequality, and the Role of Higher Education

Studies in Critical Social Sciences Book Series

Haymarket Books is proud to be working with Brill Academic Publishers (www.brill.nl) to republish the *Studies in Critical Social Sciences* book series in paperback editions. This peer-reviewed book series offers insights into our current reality by exploring the content and consequences of power relationships under capitalism, and by considering the spaces of opposition and resistance to these changes that have been defining our new age. Our full catalog of *SCSS* volumes can be viewed at https://www.haymarketbooks.org/series_collections/4-studies-in-critical-social-sciences.

Series Editor
David Fasenfest (York University, Canada)

Editorial Board
Eduardo Bonilla-Silva (Duke University)
Chris Chase-Dunn (University of California–Riverside)
William Carroll (University of Victoria)
Raewyn Connell (University of Sydney)
Kimberlé W. Crenshaw (University of California–LA and Columbia University)
Heidi Gottfried (Wayne State University)
Alfredo Saad-Filho (King's College London)
Chizuko Ueno (University of Tokyo)
Sylvia Walby (Lancaster University)
Raju Das (York University)

Social Mobility, Social Inequality, and the Role of Higher Education

Edited by
Elena G. Popkova, Bruno S. Sergi
and Konstantin V. Vodenko

Haymarket Books
Chicago, IL

First published in 2023 by Brill Academic Publishers, The Netherlands
© 2023 Koninklijke Brill NV, Leiden, The Netherlands

Published in paperback in 2024 by
Haymarket Books
P.O. Box 180165
Chicago, IL 60618
773-583-7884
www.haymarketbooks.org

ISBN: 979-8-88890-238-7

Distributed to the trade in the US through Consortium Book Sales and Distribution (www.cbsd.com) and internationally through Ingram Publisher Services International (www.ingramcontent.com).

This book was published with the generous support of Lannan Foundation, Wallace Action Fund, and the Marguerite Casey Foundation.

Special discounts are available for bulk purchases by organizations and institutions. Please call 773-583-7884 or email info@haymarketbooks.org for more information.

Cover design by Jamie Kerry and Ragina Johnson.

Printed in the United States.

Library of Congress Cataloging-in-Publication data is available.

Contents

List of Tables, Figures, Charts and Graphs XI
Notes on Contributors XVI

Introduction
Role of Higher Education in Enhancing Social Mobility and Reducing Social Inequality 1
   Elena G. Popkova, Bruno S. Sergi and Konstantin V. Vodenko

PART 1
Cultural Openness of the Knowledge Society and Its Contribution to Reducing Social Inequality

1 Benefits of Distance Education for Overcoming Cultural Disparities, Opening Universities to Persons with Disabilities, and Ensuring Inclusive Higher Education 7
   Elena G. Popkova

2 Forming Multicultural Competency of Students in the Context of Convergence Culture 20
   Elena V. Volkova, Olga Y. Khatsrinova, Rustem I. Biktashev and Mostafa M. Keruly

3 Visual Culture and Ways of Its Development among Students in the System of Higher Education 32
   Natalia V. Vinogradova, Claudio Tomazzoli, Sergey V. Bykov, Galina M. Zemlyakova and Igor G. Panov

4 Forms of Manifestation of Cultural Differences in Higher Education and Their Impact on the Inclusiveness of Universities 46
   Lyudmila A. Shvachkina, Valentina I. Rodionova, Zarema Y. Emtyl and Asker R. Kasparov

5 Cultural Differences as Barriers to Improving Positions in the International Rankings of Universities from Less Developed Countries 62
   Irina V. Lipchanskaya, Angela A. Bezrukova, Saida G. Dzybova and Ibragim K. Shaov

6   Conceptual Fundamentals and Indicators of Knowledge Economy   75
    *Nataliya A. Tovma, Igor Fernández-Plazaola, Liudmila V. Popova,
    Rasulya R. Aetdinova and Ashirgul K. Seidildayeva*

7   Cultivating a Novel Culture for Higher Education
    Successes from a Social Learning Service Program   87
    Pennee Narot and Narong Kiettikunwong

PART 2
Inclusive Higher Education in Support of Social Mobility

8   Assessment of the Level of Cultural Differences and Openness to People with Disabilities and the Impact of These Characteristics on the Inclusiveness of Russian Universities   107
    Ludmila L. Shtofer, Nafiset Z. Daurova, Inna N. Gaidareva and Zara A. Mamisheva

9   The Value of Higher Education Inclusiveness for Sustainable and Innovative Development of the Knowledge Economy   120
    Larisa V. Popova, Tatiana A. Dugina, Svetlana Yu. Shaldohina and Elena A. Nemkina

10 The Concept of Inclusive Higher Education and Approach to Its Implementation Based on Openness to Persons with Disabilities   144
    Svetlana A. Popova, Elena Kzh. Pilivanova, Evgeny A. Likholetov and Galina N. Zvereva

11 Best Practices for Inclusiveness by Top Universities and Their Openness to Persons with Disabilities in the More Developed Countries   169
    Elena S. Akopova, Daria O. Zabaznova, Irina A. Tarasova and Marietta A. Bolokova

12 Progressive Practices for Achieving Inclusiveness and Openness for People with Disabilities by Top Universities in Less Developed Countries   180
    Aminat Sh. Khuazheva, Elena A. Buller, Larisa T. Tlekhurai-Berzegova and Svetlana K. Chinazirova

13 Inclusiveness of Universities as the Basis for Achieving Strategic Academic Leadership in Russia   191
   Konstantin V. Vodenko, Margarita A. Meretukova, Irina B. Khakonova and Marina G. Shadzhe

14 Differences in Approaches to Achieving Inclusiveness between Leading and Regional Universities in Russia
   Legal Aspects   205
   Olesya P. Kazachenok, Aziza B. Karbekova, Zuriet A. Zhade and Azamat M. Shadzhe

15 Enroute towards Inclusive Technical and Vocational Education and Training Colleges
   South African Case   218
   Selina Kungwane and Anneline Korf-Taljaard

PART 3
Digital Technology in Higher Education and Its Importance for Increasing Social Mobility

16 Key Factors to Increase Attractiveness of Digital Socio-oriented Clusters in Pandemic Conditions
   Views of Generation Z Students   237
   Mikhail V. Vinichenko, Marina V. Rybakova, Oksana L. Chulanova, Sergey A. Barkov and Sergey A. Makushkin

17 Education Platforms in Pandemic Conditions   248
   Liliya V. Samosudova, Nadezhda V. Eremkina, Irina I. Kondrashkina and Sergey M. Imyarekov

18 Using VR and AR Technologies for the Sustainable Social Development of Intercultural and Inter-language Exchange in the Area of Education in the Conditions of International Cooperation   258
   Julia Yu. Rybasova, Flera L. Mazitova, Asiya G. Nizamieva, Zarema M. Zaripova and Elmira N. Uteeva

19 Digitalization of Education
   Student Assessments and Factors of Its Formation in a Pandemic   266
   Elena V. Frolova, Olga V. Rogach and Natalia V. Medvedeva

20 Education for Sustainable Development in Modern Conditions of
    Digitalization   281
    *Elvira K. Samerkhanova, Olga V. Smyshliaeva, Irina V. Panova, Lyudmila
    N. Bahtiyarova and Alexander V. Ponachugin*

PART 4
Educational Management to Reduce Social Inequality

21 Progressive School as an Implementation of Current Trends in the
    Development of Education   295
    *Zhanna Y. Bakaeva, Ella N. Shchegoleva, Galina V. Kalinina, Ljudmila
    Yu. Alexandrova and Galina M. Lokhonova*

22 Inclusiveness and Competitiveness vs. Quality and Efficiency of
    Universities
    Conflicts of Interest and Common Ground   305
    *Svetlana A. Lyausheva, Bella Kh. Khamukova, Zarema Kh. Kurmalieva
    and Fatima K. Tuguz*

23 The Dilemma of Choice in the Direction of Development of the
    National Education System
    An Educated or Professionally Trained Person   318
    *Eugenia A. Neretina, Natalya S. Komleva, Evgeniy A. Leonenko and
    Elena G. Shcherbakova*

24 Trends in the Development of the State Educational Standard of Higher
    Professional Education of the Kyrgyz Republic   329
    Elvira E. Samatova, Baktyyar M. Asanov and Diloram I. Khasanova

25 Professional Training of a Contemporary Teacher of Mathematics
    *Designing an Educational Program for a Bachelor's Degree in the
    Direction of "Physics and Mathematics Education" on a Modular-
    Competency Basis*   349
    Anarkan Dj. Attokurova

26 Russian Education in the Pandemic
    Challenges and Responses   359
    Anna A. Arinushkina, Olga A. Mashkina and Valentina V. Kuznetsova

27 Socio-economic Development of Educational Activities in the Context of the Modernization of Lifelong Education   378
Zhanna V. Smirnova, Igor E. Mizikovsky, Michael N. Pavlenkov, Elena V. Romanovskaya and Lyubov I. Kutepova

Conclusion

Worsening of Social Inequalities in the Fifth Industrial Revolution
The New Role of Higher Education in Social Mobility   387
  Elena G. Popkova, Bruno S. Sergi and Konstantin V. Vodenko

Index   389

Tables, Figures, Charts and Graphs

Tables

1.1	Statistics on distance learning and openness of universities to persons with disabilities	10
1.2	Success of leading universities in overcoming cultural differences, gender neutrality, and overall inclusiveness in higher education in 2022	11
1.3	Comparative analysis of the achievement of inclusiveness in traditional and distance learning in universities	14
4.1	Cultural differences in higher education and the inclusiveness of universities in the USA in 2021	51
4.2	Forms of cultural differences in higher education and inclusiveness of Russian universities in 2021	52
5.1	The position of the top 10 universities of developing countries in the QS international University ranking in 2022	66
6.1	Distinguished features of the economy of knowledge from the traditional economy	77
6.2	Knowledge index for 2021 by countries	78
6.3	Economics index for 2021 by countries	79
6.4	Index of human development by countries for 2021	79
6.5	Country rankings according to education index for 2021	80
6.6	Expenditures on R&D (% of GDP) for 2021	80
6.7	Country rating by the level of health expenditures in 2021	81
6.8	Rating countries by level of innovation for 2021	81
6.9	Rankings on the level of digitization in 2021 by countries	82
6.10	Rankings on the level of globalization in 2021 by countries	83
6.11	Rating of the level of creativity in 2021 by countries	84
8.1	Cultural differences and inclusiveness of Russian universities that are most open to persons with disabilities in 2022	111
9.1	Research strategy	126
9.2	Statistics and inclusiveness of higher education in low-10 countries by the level of its development in 2021	128
9.3	Statistics of sustainable and innovative development of the knowledge economy in low-10 countries by the level of the development of higher education in 2021	129
9.4	Statistics on the knowledge economy and the inclusiveness of higher education in the top-10 countries by its development in 2021	130

9.5 Regression statistics on the dependence of the knowledge economy on the inclusiveness of higher education in countries with the moderate development of the knowledge economy   132

9.6 Regression statistics of the dependence of the knowledge economy on the inclusiveness of higher education in countries with a high level of its development   134

9.7 Contribution of the research results to the increase in scientific knowledge   138

10.1 Research strategy   150

10.2 Tertiary educational attainment (age group 30–34), by disability status, by country, in %   152

10.3 Factors of inclusiveness in higher education in 2021, score 0–100   153

10.4 Regression statistics on the dependence of the openness of higher education for people with a disability experiencing difficulties in basic activities on inclusiveness factors   154

10.5 Regression statistics on the dependence of the openness of higher education for persons with disabilities experiencing no difficulty in basic activities on inclusiveness factors   155

10.6 Regression statistics on the dependence of the openness of higher education for people with a work disability caused by a LHPAD on inclusiveness factors   156

10.7 Regression statistics on the dependence of the openness of higher education to persons with no work limitations caused by a LHPAD on inclusiveness factors   158

10.8 Contribution of the research results to the increase in scientific knowledge   162

11.1 Dare index and the position in THE rating in the top ten countries for digital accessibility implementation and outcomes for persons with disabilities   172

11.2 Best practices for inclusion and openness to persons with disabilities by top universities from developed countries   174

12.1 Distance learning, social inclusiveness and the position of the top universities from developing countries in the THE rankings in 2020 (by the end of 2019)-2021 (by the end of 2020), points 1–100   184

12.2 Contribution of distance learning to inclusiveness for people with disabilities top universities in developing countries   185

13.1 The position of the top 10 Russian universities in the Times Higher Education ranking in 2022   196

13.2 Regression analysis of the dependence of rank on the indicators of internationalization of Russian universities in 2022   199

13.3 Regression analysis of the dependence of the overall score on the indicators of internationalization of Russian universities in 2022   200
14.1 Indicators of inclusiveness of Russia's leading and regional universities in 2022   209
16.1 Socio-demographic characteristics of respondents, %   240
19.1 Correlation analysis of the impact of assessments of the level of digital literacy of students on the perception of digitalization processes, person   272
19.2 Correlation analysis of answers to the questions "Assess the level of your digital literacy" and "Do you agree with the statement that the use of digital technologies causes overload of students?", person   274
22.1 Quality, efficiency, and inclusion of the top three Russian universities from QS Rankings 2013–2021: detailed statistics   310
22.2 Quality, efficiency, inclusiveness, and competitiveness of the top three Russian universities from the QS rankings in 2013–2021: summary statistics   311
22.3 Regression statistics on the dependence of the quality of educational activity on the inclusiveness of the top three Russian universities   312
22.4 Regression statistics on the dependence of the quality of scientific activity on the inclusiveness of the top three Russian universities   313
22.5 Regression statistics on the dependence of efficiency on the inclusiveness of the top three Russian universities   314
22.6 Regression statistics of the dependence of inclusiveness on the quality and efficiency of the top three Russian universities   315
23.1 Ideas about education and an educated person   320
24.1 Data on the conducted sociological survey among full-time students in the 1st-4th years at the Department of "Business and Management" of the Osh State University conducted on January 3, 2022   334
25.1 Learning outcomes (LO) of educational program (EP) training of bachelors of Physics and Mathematics education, training profile "Mathematics"   354

Figures

6.1 Model of economic development of knowledge in the Republic of Kazakhstan   85
7.1 Key features of a Teal organization   88
7.2 The proposed use of an SLSP to give students skills useful to new organizations   94
7.3 Development model for implementation for the SLSP to create diversity experiences   100

10.1	An approach to implementing the concept of inclusive higher education based on openness to persons with disabilities	159
14.1	The institutional model of inclusiveness of Universities in Russia	212
23.1	Characteristics of an educated and professionally trained person	321

Charts

1.1	The average level of inclusiveness in higher education and leading universities and its correlation with the level of development of distance learning	12
3.1	The level of visual culture. Ascertaining stage, 2020	38
3.2	The level of visual culture. Developmental stage, 2021	41
5.1	Factor analysis and analysis of the variation of competitiveness of top universities from developing countries in 2022	68
5.2	Scenario for improving the positions of universities from developing countries in international rankings based on the management of cultural differences (internationalization)	70
8.1	Overall level of inclusiveness and its connection with openness and cultural differences of Russian universities in 2022	113
8.2	Dynamics of social inclusion in Russia in 2013–2020	114
9.1	The average level of development of the knowledge economy of inclusiveness of higher education in the countries with moderate levels of its development in 2021	131
9.2	The average level of development of the "knowledge economy" of inclusiveness of higher education in the countries with high levels of its development in 2021	133
9.3	Prospects for optimizing the manifestations of inclusiveness of higher education, their ratio and increase compared to 2021 in countries with the moderate development of higher education	135
9.4	Benefits of optimizing the manifestations of inclusiveness of higher education for the knowledge economy in countries with the moderate development of higher education	136
9.5	The benefits of optimizing the manifestations of inclusiveness of higher education for the knowledge economy in countries with a high level of the development of higher education	137
10.1	Benchmark values of the inclusiveness factors in both scenarios compared to the baseline values of these indicators	159
10.2	The benefits of optimization to increase inclusiveness in higher education for people with disabilities in the first scenario	160

10.3   The benefits of optimization to increase inclusiveness in higher education for people with disabilities in the second scenario   160
13.1   The place of internalization in the system of global competitiveness of Russian universities in 2022   198
13.2   Scenario for improving the positions of Russian universities in international rankings based on the management of cultural differences (internationalization)   201
14.1   Relation of inclusiveness indicators to the competitiveness of Russian universities in 2022   211
16.1   Options for answering the question: "What attracts you the most in digital socially-oriented cluster?"   242
19.1   Distribution of answers to the question: "What do you think the digitalization of education in general is …?" %   272
24.1   Answers to the question: "Are you satisfied with the quality of education at the Department of "Business and Management" at the Osh State University?"   343

Graphs

4.1   Regression curve of the dependence of the inclusiveness of higher education on internal cultural barriers to higher education in the USA in 2021   54
4.2   Regression curve of the relationship between inclusiveness of higher education and cultural neutrality of the educational process in the USA in 2021   54
4.3   Regression curve of the dependence of inclusiveness of higher education on the cultural openness of the organizational and managerial process in universities in the USA in 2021   55
4.4   Regression curve of the dependence of inclusiveness of higher education on the cultural neutrality of the educational process in Russia in 2021   56
4.5   Regression curve of the dependence of inclusiveness of higher education on cultural openness of organizational and managerial process in universities in Russia in 2021   56

Notes on Contributors

Rasulya R. Aetdinova
Ph.D of Pedagogical Sciences, Associated Professor, Deputy Director for Science of the Higher School of Economics and Law of the Kazan Federal University, Visiting Professor of University of Trento (Italy). Research interests: risks in education, education management. Activities: training program "Valuation of Prior learning (VPL), Portfolio and Personalized Learning" at the European Center for VPL (Netherlands); project coordinator of the working group of TEMPUS and ERASMUS projects (2013–2021); coordinated and scheduled the work with foreign and Russian practitioners and researchers of education. Wrote 72 publications and scientific and academic articles (Education).

Elena S. Akopova
Professor of Rostov State University of Economics, the author of more than 180 publications. Her research interests include sustainable development, logistics systems, a corporate culture of an organization, the era of digitalization, international business, marketing, and transport and logistics infrastructure. Special attention in scientific work is paid to the Eurasian economic integration based on the EAEU. The author has published several textbooks on foreign economic activity.

Ljudmila Yu. Alexandrova
Candidate of Pedagogical Sciences, Associate Professor, Head of the Department of Economics and Management, Cheboksary Institute (branch) of the Moscow University for the Humanities and Economics, Cheboksary, 428038, RF. Author of more than 130 scientific and educational works, including 3 monographs. Directions of research: pedagogical diagnostics at school and university, scientific potential of higher education; business communications in the information and educational environment of the educational institution; theory and practice of lecturing skills; socio-pedagogical victimology; competitiveness of enterprises; marketing analysis of the enterprise; logistic approach to increase the economic sustainability of the enterprise; ensuring economic security in logistics; development of the marketing logistics system.

Anna A. Arinushkina
Doctor of Pedagogical Sciences, Chief Researcher at the Center for Content and Technology of Education, Institute of Education Management of the Russian Academy of Education, Editor-in-Chief of the journal "Pedagogy

and Education" (included in VAK). She is the author of 85 publications in VAK, Scopus, and WoS. She participated in the fulfillment of the state task No. 073-00089-19-01 "Optimization of the Hot-Food System in Educational Organizations Implementing General Education Programs (Regional Aspects, Best Practices)" the state task for the "Program of Fundamental Scientific Research of the State Academies of Sciences for 2013–2020" (in the part of RAO) (approved by the Decree of the Government of the Russian Federation of December 3, 2012 No. 2237-r) on the theme: "Development of the Informatization of Education in the Context information security of the person" (state registration No. 14.07.00.20.01.04). Her scientific interests include management in general education system, underfilled educational organizations, quality of education, geoinformation systems in education, and big data in general education system in making management decisions.

Baktyyar M. Asanov
Candidate of Economic Science, Associate professor of the Economics and Enterprise Management Department of the Osh State University (Kyrgyzstan). His scientific interests include economy, investment, market economy, education. Baktyyar M. Asanov conducts scientific and educational activities aimed at teaching bachelor students in the direction of 580 100 "Economics". Conducts research work in the field of economics, investment and business. He has published about 10 works in the Kyrgyz Republic and abroad.

Anarkan Dj. Attokurova
Candidate of Pedagogical Sciences, Associate Professor, co-founder of the "Agartuu Akademiyasy" laboratory at Osh State University, where qualifications of the teaching and administrative staff of universities, of the secondary specialized educational institutions teachers, of the secondary school teachers are being upgraded. Attokurova's scientific interests include the design of educational programs of higher professional education, the methodology of learning outcomes, the formation of competently significant qualities of a future teacher of mathematics, pedagogical technology. Anarkan Attokurova organizes the "Nazar readings" and speaks at republican and international scientific and practical conferences, was a member of the editorial board of the scientific journal of Osh State University. She has published more than 40 scientific articles in peer-reviewed scientific journals of the Kyrgyz Republic and abroad, more than 10 textbooks and study guides.

Lyudmila N. Bahtiyarova
Ph.D. in Pedagogy, Associate Professor of the Department Teacher of the Department of Applied Informatics and Information Technologies in Education of *Minin Nizhny Novgorod State Pedagogical University* (Nizhny Novgorod, Russia). Scientific interests: Application of digital technologies in education, artificial intelligence. She has publications in Russian and foreign publications.

Zhanna Y. Bakaeva
Professor of Accounting and Electronic Business Department of *I.N. Ulyanov Chuvash State University (Cheboksary, Russia)*. She graduated from the Faculty of Economics of Mordovia University, specialty "Finance and Credit" (1999). Defended: dissertation for the degree of Candidate of Philosophical Sciences in the specialty 09.00.01 Ontology and theory of cognition on the topic "Basic concepts in the structure of computer science" at Nizhny Novgorod State University named after N.I. Lobachevsky (1999), dissertation for the degree of Doctor of Philosophy in the specialty 09.00.01 Ontology and theory of Cognition on the topic "Phenomenon Information in the semantic aspect" at the I.N. Ulyanov Chuvash State University (2010). Area of scientific interests: anthology and theory of cognition, philosophy of consciousness, problems of the information society.

Sergey A. Barkov
Doctor of Sciences in Sociology, Professor, Head of the Department of Economic Sociology and Management, Faculty of Sociology of the Lomonosov Moscow State University, the author of more than 150 works on the sociology of management, economic sociology, management, and human resource management. Research interests include current trends in the development of companies, organizations, and markets as tools of social management, changing economic thinking and behavior in post-industrial society. He has been teaching since the early 1990s, constantly analyzing changes in socio-economic processes and phenomena in the postmodern era. The author has initiated and participated in numerous educational programs at the Lomonosov Moscow State University, Higher School of Economics, and Russian University of Transport. He also leads international projects on the management and analysis of the labor market. Sergey A. Barkov repeatedly acted as a teacher, trainer, and moderator at seminars and advanced training courses for executives of Russian organizations (Central Bank, Russian Railways, Severstal, etc.).

Angela A. Bezrukova
Candidate of Sociology, Associate Professor at the Department of Philosophy, Sociology, and Pedagogy, Maikop State Technological University. Her research interests include issues of gender studies, traditional Adyghe culture, and the social status of women in today's society. She has published more than 105 works in Russian and foreign peer-reviewed scientific journals, including five monographs and 15 study guides. She has also been a scientific advisor for two Candidates of Sociological Sciences.

Rustem I. Biktashev
Candidate of Science (Philology). Works in the *Kazan Cooperative Institute (Branch) of the Russian University of Cooperation* (Russia). His scientific interests include the theory of English linguistics. Rustem I. Biktashev organizes Russian and international scientific and practical conferences and is the editor and author of collective monographs and serves as a guest editor of international scientific journals. He has published more than 100 works in Russian and foreign peer-reviewed scientific journals and books.

Marietta A. Bolokova
Candidate of Philosophy, Associate Professor, Head of the Department of Constitutional Building and State and Municipal Management of the Maikop State Technological University. Her scientific interests include issues of formation of the public practice of cultural heritage preservation at the level of state and municipal administration, management in the sphere of culture, problems of interpretation of culture in conditions of civilizational contradictions, and the impact of modernization technologies on mass culture. She has published more than 60 works in Russian and foreign peer-reviewed scientific journals.

Elena A. Buller
Candidate of Economic Sciences, Associate Professor of the Department of Management, of Adyghe State University (Maikop, Republic of Adygea, Russia). In her works, she develops scientific research in the field of creation and effective functioning of personnel management systems at enterprises of various industries and sectors of the economy, integrated management systems, measuring systems in innovative personnel management, labor economics, development of strategic personnel management and competitiveness of enterprises, analysis and assessment of the quality of life of the population of the region. Her research interests include economics and human resource management, sustainable development of the region, humanization of labor relations, economic security of the national economy. She takes part in Russian

and international scientific and practical conferences. Elena A. Buller has published more than 120 scientific papers in Russian and foreign peer-reviewed journals.

Sergey V. Bykov
Doctor of Psychology, Associate Professor, Professor of the Department of Painting and Art Education, Togliatti State University. The author's scientific interests are associated with the psychology of culture and art, history of art, social psychology of the urban environment, "mass culture" and its perception by young people, the practice of contemporary art, art education, and culture of everyday life. In his works, the author pays much attention to the search for personal values and meanings acting as internal determinants of culture, the problems of patriotic education, emotional and aesthetic attitude, and finding one's own sense of history and modernity in the art on the basis of integral artistic consciousness. Sergey V. Bykov is a participant in international and all-Russian conferences. He is the author of more than 90 scientific publications in Russian and foreign journals and books.

Svetlana K. Chinazirova
Candidate of Economic Sciences, Associate Professor of the Department of Management of Adyghe State University (Maykop, Russia). His research interests include the organization of production, corporate social responsibility, competitiveness management, forecasting and planning, as well as the digital economy. She has published more than 100 papers in Russian and foreign peer-reviewed scientific journals, including 3 articles in collections of collective monographs and 24 scientific articles in publications accredited by the Higher Attestation Commission, including textbooks "Managing the competitiveness of an organization", "Commodity management", "Organization of production at a food industry enterprise". The Hirsch index is 9.

Oksana L. Chulanova
Doctor of Economics, Associate Professor, Professor of the Department of State and Municipal Administration and Human Resources Management of the Surgut State University, the author of more than 400 works on labor economics and human resource management. Research interests include the methodology of a competence-based approach in work with personnel; formation and development of soft skills; emotional intellect; contemporary HR technologies in the context of the digital paradigm, the use of artificial intelligence in HR, and the opportunities and risks of using HR analytics; gig economy as a trend of digital globalization; features of integrating well-being technology in

working with personnel in conditions of remote work and hybrid office during the COVID-19 pandemic, etc. The author participates in collaborative studies of the opportunities and risks of introducing artificial intelligence from the standpoint of representatives of various faiths and Generation Z, as well as the formation and development of soft skills in students of various areas of training in accordance with the demands of the labor market and large business entities.

Nafiset Z. Daurova
Candidate of Economic Sciences, Associate Professor, Employee of the Department of Accounting and Finance, *Adyghe State University* (ASU) (Maykop, Russia). Her research interests include money, credit, banks, investments, marketing research. Participated in the All-Russian annual educational campaign "All-Russian economic dictation" LLC "Free Economic Society of Russia". Daurova N.Z. participates in Russian scientific and practical conferences. She has published more than 150 papers in Russian and foreign peer-reviewed scientific journals and books.

Tatiana A. Dugina
Candidate of Economic Sciences, Associate Professor, Head of the Department "Economic Security" of the Volgograd State Agricultural University (Volgograd SAU). The directions of scientific research are related to innovation in the agricultural sector and the economic growth of agricultural production. She has more than 130 publications in Russian and foreign peer-reviewed scientific journals and books, including on the development of the agricultural sector.

Saida G. Dzybova
Associate Professor of the Department of Theory and History of State and Law, Constitutional Construction and Political Science, *Adyghe State University* (*Maykop, Russia*), the author of more than 120 publications. Her research interests include strategic development of tourism, socio-economic development, municipal education, digital transformation, cluster structures, regional economy, municipal image, agglomeration processes, human resource policy, public-private partnership, regional sustainability, and small business.

Zarema Y. Emtyl
Doctor of Science (Historical), Professor of the Department of History, Philosophy, and Psychology of The Kuban State University of Technology. Her scientific interests include the sociocultural and sociopolitical history of the North Caucasus. Zarema Y. Emtyl is the author of three monographs on the

history of the Adyghe Intelligentsia and more than 60 publications in Russian and foreign journals. She is a member of Russian and international scientific conferences.

Nadezhda V. Eremkina
PhD (Philology), Associate Professor, Department of Management and Food Industry of *Saransk Cooperative Institute (Branch) of the Russian University of Cooperation.* Her scientific interests include contemporary techniques in teaching the Russian language and speech culture. She also does research work in the area of different aspects of international cultural exchange and business communications. Her scientific papers are published in leading indexed journals.

Igor Fernández-Plazaola
Doctor of Architecture, Building, Urban Planning and Landscape, Associate Professor at Universidad Politecnica de Valencia (*Valencia, Spain*), director of the Master in Building Management and Technologies, data scientist of the Cathedra housing observatory. His research interest includes housing price, and offer and demand relations, and new ways of house promotions for social needs, also business management tools in the building and real estate companies and innovative entrepreneurship. On the educational side his research is how to implement new practical tools into the university process. Prof. Igor Fdz. promotes different periodical reports related with house pricing, offer and real estate demand he also organises different congresses as AIRE, EDIFICATE, COINVEDI.

Elena V. Frolova
Doctor of Sociology, Professor, Russian State Social University, Moscow, Russian Federation, head of the grant for the digitalization of Russian education, and author of training courses and educational programs. Research interests: education management, digitalization of education, sociology of management.

Inna N. Gaidareva
Candidate of Sciences in Sociology, Associate Professor, Deputy Director of the Scientific and Educational Cluster Institute of Law of the Adyghe State University (Maikop, Russia). Executor of the RFBR grant "Mechanisms for strengthening trust in authorities in the regions of Russia in the post-pandemic period: political and sociological analysis". He is a participant of international and Russian scientific and practical conferences. Author of more than 100 papers in peer-reviewed scientific publications. Research interests: information

security, digital transformation, information culture, anti-corruption, prevention of administrative offenses, administrative and legal regulation in the field of public administration.

Sergey M. Imyarekov
Doctor of Economics, Professor, Department of Management and Food Industry of *Saransk Cooperative Institute (Branch) of the Russian University of Cooperation*. The sphere of scientific interests and investigation lies in the field of management development of business, strategies for the economic development of an enterprise and educational institutions. Sergey M. Imyarekov is an author of more than 150 papers devoted to international business technologies, methods of teaching management, and modeling educational programs. The results of his research have been published in leading Russian and foreign scientific journals.

Galina V. Kalinina
PhD in Economics, Doctor of Philosophical Sciences, Professor, Director of the Cheboksary Institute (branch) of the *Moscow Humanitarian Economic University*. Laureate of the State Prize of the Chuvash Republic, Honored Scientist of the Chuvash Republic, Cheboksary, 428038, Russian Federation. She completed an internship in marketing and management at the Universities of Bologna and Cremona in Italy. Author of more than 100 scientific and educational works, including 7 monographs. Directions of research: co-evolutionary development of socio-economic systems in the information society; ensuring the economic security of the cooperative sector in the context of the reindustrialization of the Russian economy; program-target approach in managing the socio-economic development of the region; directions of development of ecological philosophy; philosophical aspects of social development management; social development and quality of life.

Aziza B. Karbekova
Doctor of Economics, Acting Professor of the Department of Economics, Accounting and Finance, Coordinator of the Technology and Innovation Support Center of *Jalal-Abad State University named after B. Osmonov* (TISC JAGU) (Jalal-Abad, Kyrgyzstan). Her research interests include national economic theory, social entrepreneurship, digital economy, sustainable development. Aziza B. Karbekova participates in Russian and international scientific and practical conferences, is the author of collective monographs, an invited reviewer of international scientific journals. She has published more than

100 papers in Kyrgyz, Russian and foreign peer-reviewed scientific journals and books.

Asker R. Kasparov

Candidate of Sociological Sciences, Senior Lecturer at the Krasnodar University of the Ministry of Internal Affairs of Russia. His research interests include the sociology of conflict, conflicts in small professional groups, the conflict potential of the Russian police, the role of internal affairs agencies in the prevention and resolution of conflicts of various origins in modern society. He is a participant in a number of international and all-Russian scientific and practical conferences. He has published more than 30 papers in Russian and foreign peer-reviewed scientific journals and books.

Olesya P. Kazachenok

Associate professor of the civil and private international law Department in Volgograd State University. In 2006 defended the PhD thesis on the topic "Peculiarities of concluding a mortgage agreement (pledge of real estate)". In 2009 graduated from Volgograd State Technological University with a bachelor degree in management. In 2001–2002 participated in the formation of the region judicial practice in the copyright field, while working in the Lower Volga branch of the Russian Copyright Society. Since 2002, working as a lawyer, she has specialized in bankruptcy of large industrial complexes in region, politically significant processes for the protection of honor, dignity and business reputation, complex arbitration processes, including shareholder disputes and invalidation of real estate transactions. Since 2009 till 2016 she was a Deputy Head of retail operations department of the Volgograd branch of the bank Vozrozhdenie, specializing in the financial planning and the analysis of the Bank's retail business. In 2016 was awarded an Honorary Diploma of the Volgograd State Duma for her significant contribution to ensuring the protection of rights, freedoms and legitimate interests of the Volgograd residents. In 2017 and 2018 she received the gratitude from the Public Chamber of Volgograd region for active citizenship and fruitful activity. In 2018 was awarded an Honorary Diploma of the Volgograd regional Duma. Since 2018 has been a regional expert of the agency for strategic initiatives.

Mostafa M. Keruly

Phylologian, the researcher of the linguistics, Professor at *Kazan Cooperative Institute (Branch) of the Russian University of Cooperation,* has more than 20 Russian-Turkish grammar comparative studies published in the linguistic journals and books. He has worked in KFU (Kazan Federal University) as a leading teacher of the Turkish language and literature. He is a founder and a director of Turkish Language Center in the KFU. His scientific interests include the methodology of language teaching and comparative grammar studies.

Irina B. Khakonova
Candidate of Law, Associate Professor of the Department of Civil and Arbitration Process of *Adyghe State University (Maykop, Russia)*. Conducts classes in civil law disciplines, is the supervisor of student papers, participates in conferences, and is the author of more than 50 publications.

Bella Kh. Khamukova
Associate Professor of the Department of Pedagogy and Pedagogical Technologies of the *Adyghe State University (Maykop, Russia)*, the author of about 20 publications. Her research interests include multi-ethnic society, educational environment, youth education, civil society, spiritual and moral education, personal tolerance, and inclusive education.

Diloram I. Khasanova
Master of Economics of the Economics and Taxes Department of the Osh State University (Kyrgyzstan). Her research interests include education, economics, taxes, international standards, market economy. Diloram I. Khasanova conducts scientific and educational activities aimed at teaching students in Economics, instilling in students all the necessary knowledge and skills. Conducts research work in the economics and business field. She has published about 10 works in the Kyrgyz Republic and Russia.

Olga Y. Khatsrinova
Candidate of Technical Sciences, Associate Professor of the Department of Engineering Pedagogy and Psychology, Institute of Additional Professional Education, *Kazan National Research Technological University*. The sphere of interests isthe methods of organizing educational events that deal with the development of culture and the development of worldview functions among students. She has more than 200 papers in Russian and foreign peer-reviewed scientific journals.

Aminat Sh. Khuazheva
Doctor of Economics, Professor, Head of the Department of Adyghe State University (Russia); ex-Minister of Education and Science of the Republic of

Adygea (Russia), corresponding member of the Russian Academy of Natural Sciences (Russia) and corresponding member of the Adygea (Circassian) International Academy of Sciences (Russia). Her research interests include the study of problem areas in the management of educational systems and factors affecting the effectiveness of this process; conceptual justification of the mechanism for ensuring economic security at various levels. Aminet Sh. Khuazheva is the author of a fundamentally new conceptual structural and functional model of the mechanism for ensuring the sustainable development of the regional agro-industrial complex by forming agro-industrial clusters and transforming the organizational and institutional structure of the regional agro-industrial complex, and also the author of the methodology of expert-analytical ranking assessment of regional agro-industrial complex. She has published over 120 scientific and educational works in Russian and foreign peer-reviewed scientific journals and books.

Narong Kiettikunwong
Associate Professor in the College of Local Administration at the Khon Kaen University where he has been a faculty member since 2014. He completed his undergraduate studies at Eastern Connecticut State University (BSc. in Business Administration) and Chulalongkorn University (LL.B.), postgraduate studies at Chulalongkorn University (Master of Public Administration) and Leuphana Universität Lüneburg (LL.M. in Competition & Regulation). He is also an attorney-at-law. Prior to joining the college, he had worked with the U.S. Department of State and several other private companies including his own – where he was a founder and CEO. Narong Kiettikunwong serves as an editor and author of collective monographs. His latest scientific peer-reviewed book relevant to this topic was Education for the Elderly in the Asia Pacific. Narong Kiettikunwong current research interests lie in the topic of competition & regulation in energy sector, energy transition (Energiewende), e-Government, and special and inclusive education.

Natalya S. Komleva
Graduated from the Faculty of Economics of the Mordovian University (1994). PhD in Economics (2003). Associate Professor of the Department of Management of the National Research Ogarev Mordovia State University (2007). Scientific interests: Management of marketing activities of an industrial enterprise, consumer behavior in the markets of goods and services, formation of a client-oriented management system for an industrial company. 150 scientific and educational works, including 9 teaching aids.

Irina I. Kondrashkina

PhD (Economics), Associate Professor, Department of Management and Food Industry of *Saransk Cooperative Institute (Branch) of the Russian University of Cooperation*. Her scientific interests cover a wide range of areas such as innovative management, the economics of management, and economics of education. Irina I. Kondrashkina has performed some studies in the field of contemporary educational technologies, strategies in higher education development, educational models, and communication and interaction with various social audiences. She has published more than 100 papers in Russian and foreign scientific journals.

Anneline Korf-Taljaard

holds a Masters degree in Education (Adult Education) from the University of KwaZulu-Natal. The focus of research was an investigation on the predictive validity of a placement tool for TVET Colleges (https://goo.su/zRAL1C) . Anneline Korf-Taljaard is registered with the Health Professions Council in South Africa as a psychometrist. She serves as an executive committee member of the Higher and Further Education Disability Services Association, an umbrella advocacy organisation for the Disability Rights and Support Units at all Higher Educational institutions in South Africa. She took up the responsibility to spearhead inclusive education at *Boland Technical and Vocational Education and Training College (Stellenbosch, South Africa)* and became an activist towards changing the educational environment in South Africa to include students with disabilities. Often invited by organisations, she shares best practices learned. She is involved in research projects to develop tools for the early identification of academically vulnerable students which will form the foundation of further academic studies.

Selina Kungwane

graduated with a master's degree from Hiroshima University in Japan. Currently she is pursuing her doctoral studies with University of South Africa focusing on disability support in technical vocational education and training (TVET) sector. She has been involved in the promotion of the rights of persons with disabilities in various Departments she has worked in. She obtained an opportunity to work at the Department of Higher Education and Training in South Africa, TVET branch, Student Development and Support unit focusing on student support. She is involved in non-academic support and her focus area is support for students with disabilities in TVET Colleges. She sees herself as a future academia and disability rights activist within the TVET space as a growing sector is South Africa.

Zarema Kh. Kurmalieva
Associate Professor of the Department of Economic Theory and Personnel Management of *Adyghe State University (Maykop, Russia)*, the author of about 20 publications. Her research interests include monetary policy, anti-crisis regulation, implementation of cluster initiatives in entrepreneurship, currency regulation, social economy, and social and labor sector of the region. She is the author of textbooks on macroeconomics, economic theory, and the economic foundations of social work.

Lyubov I. Kutepova
Candidate of Pedagogical Sciences, Associate Professor of the Department of Service Technologies and Technological Education, Minin Nizhny Novgorod State Pedagogical University, has been working in the field of higher education since 1993. In 2002 she defended her Ph.D. thesis on the topic "Theory and methodology of vocational education. Didactic conditions for the formation of design skills of students of construction specialties of secondary vocational education". She is the author of more than 50 publications. Has 18 scientific articles indexed by the international database Scopus. Main scientific interests: organization of professional activity of a teacher in the structure of the university, the system of development of additional education. Actively participates in scientific conferences, seminars and round tables, supervises the research work of students.

Valentina V. Kuznetsova
Associate Professor, Department of World Economy and Foreign Economic Management, Faculty of Public Administration, Lomonosov Moscow State University. She previously worked at the Institute of Scientific Information on Social Sciences of the USSR Academy of Sciences in the China sector. Valentina Kuznetsova developed programs for the courses "International Settlement and Payment Operations," "Modern Methods of Financial Regulation of Cyclicality of the World Economy," and "Public Administration in China" for graduate students in the Department of Public Administration. She published textbooks "Inflation Targeting: International Discussions and Practices," "Central Banks in the World Economy" (co-authored with S. A. Andryushin); "International Currency and Credit Relations. Practicum"; "Banking. Practicum" (co-authored with O. I. Larina and V. P. Bychkov). The textbook "Sovereign Debt Management" was the winner of the II All-Russian competition for the best scientific and educational publication "Akademus." Valentina. V. Kuznetsova has published two monographs and more than 100 articles.

Evgeniy A. Leonenko
since 2003 lecturer in the Department of Management, since 2006 Senior Lecturer in the Department of Management, since 2007 Associate Professor in the Department of Marketing, since 2015 Associate Professor in the Department of Management of National Research Ogarev Mordovia State University *(Saransk, Russia)*. Scientific interests: Issues of the efficiency of using the potential of enterprises, the development of domestic and foreign pharmaceutical drug makers, the globalization of the world economy and the problems of modern education, etc.

Evgeny A. Likholetov
Associate Professor of the Department of Economics and Foreign Economic Activity of *Volgograd State Agricultural University (Volgograd, Russia)*, the author of about 60 publications. His research interests include pricing, agriculture, economic growth, digital transformation, economic security, investment, enterprise taxation, a market economy, crisis management, and innovative technologies.

Irina V. Lipchanskaya
Associate Professor of the Department of Philosophy and Cultural Studies of *Rostov State University of Economics (Rostov-on-Don, Russia)*, the author of more than 60 publications. Her research interests include intellectual (spiritual) elite, scientific community, digital transformation, women's independence, human self-identity, scientific innovation, social communication, academic capitalism, humanitarian knowledge, and the social responsibility of a scientist.

Galina M. Lokhonova
Candidate of Pedagogical Sciences, Assistant Director of the *Cheboksary Institute (Branch) of the Moscow Humanitarian Economic University*, Cheboksary, 428038, RF. Winner of the competitions "Postgraduate Student of the Year of the Chuvash Republic" (2011), "Best Young Scientist of the Russian University of Cooperation" (2013). Member of the Russian Union of Young Scientists. Has acts on the implementation of the results of scientific research of the Cheboksary Cooperative Institute and the Karaganda Economic University of Kazpotrebsoyuz. She was the executor of grant projects of the Russian Humanitarian Foundation, the Russian Foundation for Basic Research, the project manager of the international grant competition "Orthodox Initiative – 2018". Author of 102 scientific and educational works, incl. 1 monograph and 10 articles published in journals recommended by the

Higher Attestation Commission. Directions of research: theory and methodology of vocational education, corporate culture and its role in the formation of professional and personal qualities of a future specialist, spiritual and moral development of students, the formation of a multicultural personality of a student of a modern university.

Svetlana A. Lyausheva
Professor of the *Adyghe State University (Maykop, Russia)* is the author of more than 120 publications. Her research interests include information openness, multicultural region, distance learning, regional public authorities, economic integration, social inertia, and migration.

Sergey A. Makushkin
Candidate of Historical Sciences, Associate Professor, Associate Professor of the Faculty of Humanities of the Russian State Social University, the author of more than 326 works on the socio-economic aspects of management, the use of digital technologies, the development and use of educational technologies, personnel management, and history. The results presented in the author's papers are based on research conducted jointly with colleagues. Research results are periodically published in journal articles included in the Scopus and Web of Science databases, reflected in research reports and fundamental works. Recently, the focus has been made on the activities of socio-economic systems in the context of the COVID 19 pandemic using digital technologies.

Zara A. Mamisheva
PhD in Law, Associate Professor, Associate Professor of the Department of Theory and History of State and Law, Constitutional Building and Political Science of the Scientific and Educational Cluster Institute of Law of the Adyghe State University (Maikop, Russia). He is the author of more than 60 papers in Russian and foreign peer-reviewed scientific publications. Research interests: legal regulation of cooperation, the principle of separation of powers, anti-corruption policy, human rights.

Olga A. Mashkina
PhD, Associate Professor, Chinese Department of Institute of Asian and African Studies, Lomonosov Moscow State University *(Moscow, Russia)*. She is a former Deputy Dean of the Faculty of Educational Study of the Lomonosov Moscow State University and a former associate professor of the Department of Chinese Philology of the Institute of Asian and African Studies; Head of the Department of Academic Affairs of the joint University of MSU-PPI in

Shenzhen (China). Olga A. Mashkina has more than 30 years of experience of scientific and pedagogical work in higher educational institutions. She is a scientific supervisor of the postgraduate students (20 master's theses, 16 diplomas, and one candidate's thesis (PhD) in pedagogical sciences). Olga A. Mashkina is the author of about 150 publications in development of education abroad and in Russia; international cooperation in the field of higher education; education as a factor of modernization (on the example of China, Russia, and Central Asian countries); influence of the worldview and traditions on the educational motivation of students.

Flera L. Mazitova
Associate Professor of *Kazan Cooperative Institute (Branch) of Russian University of Cooperation (Kazan, Russia)*. She graduated from the Kazan State Pedagogical Institute with a degree in German and English. In 1986, she defended her thesis for the degree of Candidate of Philological Sciences. In 2001, she received the academic title of Associate Professor in the Department of Foreign Languages. In 2013, she was awarded the honorary title "Honorary Worker of Higher Professional Education of the Russian Federation" for merits in the area of education (Order of the Ministry of Education and Science of Russia dated March 5, 2013 No. 131/k-n). Flera L. Mazitova improves her scientific and professional qualifications under the programs "Use of EIET resources in the implementation of educational programs" and "Information and communication technologies in the professional activities of higher education teacher." She completed an internship at the Department of European Languages: "Modern views on teaching English today and tomorrow" (Kazan Federal University, Institute of International Relations, History and Oriental Studies; advanced training at the University of George Washington, USA). She has also won a grant for advanced training in Germany at the University of Potsdam. She has more than 100 publications, including on intercultural and interlingual exchange in the area of education.

Natalia V. Medvedeva
Candidate of Social Sciences, Associate Professor, Russian State Social University, Moscow, Russian Federation, head of the educational program, participant in projects, including on the topic of education in higher education, the author of a series of articles on the digital transformation of education in a pandemic. Interests: education management in higher and secondary schools, sociology of management.

Margarita A. Meretukova
Senior Lecturer of the Department of Civil Law and Civil Process of the *Adyghe State University (Maikop, Russia)*. Conducts classes in civil law disciplines, is the supervisor of student work, participates in conferences, is the author of scientific articles.

Igor E. Mizikovsky
Doctor of Economics (2006), Professor (2009), Academician of the Russian Academy of Natural Sciences. Head of Accounting Department, Lobachevsky State University of Nizhni Novgorod (*Nizhny Novgorod, Russia*). Deputy Chairman of the Dissertation Council D 212.166.23. Active member of the Russian Academy of Natural Sciences. Head of educational programs of higher education: Bachelor's degree 38.03.01 "Finance and credit. Accounting"; Masters 38.04.01 "Accounting, analysis and audit"; Postgraduate studies 08.00.12 "Accounting, statistics". Head of the educational program of secondary vocational education 38.02.01 "Economics and accounting (by industry)". Research interests: accounting, control and revision, economic security, information systems in the economy, security of accounting information. Scientific activity: published scientific works – more than 130; textbooks, educational and teaching aids – more than 60.

Pennee Narot
Retired after 30 years as Associate Professor in International and Development Education at the Faculty of Education, Khon Kaen University, Thailand. After receiving Ph.D. in International and Development Education from University of Pittsburgh, she has been teaching and conducting research in various areas such as teachers' development, non-formal, informal education and, inclusive education, and aged situations society analysis. She has continuously been conducting research intensively in inclusive education, with the work like: a professional learning program for enhancing the competency of students with special needs, a model professional learning program for enhancing the competency of students with special needs, inclusive education in Thailand, understanding inclusive education practices in schools under local government jurisdiction, and different paths for inclusion in Thailand: improving , and special teachers as leaders in the development of inclusive education.

Elena A. Nemkina
Candidate of Economic Sciences, Associate Professor at the Department of Economic Analysis and Finance, Volgograd State Agricultural University (Volgograd SAU). She has more than 60 publications in Russian and foreign

peer-reviewed scientific journals and books, including on the issues of import substitution and economic security in the context of digitalization of the agro-industrial complex.

Eugenia A. Neretina
PhD in economics, Professor of National Research Ogarev Mordovia State University (*Saransk, Russia*). "Graduated from the Kuibyshev Planning Institute with a degree in National Economy Planning" (1972). Doctor of Economic Sciences (2001). Professor (2003). In 1972–1976 Senior Economist of the State Planning Committee of the MASSR. In 1976–1978 – junior employee of NISa, assistant of the Department of Economics and Organization of Production, Mordovian University. In 1979–1991 – Senior Lecturer, Associate Professor, Head of the Department of Economics of Cooperative Trade of the Saransk Branch of the Moscow Cooperative Institute. In 1991–2004 – Associate Professor, Professor of the Department of Management. Since 2004 – Professor, Head of the Department of Marketing. Active member of the Academy of Quality Problems, member of the Russian Marketing Association. Scientific interests: modern problems of marketing and management; system innovation, the problems of modern education. Publications: More than 300 scientific and educational works, including 23 monographs, 7 manuals, 25 educational and methodological developments.

Asiya G. Nizamieva
Deputy Head of the Department of Humanities and Foreign Languages of the *Kazan Cooperative Institute (Branch) of Russian University of Cooperation (Kazan, Russia)*. She graduated from the Kazan State Pedagogical University with a degree in Tatar language, Tatar literature, and English. In 2002, she completed training courses for the reserve of the teaching staff at the Kazan State Pedagogical University. From 2002 to 2018, she worked as a foreign language teacher in secondary schools in Kazan. Asiya G. Nizamieva improves her scientific and professional qualifications in the programs "Relevant problems and current approaches to teaching foreign languages in the context of the implementation of the Federal State Educational Standard of Education," "Tutorial support of the individual educational trajectory of a gifted child," "Current approaches to the implementation of innovative educational technologies in accordance with the Federal State Educational Standards of secondary vocational education," and "Information and communication technologies in the professional activities of teacher of higher education." In 2019, she underwent professional retraining at the Autonomous Non-Profit Organization for Higher Education of the Central Union of the Russian Federation "Russian

University of Cooperation" under the program of additional professional training "Teacher of foreign language of higher school (Turkish language)." Since 2020, she has been an applicant for the Department of Social Work, Pedagogy, and Psychology of the Kazan National Research Technological University. She has more than 20 publications, including on intercultural and interlingual exchange in the area of education.

Igor G. Panov
Professor, painter, Director of the Institute of "Fine and Applied Arts," Togliatti State University. The area of scientific interests is connected with the practical application of traditional art styles in contemporary forms of painting. Igor G. Panov leads an active exhibition activity at international, all-Russian, and regional levels; 40 of more than 300 exhibition projects are personal. He is the curator of the art projects "New Look" and "Northern Latitudes," successfully held in many cities of Russia. He made several art trips to Germany, Norway, Tanzania, China, Egypt, Italy, Montenegro, and India to popularize traditional realistic art. The main task of his creative activity is the development and preservation of the traditions of the system of artistic academic education.

Irina V. Panova
Ph.D. in Pedagogy, Associate Professor of the Department Teacher of the Department of Applied Informatics and Information Technologies in Education of *Minin Nizhny Novgorod State Pedagogical University* (Nizhny Novgorod, Russia). Head of the Educational program of the direction of preparation 44.04.01 "Pedagogical education" profile "Information technologies in education". Member of the expert group for certification of teachers of pedagogical colleges in the Nizhny Novgorod region. Scientific interests: Methods of teaching informatics, informatization of education, e-learning, ICT competence of a teacher and head of an educational organization. In 2020, she took advanced training courses under the program "End-to-End Technologies. Information infrastructure, digital environment and artificial intelligence" at Tomsk State University. She has publications in Russian and foreign publications.

Michael N. Pavlenkov
Doctor of Economics (2009), Professor (2018), Professor of the Department of Information Technologies and Instrumental Methods in Economics, Lobachevsky State University of Nizhni Novgorod. Research interests: modeling of socio-economic processes; controlling socio-economic processes. Scientific activity: the number of published works – over 150, the number of published

monographs – 14, the number of published manuals – 5. Supervises postgraduate and doctoral students, is a member of dissertation councils: D.212.141.21 of the Moscow State Technical University. N.E. Bauman and D.212.166.23 Nizhny Novgorod State University. N.I. Lobachevsky, a member of the editorial board of the journals "Controlling", "Innovations in Management" (the journals are included in the list of VAK).

Elena Kzh. Pilivanova

Associate Professor of the Department of Commerce and Logistics of the *Rostov State University of Economics (Rostov-on-Don, Russia)*, the author of more than 30 publications. Her research interests include regional economics, green economy, green technology, transport and logistics infrastructure, marketing, retailing, and competitiveness. She is the author of a textbook on logistics.

Alexander V. Ponachugin

PhD in Economics, Associate Professor of the Department of Applied Informatics and Information Technologies in Education of *Minin Nizhny Novgorod State Pedagogical University* (Nizhny Novgorod, Russia). Scientific interests: Network economy, Network design, artificial intelligence. Head of the educational program of the bachelor's degree in the direction 09.03.03 "Applied Informatics". In 2020, he completed advanced training courses under the program "End-to-End Technologies. Information infrastructure, digital environment and artificial intelligence" at Tomsk State University. In 2021, he was trained as part of the Intel® AI for Youth Trainer Training Initiatives "AI Technologies for Everyone" training initiatives with the status of a certified teacher in the Intel® Skills for Innovation program (Skills for Innovation). He has over 100 publications in Russian and foreign publications.

Elena G. Popkova

Doctor of Science (Economics), the founder and president of the Institute of Scientific Communications (Russia) and Doctor of Science (Economics), the founder and president of the Institute of Scientific Communications (Russia) and Professor of RUDN University, Moscow, Russia. Her scientific interests include the theory of economic growth, sustainable development, globalization, humanization of economic growth, emerging markets, social entrepreneurship, and the digital economy and Industry 4.0. Elena G. Popkova organizes Russian and international scientific and practical conferences and is the editor and author of collective monographs, and serves as a guest editor of international scientific journals. She has published more than 300 works in Russian and foreign peer-reviewed scientific journals and books.

Liudmila V. Popova

Doctor of Economics, Professor, Head of the Department of Economics, Finance and Accounting of *Orel State University named after I.S. Turgenev*, President of the Oryol regional branch of the public organization "Free Economic Society of Russia", editor-in-chief of the journal "Economic and Humanitarian Sciences", current corresponding member of the Oryol regional branch of the "Academy of Military Sciences". Her scientific interest includes such areas as: accounting, analysis and audit, public audit, finance, Popova Liudmila Vladimirovna organized Russian and international scientific and practical conferences, was an editor and author of collective monographs, and was also invited to be an editor of international scientific journals. Liudmila Vladimirovna has published more than four hundred papers in Russian and foreign peer-reviewed scientific journals and books.

Larisa V. Popova

Doctor of Economic Sciences, Professor of the Volgograd State Agricultural University (Volgograd SAU). Under her leadership, a scientific school "Financial and Economic Relations of Agricultural Formations" was opened, where research is carried out in the areas of innovative development of agriculture in the context of digitalization. L. V. Popova is a member of the Dissertation Council at the Volgograd State University for the defense of doctoral and candidate dissertations in economic specialties. Under her leadership, 11 graduate students and applicants received their degrees. She has more than 300 publications in Russian and foreign peer-reviewed scientific journals and books, including on innovative development and digitalization of the agricultural sector.

Svetlana A. Popova

Associate Professor of the Department of Agricultural Production Organization of *Volgograd State Agricultural University* (*Volgograd, Russia*), the author of about 90 publications. Her research interests include rural development, social infrastructure, accounting, globalization, and innovation. S. A. Popova developed and published methodological recommendations for the organization and conduct of industrial practice for students studying in the direction 38.04.02 "Management," master's program (applied) "Production Management," as well as teaching materials on the basics of research activities.

Valentina I. Rodionova
Doctor of Philosophy, Associate Professor, Professor of the Department of Social and Humanitarian Disciplines of the Institute of Service and Entrepreneurship (branch) of Don State Technical University in Shakhty. Her research interests include the theory of technologization of today's society, social and cultural problems of various social groups, and processes of sociocultural transformations. She has published more than 180 papers in Russian and foreign peer-reviewed scientific journals and books.

Olga V. Rogach
Candidate of Social Sciences, Associate Professor, Russian State Social University, Moscow, Russian Federation, head of the educational program, participant in projects on digitalization of education, and author of monographs and series of articles on the digital transformation of education in a pandemic. Areas of interest: management of education in higher education, sociology of management, digital transformation of higher education.

Elena V. Romanovskaya
Candidate of Economic Sciences, Associate Professor of the Department of "Enterprise Economics" of Minin Nizhny Novgorod State Pedagogical University, has been working in the field of Higher Education since 2008. In 2011, she defended her PhD thesis on the topic "Formation of an organizational and economic mechanism for restructuring machine-building enterprises". She is the author of 263 publications, 256 of them scientific and 7 of an educational and methodological nature. He has 82 scientific articles indexed by the international database Scopus. Directs the main professional educational program in the direction of "Economics". She is the organizer of the annual international scientific and practical conferences "Industrial development of Russia: problems, prospects", "Economic development of Russia: trends, prospects", held on the basis of Minin University. Actively participates in scientific conferences, seminars and round tables, directs the research work of students.

Marina V. Rybakova
Doctor of Sociology, Professor of the Department of Sociology of Management of the Faculty of Public Administration of the Lomonosov Moscow State University, the author of more than 160 works on the sociology of management, the sociology of education, the digitalization of society, the use of artificial intelligence in the socio-cultural sphere, the development of the Russian and international educational environment, personnel management, public administration, social ecology, ecological settlements, environmental

sociology, and environmental problems. Her works are of interest in Russia and abroad. The conducted studies are based on the author's empirical and secondary empirical data. Her studies consider current trends and patterns of socio-economic development of society. Sociological research is organized and conducted in Russia and other countries of the world and is reflected in articles in the journals of the Scopus and Web of Science databases. Scientific works of Marina V. Rybakova pay particular attention to the problems of dynamic digitalization of society and the introduction of artificial intelligence from the standpoint of representatives of various faiths, today's youth (Generation Z).

Julia Yu. Rybasova

Associate Professor of the Department of Humanities and Foreign Languages of *Kazan Cooperative Institute (Branch) of Russian University of Cooperation (Kazan, Russia)*. She graduated from the Kazan State Pedagogical Institute as a music teacher. From 1991 to 1992, she underwent retraining in the specialty "Psychology and Social work," with the obtainment of qualification "Psychologist and social teacher." In 1996, she defended her dissertation on the topic: "General cultural training of students of a technical university" and obtained the degree of Candidate of Pedagogical Sciences. In 2000, she completed a short-term study at the Academy of Social Work of the Moscow State Social University on the problem of social policy, history, and theory of social work. In 2005, he was awarded the academic title of Associate Professor of Social Work. Julia Yu. Rybasova improves her scientific and professional qualifications under the programs "Educational and methodological support for the implementation of Federal State Educational Standards in specialties and areas of training," "Information and communication technologies in the professional activities of teacher of higher education," "Technologies for supporting persons with disabilities," and "Designing an integration platform and lifelong education services as a tool to accompany and support the system of lifelong education of citizens." She has more than 100 publications, including on intercultural and interlingual exchange in the area of education.

Elvira E. Samatova

Candidate of Economic Science, Associate professor of the Economics and Enterprise Management Department of the Osh State University (Kyrgyzstan). Her science interests include education, university, quality, quality of educational services, system of management quality, international standards, and digital economy. Elvira E. Samatova conducts the students and masters teaching and instilling competencies and skills for mastering economic and management knowledge. Conducts research work in the quality management and educational services field. She has published about 100 works, including the scientific papers, monographs and collective monographs, in the Kyrgyz Republic, Russia and abroad.

Elvira K. Samerkhanova
Doctor of Pedagogy, Professor, First Vice-rector of *Minin Nizhny Novgorod State Pedagogical University* (Nizhny Novgorod, Russia). Head of Master's programs in the direction 44.04.01 "Pedagogical education", profile "Information technologies in education", "Digital pedagogy". Research interests: Designing an information and educational environment, informatization of education, e-learning, project management in education. Chairman of the Regional Association of Informatics and ICT Teachers. In 2020, she took advanced training courses under the program "End-to-End Technologies. Information infrastructure, digital environment and artificial intelligence" at Tomsk State University. She has more than 100 publications in Russian and foreign publications.

Liliya V. Samosudova
PhD (Philology), Associate Professor, Department of Management and Food Industry of *Saransk Cooperative Institute (Branch) of the Russian University of Cooperation (Saransk, Russia)*. Her scientific interests include contemporary methods and approaches to teaching foreign languages, as well as research in the field of linguistics. She constantly takes part in different scientific conferences relating to contemporary methods of teaching and training foreign languages at the stage of higher education in non-linguistic institutions. Liliya V. Samosudova has published some articles on comparative analysis of temporal and local means in different languages, innovative techniques in foreign languages teaching in leading scientific journals.

Ashirgul K. Seidildayeva
candidate of Technical Sciences Assoc. Professor, 2010 defended her PhD thesis in the specialty 05.02.18 – Theory of mechanisms and machines; 2011 received a diploma of Candidate of Technical Sciences. 1991–2011 Al-Farabi Kazakh National University, Faculty of Mechanics and Mathematics, Department of Mechanics, Engineer, specialist, teacher, Senior lecturer; 2011–2013. Al-Farabi Kazakh National University, Faculty of Chemistry and Chemical Technology, Department of Chemical Physics and Materials Science, Senior Lecturer; From 2013 to the present, she has been working as a head at the Department of General Scientific Disciplines of the Academy of Civil Aviation (*Almaty, Kazakhstan*).

Bruno S. Sergi

Ph.D., is Professor of International Economics, University of Messina, and Associate, Davis Center for Russian and Eurasian Studies, Harvard University. Bruno S. Sergi teaches at the Harvard Extension School on the economics of emerging markets and the political economy of Russia and China. Sergi is Associate of Harvard University's Davis Center for Russian and Eurasian Studies and the Harvard Ukrainian Research Institute. He also teaches political economy and international finance at the University of Messina, Italy. He is Series Editor of Cambridge's Elements in the Economics of Emerging Markets (Cambridge University Press), as well as Editor for Entrepreneurship and Global Economic Growth and Co-Series Editor of Lab for Entrepreneurship and Development (Emerald Publishing). He is Founder and Editor-in-Chief of the International Journal of Trade and Global Markets, the International Journal of Economic Policy in Emerging Economies, and the International Journal of Monetary Economics and Finance. He is Associate Editor of The American Economist. He has published several articles in scholarly journals and many books as Author, Co-Author, Editor, or Co-Editor. Sergi's academic career and advisory roles have established him as a frequent guest and a commentator on matters of contemporary developments in political economies and emerging markets in a wide range of media. Sergi holds a Ph.D. in Economics from the University of Greenwich Business School, London.

Azamat M. Shadzhe

Doctor of Law, Professor, Director of the Scientific and Educational Cluster Institute of Law of the Adyghe State University (Maikop, Russia). Azamat M. Shadzhe takes an active part in Russian and international scientific and practical conferences. Member of the editorial board of two Russian peer-reviewed journals. He is the author of more than 150 papers in Russian and foreign peer-reviewed scientific journals. Research interests: Russian legislation, constitutional and legal policy, national security, human rights, biological security, bioterrorism, anti-corruption, legal support of national security.

Marina G. Shadzhe

Candidate of Law, Associate Professor of the Department of Civil and Arbitration Process of *Adyghe State University (Maykop, Russia)*. Conducts classes in civil law disciplines, is the supervisor of student papers, participates in conferences, and is the author of more than 50 publications.

Svetlana Yu. Shaldohina
Candidate of Economic Sciences, Associate Professor in Finance, Money Circulation and Credit, Volgograd State Agricultural University (Volgograd SAU). She has more than 60 publications in Russian and foreign peer-reviewed scientific journals and books, including on issues of ensuring economic security and digital transformation of agricultural production and the financial sector.

Ibragim K. Shaov
Candidate of Legal Sciences, Associate Professor of the Department of Constitutional and Administrative Law of *Adyghe State University (Maykop, Russia)*. His research interests include international law; European law; social partnership and building civil society. He is the author of more than 30 scientific articles in Russian and foreign scientific journals.

Ella N. Shchegoleva
Associate Professor of *I.N. Ulyanov Chuvash State University (Cheboksary, Russia)*. In 1985, she graduated from the Leningrad Institute of Finance and Economics. From 1987 to 1990, she studied at the full-time postgraduate course of the Leningrad Financial and Economic Institute, after which she defended her dissertation for the degree of Candidate of Economics, specialty 08.00.05 ("Economics and management of the national economy"). At present, the sphere of her scientific interests is connected with the theory of industry markets, corporate planning, organization of commercial activities of an enterprise, diagnostics of the economic potential of a business, and the assessment of the competitiveness of a business and the sustainability of its functioning.

Elena G. Shcherbakova
Associate Professor of the Department of Management of National Research Ogarev Mordovia State University *(Saransk, Russia)*. Graduated from the Faculty of Economics of the Mordovian University (1993). PhD in Economics (2004). Associate Professor (2007). Scientific interests: research of marketing problems in the markets of goods and services, competitiveness of organizations. More than 100 scientific and educational works, including 10 manuals.

Ludmila L. Shtofer
Candidate of Philosophy, Associate Professor, Head of the Philosophy and Culturology Department of the Rostov State University of Economics. Member of the Editorial Board of the journal "Bulletin of Don State Agrarian University". Her research interests include military-political conflicts, information war,

spiritual security, ecological culture, cultural identity, historical memory, digitalization of education, public health, social inclusion. The author of over than 100 works, including those which are indexed by Scopus and Web of Science.

Lyudmila A. Shvachkina
Doctor of Science (Philosophy), Professor of the Department of Social and Humanitarian Disciplines of the Institute of Service and Entrepreneurship (branch) of Don State Technical University in Shakhty. Her scientific interests include the history and theory of culture, social anthropology, philosophical anthropology, and globalization processes. Lyudmila A. Shvachkina participates in Russian and international scientific and practical conferences, is the editor and author of collective monographs, and serves as a guest editor of international scientific journals. She has published more than 100 works in Russian and foreign peer-reviewed scientific journals and books.

Zhanna V. Smirnova
Candidate of Pedagogical Sciences, Associate Professor of the Department of Service Technologies and Technological Education, Minin Nizhny Novgorod State Pedagogical University, has been working in the field of higher education since 1996. In 2004 she defended her Ph.D. thesis on the topic "Training a master of vocational training in the structure of an engineering and pedagogical university". She is the author of more than 300 publications, 15 of them are educational and methodological. Has 122 scientific articles indexed by the international database Scopus. Supervises the main professional educational program in the direction of "Service". Main scientific interests: Problems of technological training of university students Organization of independent work of students at the university Application of information technologies in the learning process. Organization of professional activity of a teacher in the structure of the university. The system of development of additional education. Actively participates in scientific conferences, seminars and round tables, supervises the research work of students.

Olga V. Smyshliaeva
Senior Lecturer of the Department of Applied Informatics and Information Technologies in Education of *Minin Nizhny Novgorod State Pedagogical University* (Nizhny Novgorod, Russia). Scientific interests: possibilities of information technologies in special education. In 2020, she took advanced training courses under the program "End-to-End Technologies. Information infrastructure, digital environment and artificial intelligence" at Tomsk State University. In 2021, she was trained as part of the Intel® AI for Youth Trainer Training

Initiatives "AI Technologies for Everyone" with the status of a certified teacher in the Intel® Skills for Innovation program (Skills for Innovation). She has publications in Russian editions.

Irina A. Tarasova
Associate Professor of the Department of Applied Mathematics of *Volgograd State Technical University* (*Volgograd, Russia*), the author of about 100 publications. Her research interests include robotization, recycling, artificial intelligence, entrepreneurship, automation, and economic and mathematical modeling. She has published textbooks on optimization in engineering and management problems, risk modeling, information security, and statistical data processing.

Larisa T. Tlekhurai-Berzegova
Head of the Department of Personnel Management of *Adygea State University* (*Maykop, Russia*), the author of more than 100 publications. Her research interests include human resource management (HRM), business-university collaboration, HR policy of an organization, personnel training, effective contract in the university, and personnel development. She has published educational and methodological manuals on human resource management and the basics of work organization.

Claudio Tomazzoli
Ph.D. in Computer Science, Fellow of the University of Verona, Member of the Order of the Institute of Electrical and Electronics Engineers. The author's research interests are related to information communications, human behavior in social networks, information terrorism, and the improvement of energy-saving methods of the environment using artificial intelligence. Most of the author's research focuses on intelligent innovations, software development, a multi-agent approach to environmental monitoring, bioinformatics, and the study of computer methods aimed at data storage, analysis, and visualization. Claudio Tomazzoli is the author of more than 100 scientific publications in foreign publishing houses and a participant in various international conferences in the field of advanced digital transformations and information technologies.

Nataliya A. Tovma
doctor (PhD), candidate of economic sciences, deputy head of the "Business Technology" department of *Al-Farabi Kazakh National University* (*Almaty, Kazakhstan*); academician of the International Academy of Informatization, professor of the Russian Academy of Natural Sciences. He has 4 foreign and

8 Kazakh awards, three-time winner of state scientific scholarships of MON RK for talented young scientists (2008–2010, 2012–2013, 2013–2014). 12 research internships were held abroad: in Turkey, the Russian Federation, the Czech Republic, Great Britain, Poland, Spain, Italy, Germany, Switzerland and the USA. Published more than 100 scientific works, including 19 in journals indexed by the Scopus database, 3 of them with a percentile higher than 50. The Hirsch index is 4. Scientific interests are related to the processes of digitization of the economy, information economy, knowledge economy. Was a manager in two projects and a responsible executor in 6 fundamental projects of grant funding of MES RK. Supervised the following projects for grant financing of scientific researches of the MES RK: (1) 2021–2023 – AP09057847 "Formation and development of the knowledge economy in the conditions of digitalization of the Republic of Kazakhstan: conceptual foundations and implementation prospects"; (2) 2018–2020 – AP05135078 "Formation and development of digital economy in the Republic of Kazakhstan: theory and practical implementation measures".

Fatima K. Tuguz
Director of the Institute of Arts of the Adyghe State University, Advisor to the Rector of the Adyghe State University on Cultural Affairs (Maikop, Republic of Adygea, Russian Federation), Doctor of Philosophy, Honorary Worker of Education of the Russian Federation. The scientific interests of the author relate to the role and potential of the classical university in the formation of personality and the problems of the development of the regional classical university as a space for the preservation of culture and the socialization of young people. She has published more than 40 scientific articles and monographs on this issue. Fatima K. Tuguz takes an active part in organizing and holding major scientific, cultural, and youth events at the Adyghe State University.

Elmira N. Uteeva
graduated from the Kazan State Medical University with a degree in Social Work; Kazan (Privolzhsky) Federal University in the direction of training "Pedagogical education" and "Pedagogy of higher education." Elmira N. Uteeva works at the *Kazan State Medical University of the Ministry of Health of the Russian Federation (Kazan, Russia)* as a deputy head of the educational and methodological department and senior lecturer in the department of economic theory and social work. She analyzes the innovative processes occurring in the educational sector to introduce them into the educational process and control the educational and methodological work of the departments. She participates in creating software, information and methodological tools,

and automated systems for educational purposes. Moreover, she improves the methodological documentation that regulates the educational process. She improves her scientific and professional qualifications under the programs "Current requirements for medical education. Methods of e-learning using distance technologies," "Digital technologies in the professional activities of scientific and pedagogical workers of higher education institutions in the context of digitalization of education," "Digital literacy of a contemporary teacher," and "Digital education trends." She has more than 60 publications, including on the problems of introducing digital technologies into the educational process.

Mikhail V. Vinichenko
Doctor of Historical Sciences, Professor, Professor of the Faculty of Humanities of the Russian State Social University, the author of more than 530 works on the sociology of management, digitalization of society, the use of artificial intelligence in socio-economic systems, the development of the Russian and international educational environment, personnel management, efficiency improvement technologies, and world history. His works are of interest in Russia and abroad. The conducted studies are based on the author's empirical data and those obtained by other scientists. His studies consider current trends and patterns of socio-economic development of society. Sociological research is organized and conducted in Russia and other countries of the world and is reflected in scientific articles in the journals of the Scopus and Web of Science databases, materials of international conferences, monographs, and fundamental works. Scientific works of Mikhail V. Vinichenko pay particular attention to the problems that have arisen in the context of the COVID-19 pandemic, the dynamic digitalization of society, and the introduction of artificial intelligence from the standpoint of representatives of various faiths and the future of civilization – Generation Z.

Natalia V. Vinogradova
Candidate of Pedagogical Sciences, Associate Professor at the Department of Painting and Art Education, Togliatti State University, Head of Master Program 44.04.01 "Pedagogical Education (Art Education)." The author's research interests are related to art pedagogy, the search for methods and technologies to develop and educate children and adults in the artistic perception of color, imaginative thinking, a sense of color, and visual culture. In her works, the author pays much attention to the problems of digitalization, humanitarianization, and ecologization of education, the prospects of vocational training of students in an industrial revolution, the formation of a system of values and semantic orientations, and the development of personal spiritual culture

and its familiarization with national traditions through art and art activities. Natalia V. Vinogradova participates in international and all-Russian conferences. She is the author of more than 40 scientific publications in Russian and foreign books and journals.

Konstantin V. Vodenko

Konstantin V. Vodenko – Doctor of Philosophy, Head of the Department of Philosophy and Cultural Studies of *Platov South-Russian State Polytechnic University (NPI) (Novocherkassk, Russia)*, professor in the scientific specialty "Social structure, social institutions and processes." Master of Public and Municipal Administration; Master of Sociology.

He is the head of the master's program "State and Municipal socio-economic policy in the field of State and municipal Administration". Actively participates in research work and is engaged in the study of socio-cultural and socio-economic institutions in the context of the formation of a national model of social development and public administration. He is the first deputy editor-in-chief of the scientific journal "Humanities of the South of Russia". He is a member of the organizing committees of various international conferences. The total number of publications is more than 290. He was the responsible editor of the book (collection of articles) indexed in the Scopus and Web of Sciense databases: Public Administration and Regional Management in Russia – Challenges and Prospects in a Multicultural Region [Springer International Publishing AG]. 15 PhD theses have been defended by the scientific leadership. Member of the Dissertation Council at the Southern Federal University. Member of the Dissertation Council at the Southern Federal University. 15 PhD theses have been defended by the scientific leadership.

Elena V. Volkova

Candidate of Pedagogical Sciences, the executive in charge of career guidance counseling at the department of foreign languages of Kazan national research technological university (KNITU) (Kazan, Russia), the participate and organizer of international programs. Her scientific interests include the theory of sociocultural sphere in pedagogy, intercultural communication, competences development in higher education, sustainable development, and globalization. The last researches were devoted in social typology of a personality and digitalization in education. Elena V. Volkova took part in Russian and international scientific and practical conferences and is the author of a monograph and school books. She has published more than 70 works in Russian and foreign peer-reviewed scientific journals and books.

Daria O. Zabaznova
Associate Professor of the Department of Accounting and Audit of *Volgograd State Agricultural University* (*Volgograd, Russia*), the author of more than 60 publications. Research interests include holdings, agro-industrial complex, agricultural holdings, accounting policy, agricultural producers, accounting, enterprise credit portfolio, and financial infrastructure. She is the author of a monograph on economic analysis.

Zarema M. Zaripova
Associate Professor of the Department of Theory and Practice of Teaching Foreign Languages of *Kazan Federal University* (*Kazan, Russia*). She graduated from the Kazan State Pedagogical Institute with a degree in German and English. In 1988, she defended her thesis for the degree of Candidate of Philological Sciences. In 2005, she received the academic title of Associate Professor in the Department of Foreign Languages: German teacher in the following disciplines: the practice of German speech, the theoretical foundations of second foreign language (German), regional studies, linguistic and regional studies, and stylistics. Zarema M. Zaripova improves her scientific and professional qualifications in the programs "Theory and practice of using LMS MOODLE in teaching," "Information competence of teachers in the field of IT application in the educational process of the university," "Digital technologies in prof. activities of scientific and pedagogical workers of institutions of higher education in the conditions of digitalization of KFU," and "Electronic information educational environment of the university: digital resources." She has also developed an online course "Interactive approaches to teaching German as a second foreign language." Zarema M. Zaripova has more than 80 publications, including on intercultural and interlingual exchange in the area of education.

Galina M. Zemlyakova
Candidate of Pedagogic Sciences, Associate Professor in the Department of Painting and Art Education, Togliatti State University. The field of scientific interests of Galina M. Zemlyakova is associated with the history and theory of the development of art education from the historical and contemporary perspective. In her works, the author pays great attention to the quality of higher art education, targeted training of students in the context of modernization and transformation of the education system, the definition of the content side of the educational process, the development of intellectual potential and spiritual and moral aspects of personality. Galina M. Zemlyakova cooperates with the heads of art schools and institutions of general and additional

education. She is the organizer of creative competitions and Olympiads in the field of artistic disciplines among young people.

Zuriet A. Zhade

Doctor of Political Sciences, Professor, Head of the Department of Theory and History of State and Law, Constitutional Construction and Political Science of the Scientific and Educational Cluster Institute of Law, Head of the Laboratory of Ethnocultural Problems of the Research Institute of Complex Problems of the Adyghe State University (Maikop, Russia). Honored Scientist of the Republic of Adygea. Honorary Worker of Education of the Russian Federation. Head of RFBR grants "Construction of the image of the Republic of Adygea in the space of social media"; "Interaction between government and society in the context of a new global risk: tendencies of (dis)integration"; "Mechanisms for strengthening trust in authorities in the regions of Russia in the post-pandemic period: a political and sociological analysis". Member of the editorial board of journals: Bulletin of the Adyghe State University. Regional Studies Series (Maikop), South Russian Journal of Social Sciences (Krasnodar), Theory and Practice of Social Development (Krasnodar), Society: Sociology, Psychology, Pedagogy (Krasnodar), Theory and Problems of Political Research (Moscow). He is an organizer and participant of international scientific and practical conferences, is a co-author of a number of collective monographs. Author of more than 450 papers in Russian and foreign peer-reviewed scientific publications. Research interests: multi-level identity, identity politics, political identity, ethno-social processes, inter-ethnic tension, trust in power.

Galina N. Zvereva

Associate Professor of the Department of Management of *Volgograd State Agricultural University* (*Volgograd, Russia*), the author published more than 60 publications. Research interests include agribusiness, organic agricultural production, lean production, business organization and management, regional economics, production cooperation, management efficiency, and agribusiness. The author issued methodological recommendations on design and technological practice and on the feasibility study of the project.

Introduction
Role of Higher Education in Enhancing Social Mobility and Reducing Social Inequality

Elena G. Popkova, Bruno S. Sergi and Konstantin V. Vodenko

Social inequality is a manifestation of an imperfect social model. It is the result of "institutional traps" – unfair traditions that have lost their relevance but continue to exist based on self-sustaining institutions: gender inequality, ageism, and cultural inequality. Social inequality is a considerable barrier to the development of society.

Thus, gender inequality hinders women's employment, career development, and human potential, which reduces the overall productivity of the economic system and hampers its economic growth. Ageism causes unemployment among workers of pre-retirement age, inhibiting the transfer of experience in society and the economy. Another manifestation of ageism is the difficulty in finding jobs faced by talented young people who have just graduated from universities; these difficulties are associated with the lack of work experience required by employers. Cultural inequality hinders employment and the formation of multicultural work teams.

The essence of social inequality is the unfair selection of candidates for jobs, due to which employment opportunities, career building, and salary levels are determined not by objective (skill level, work experience, abilities, and talents) but by subjective characteristics (gender and cultural background, age). The results of social inequality are unemployment and income inequality. To maintain social stability, protect the rule of law, and fight poverty, the government has to assume the function of smoothing social inequality through the payment of social benefits, including unemployment benefits.

The problem of social inequality is exacerbated by the fact that it is often systemic in nature, covering the labor market and the market for higher education. This is manifested in the unfair selection of applicants and the inaccessibility of higher education to applicants from low-income and vulnerable social groups. Inaccessibility of education reduces competitiveness in the labor market. This is how social inequality is institutionalized in today's context, where traditions that have lost relevance are reinforced by economic justification.

Social mobility is a way of overcoming social inequality. It creates social elevators on terms of equal opportunity for all members of society, erasing the boundaries between social categories. Higher education with equal access and objective selection of applicants plays an important role in social mobility. Equal development of the human potential of students contributes to their equally high competitiveness in the labor market and forms a "healthy" competition of human resources in this market. This is how social differences are erased, and social inequalities are overcome.

Deep social shifts are now taking place, replacing "institutional traps" with new progressive institutions that support the Sustainable Development Goals (SDGs), such as SDG 1, SDG 4, SDG 5, SDG 8, and SDG 10. The first institution is the knowledge society. The advantage of this institution, which is at the heart of the equitable model of social structure, is that it is knowledge and natural talents that determine opportunities for university entrance, higher education, employment, and career building.

The philosophy of lifelong learning and the universal availability of knowledge and its role as a factor in the competition of human resources (the competition of knowledge) ensure cultural openness – the social justice of the knowledge society. This makes it possible to achieve a social equilibrium (Pareto-optimum) in which everyone can unlock their human potential according to their current abilities and, if they wish, can upgrade their skills and achieve new professional successes, as well as increase their income.

The second institution is inclusive higher education. This institution is closely related to the previous one because inclusive higher education is a crucial feature and advantage of the knowledge economy. Nevertheless, it is singled out as a separate institution because it is not only about the fair selection of students but also about ensuring the flexibility of the higher education system in general and universities in particular, which adjust to the individual characteristics and needs of each student.

In particular, inclusiveness implies the creation of favorable and comfortable conditions for the education of persons with disabilities, adjusting the educational process to them for the development of their human potential and their subsequent successful employment. Inclusive higher education makes "healthy" competition in the labor market accessible to people with disabilities, creating unprecedented opportunities for social mobility.

The third institution is high-tech higher education (EdTech). The digital economy has opened up new technological opportunities actively implemented in higher education. A striking example is distance learning, which supports social mobility by allowing students to study on their own schedule at a convenient time (allowing them to combine work and study) with individual remote (and, therefore, devoid of subjective evaluations) interaction with teachers.

The fourth institution is flexible and highly efficient management of higher education. The management of today's universities is based on marketing tools. This makes it possible to consider the priorities of all stakeholders. Universities have become wide open for all applicants and students, as well as for graduates to continue their education. Employers get opportunities for corporate training and filling gaps in their employees' competencies. Thus, high expectations and the state's strict standards for university quality and efficiency are met.

A shortcoming of the existing literature is the consideration of these institutions in isolation. This approach does not provide a holistic view of the current situation in the higher education market and the labor market. Moreover, it does not allow assessing the prospects for increasing social mobility and reducing social inequality. This lack of existing literature is overcome in this book, which systematically examines all institutions and provides a comprehensive view of social mobility and progress toward reducing social inequality.

The book aims to explore the role of higher education in increasing social mobility and reducing social inequality in today's world. This goal determined the logic and structure of the book, which is divided into four parts. The first part examines the cultural openness of the knowledge society and identifies its contribution to reducing social inequality. It examines multicultural competencies and best practices for overcoming cultural differences in higher education. Additionally, the first part outlines the guidelines for a new culture of higher education consistent with the philosophy of the knowledge society.

The second part focuses on inclusive higher education in support of social mobility. It focuses on the openness of universities to people with disabilities. The third part reveals digital technologies in higher education and their importance for the growth of social mobility. It covers distance learning during the COVID-19 pandemic, virtual and augmented reality technologies in higher education and other technical innovations. The book concludes with the fourth part, which focuses on managing education to reduce social inequalities. It strikes the right balance between the quality and efficiency of universities in support of their openness to encourage social mobility and reduce social inequality.

The novelty of this book is that it offers a new perspective on social inequality from the perspective of institutions. This new perspective allows us to most authentically define the role of higher education in increasing social mobility, and to propose an institutional approach to overcoming social inequalities in the knowledge society. The book is also unique in that it covers various forms of social inequalities, including the least explored cultural inequalities and educational and employment barriers for people with disabilities, which are successfully overcome in the knowledge society.

The practical relevance of the book lies in the fact that it highlights and discusses the best practices for overcoming social inequality through social mobility based on higher education. In particular, the book presents empirical evidence and cases from Russia and Kyrgyzstan, as well as other developed and developing countries. The book focuses separately on the advantages and disadvantages of university rankings, as well as the prospects for overcoming them.

The primary target audience for this book is scholars who study manifestations of social inequality in contemporary society and ways to overcome it. In this book, they will find a systemic view of the most common forms of social inequality. The book also presents a scientific concept of a comprehensive solution to current problems of social inequality through increased social mobility based on ensuring the inclusiveness of higher education. The book is of interest to representatives of various social sciences and humanities, including sociology, cultural studies, political science, law, psychology, pedagogy, economics, and management.

The secondary target audience for this book is practicing experts, for whom the book presents current international experience and case studies. In this book, government regulators of higher education and labor markets will find recommendations for making these markets inclusive and fostering the cultural openness of the knowledge economy. University administrators will find practical recommendations for improving educational management, particularly through greater use of digital technology, in support of reducing social inequality.

PART 1

*Cultural Openness of the Knowledge Society and
Its Contribution to Reducing Social Inequality*

CHAPTER 1

Benefits of Distance Education for Overcoming Cultural Disparities, Opening Universities to Persons with Disabilities, and Ensuring Inclusive Higher Education

Elena G. Popkova

Abstract

This chapter aims to explore the benefits of distance learning in bridging cultural differences, opening universities to people with disabilities, and making higher education inclusive. The chapter reveals a significant contribution of distance learning to the inclusiveness of universities. Distance learning creates advantages (compared to traditional learning) to achieve all manifestations of inclusiveness in higher education and universities. The theoretical significance of the research results is that they quantified the extent to which the potential of distance learning to increase the inclusiveness of universities is realized in practice and showed that special management measures are needed to unlock this potential fully. The chapter's contribution to the literature is that it uncovered the social aspects of distance learning and that its significant contribution to the inclusiveness of universities and higher education is unknown. The practical significance of the research results is that the experience of leading universities from developed countries discussed in this chapter will be useful for other universities, including those in developing countries. The social significance is that the development of distance learning will increase the overall inclusiveness of higher education globally and contribute to the systemic implementation of SDG 4, SDG 5, SDG 8, and SDG 10.

Keywords

distance learning – overcoming cultural differences – openness of universities to people with disabilities – inclusiveness of higher education – competitiveness of universities

1   Introduction

In the digital economy, the Fourth Industrial Revolution has made distance learning possible and increasingly widespread around the world. Distance learning represents a new format of training, the feature of which is the remote interaction of teachers and students. Moreover, it provides the widest possible range of automation in the process of providing and receiving higher education services (*Forlin and Lian*, 2008; *Forlin and Tierney*, 2006; *Sibirskaya* et al., 2019). These tools include repetitive on-demand e-lectures that are scalable to any number of students, automatically tested online lectures, educational chatbots and robots, and others.

Distance learning has the potential to make universities more inclusive. First, distance learning overcomes cultural differences in higher education. It contributes to the internationalization of universities because it allows the university's educational courses to be broadcast worldwide in different languages, as well as online communication between students and faculty through auto-translators. Distance learning can also help achieve a gender-neutral learning process at universities (*Abdul-Rahaman* et al., 2022; *Hrebeniuk* et al., 2022).

Second, distance learning can support the openness of universities to people with disabilities because it does not require these people to adjust to the lack of flexibility of universities, but universities begin to consider the individual characteristics of people with disabilities and adapt the distance learning process for them (*Alexandra Da Fonte* et al., 2020; *Correia* et al., 2022; *Forlin*, 2007; *Maconi* et al., 2019).

Third, distance learning can increase the overall inclusiveness of universities and higher education for applicants and students due to the increased flexibility and convenience of the educational process (e.g., the ability to combine study with work) and the reduced cost of tuition in the university (*Abdullah and Mohamad Said*, 2022; *Karipi* et al., 2022).

The problem lies in the uncertainty of the extent to which the noted potential of distance learning to increase the inclusiveness of universities is realized in practice and how to realize this potential fully. This chapter addresses the problem and aims to explore the benefits of distance learning in bridging cultural differences, opening universities to people with disabilities, and making higher education inclusive.

2   Literature Review

This chapter is based on the Theory of Distance Learning, which considers distance learning from the perspective of technology – as a promising direction for developing high-tech education (EdTech). *Antonova and Kashevarova* (2022), *Benčič* et al. (2020), *Frolova and Rusakova* (2022), *Kamenkov* (2022), *Segbenya* et al. (2022), *Shabaltina* et al. (2021), *Shi-Hui* et al. (2022), *Vanchukhina* et al. (2019) note that distance learning is not intended to replace but rather to supplement and substitute for traditional learning when traditional learning is not available. The COVID-19 pandemic is a case in point: most countries worldwide switched to temporary distance education due to the strict requirements of social distancing (in 2020), returning to the traditional format of higher education by now (2021–2022).

Alnasraween and Shahadab (2022), *Fujs* et al. (2022), and *Gnawali* et al. (2022) point out that the key advantage of distance learning from a technical point of view is its high efficiency due to the reduction in the number of teachers per student and the significant increase in the productive capacity of the university while its infrastructure (campuses, etc.) remains the same. However, the quality of learning may be diminished.

Thus, according to an international survey conducted by Research Portal for Scientists "Research" (2020) in the academic year 2021–2022, 50% of students (undergraduate) indicated the same quality of higher education as in traditional education. It should be noted that 11% of students (undergraduate) and 10% of graduates felt that the quality of distance learning is lower than the quality of traditional education. In this regard, distance learning can reduce the competitiveness of universities and is, therefore, preferable for local universities but not for the world's leading universities.

Abdullah Alkhabra (2022), *Abrantes* et al. (2022), *Domínguez-Figaredo* et al. (2022), and *Salta* et al. (2022) write that the inclusiveness of higher education through distance learning is self-assured and guaranteed. This process does not require any government intervention or managerial action on the part of university authorities. From a technical point of view, the transition to distance learning does contribute to a more rational learning process and a more objective assessment of knowledge. However, from a social point of view, remote interaction between teachers and students definitely has psychological peculiarities, especially if it does not involve their offline contacts.

The literature review revealed that the social aspects of distance learning are not fully disclosed, and its actual contribution to the inclusiveness of universities and higher education is unknown, which is a research gap. The identified research gap is filled in this chapter through an empirical study of the current

TABLE 1.1 Statistics on distance learning and openness of universities to persons with disabilities

Country	Conditions for e-learning, score 0–100	Persons aged 15–64 participating in education and training, having no work limitation caused by a LHPAD, %	Persons aged 15–64 participating in education and training, having a work limitation caused by a LHPAD, %
Norway	100.00	44	28
Switzerland	95.4	38	26
Luxembourg	94.4	28	14
Netherlands	84.8	31	14
Sweden	97.0	37	32
Austria	75.8	24	9
Finland	71.0	37	20
Germany	60.8	22	6
France	57.3	19	9
Hungary	52.7	18	3

SOURCE: COMPILED BY THE AUTHOR BASED ON EUROSTAT (2014) AND HR NEWS (2020)

experience of extracting the benefits of distance learning for inclusiveness of leading universities from developed countries that have achieved outstanding success in the field of inclusiveness.

3   Materials and Methods

To determine the benefits of distance learning for the inclusiveness of higher education, the author selected ten (developed) countries included in the top 16 countries with the best infrastructure for e-learning according to *HR News* (2020) estimates, for which statistics are available for persons aged 15–64 participating in education and training, by country and disability status (*Eurostat*, 2014). The statistics for these countries are shown in Table 1.1.

One top university with the best ranking in the *Times Higher Education* (2022) in 2022 and an outstanding record of inclusiveness is selected for each country in the sample. Statistics on international activities (overcoming cultural differences), gender neutrality, and overall inclusiveness (overall score) of the selected universities for 2022 are collected in Table 1.2.

This chapter conducts a quantitative-qualitative study to obtain the most reliable and valid results. Based on the statistics from Table 1.1 and Table 1.2, the author applied a correlation analysis to quantify the contribution of distance learning to the inclusiveness of universities. The arithmetic mean and correlation coefficients of indicators of inclusiveness of higher education and universities with conditions for e-learning are calculated. The method of comparative analysis qualitatively identifies the advantages of distance learning for the inclusiveness of universities compared with traditional training.

TABLE 1.2 Success of leading universities in overcoming cultural differences, gender neutrality, and overall inclusiveness in higher education in 2022

Country	The university with the best ranking on THE	International students, %	Female: Male ratio (share of women among students), %	Overall score, 0–100
Norway	University of Oslo	19	66	60.1
Switzerland	ETH Zurich	41	32	88.2
Luxembourg	University of Luxemburg	52	53	50.3 (48.1–50.3)
Netherlands	Wageningen University & Research	27	53	70.1
Sweden	Karolinska Institute	24	69	74.3
Austria	University of Vienna	29	66	58.4
Finland	University of Helsinki	6	67	62.2
Germany	LMU Munich	18	61	78.6
France	Paris Sciences et Lettres – PSL Research University Paris	25	47	74.1
Hungary	Semmelweis University	33	72	50.3 (48.1–50.3)

SOURCE: COMPILED BY THE AUTHOR BASED ON TIMES HIGHER EDUCATION (2022)

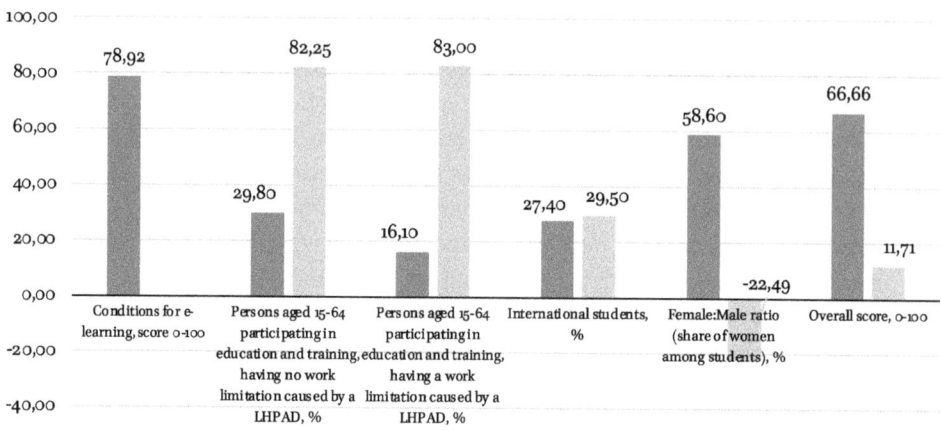

CHART 1.1 The average level of inclusiveness in higher education and leading universities and its correlation with the level of development of distance learning
SOURCE: CALCULATED AND COMPILED BY THE AUTHOR

4 Results

4.1 The Contribution of Distance Learning to the Inclusiveness of Universities

Based on the statistics from Table 1.1 and Table 1.2, using the method of correlation analysis in Chart 1.1, the author determined the overall level of inclusiveness of higher education and the contribution of distance learning to the achievement of inclusive universities.

According to Chart 1.1, the leading universities from developed countries have an overall favorable environment for e-learning, which averaged a score of 78.92. The share of persons aged 15–64 participating in education and training and having no work limitation caused by an LHPAD averages 29.80%. It is 82.25% determined by the development of distance learning (a very close relationship). The share of persons aged 15–64 participating in education and training and having a work limitation caused by a LHPAD averages 16.10% (2 times less). Its connection with distance learning is even stronger: the correlation is 83%.

The share of international students averages 27.40%; it is 29.50% determined by the development of distance learning. Female:Male ratio (the share of women among students) averages 58.60% (very high). Nevertheless, distance learning does not contribute to its improvement (the correlation is negative: -22.49%). The overall level of inclusiveness and competitiveness of universities (overall score) is estimated at 66.66 points. It is 11.71% determined by the development of distance learning. Consequently, the development of distance learning does not guarantee the growth of inclusiveness. However, it can significantly increase inclusiveness under certain conditions and appropriate measures of state regulation and university management.

4.2   Advantages of Distance Learning for Inclusive Universities Compared to Traditional Learning

The advantages of distance learning for university inclusiveness over traditional learning are reflected in the results of their comparative analysis presented in Table 1.3.

As shown in Table 1.3, overcoming cultural differences in higher education and the internationalization of universities in traditional teaching involves high demands on faculty, not only from a teaching perspective but also from an international teaching perspective. In this case, preference may be given to teachers better versed in foreign languages and international instructors rather than to leading professionals in their subject area. Distance learning allows achieving this through the one-time involvement of experts (e.g., professional translators, foreign teachers, and programmers) to create international educational courses with the teachers' focus on the quality of learning.

Achieving gender neutrality in traditional education requires increasing the number of teachers per student when creating educational commissions to assess students' knowledge objectively. Distance learning provides an individual approach and a gender-neutral assessment of knowledge, which is implied in this form of education.

The openness of universities to people with disabilities in traditional education requires the development of infrastructure (campuses, etc.) of universities. Nevertheless, this only partially increases inclusiveness; for example, university buildings can be well-equipped while dormitories may not be equipped or equipped not for all types of disabilities, etc. Distance learning achieves full inclusiveness while preserving the usual lifestyle of people with disabilities (they live at home).

General inclusiveness as the attractiveness and competitiveness of universities and higher education in traditional teaching implies a slow modernization of educational programs with high resistance to change on the part of university staff. In traditional education, it is facilitated by the flexibility and openness of educational programs to change.

TABLE 1.3 Comparative analysis of the achievement of inclusiveness in traditional and distance learning in universities

Manifestation of inclusiveness	Traditional learning	Distance learning
Overcoming cultural differences in higher education and the internationalization of universities	High requirements for teachers in terms of training and teaching on an international level	One-time use of experts to create international educational courses with a teachers' focus on the quality of teaching
Achieving a gender-neutral learning process	Increasing the number of teachers per student in the creation of educational commissions to achieve objectivity	Individual approach and gender-neutral assessment of knowledge, which is implied by distance learning
Openness of universities to people with disabilities	The need to develop the infrastructure (campuses, etc.) of universities; this only partially increases the inclusiveness	Full inclusiveness while maintaining the usual lifestyle of people with disabilities
Overall inclusiveness as the attractiveness and competitiveness of universities and higher education	Slow modernization of educational programs with high resistance to change on the part of university staff	Flexibility and openness of educational programs to change

SOURCE: DEVELOPED BY THE AUTHOR

5 Discussion

The chapter contributes to the development of the Theory of Distance Learning by revealing its new – social aspect. In contrast to *Antonova and Kashevarova* (2022), *Benčič* et al. (2020), *Frolova and Rusakova* (2022), *Kamenkov* (2022), *Segbenya* et al. (2022), *Shabaltina* et al. (2021), *Shi-Hui* et al. (2022), and *Vanchukhina* et al. (2019), the author revealed that distance learning could completely replace traditional learning. From the perspective of social interaction between teachers and students (e.g., for persons with disabilities), distance learning is preferable and sufficient for the full and successful completion of their educational course and mastery of all necessary competencies.

In contrast to *Alnasraween and Shahadab* (2022), *Fujs* et al. (2022), and *Gnawali* et al. (2022), the chapter found that the quality of distance learning is not lower and may even be higher than that of traditional education but only with a high level of organization of the distance learning process. The development of distance learning increases the competitiveness of universities, as proven by leading universities in developed countries. Consequently, distance learning can and should be developed not only by local universities but also by leading universities to increase their inclusiveness and competitiveness while increasing the quality of providing higher education services.

In contrast to *Abdullah Alkhabra* (2022), *Abrantes* et al. (2022), *Domínguez-Figaredo* et al. (2022), and *Salta* et al. (2022), it is substantiated that the inclusiveness of higher education in distance learning is not increased independently and is not guaranteed. For example, the gender neutrality of the educational process at leading universities decreases in developed countries as distance learning develops. Consequently, the development of distance learning requires state intervention and special management measures on the part of the university to obtain the benefits of inclusiveness.

6   Conclusion

The chapter reveals a significant contribution of distance learning to the inclusiveness of universities. The conditions for e-learning were found to determine the share of persons aged 15–64 participating in education and training and having no work limitation caused by a LHPAD by 82.25%, and the share of persons aged 15–64 participating in education and training and having a work limitation caused by a LHPAD by 83%. Conditions for e-learning also determine the share of international students by 29.50% and the overall level of inclusiveness and competitiveness of universities (overall score according to Times Higher Education in 2022) by 11.71%.

Distance learning creates advantages (compared to traditional learning) to achieve all manifestations of inclusiveness in higher education and universities. To overcome cultural differences in higher education and ensure the internationalization of universities, a one-time involvement of experts to create international educational courses for distance learning is enough, allowing one to maintain teachers' focus on the quality of teaching.

The individualized approach and gender-neutral assessment of knowledge assumed by distance education are available to achieve gender-neutrality in the learning process. To ensure that universities are open to people with disabilities, distance learning is fully inclusive while preserving the familiar lifestyles of people with disabilities. To increase overall inclusiveness as the attractiveness and competitiveness of universities and higher education, distance learning provides the flexibility and openness of educational programs to change.

It is important to note that with traditional education, full inclusiveness is difficult to achieve because it requires a serious expense that most universities cannot afford. In contrast, distance learning requires minimal costs, is even more economical, and makes it possible to achieve full inclusiveness in all its manifestations. The theoretical significance of these results is that they quantified the extent to which the potential of distance learning to increase the inclusiveness of universities is realized in practice. Moreover, the research results also showed that special management measures are needed to unlock this potential fully.

The chapter's contribution to the literature is that it uncovered the social aspects of distance learning and that its significant factual contribution to the inclusiveness of universities and higher education is unknown. The practical significance of the research results is that the experience of leading universities from developed countries discussed in this chapter will be useful for other universities, including those in developing countries. The social significance is that the development of distance learning will increase the overall inclusiveness of higher education globally and contribute to the systemic implementation of SDG 4, SDG 5, SDG 8, and SDG 10.

References

Abdullah Alkhabra S (2022) An exploration of applicability of social constructivism approach in distance learning amid the COVID-19 pandemic; the case study of Hail University (UOH). *International Journal of Information and Learning Technology* 39(3): 282–304. DOI: 10.1108/IJILT-11-2021-0166.

Abdullah Z, and Mohamad Said MNH (2022) Engaging and empowering Malaysian students through open and distance learning in the post-COVID era. *Frontiers in Education* 7: 853796. DOI: 10.3389/feduc.2022.853796.

Abdul-Rahaman N, Terentev E, and Arkorful VE (2022) COVID-19 and distance learning: International doctoral students' satisfaction with the general quality of learning and aspects of university support in Russia. *Public Organization Review*. DOI: 10.1007/s11115-022-00608-x.

Abrantes P, Silva AP, Backstrom B, Neves C, Falé I, Jacquinet M, ... Henriques S (2022) Transversal Competences and Employability: The impacts of distance learning university according to graduates' follow-up. *Education Sciences* 12(2): 65. DOI: 10.3390/educsci12020065.

Alexandra Da Fonte M, Boesch MC, and Clouse K (2020) Aided communication systems: Using assistive technology to support individuals with complex communication needs. *International Perspectives on Inclusive Education* 14: 69–91. DOI: 10.1108/S1479-363620200000014008.

Alnasraween MS, and Shahadab FH (2022) Obstacles of teaching distance universities courses in light of E-learning quality standards. *Cypriot Journal of Educational Sciences* 17(4): 1244–1257. DOI: 10.18844/cjes.v17i4.7145.

Antonova NV, and Kashevarova YN (2022) Industry 4.0 as the basis for the transformation of social relationships in the field of labor and employment in the EEU countries. In: Inshakova AO, and Frolova EE (eds) *The transformation of social relationships in industry 4.0: Economic security and legal prevention.* Charlotte, NC: Information Age Publishing, 333–345.

Benčič S, Kitsay YA, Karbekova AB, and Giyazov A (2020) Specifics of building the digital economy in developed and developing countries. In: Popkova E, and Sergi B (eds) *Digital economy: Complexity and variety vs. rationality.* Cham, Switzerland: Springer, 39–48. DOI: 10.1007/978-3-030-29586-8_5.

Correia AM, Forlin C, and Sio E (2022) Exploring the participation and agency of students with special education needs in a Macau-Chinese secondary school. *Journal of Research in Special Educational Needs* 22(3): 288–296. DOI: 10.1111/1471-3802.12566.

Domínguez-Figaredo D, Gil-Jaurena I, and Morentin-Encina J (2022) The impact of rapid adoption of online assessment on students' performance and perceptions: Evidence from a distance learning university. *Electronic Journal of e-Learning* 20(3): 224–241. DOI: 10.34190/ejel.20.3.2399.

Eurostat (2014, August 27) *Persons aged 15–64 participating in education and training, by country and disability status (1), in %.* Available (consulted 20 June 2022) at: https://ec.europa.eu/eurostat/statistics-explained/index.php?title=File:Persons_aged_15-64_participating_in_education_and_training,_by_country_and_disability_status_(1),_in_%25,_2011.JPG.

Forlin C, and Lian M-GJ (2008) Contemporary trends and issues in education reform for special and inclusive education in the Asia-Pacific region. In: *Reform Inclusion and Teacher Education: Towards a new era of special education in the Asia-Pacific Region.* London, UK: Routledge, 3–12. DOI: 10.4324/9780203895313.

Forlin C, and Tierney G (2006) Accommodating students excluded from regular schools in schools of isolated and distance education. *Australian Journal of Education* 50(1): 50–61. DOI: 10.1177/000494410605000105.

Forlin CL (2007) Inclusive educational practices: A way forward for Hong Kong. *Chinese Education and Society* 40(4): 63–75. DOI: 10.2753/CED1061-1932400405.

Frolova EE, and Rusakova EP (2022) Development of digital technologies for dispute resolution of economic entities as a means of increasing economic stability. In: Inshakova AO, and Frolova EE (eds) *The transformation of social relationships in industry 4.0: Economic security and legal prevention.* Charlotte, NC: Information Age Publishing, 65–73.

Fujs D, Vrhovec, S., Žvanut B, and Vavpotič D (2022) Improving the efficiency of remote conference tool use for distance learning in higher education: A kano based approach. *Computers and Education* 181, 104448. DOI:10.1016/j.compedu.2022.104448.

Gnawali YP, Upadhayaya PR, Sharma B, and Belbase S (2022) Access, efficiency, inconvenience, and scarcity as issues of online and distance learning in higher education. *European Journal of Educational Research* 11(2): 1115–1131. DOI: 10.12973/eu-jer.11.2.1115.

HR News (2020, October 14) *The countries with the best infrastructure for e-learning.* Available (consulted 20 June 2022) at: https://hrnews.co.uk/the-countries-with-the-best-infrastructure-for-e-learning/.

Hrebeniuk L, Motsak S, Ruzhytskyi V, Kalabska V, and Tepla O (2022) Students' preparation for international cooperation in distance learning with role-playingt. *Youth Voice Journal* 4(SI): 17–30.

Kamenkov VS (2022) Interaction of neo-industrialization subjects in the context of intensification of digital technologies: A system of sources of legal regulation in the Republic of Belarus and the Russian Federation. In: Inshakova AO, and Frolova EE (eds) *The transformation of social relationships in industry 4.0: Economic security and legal prevention.* Charlotte, NC: Information Age Publishing, 221–236.

Karipi E, Mawela AS, and Van-Wyk MM (2022) Exploring faculty members' views on the use of open education resources: A case of the Namwibian open distance learning institutions. *International Journal of Educational Methodology* 8(1): 107–116. DOI: 10.12973/IJEM.8.1.107.

Maconi ML, Green SE, and Bingham SC (2019) It's not all about coursework: Narratives of inclusion and exclusion among university students receiving disability accommodations. *International Perspectives on Inclusive Education* 13: 181–194. DOI:10.1108/S1479-363620190000013014.

Research Portal for Scientists "Research" (2020, June 30) *50 Online education statistics: 2021/2022 data on higher learning & corporate training.* Available (consulted 20 June 2022) at: https://research.com/education/online-education-statistics.

Salta K, Paschalidou K, Tsetseri M, and Koulougliotis D (2022) Shift from a traditional to a distance learning environment during the COVID-19 pandemic: University students' engagement and interactions. *Science and Education* 31(1): 93–122. DOI: 10.1007/s11191-021-00234-x.

Segbenya M, Bervell B, Minadzi VM, and Somuah BA (2022) Modelling the perspectives of distance education students towards online learning during COVID-19 pandemic. *Smart Learning Environments* 9(1): 13. DOI: 10.1186/s40561-022-00193-y.

Shabaltina LV, Karbekova AB, Milkina E, and Pushkarev IY (2021) The social impact of the downturn in business and the new context of sustainable development in the context of the 2020 economic crisis in developing countries. In: Popkova EG, and Sergi BS (eds) *Modern global economic system: Evolutional development vs. revolutionary leap.* Cham, Switzerland: Springer, 74–82. DOI: 10.1007/978-3-030-69415-9_9.

Shi-Hui S, Chaw LY, Aw, EC-X, and Sham R (2022) Dataset of international students' acceptance of online distance learning during COVID-19 pandemic: A preliminary investigation. *Data in Brief* 42: 108232. DOI: 10.1016/j.dib.2022.108232.

Sibirskaya E, Popkova E, Oveshnikova, L, and Tarasova I (2019) Remote education vs traditional education based on effectiveness at the micro level and its connection to the level of development of macro-economic systems. *International Journal of Educational Management* 33(3): 533–543. DOI: 10.1108/IJEM-08-2018-0248.

Times Higher Education (2022) *World University Rankings 2022.* Available (consulted 20 June 2022) at: https://www.timeshighereducation.com/world-university-rankings/2022#!/page/0/length/50/locations/RUS/sort_by/rank/sort_order/asc/cols/stats.

Vanchukhina L, Leybert T, Rogacheva A, Rudneva Y, and Khalikova E (2019) New model of managerial education in technical university. *International Journal of Educational Management* 33(3): 511–524. DOI: 10.1108/IJEM-08-2018-0270.

CHAPTER 2

Forming Multicultural Competency of Students in the Context of Convergence Culture

Elena V. Volkova, Olga Y. Khatsrinova, Rustem I. Biktashev and Mostafa M. Keruly

Abstract

The chapter focuses on forming multicultural competency of students in terms of the convergence culture in the educational process. The combination of new and old forms of cultural heritage in a teaching situation provides the basis for intercultural communication and interaction. An accredited educational process that engages students in learning new knowledge can be built on top of the skills mastered. The binding space based on studying folklore, contemporary literary works, and popular media content provides significant opportunities for training because different types of dissimilarities in the levels of education (age, class-specifics, and race) are overcome through joint efforts. The formation of multicultural competency of students occurs quicker if they use access to folklore and contemporary cultural space, crossing the line of formal educational preferences. Using creative initiatives of students in studies of public and contemporary culture is the main linking element for students and teachers, opening new space for their intercultural interaction.

Keywords

multicultural competency – Folklore environment – cultural specifics – national characteristics

1 Introduction

1.1 *Actualization*

The relevance of this problem is determined by the fact that the second half of the 20th century was marked by radical changes in all areas of social life, such as economic, labor, political, demographic, cultural, educational, spiritual, etc.

Now, forming multicultural competence occurs in terms of convergent culture. We define a convergent culture as the conjugation of the old and the new culture, the right to develop and borrow cultural values and traditions from other peoples while preserving our own identity. This fact is especially important now when practically every European country and the Russian Federation carry the burden of receiving migration streams in their territories. With children of different linguistic groups and nationalities studying at the same school, it is necessary to form sociocultural and multicultural competencies among young people to resolve all conflicts in a non-violent way. English serves as a guiding star in this matter. First, English is international. Second, all world bestsellers and media franchises that are interesting for young people of all nationalities and language groups are published in English. This fact forces young people to involuntarily study English and develop intercultural and social skills in a new society. These issues are guaranteed in the international document "UNESCO Universal Declaration on Cultural Diversity" (UNESCO, 2001). It is necessary not to develop the universality of one culture and predominance over all others but to promote the principles of compatibility, borrowing and convergence of cultural values of different peoples in pedagogical education.

The relevance of multicultural education is one of the state policy directions. The Kazan National Research Technological University (KNRTU) has 2000 international students. It is necessary to warn them against conflict situations, rash acts committed in anger, and emotional responses. Plenty of information in social networks calls for stirring up interethnic hatred. Multicultural education is unthinkable without knowledge of the culture of other nations.

Mastering a foreign language at a high level at the university provides continuing education, advanced training abroad, and further business and professional cooperation with foreign specialists, colleagues, and partners through the use of contemporary means of communication. Moreover, it contributes to the formation of culture. If the university does not form a spiritual center for its graduate by any means, combining its various qualities and properties, then there will be new Chernobyl, submarine accidents, and other technogenic and social disasters, the size of which will beat everything we know until the present.

For written or oral communication, it is necessary to acquire not only the language itself but also the image of the world of the interlocutor (i.e., to be able to understand the logic of behavior, know and understand a minimum of what surrounds the interlocutor in every day, social, and professional activities). The movement and the character of social development, the increasing scales of international relations and wide verbal intercultural communication, and the internationalization of spheres of life contribute to the formation of the great demand for specialists with knowledge of a foreign language and increase the motivation of students to study a foreign language.

The Kazan National Research Technological University is involved in international activities and pursues an active policy of developing foreign language training among students and teachers. One of the focus areas of scientific and educational activities of the KNRTU is petrochemistry and oil refining. The question of creating competitive petrochemical products in the territory of the Russian Federation arises in the rapidly changing conditions of economic development and an active policy of import substitution. The necessary conditions for fulfilling this task are the training of highly qualified personnel with the skills of business and professional foreign language communication, capable of working in an international environment. This question is mentioned in the articles of E. Volkova (*Volkova* et al., 2015).

This chapter aims to form the multicultural competence of students when studying the English language based on popular bestsellers among young people and folk classics. Identifying commonalities in spiritual and moral values in the native language and English helps create the conditions for students to experience interaction in the intercultural space.

2   Methods and Approaches

The special task of multicultural education, determined by the necessity of dialogue and unity in the united global universe, is proved by fundamental works of researchers.

The ideas of N. K. Roerich about the "beneficent synthesis," which he understands as the "unity of cultures," creating beneficial cooperation of people (*Roerich*, 2010), and the ideas of outstanding philosophers and historians of our time (N. A. Danilevsky, E. Mailer, A. Toynbee, Y. Yakovets) about the integrity of cultural and historical development of humankind and the presence of some similar principles in the functioning cultures of different peoples help to understand entity, targets, and functions of multicultural education.

The ideas of interrelation between the national and the universal views in pedagogy are continued by the Russian scientist, educator, and psychologist P. F. Kapterev. He writes about the role of multicultural education in personality development (*Kapterev*, 1982). P. F. Kapterev attributed language, religion, and everyday life to the peculiarities of the pedagogical process determined by national values. In his research, he emphasized the necessity of developing the belonging to everything human and the inadmissibility of dividing culture into primary and secondary in the consciousness of young people. According to P. F. Kapterev, the pedagogical activity is initially carried out based on the national ideal, and then it is transformed into activities for achieving the universal human ideal. In upbringing, he emphasized the need to fill one's culture with universal human values and borrow moral norms from other cultures to join the world experience of socialization. In this chapter, we used cultural and conversational approaches when studying the formation of multicultural competence. In our understanding, a cultural approach is a scientific direction that makes it possible to consider multicultural education as creative, affirming, and developing harmony in relations between members of different ethnic groups. In our opinion, the statement of U. Sandfuchs is a catch-all: "Multicultural education considers cultural change and cultural diffusion as ongoing and necessary processes" (*Sandfuchs*, 1986). The cultural approach focuses on the question of human cultural identity (the set of cultural forms, features, and characteristics). In the framework of the cultural approach, we consider multicultural education as oriented on the ideas of free choice and human perception of a person by a person.

As for a dialogue approach, just principles of openness, dialogue of cultures, and cultural pluralism are of practical use for our research. The essence of this approach is to familiarize students with different cultures without destroying and devaluing them, but by absorbing and developing. The purpose of implementing this approach is the education of the world citizen and the formation of the common planetary consciousness of the younger generation. These qualities will allow the young generation to integrate into the modern global educational environment and communicate with people of different nationalities (*Sandfuchs*, 1986).

The theme of dialogue in regard to culture first appeared at the beginning of the 20th century in the works of K. Jaspers (*Maslov and Nikitina*, 2020), O. *Spengler* (1926), *M. Buber* (2005), and *M. Bakhtin* (1986a). Later, the problem of "dialogue of cultures" was raised in the works of *L. Batkin* (2020) and *M. Kagan* (1988) and, at the turn of the 1980s–1990s, in the works of *P. Gaidenko* (1963), *V. Bibler* (1989), and others.

Thus, K. Jaspers raised the ability of communication to the rank of "gnosiological criterion of truth" (*Maslov and Nikitina*, 2020). M. Bakhtin transferred the concept of "dialogue" from a literary genre to a philosophical category (*Bakhtin*, 1986b). However, this connection is followed in the research of other scientists such as L. G. Vedenina, G. Pommerin, and M. Hohmann (*Vedenina*, 1993). They focus on training students to understand other cultures and recognize the surrounding diversity. Using the concept of "intercultural training," L. G. Vedenina connects it directly with teaching a foreign language and defines it as "a polylogue of languages and cultures, learning which is aimed at integrating a student into the system of the world culture" (*Vedenina*, 1993).

In our view, multicultural education is in the situation when a certain person aims to communicate with people of another culture, understand their value system, actions, and specific system of perception, cognition, and thinking, integrate new experiences into their own cultural system, and change this cultural system in accordance with a foreign culture.

New educational programs should provide the opportunity of expanding the boundaries of learners' worldviews, ensure the ability to understand the relativity of opinions and judgments, and teach how to approach critically to prevailing beliefs in society.

The key concept of this chapter is "multicultural competence." Multicultural competence is characterized as an integrative set of socially significant qualities of a student's personality, forming a complex system of components and reflecting the process, the result of the forming a set of fundamental competencies such as motivational-target, value-semantic, general cultural, and communicative.

The formation of multicultural competence of students at the university is a purposeful and organized process of active involvement of students in a multicultural folklore environment. This process will be effective if the following pedagogical conditions are implemented:
- Developing a special, scientifically grounded system of classes based on the intercultural dialogue of English and Russian cultures;
- Using a variety of contemporary teaching technologies such as interactive technologies;
- Informative and communicative educational technologies;
- A person-centered approach to training.

Nowadays, one of the possible ways of forming the multicultural competence of students is reading contemporary bestsellers, which are of interest to the circle of young readers and viewers around the world. Even though the authorship of these youth bestsellers belongs to such famous writers as John Tolkien and Joanne Rowling, they have already become a part of the modern folk genre. Young people perceive these works as a kind of favorite fairy tale of our time: "The Marvel Empire," "Harry Potter," "The Lord of the Rings," and "The Hobbit, or There and Back Again." Books have been written on all these works, films have been produced, and interesting video games have been released, uniting the youth of all countries. They are the subject of discussion on the Internet, in playgrounds, schools, and universities. They reflect the spiritual and moral values, cultural characteristics, and everyday life of people in a different time and storyline mode.

Combining common ideas in the entertainment industry contributes to the creation of pedagogical conditions for students to gain experience of interaction in a multicultural space. We can call it a contemporary educational folklore environment. This is a special system of pedagogical conditions for forming a student's personality implemented by means of contemporary science fiction literature, the film industry, and digital space, based on the culture of different nations, realized under the influence of globalization and reflected in fantastic reality.

We identified the following key components of the pedagogical potential of the so-called contemporary educational folklore environment:
- Acquaintance with the cultural and national specifics of Western countries and multicultural communities, in which folklore acts as a catalyst for the interest of students and expands their understanding of the traditions and customs;
- The study of the harmony of genre diversity stimulates interest in the elements of imagery in contemporary literature and cinema and contributes to the development of literary and artistic taste;
- Studying and viewing contemporary science fiction works and media franchises positively affect the development of the basic thought processes of students, such as analysis, synthesis, comparison, generalization, concretization, and abstraction, and contributes to the assimilation of general cultural and moral norms and values.

The creation of global fan communities, united by one storyline, creates conditions for students from all countries to communicate in English. A new popular story is a subject of discussion; it contributes to establishing relationships and creating special information, communication, and multicultural space, pedagogical conditions for students. In other words, studying contemporary fantastic bestsellers influences the formation of multicultural competence in students.

Our research used competence-based and personality-oriented approaches to organize a contemporary educational folk environment. "In the framework of the competence-based approach, we organized the educational process" in such a way that the teaching material of the Foreign Language discipline was filled by modern popular works of the fantastic genre, such as "Harry Potter," "The Lord of the Rings," "The Marvel Empire," and by works of the folklore genre of world literature (*Volkova* et al., 2021).In our research, the personality-oriented approach was realized through reading well-known world bestsellers by students and their ability to communicate in a given contemporary fantastic folklore educational environment.

3   Progress of Work

One of the possible means of forming multicultural competence is contemporary English bestsellers and popular media franchises that reflect all features of British folklore. It can serve as a means of forming the multicultural competence of students in studying English.

In our opinion, in this situation, an important problem arises for an English teacher, it is necessary to teach the language as a means of communication and present the whole process of mastering a foreign language in such a way that students can turn to the origins, traditions, folk culture, and the contemporary cinematograph art. They should appreciate the spiritual and the material heritage of the native and foreign language culture and understand the differences between them because these things create a stable value system and form the national identity and students' culture. Due to its complexity, multicultural competence can be represented as a set of four interconnected components: motivational-value, cognitive, activity-based, and emotional, which form its structure.

The main element of the work on forming multicultural competence was the study of English folklore and foreign bestsellers in the context of its comparison with Russian folklore, films, and cartoons. This typology was modified by our teachers; the English-language folklore corpus was used as a cultural material, which defined three groups of tasks:

1   To compare and collate folklore genres of co-studied cultures to identify cultural similarities between countries and peoples of co-studied languages and cultures;
2   To search and interpret cultural information in folklore texts that confirm the similarities between the studied multicultural communities;
3   To produce a detailed statement and a schematic presentation of cultural information about the similarities between the native culture and the culture of the target language country.

The set of lessons included four thematic blocks; five lessons were devoted to implementing each block: contemporary folklore forms – songs, fairy tales, folk ballads, and fantasy. The main characteristics of this genre are magic, magical creatures, and a unique fantasy world. At the heart of the English-language fantasy, folklore motives and images of good and evil are transformed.

In popular modern British fiction, one can find such fairy-tale characters as dragons, giants, elves, kobolds, fairies, mermaids, and all kinds of ghosts and evil spirits, which makes it possible to maximize the fabulous atmosphere of England and better understand the national culture.

Russian and English literary works were compared based on the identification of differences in the plot structure of the content under several characteristics: characters, a place and time of action, main events, and the moral of the work. Then, working in micro groups, students identified common motives of Russian and English books, analyzing the same components. The study of British literary works involved several sequential tasks:
– Tasks for consolidating small literary forms: to choose a riddle that is suitable for the plot content of a book, containing phrases from the text;
– Tasks for activating vocabulary: to insert missing letters, find a match, continue sentences, and answer questions;
– Tasks for depicting the path of the fairy tale character, the cartoon, or the film.

Students were offered to watch British videos to compare the national and cultural characteristics of Russian and English cultures to develop an interest in the study of the British heroic epic and learn about the main historical periods of Great Britain.

Children and adults from all over the world are reading books about Harry James Potter written by Joanne Rowling. Thus, we can conclude that contemporary English-language fantasy combines folklore, modern views of the world, and the author's understanding of reality.

The peculiarities of the culture and mentality of the British people were analyzed in the final projects, presented in the chosen folklore genre or work, compared with the similar genre of Russian folklore. All projects prepared by the students demonstrated common cultural roots reflected in folklore works, such as a subject matter, a compositional structure, a storyline, characteristics of characters, symbolism, and moral and ethical issues. The students used approximate "spider grams" (varieties of mind maps). The preparation of the project and its final defense required students to work in a team, a tolerant attitude towards each other during the subsequent project discussion. It contributed to the development of empathy and the skills of respectful discussion, which also met the objectives of the implemented program for forming multicultural competence in students.

It has been proved as a part of a study that forming students' multicultural competence improves the educational process at the university by implementing the following pedagogical conditions:
– The organization of textual activity and the gradual implementation of the "dialogue of cultures" idea in the classroom of the English language;
– Working out a program for forming a student's multicultural competence and determining links with future professional activities, including language educational projects;

– Creating an atmosphere in the classroom is most closely approximated to natural communicative conditions.

The research was carried out using questionnaires, testing, conversations, observation, analysis of projects, and mini-essays. The methodology "Motivation for studying at the university" developed by T. I. Ilyina allows revealing the prevalence of education factors at a university. Students' motivation increased from 72% to 86% during the learning process. The methodology "The strategy and tactics of behavior in a conflict situation" developed by K. Thomas make it possible to determine the type of behavior of students in conflict situations. The study of behavior in conflict situations allowed us to establish that the average level of avoidance of conflict situations prevails. Perhaps, the results obtained "on paper" embellish the picture of the behavior of young people significantly in real conflict situations. The increasing value of this component to 8% indicates the contribution to avoiding conflict situations. During the study, there was a large percentage of students with an average of 32% and a high level of 48% empathy, which allows us to consider this fact as a positive factor for developing students' multicultural competence. Indicators of the development of reflexive abilities were increased to 23%, i.e., the number of students, who are inclined to analyze their own activities and collect their thoughts about current events, has increased too. This factor also positively affects the formation of multicultural competence. In September of the last year, we received the following results of the development of students' multicultural competence: low – 54%, medium – 33%, and high – 13%. Measurements in May showed the following results: low – 20%, medium – 38%, and high – 42%. The conducted research proves the fact that the developed training program is effective and influences the formation of multicultural competence in students.

4 Conclusion

The technological progress and activating international contacts are significantly ahead of the development of knowledge and skills of interaction between representatives of different cultures. Therefore, knowledge of the foundations of the cultural realities of other countries and continents is becoming the main component of the multicultural competence of a contemporary person.

Under such conditions, the goal of the educational process is determined precisely by the tasks of developing a personality, ready for active, creative activity in a contemporary multicultural environment, preserving its sociocultural identity, respecting and accepting other cultural and ethnic communities, living in peace and harmony with representatives of other nationalities, and implementing a strategy of responsibility for engineering decisions.

The analysis of the results of diagnostics of the multicultural competence of students allowed us to conclude about the insufficient formation of a high level of multicultural competence of students in the first year of study. Therefore, working with groups of the same students, we identified three stages of forming a multicultural competence.

The first stage is motivational. At this stage, it is important to arouse interest in the studying subject, which should be based on thematic communication and the study of the traditions and customs of different peoples. This idea was introduced in the research of *O. Khatsrinova* (2020). In this matter, the most important thing is that topics should be interesting for young people and should be discussed by them every day. These steps will help create a certain mood and adjust the work in accordance with the characteristics of the audience that will be the result of this stage.

The second stage is cognitive. This stage aims to determine the following directions and tasks:
- To introduce students to universal human values, critical analysis of materials from Russian and English sources and the media;
- To teach students to see the main idea of the context, see universal values in the storylines of famous bestsellers, and develop abilities to appreciate historical experience and traditions;
- To direct students to develop the qualities necessary for positive interaction with people of different nationalities. The means of achieving these goals will be universal human values included in the educational process. As a result, students should develop a conscious attitude to this problem, a respectful attitude towards different ethnic groups and religions, and the ability to communicate with people of different confessions.

The third stage is the final one. Its purpose is to summarize the results obtained and develop a program of further actions.

Solving the problems of multicultural education requires a wide application of active methods of teaching and upbringing. Among all methods of teaching and upbringing, the leading place is taken by the creative activity of students, discussions, group and individual independent work, and participation in games on the Internet from the side of teachers and students. Joining fan communities of popular media franchises creates opportunities for students to interact in a multicultural environment using the communication culture. A project-based approach involving multimedia, information, and communication technologies and thematic sites will be the most productive of the methods in solving the problems of forming multicultural competence.

Correctly organized classes and extracurricular activities in the system "teacher – student," "student – student," and "teacher – student group" reveal to students the cultural characteristics of communication between different peoples, the rules of behavior adopted in the society of peers and representatives of the older generation.

Summing up, we can note that multicultural education is a process that consists of creating conditions for developing a personality and ideological attitude towards constructive cooperation based on familiarization with world cultures.

References

UNESCO (2001) *Universal Declaration on Cultural Diversity* (adopted on 2 November 2001 by the General Conference of the United Nations Educational, Scientific and Cultural Organization). Paris, France. Available (consulted 1 January 2022) at: https://www.un.org/ru/documents/decl_conv/declarations/cultural_diversity.shtml.

Bakhtin MM (1986a) *To philosophy of an action.* Moscow, USSR: Nauka.

Bakhtin MM (1986b) *Speech genres and other late essays* (Transl. McGee VW; Emerson C, and Holquist M ed.). Austin, TX: University of Texas Press.

Batkin LM (2020) *History resuming: Reflections on politics and culture.* Moscow, Russia: *Moscow worker,*.

Bibler VS (1989) Culture. Dialogue of cultures (experience of definition). *Questions of Philosophy* 6: 31–42.

Buber, M. (2005) In: Mendes-Flohr, PR (ed) *A land of two peoples: Martin Buber on Jews and Arabs.* Chicago, IL: *University of Chicago Press.*

Gaidenko PP (1963) *Existentialism and the problem of culture.* Moscow, USSR: Higher School.

Kagan MS (1988) *The world of communication: The problem of intersubjective relations.* Moscow, USSR.

Kapterev PF (1982) *Selected pedagogical writings.* Moscow, USSR: Nauka.

Khatsrinova O, Galikhanov M, and Khatsrinova Y (2020) The method of formation of the students of the engineering university competence to innovative professional activity. In: Auer M, Hortsch H, and Sethakul P (eds) *The impact of the 4th industrial revolution on engineering education.* Cham, Switzerland: Springer, 818–829. DOI: 10.1007/978-3-030-40274-7_79.

Maslov ES, and Nikitina SE (2020) Karl Jaspers "philosophical narrative: Historical process structure." *Utopia y Pxaxis Latinoamericana* 25(12): 208–214. Available (consulted 1 January 2022) at: https://produccioncientificaluz.org/index.php/utopia/article/view/34565.

Roerich NK (2010) *Epistolary heritage of N.K. Roerich from the archives of the Odessa House-Museum of N. K. Roerich. Issue series 22–23b Series "The legacy of the Roerich family."* Odessa, Ukraine: Odessa House-Museum. N.K. Roerich.

Sandfuchs U (1986) *Lehren und Lernenmit Ausländerkindern.* Bad Heilbrunn, Deutschland.

Spengler O (1926) *The decline of the West. Vol. 1: Form and actuality.* New York, NY: Alfred A. Knopf, 46–47.

Vedenina L (1993) Intercultural education as polylogue of languages and cultures. In: Kalentyeva TL (ed) *Intercultural communication: Theses of reports.* Irkutsk, Russia: Irkutsk State Institute of Foreign Languages.

Volkova E, Semushina E, and Tsareva E (2021). Developing cross-cultural communicative competence of university students in the globalized world. In: Auer ME, and Rüütmann T (eds) *Educating engineers for future industrial revolutions.* Cham, Switzerland: Springer, 405–416. DOI: 10.1007/978-3-030-68198-2_38.

Volkova E, Zinurova R, and Tuzikov A (2015) Formation experience of sociocultural competence in the system of additional foreign education. In: Lcc G, and Schaefer G (eds) Proceedings of the ICSSS: *4th International Conference on Social Sciences and Society.* Paris, France, 144–147.

CHAPTER 3

Visual Culture and Ways of Its Development among Students in the System of Higher Education

Natalia V. Vinogradova, Claudio Tomazzoli, Sergey V. Bykov, Galina M. Zemlyakova and Igor G. Panov

Abstract

Purpose: The paper aims to search for means and methods of developing a visual culture in university students in the discipline of "History of Fine Art." The research objects are the pedagogical mechanisms that influence the development of the visual culture of young people.

Methodology: The study is of world outlook, culturological, and aesthetic nature. It represents a sociological analysis of several issues: what factors influence the development of visual culture and what objective and subjective conditions are necessary for this; whether art is a contemporary means of communication, information, and cognitive sphere, which forms social activity and spiritual and aesthetic positions; whether young people have structural and functional methods and skills of critical analysis or their ways of knowing the world are prejudicial. The paper analyzes visual culture as an important component of social, behavioral, and cognitive activity and emotional and aesthetic experience of evaluation, in which the individual can master new possibilities and methods of analysis, perception, and interpretation of information, texts, and images.

Results: On the one hand, the authors identify shortcomings and cause-effect relationships that lead to a change in the vision and understanding of information by students. On the other hand, these changes serve as a promising model for developing visual activity, designing and implementing search, creative, and interactive methods in the educational process of higher education. These methods allow the individual to interact with the environment and contribute to a personal understanding of the information and knowledge received, playing a significant role in developing emotional, behavioral, cognitive, and motivational spheres. The obtained results indicate a change in the forms of cultural inclusion and the individual's visual abilities, as well as in the development of a new visual paradigm based on the integration of human-computer interaction.

Practical relevance: During the experiment, indicators of the development of visual culture were determined. Various research activities were carried out, including questionnaires, tests, discussions, practical conferences, master classes, and virtual tours, which prove the relevance of visual culture. Additionally, the authors reviewed scientific articles by Russian and foreign authors relating to the spiritual and aesthetic demands of society, current trends in art, and means of creative development of the individual.

Keywords

visual culture – communicative and visual space – social activity – aesthetic values – cognitive sphere – critical thinking – structural and functional analysis

1 Introduction

The construction of a new model of a picture of the world – an integrated space: social-virtual, informative-interactive, and communicative-visual, which has its own values and meanings – has led to radical changes in knowledge and perception of the world, combining the visual-graphic, audio, video, and written language in a new form of the expression of information. Artificial intelligence synthesized human actions and thought operations, turning the traditional form of perception toward computer-mediated, networked communication. Having formed its own norms, evaluations, ways of being, and social and virtual reality with its communication experience, a smart society becomes a means of learning, education, and development (*Mitrofanova* et al., 2020).

Smart technology places art in a space that has gone beyond the canvas. Screen culture has come to dominate communicative, verbal, and textual culture. Visual content has become convenient, simplified, and accessible as a form of information transfer. However, freedom, dynamism, and openness become "informational chaos," an order infinite and immanent, with no meaning. Visually "saturating" a person, the information labyrinth becomes a means of manipulating peoples' behavior, will, emotions, and thinking. It brings entirely new forms of knowledge, values, and perceptions. Will the multiplicity of entertainment channels and the polyvalence of visual information lead to the generation of views, the deconstruction of meaning, its imitation, the "sliding on the surface," simulacrum, and the emergence of a new aesthetic order?

Visual culture has repeatedly been the subject of socio-humanitarian research. It was considered a process of cognition, "visual thinking," and part of the cultural context visually and verbally related to understanding the content of information. It was defined as the social position, behavior, attitude, and personal culture of the individual. The semiotic approach, iconological, hermeneutic, and phenomenological methods used to analyze text and art reflected the search for social and attitudinal meanings. Mass culture also became the subject of research, including fashion, design, and advertising as areas of influence on human sensory perception. The investigated field includes not only the artistic and aesthetic meanings but also the problem of vision, the experience of analysis, and evaluation relations, revealing the ideological content of visual culture (*Suminova*, 2006).

The interdisciplinary nature of the research explains the fact of scientific attention to the impact of art and products of the art and media market on the visual development of youth culture. Digital technology has contributed to the merger of the "human being watching and the human being listening," bringing to the fore the problem of developing critical thinking, the cognitive abilities of the individual, and the ability to navigate in visual space. The authors think that visual culture is related to consciousness and understanding, the socio-psychological activity of people. It reflects the intellectual and emotional state of a person. It is a criterion of aesthetic evaluation; it provides the social adaptation of the individual and regulates the processes of semantic comprehension and transformation of information. Visual culture is the most active form in the designated processes: communication and perception, cognition and understanding, analysis and comparison, and interpretation and classification. Art is an area of visual-image comprehension, which performs a visual-communicative function, where the image is a "cognitive map" through which a person at the emotional and aesthetic level receives the experience and comprehends the system of value concepts and relations necessary for its interaction in society. What are the human meanings of an individual's visual culture today? Is an individual capable of cultural self-development and the definition of spiritual and aesthetic values?

2   Materials and Method

Publications by foreign authors represent the vanguard of research on the visual experience of perception, the study of the art market, and the culture of behavior in social networks. Art is seen as an entrepreneurial model that leads to career success. Foreign authors are interested in the value of art from the perspective of perception (tactile and visual, cognitive and emotional). As a result, various experiments in psychology and neurobiology are emerging, such as Greated's article "Painting in extreme environments" (*Greated*, 2019).

Of particular interest is the experience of Italian colleagues, whose research is related to the semantic space of the new, digital Web culture and the introduction of intelligent analysis of Web content as a method to identify and structure visual information, making it accessible, understandable, and interpretable (*Scannapieco* et al., 2021). Alain Quemin, Professor of Sociology of Art at the University of Paris, addresses various issues of the formation of an art market where famous galleries and museums influence and control current trends in art and strengthen their position in shaping new artistic values (*Quemin*, 2020). *Brown* (2020), Professor of Social Sciences and Humanities at Oxford University, notes that the evolving concept of "aesthetic atheism" and the art market are displacing values associated with art, becoming "fictitious capital" that threatens the ontological status of society.

Many scholars analyze and debate what art and "non-art" is. If we proceed from political and cultural influences, this analysis leaves the sensory-emotional side of the perception of a work of art behind (*Wong*, 2019). Most of the publications of foreign authors prove that art classes contribute to the development of aesthetic perception, influence behavior, and motivate to engage in the creative activity (*Miralay and Egitmen*, 2019). There is evidence of a correlation between behavior and aesthetic values, which raises the question of the need to introduce special activities at the university, promoting them and playing an important role in the intellectual and emotional development and the formation of a coherent and harmonious personality (*Fallouh and Al-Qudah*, 2020). For example, *Hjelde* (2020), Professor of Art at the University of London, emphasizes the role of student exhibitions as a link between the development of artistic vision, visual culture, and the reputation of the institution, between the work of students and their future careers. In researching people with visual impairment, *Lauwrens* (2019) points out that the viewer, seeing but not being able to touch the work, will not receive aesthetic enjoyment because there is no language adequate to aesthetic touch that is both visual and tactile. For *Frank-Witt* (2020), Professor of Art at New York University, a work of art is a property of the human mind. By searching for an artistic idea, an individual comes to an understanding of it, which forms an aesthetic appreciation and imaginative perception. The problem of the commercialization of art is discussed in the work of *Kenning* (2019); the author asks whether the reality of social media can define the role of aesthetic responsibility, appreciating the value of art by addressing real problems in personal development, work, career, and finances. *McCartney and Tynan* (2021) illustrate the disturbing impact of neoliberalism on cultural space. Thus, the interaction of art and fashion and the emphasis on the spectacular reflect the changes in the world's perception. This is especially relevant concerning pop art, which signals the emergence of a new interdisciplinary aesthetic. In his research, *Riley* (2021) notes that neoliberalism, having become the dominant policy while embracing all governance systems, including education, is undermining the foundations of the fine arts pedagogy. The author argues that drawing as an educational activity is more important than the market, especially in the formation of visual and aesthetic culture (*Riley*, 2021). In another work, *Riley* (2018) argues that visuality is fundamental to developing human culture, perception, and communication. In a general sense, the author focuses on the fact that art acts as a system-functional, semiotic language and a driving force of creativity, facilitating the understanding of meaning. It is "visual intelligence," the ability to see, that speaks to the flexibility of vision to go beyond and extract information from the observed and analyzed object (*Riley*, 2018).

Russian authors focus on the search for methods and means of personal development, socio-psychological and humanitarian aspects, and the creation of models of developmental space. *Tagiltseva* (2021) presents the experience of forming an aesthetic worldview in children by integrating masterpieces of musical culture with the visual arts. According to *Kashekova* (2019), the development of visual culture correlates with art characterized by the following components: imagery, symbolism, associativity, and semantic diversity, which determines the introduction of mechanisms of integration of scientific (memory, logical thinking) and artistic (feelings, imagination, associative memory) ways of knowledge in the educational process. Rusakova and her co-authors present a model of competence – a behavioral indicator that provides the universality of the value foundations of the spiritual and moral culture of the individual (*Rusakova* et al., 2019). Shafazhinskaya and her co-authors consider the formation of universal competence – intercultural communication related to understanding the meaning of the most important aesthetic categories, which requires conscious effort in practical and spiritual activities of university students (*Shafazhinskaya* et al., 2019).

Syrova (2018) represents visual culture as the ability of an individual to analyze, compare, and evaluate. *Gabova* (2017) notes that the emergence of virtual reality (VR), augmented reality (AR), and 3D technologies in the contemporary information world is due to the state of the intellectual and spiritual life of society. Technology has become a factor in the emergence of new kinds of art, leading to the mixing of cultures, creating "transcultural," and weakening critical thinking. That is, the visual culture of society is characterized by a state of "in-between," changing ideas about space in the direction of show culture and giving birth to new forms of leisure. Research by Russian authors is based on the main figure – a person who, through communication, builds a system of views and the ability to experience and create values that are significant to the psychological culture of the individual (*Burenina and Konovalova*, 2020).

We face completely different worldviews. However, in many opinions, there is an idea that in the age of rapidly developing technology and the enormous flow of visual information, uncontrolled spontaneous perception can lead to a deformation of cultural meanings and aesthetic taste in young people, primitivize consciousness, and affect the development of completely different value and semantic orientations.

3   Results

When developing the research plan, the authors proceeded from the fact that visual culture is a process that involves the emotional-sensory and rational-logical spheres of thought, expressed by the ability to feel, analyze, understand, and evaluate. As a mental and cognitive process, cognition is conditioned by the laws of thinking. Evaluation and analysis are related to the ability to see, recognize, and distinguish the main aspect. An essential role in the development of visual culture is played by existing values, as well as the environment and the conditions in which an individual is active. The criteria of visual culture are represented by three components of activity: social, cognitive, and emotional. The social (normative, behavioral) component is characterized by the manifestation of spiritual and moral guidelines and meanings, communication skills, active life, civic positions, and awareness of actions. The cognitive component is based on a scientific picture of the world and is represented by the following descriptors: objectivity, critical judgment, and the ability to classify, distinguish, analyze, compare, systematize, recognize, and understand the depth of knowledge obtained. The emotional (volitional, practical) component is a motivating link in reflection and cognition of artistic aspects, semantic content, and the aesthetic evaluation of one's emotions and expression of an emotionally sensitive attitude.

Based on compilation-systematizing, culturological, activity-based, and integrated approach, art pedagogy, as well as the development of visual culture, we developed visual culture, various sociological (monitoring, questioning), explanatory-illustrative, problem-searching, and interactive methods that stimulate social, cognitive, and emotional activity in seminars, during masterclasses, discussions, group discussions, projects, writing a creative essay, and visiting virtual exhibitions and workshops of artists. The experimental study was conducted using in Google Forms platform on the basis of the information and educational center "Russian Museum: Virtual Branch" of the

Volga Academy of Education and Arts in honor of St. Alexis, Metropolitan of Moscow. The experiment involved 81 students (bachelors) aged from 17 to 21 years. Students of creative (EG1-P) and other humanities (EG2-H) areas were involved. The experiment was held within the discipline of "History of Fine Arts" in several stages and lasted for the academic year 2020–2021.

At the ascertaining stage, we determined the system of views and interests of students in the field of art through a questionnaire consisting of two blocks of 20 questions, each with suggested options for answers (multiple choice). The first block contained questions revealing the specifics of young people's understanding of the role and importance of art and culture for society and individuals (https://docs.google.com/forms/d/1cZsipPLq_WECQbD1_EgP SHMWvCs_dGevLOF2A9DnStc/viewform?edit_requested=true). Questions from the second block were aimed at identifying artistic criteria and aesthetic ideals of young people (https://docs.google.com/forms/d/1p3-niphIcCxV7xS lkMbLov-o-Ziz70RTDMzKd2r1-KA/edit).

The survey results indicate that the visual culture of today's youth is characterized by screen nature, lack of skills in structural and functional analysis, weakening of critical evaluation skills, consumer attitude, the weak concentration of attention, and the formation of fragmented perception. The ability to critically analyze, conduct vertical and horizontal evaluations, apply synchronic and diachronic analysis, and understand and express an aesthetic attitude toward works of art, is below average (Chart 3.1).

Nevertheless, the study also identified positive aspects. The group (EG-2H) named contemporary art figures and artists belonging to the category of "relational aesthetics" and "participatory art," working in the genre of installation, pop art, neo-pop, social and public art, abstractionism, expressionism, graffiti, performance art, and art brut (Artem Filatov, Anish Kapoor, Keith Haring, Yayoi Kusama, and Takashi Murakami); art video, video installations,

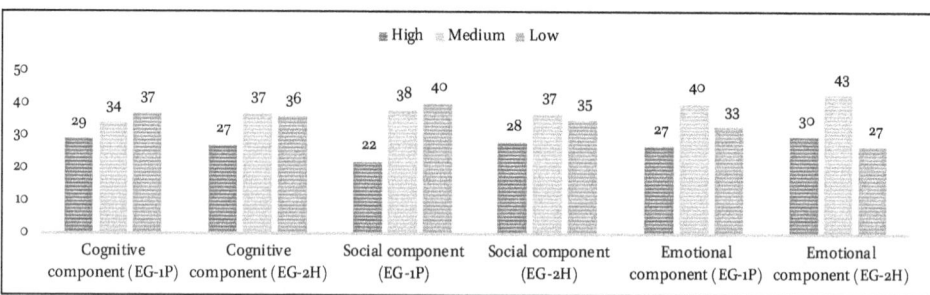

CHART 3.1   The level of visual culture. Ascertaining stage, 2020
SOURCE: COMPILED BY THE AUTHORS

and deconstructivism (Pierre Huyghe, Zaha Hadid, Stuart Campbell, and John Raffman). Sometimes students called celebrities whose field of activity is not related to the fine arts (Anton Belov, Leonid Mikhelson, Egor Kuvaldin, and Sergey Shnurov). Questionnaires (EG-1P) showed that students are fascinated by biographical paintings, demonstrating a high level of technical skill (Alekasander Balos, Wojciech Babski, Warren Chang, Aurelio Bruni, and Antonio Finelli) close to the work of masters of the 16th century (Caravaggio and Jan Vermeer), working in the directions of hyperrealism, surrealism, in the genre of illustration and fantasy, seeking to convey the lively, real feelings of people absorbed in their daily routine with their simple joys of everyday life. Nevertheless, there were difficulties in identifying styles and trends, the inability to explain the difference between pop art and Sots Art, and a poor grasp of information about ongoing cultural events on a city, regional, and all-Russian scale.

In the search phase of the research, the groups (EG-1P and EG-2H) analyzed the CBS logo and R. Magritte's painting "The Son of Man." The task was aimed at mastering the methods of horizontal and vertical analysis and the ability to contemplate, reflect, conduct artistic interpretation, constructively exchange information, and form independent judgments. The analysis consisted of three elements: "author's reading," "how I perceive it," and "what should be seen." Students were asked to express their associations and identify the content-significant (the idea and the plot) and the formal and figurative (expressive language, metaphor, and hyperbole) sides of the works. About 25% of the respondents turned out to be not ready to master the products of visual culture. Thus, due to the lack of information, they are afraid to make a mistake and feel insecure about their knowledge. Subsequently, a creative essay was written on one of the following topics:
- "The role and importance of art in personal, social, and professional life";
- "What themes of art, history, and philosophy excite you and why?"

The aim of the task was to find out what criteria are the most essential: beauty, harmony, and ideal; whether students can characterize them; what is meant by the words "art" and "non-art." Analyzing the essays, the authors noted the lack of conceptual frameworks between ethics and aesthetics; the boundaries between beauty and vulgarity, good and evil were blurred. The argumentation was still rather weak.

The third stage of the research was a test that consisted of general questions on the history and theory of art. Cultural appreciation begins with spiritual and moral enrichment and comprehension of historical facts. Respondents found it difficult to answer questions about Russian art of the 12th–13th and 20th centuries, related to its religious aspects: a type of art characteristic of medieval Russia; literary genres of ancient Russia; characteristics of the works of Andrei Rublev; authors of the architectural projects The Winter Palace and St. Isaac's Cathedral. Respondents had difficulty in answering the questions that required the names of Soviet sculptors and artists whose work is devoted to the theme of patriotism: the author of the monumental composition "Worker and Kolkhoz Woman" and the poster "Did you volunteer."

Online conferences were held during the experiment. The goal of these conferences was to make the students understand that not only the visual analyzers are involved in comprehending the world but also the sensory-intellectual structures of thinking. Professors prepared presentations and lecture materials, allowing students to master the skills of emotional and aesthetic evaluation, the basics of art morphology, semiotics, and hermeneutics, formal, stylistic, and iconological analysis, and reveal the specific features of contemporary trends and art practices. Masterclasses were held on painting still life, easel compositions, and genre paintings. Personal exhibitions and meetings in the workshops of such artists as I. G. Panov, S. N. Kondulukov, and A. V. Zuev, where they talked about their creative projects, were organized.

The fourth stage was a creative essay. The goal of this stage was to compare two or three works, express an opinion, and give an aesthetic, artistic, ideological, and semantic description of works of art by A. Rublev ("The Trinity"), V. V. Vereshchaginn ("The Apotheosis of War"), A. I. Ivanov ("The Appearance of Christ Before the People"), V. S. Surikov ("Boyarynya Morozova"), M. A. Vrubel ("Demon Sitted"), V. V. Kandinsky ("The Blue Rider"), and V. F. Stozharov ("Bread, Salt, and the Love Cup"). Reproductions were presented and shown on the screen. Almost 28% of the respondents chose the creative essay. The outward beauty of the work was brought to the forefront. The expression of emotion was very discreet. The works of V. V. Vereshchagin, V. F. Stozharov, and M. A. Vrubel were the least appreciated.

Formal characteristics dominated the evaluation of the work. The difficulty of this task consisted in mastering the skills of structural-functional analysis, where the work was viewed as an integral structure (composition and decomposition) with its interconnected elements (attitude, means, and reflection) subject to the laws of representation (ideological intent, artistic means, tropes, and associations).

At the end of the experiment, respondents presented their project "Art and Me," filled with information about their interests and hobbies, quotes, a short essay, videos, and photos from the family archive. More than 86% of students in the experimental groups participated in the project, acquiring the knowledge and skills to navigate in an educational environment using means of interpersonal communication (*Popova* et al., 2021). In the experimental groups (EG-1P

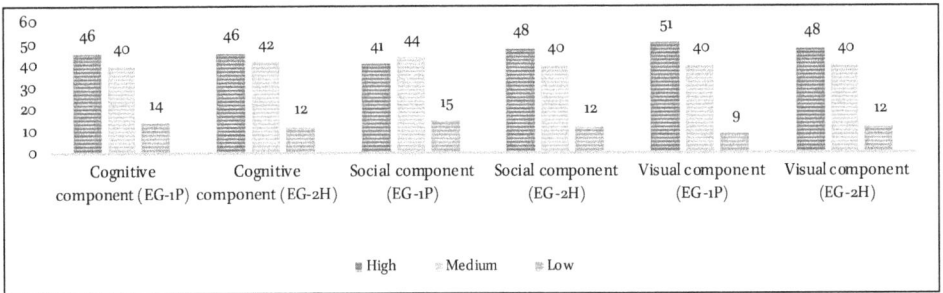

CHART 3.2   The level of visual culture. Developmental stage, 2021
SOURCE: COMPILED BY THE AUTHORS

and EG-2H), the level of cognitive, social, and emotional activity increased by 22% (Chart 3.2). The development of visual culture was preceded by various theoretical and practical exercises to express an emotional and aesthetic attitude and master the skills of critical analysis, evaluation, and the ability to interpret and conclude. According to the authors, this was facilitated by analytical discussions held after each stage of the study, where subjects expressed their opinions and learned rational argumentation.

4   Discussion

The results demonstrate the imperfection of the educational system, which, in changing socio-economic conditions, raises the question of designing educational programs that can express the relevant problems of education, culture, art, and ecology of relations to master a holistic vision, analysis skills, and structural and functional methods, form a deep understanding of the occurring cultural processes, acquire the skills of discussion, methods of creative activity, critical analysis of information, systemic methods, and develop methodological thinking. The ability to think about what we see and the ability to evaluate, compare, and consider are the specific properties of visual culture. It is the factor where the processes of cognition, comprehension, and reflection are an alternative for developing thinking, speech, memory, figurative perception, and aesthetic attitude.

Against the backdrop of the current social and political situation, the thinking activity of the younger generation is quite atrophied. Young people are preoccupied with the consumption of available resources and the idea of getting money. The process of self-cultivation and self-education takes place in social networks. Under the influence of external factors of the media and the Internet, the minds of young people form a consumer attitude towards life, the secondary importance of spiritual values and aesthetic ideals, and illusory judgments and assessments that affect the emotional and volitional sphere (*Vinogradova*, 2021). Young people stop thinking and critically perceiving information. The development of visual culture involves intellectual activity, an aesthetic attitude, and a search for meaning. The obtained results confirm the idea of many researchers that there are changes in the forms of cultural involvement and visual abilities of the individual; a new paradigm based on the integration of human-computer interaction is developing, which will lead to new means and technologies for the development of the visual activity.

5   Conclusion

Art undoubtedly influences the development of visual culture, forms the artistic taste, value orientations, aesthetic norms, cognitive and communicative skills, and regulates motives of behavior. Reducing the role of art at the public and state levels can lead to a decline in its position as the most important institution for the spiritual development of a person, their visual culture. If artistic culture does not serve the high, spiritual ideals of society and contributes to the formation of primitive stamps and stereotypes in the educational sector, it will lead to the collapse of the moral consciousness of people. Large-scale transformations in education are possible only with the support of historical and spiritual traditions and respect for language, customs, and folklore while preserving civilization's identity.

The topic of the development of visual culture has opened many problems, including psycho-pedagogical, methodological, sociological, cultural, national, anthropological, and epistemological problems (*Vinogradova* et al., 2020). The development of critical, visual-actual, and visual-imaginative thinking is at the heart of visual culture. This is closely related to the definition of spiritual and moral ideals of a person and education of emotional and aesthetic feelings and analytical judgments. This draws the authors' attention to the rethinking of the role that faces the educational sector as a sector capable of giving value and meaning to the education and development of the individual, citizen, patriot, and professional. The reevaluation of the teaching of art history and other creative disciplines is possible only in view of the changing conditions and existing problems of our time, in conjunction with the cultural, philosophical, socio-economic, and political processes occurring in society. The educational sector should become a methodological regulator, where its mechanisms ensure the creation of cultural space filled not with "matter of nothingness" but with interdependent, determinative behavioral processes that determine the individual development and aesthetic education of the individual. Socio-economic conditions, globalization, transformation, informatization, and commercialization form a new innovative model of the university of an entrepreneurial type, in which the cultural and intellectual meanings of society are more consistent with pragmatic aspirations than the model of the classical university, which implies a set of aesthetic values, spiritual guidelines and knowledge, and established educational traditions (*Chehri* et al., 2021). This further draws the authors' attention to the development of the visual culture of the individual and its preparation for the new socio-cultural realities of today's world.

References

Brown K (2020) Disappearing acts: Fictitious capital, aesthetic atheism, and the art world. *Journal of Visual Art Practice* 19(3): 225–240. DOI: 10.1080/14702029.2020.1808336.

Burenina VI, and Konovalova SA (2020) Internal and external conditions affecting the development of creativity. In: *The future of mechanical engineering in Russia: Collection of reports in 2 volumes.* Moscow, Russia: Publishing House of the Bauman Moscow State Technical University, 217–221.

Chehri A, Popova TN, Vinogradova NV, and Burenina VI (2021) Use of innovation and emerging technologies to address COVID-19-like pandemics challenges in education systems. In: Uskov VL, Howlett RJ, and Jain LC (eds) *Smart education and e-Learning 2021.* Singapore: Springer, 441–450. DOI: 10.1007/978-981-16-2834-4_38.

Fallouh R, and Al-Qudah M (2020) The capability to predict the behaviors of the students enrolled in Jordanian universities through their aesthetic values. *Journal of Education and Practice* 11(4): 104–114. DOI: 10.7176/JEP/11-4-11.

Frank-Witt P (2020) Intentionality in art: Empirical exposure. *Journal of Visual Art Practice* 19(4): 297–309. DOI: 10.1080/14702029.2020.1752514.

Gabova MV (2017) Visual culture of modern society (experience of typology). *Human. Culture. Education* 2(24): 30–40.

Greated M (2019) Painting in extreme environments. *Journal of Visual Art Practice* 18(1): 64–80. DOI: 10.1080/14702029.2017.1402502.

Hjelde K (2020) Showing-knowing: The exhibition, the student, and the higher education art institution. *Journal of Visual Art Practice* 19(1): 69–85. DOI: 10.1080/14702029.2020.1732613.

Kashekova IE, and Kononova EA (2019) Cognitive factors of "art+" cross-cultural pedagogical technology. *International Journal of Innovative Technology and Exploring Engineering* 9(1): 1305–1311. DOI: 10.35940/ijitee.L3624.119119.

Kenning D (2019) Art world strategies: Neoliberalism and the politics of professional practice in fine art education. *Journal of Visual Art Practice* 18(2): 115–131. DOI: 10.1080/14702029.2018.1500112.

Lauwrens J (2019). Touch as an aesthetic experience. *Journal of Visual Art Practice* 18(4): 323–341. DOI: 10.1080/14702029.2019.1680510.

McCartney N, and Tynan J (2021) Fashioning contemporary art: A new interdisciplinary aesthetics in art-design collaborations. *Journal of Visual Art Practice* 20(1–2): 143–162. DOI: 10.1080/14702029.2021.1940454.

Miralay F, and Egitmen Z (2019) Aesthetic perceptions of art educators in higher education level at art classes and their effect on learners. *Cypriot Journal of Educational Sciences* 14(2): 352–360. DOI: 10.18844/cjes.v14i2.4242.

Mitrofanova YS, Popova TN, Glukhova LV, and Tukshumskaya AV (2020) Modeling of residual knowledge estimation in smart university. In: Uskov V, Howlett R, and Jain L (eds) *Smart education and e-Learning 2020*. Singapore: Springer, 479–489. DOI: 10.1007/978-981-15-5584-8_40.

Popova TN, Yakusheva TS, and Vinogradova NV (2021) Peculiarities of teaching a foreign language to undergraduate students of the Institute of Fine and Decorative-Applied Art. In: Gorbunov YuI (ed) *Current problems of theoretical and applied linguistics and optimization of foreign language teaching: To the 70th anniversary of Professor Yu. I. Gorbunov: Collection of materials*. Togliatti, Russia: Togliatti State University, 236–242.

Quemin A (2020) The market and museums: The increasing power of collectors and private galleries in the contemporary art world. *Journal of Visual Art Practice* 19(3): 211–224. DOI: 10.1080/14702029.2020.1804705.

Riley H (2018) Drawing as language: The systemic-functional semiotic argument. *Journal of Visual Art Practice* 18(2): 132–144. DOI: 10.1080/14702029.2018.1537640.

Riley H (2021) A contemporary pedagogy of drawing. *Journal of Visual Art Practice* 20(4): 323–349. 10.1080/14702029.2021.1980278.

Rusakova TG, Muss GN, Miroshnikova DV, Zholdasova M, and Goverdovskaya E (2019) The project "spiritual and moral culture of student youth" as the basis for the theoretical modeling of the spiritual and moral competence of students of Russian and Kazakhstan universities. *Amazonia Investiga* 8(21): 33–41. Available (consulted 27 February 2022) at: https://amazoniainvestiga.info/index.php/amazonia/article/view/45/26.

Scannapieco S, Ponza A, and Claudio T (2021) Unified semantic space for a novel multimodal approach to document similarity. In: IEEE: *6th International Forum on Research and Technology for Society and Industry (RTSI)*, 457–462. DOI: 10.1109/RTSI50628.2021.9597240.

Shafazhinskaya NE, Shcherbinina VM, Ivanova EY, Belyakova ET, & Pereverzeva VM (2019) Learning about world art culture as a method of forming a universal cross-cultural communication competence. *Humanities and Social Sciences Reviews* 7(6): 1225–1229. DOI: 10.18510/HSSR.2019.76173.

Suminova TN (2006) *Artistic culture as an information system (philosophical and theoretical-methodological foundations)* (Dissertation of Doctor of Philosophy). Moscow, Russia: Academic project.

Syrova NV, and Chikishev VN (2018) Visual culture as a means of forming a common and professional culture of a person. *Vestnik of Minin University* 6(1): 5. DOI: 10.26795/2307-1281-2018-6-1-5.

Tagiltseva NG (2021) Polyartistic approach as a mechanism for organizing art education at school and university. In: Savenkova LG (ed) *Yusov Readings. Socialization of trainees in the integrated festival and competition space: Collection of scientific articles on the Materials of the XXI International Scientific and Practical Conference.* Moscow, Russia: Institute of Art Education and Cultural Studies of the Russian Academy of Education, 122–126.

Vinogradova NV (2021) Trends in the development of art under the influence of new virtual technologies. *Current Scientific Research in the Modern World* 10–13(78): 108–116.

Vinogradova NV, Zemlyakova GM, Ippolitova NV, Prikhodko AN, Valiev GH, and Thomas SM (2020) Higher education as a means of formation of innovative personality at different periods of society reform. *International Journal of Applied Exercise Physiology* 9(4): 240–252.

Wong SKS (2019) Applying an ethological perspective of art to the community arts and socially engaged arts. *Journal of Visual Art Practice* 18(3): 205–220. DOI: 10.1080/14702029.2019.1613614.

CHAPTER 4

Forms of Manifestation of Cultural Differences in Higher Education and Their Impact on the Inclusiveness of Universities

Lyudmila A. Shvachkina, Valentina I. Rodionova, Zarema Y. Emtyl and Asker R. Kasparov

Abstract

The paper aims to investigate the impact of different forms of cultural differences in higher education on the inclusiveness of universities. To achieve the research goal, the authors apply the regression analysis method. This method models the impact of cultural differences in higher education on the inclusiveness and internationalization of universities in the USA. It also models the impact of cultural differences in higher education on the inclusiveness and internationalization of universities in Russia compared with the USA. The theoretical significance of the results is that they allowed the authors to rank the forms of cultural differences in higher education by the degree of their impact on the inclusiveness of universities. This strengthened the evidence base for the critical importance of culturally inclusive universities for the internationalization of higher education. Moreover, it highlighted an unimportant and controversial factor – internal cultural barriers to higher education – allowing future research to focus on other, more significant factors. The practical significance of the research findings is related to the justification of the country-specific features of the impact of various forms of cultural differences in higher education on the inclusiveness of universities. This indicates the need to consider country specifics in the development and implementation of strategies for internationalization of higher education, as well as provides scientific and methodological support for the flexibility of these strategies. The author's conclusions are especially useful for the internationalization of higher education in Russia and the USA.

Keywords

cultural differences – higher education – inclusiveness of universities – cultural neutrality – cultural openness

1 Introduction

Under the influence of recent decades of globalization, cultural differences have become more or less characteristic of all contemporary societies. Multiculturalism provides several advantages in higher education. One of these advantages is the improved diffusion of knowledge. Each university has a unique system of knowledge, historically shaped throughout its existence and updated as the university conducts research. Knowledge exchange is the engine of world science, education, and the knowledge society. Therefore, the internationalization of universities prevents the stagnation of scientific and technological progress and stimulates the development of human potential worldwide.

Another advantage is the increased efficiency of scientific research. International research teams can conduct broader scientific research and produce more productive and innovative results by combining the perspectives of different cultures. Another advantage is the development of cultural neutrality (tolerance) competencies in students. Loyalty to diverse cultures is critical for university graduates because it allows them to successfully work and lead international workforces that are becoming increasingly common as globalization intensifies.

For universities, the cultural inclusiveness that underlies the internationalization of higher education is critical. The influx of international students expands markets and brings universities an additional and more stable income, increasing their efficiency. Additionally, international university rankings (e.g., (QS, 2022a)) focus on the internationalization of university activities, which has now become one of the main conditions for university competitiveness.

The problem is that, despite the high demand for an internationalization of higher education, it is happening at a slow pace, remaining moderate (not reaching a high level) even in the leading universities. Although the prolific efforts of universities in recent years have made significant progress in developing international higher education, most universities retain a clear territorial and cultural attachment to the country in which they are located. Thus, according to the estimates of U.S. News (2022), the most internationalized university in the USA has a 30% share of international students (The New School, New York), while a high degree of internationalization (the university's global status) implies a share of at least 50% (*Ben Abdelaziz* et al., 2021; *Lobova* et al., 2021; *Morozova* et al., 2020; *Nikolaichuk* et al., 2019).

The experience of the USA is particularly interesting because the system of higher education in this country is one of the most progressive in the world, and universities in the USA are the most represented (compared to universities in other countries). Thus, in 2021, the Massachusetts Institute for Technology (MIT) confirmed its leadership in the QS ranking, having received the maximum possible 100 points (*QS*, 2022a). The structure of the top 1000 universities from 80 countries is dominated by universities from the USA (160 universities, 16%) (*QS*, 2022a). The top ten SDG rankings for 2022 are led by MIT, followed by Stanford University, Harvard University, California Institute of Technology (Caltech), and the University of Chicago (which make up 50%) (*QS*, 2022b).

It is also necessary to mention the major strides the USA has made in recent decades in mitigating cultural differences and fostering a culturally neutral society. It cannot be ignored that the announcement of the COVID-19 pandemic and the imposition of strict social distancing measures worldwide has sparked a cultural revolution in the USA. This underscores the importance of reducing cultural inequalities for the USA and makes it a particularly important subject for study.

Russia's experience as another country with a progressive higher education system is also interesting. According to *WIPO* (2021), In Russia in 2021, 84.6% of the population had higher education (tertiary enrollment, % gross), and the level of development of higher education (tertiary education) was 14th in the world. The *Ministry of Science and Higher Education of the Russian Federation* (2022) estimates that the most internationalized university in Russia, RUDN University, had 28.90% foreign students in 2021 (which is similar to the level of the leading international university in the USA). This makes Russia's experience significant to study as well.

The research question (RQ) of this paper is as follows: What determines the cultural inclusiveness of universities and the internationalization of higher education? The RQ is answered by two hypotheses.

Hypothesis H_1: The ways in which cultural differences in higher education manifest themselves determine the inclusiveness and internationalization of universities. The basis for this hypothesis is the well-known difference in the impact of cultural differences on the cultural inclusiveness of society, noted in the works of *Alt and Raichel* (2021) and *Tebbett* et al. (2021). For example, even if internal cultural contradictions in the country persist, it may be open to international tourism, which is typical for the EU countries, where internal cultural contradictions are caused by spontaneous migration flows.

Hypothesis H_2: The impact of cultural differences in higher education on the inclusiveness and internationalization of universities varies among countries. The basis for this hypothesis is the well-known difference in approaches to achieving the overall cultural neutrality of societies. For example, in Russia, cultural neutrality is a historic feature of a multinational society (*Vodenko et al., 2021*); in the USA, it is a relatively new feature acquired during the cultural revolutions (*Graham, 2009*).

The research aims to explore the impact of different forms of cultural differences in higher education on the inclusiveness of universities. To achieve the set goal, the research solves the following tasks:
- To model the impact of forms of cultural difference in higher education on the inclusiveness and internationalization of universities in the USA;
- To model the impact of cultural differences in higher education on the inclusiveness and internationalization of universities in Russia compared with the USA.

2 Literature Review

The fundamental basis for this research is formed by the theory of the internationalization of higher education. In accordance with this theory, the available literature identifies the following main forms of cultural differences in higher education:
- Internal cultural barriers to higher education: the impact of cultural differences on student selection for university admission (*Bischoff* et al., 2021; *Olaniyan*, 2021; *Sun* et al., 2021; *Wan Husin* et al., 2021);
- Cultural neutrality of the educational process: accessibility of the university for students from different countries, each of which has its own culture (Mao et al., 2022; *Mbous* et al., 2022; *Popov* et al., 2022; *Zhang and You*, 2022; *Zhang* et al., 2022);
- Cultural openness of the organizational and managerial process in universities: the involvement of teachers from different cultures and the involvement of representatives of different countries (and, respectively, cultures) in research projects, international exchange of teachers and students, international internships, and double degrees (acting in different countries) (*Cao* et al., 2022; *Chen*, 2022; *Popkova*, 2019; *Watkins* et al., 2022).

Although the forms themselves have been extensively researched, their impact on the inclusiveness and internationalization of universities has been understudied, which represents a research gap. This paper fills this gap by modeling the impact of different forms of cultural differences in higher education on university inclusiveness and comparing the extent of this impact between forms and countries.

3   Materials and Methods

The posed hypotheses are tested using regression analysis. The research model takes the following form:

$$y = a + b^*x \tag{1}$$

where:

y – Inclusiveness (internationalization) of universities, as measured by the proportion of foreign students;

x – factor: a form of manifestation of cultural differences in higher education;

a – constant;

b – regression coefficient for factor variables.

Hypothesis H_1 is considered proven if positive values of regression coefficients (b) are obtained when the educational process is culturally neutral, and the organizational and management process in universities is culturally open, or negative values of regression coefficients (b) are obtained when internal cultural barriers to higher education are present. This would indicate the positive impact of overcoming cultural differences in higher education (in appropriate forms) on the inclusiveness and internationalization of universities.

Hypothesis H_2 is considered proven if the correlation coefficients for the regression models differ significantly among the studied countries. This would indicate the different significance of overcoming cultural differences in higher education (in appropriate forms) for the inclusiveness and internationalization of universities in different countries.

Consistent with this goal, the first objective of this research is to model the impact of cultural differences in higher education on the inclusiveness and internationalization of universities in the USA. The inclusiveness (internationalization) of universities is viewed through the prism of the share of international students, as calculated by *U.S. News* (2022).

Domestic cultural barriers to higher education are examined through the lens of racial disparity in bachelor's degrees as calculated by the SDG *Index* (2022) in the states of the USA. The cultural neutrality of the educational process is viewed through the prism of the ratio of international students, and the cultural openness of the organizational and managerial process in universities – through the prism of the international faculty ratio, as calculated by the QS (2022a). The sample of the top ten most internationalized universities for the research was formed according to the criterion of completeness of data for all indicators. The empirical basis of the 2021 study for the USA is shown in Table 4.1.

FORMS OF MANIFESTATION OF CULTURAL DIFFERENCES

TABLE 4.1 Cultural differences in higher education and the inclusiveness of universities in the USA in 2021

State	University	International students ratio, %	International faculty ratio, %	Racial disparity in bachelor's degree[a], times higher	Percentage of international students in the 2020–2021 academic year
		x_1	x_2	x_3	y
West Virginia	University of Virginia	14.3	8.1	4	1.46
Florida	University of Florida	20.6	75.3	2	1.74
New York	University of Rochester	92.9	63.5	27	2.94
Massachusetts	Boston University	88.0	30.9	21	3.49
Pennsylvania	Carnegie Mellon University	99.4	65.3	21	2.94
California	University of California-San Diego	64.3	59.9	17	4.37
Illinois	Illinois Institute of Technology	99.6	23.0	15	3.86
Ohio	Case Western Reserve University	74.5	55.3	14	1.91
Maryland	Johns Hopkins University	87.7	66.3	12	3.26
Rhode Island	Brown University	53.4	82.9	11	3.54

Note:
a How many times more likely it is that white people aged 25–34 earn a bachelor's degree than people the same age of racial group least served – the smaller the indicator's value, the better

SOURCE: COMPILED BY THE AUTHORS BASED ON (QS, 2022A, 2022B; SDG INDEX, 2022; U.S. NEWS, 2022)

TABLE 4.2 Forms of cultural differences in higher education and inclusiveness of Russian universities in 2021

City	University	International students ratio, %	International faculty ratio, %	Specific weight of the number of foreign students enrolled in bachelor's, specialist, and master's degree programs in the total number of students (the adjusted contingent)
		x_1	x_2	y
Moscow	Lomonosov Moscow State University	76.8	20.1	12.25
St. Petersburg	Saint Petersburg State University	36.8	5.9	18.37
Novosibirsk	Novosibirsk State University	47.2	9.0	5.92
Tomsk	Tomsk State University	93.4	29.1	24.47
Dolgoprudny	Moscow Institute of Physics and Technology	42.4	32.0	14.41
Moscow	Bauman Moscow State Technical University	11.5	11.0	5.50
Moscow	HSE University	17.0	8.1	11.78
Moscow	National Research Nuclear University MEPhI	82.7	49.6	27.78
Moscow	RUDN University	95.0	11.5	28.90
Yekaterinburg	Ural Federal University	43.1	16.4	13.96

SOURCE: COMPILED BY THE AUTHORS BASED ON (MINISTRY OF SCIENCE AND HIGHER EDUCATION OF THE RUSSIAN FEDERATION, 2022; QS, 2022A)

According to Table 4.1, the percentage of international students at the top ten most internationalized universities in the USA averaged 2.95% in 2021.

The second aim of this research is to model the impact of cultural differences in higher education on the inclusiveness and internationalization of universities in Russia compared with the USA. The inclusiveness (internationalization) of universities is considered through the prism of the share of foreign students, as calculated by the *Ministry of Science and Higher Education of the Russian Federation* (2022).

Internal cultural barriers to higher education are not subject to statistical accounting in Russia, so this form of manifestation of cultural differences in higher education is not studied. The cultural neutrality of the educational process is viewed through the prism of the ratio of international students, and the cultural openness of the organizational and managerial process in universities – through the prism of the international faculty ratio, as calculated by the QS (2022a). The sample of the top ten most internationalized universities for the research was formed according to the criterion of completeness of data on all indicators. The empirical basis of the 2021 study for Russia is shown in Table 4.2.

According to Table 4.2, the share of international students in the top ten most internationalized universities in Russia averaged 16.33% in 2021.

4 Results

4.1 *Modeling the Impact of Cultural Differences in Higher Education on the Inclusion and Internationalization of Universities in the USA*

Within the first task of this research, to model the effects of cultural differences in higher education on the inclusiveness and internationalization of universities in the USA, the authors built regression curves using the data in Table 4.1 and the research model (1) in Graphs 4.1–4.3.

The results from Graph 4.1 suggest that domestic cultural barriers to higher education in the USA in 2021 do not reduce the inclusiveness (internationalization) of universities (because the coefficient b took a non-negative value).

The results from Graph 4.2 show that the cultural neutrality of the educational process in the USA in 2021 had a positive effect on the inclusiveness (internationalization) of universities (because the coefficient b took a non-negative value). A 1% increase in the cultural neutrality of the educational process contributes to a 0.0185% increase in the share of international students. The 35.77% change in the share of international students in the top ten most

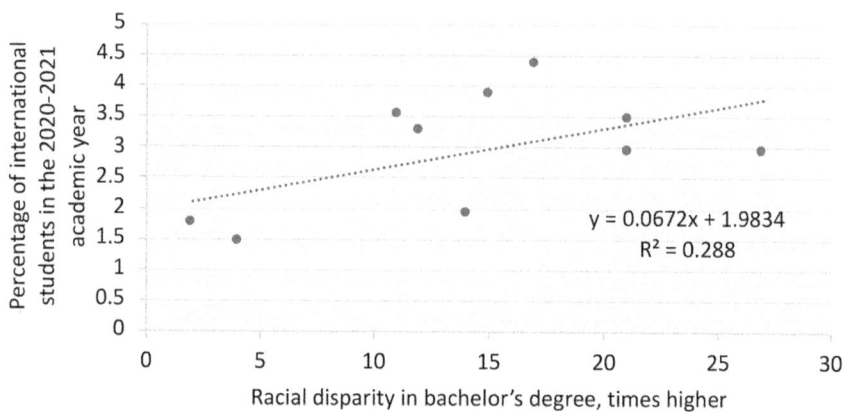

GRAPH 4.1   Regression curve of the dependence of the inclusiveness of higher education on internal cultural barriers to higher education in the USA in 2021

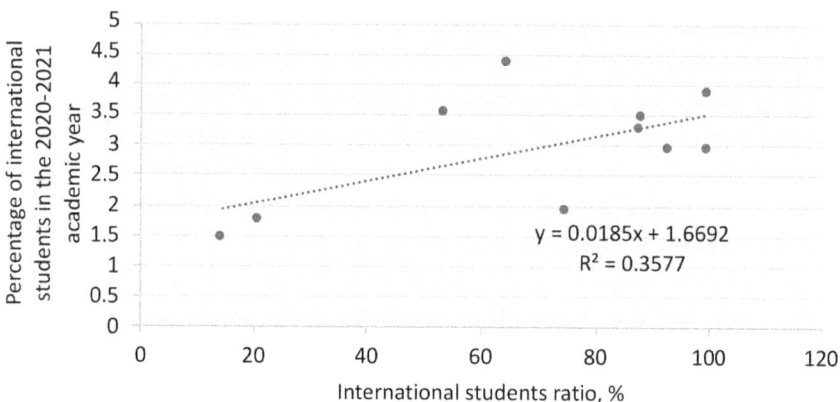

GRAPH 4.2   Regression curve of the relationship between inclusiveness of higher education and cultural neutrality of the educational process in the USA in 2021

internationalized universities in the USA is explained by the cultural neutrality of the educational process.

The results from Graph 4.3 indicate that the openness of the organizational and managerial process at universities in the USA in 2021 positively affected the inclusiveness (internationalization) of universities (because the coefficient b took a non-negative value). A 1% increase in the openness of the organizational and management process at universities increases the proportion of international students by 0.0056%.

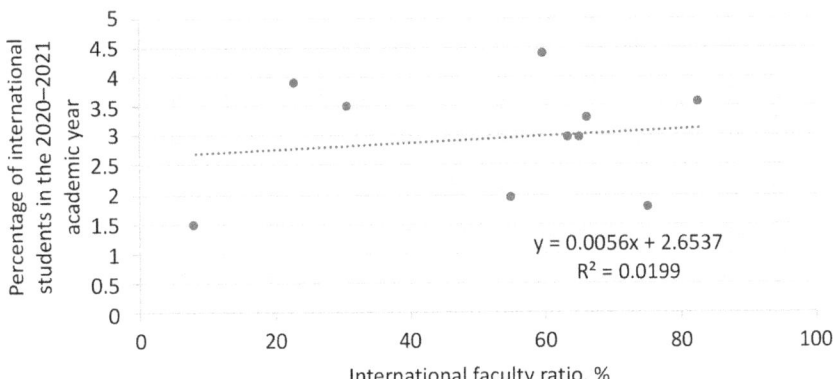

GRAPH 4.3   Regression curve of the dependence of inclusiveness of higher education on the cultural openness of the organizational and managerial process in universities in the USA in 2021

However, the change in the share of international students in the top ten most internationalized universities in the USA by only 1.99% is explained by the openness of the organizational and managerial process in universities. This points to the small role this form of cultural difference plays in the inclusiveness of universities in the USA.

4.2   *Modeling the Impact of Cultural Differences in Higher Education on the Inclusion and Internationalization of Universities in Russia Compared with the USA*

Within the second task of this research, to model the impact of cultural differences in higher education on the inclusiveness and internationalization of universities in Russia compared to the USA, the authors built regression curves using data in Table 4.2 and the research model (1) in Graphs 4.4–4.5.

The results from Graph 4.4 indicate that the cultural neutrality of the educational process in Russia in 2021 had a positive effect on the inclusiveness (internationalization) of universities (as the coefficient b took a non-negative value). A 1% increase in the cultural neutrality of the educational process contributes to an increase in the share of foreign students by 0.2138%. The change in the share of foreign students in the top ten most internationalized universities in Russia by 60.37% is explained by the cultural neutrality of the educational process.

The results from Graph 4.5 show that the openness of the organizational and management process in universities in Russia in 2021 had a positive effect on the inclusiveness (internationalization) of universities (as the coefficient

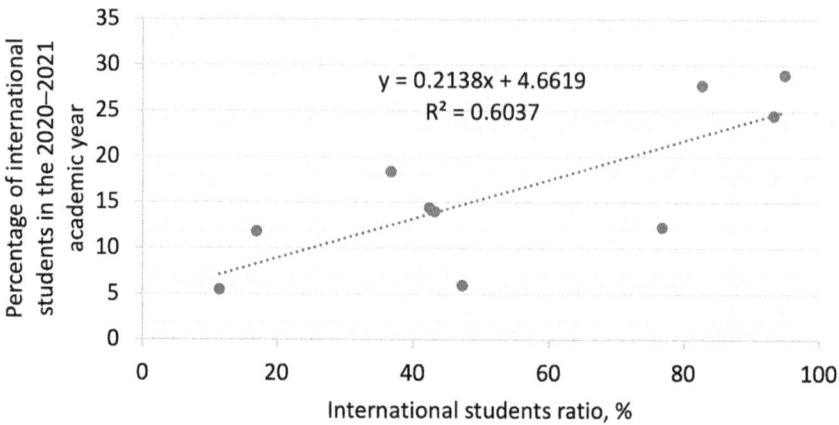

GRAPH 4.4 Regression curve of the dependence of inclusiveness of higher education on the cultural neutrality of the educational process in Russia in 2021

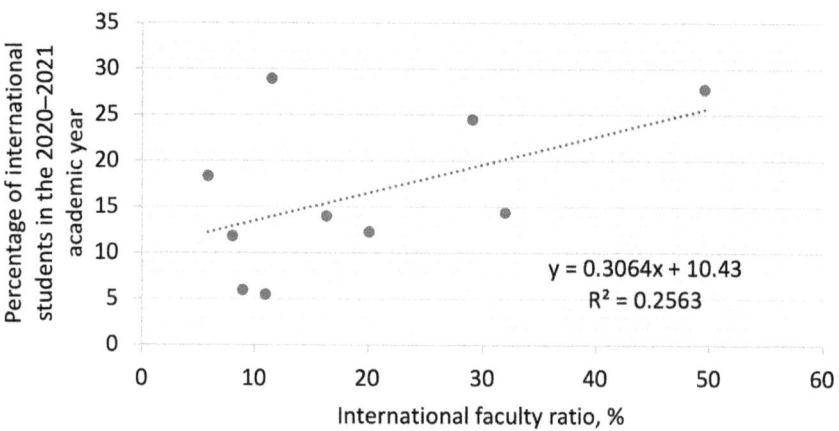

GRAPH 4.5 Regression curve of the dependence of inclusiveness of higher education on cultural openness of organizational and managerial process in universities in Russia in 2021

b took a non-negative value). A 1% increase in the openness of the organizational and management process in universities contributes to an increase in the share of international students by 0.3064%. The change in the share of foreign students in the top ten most internationalized universities in Russia by only 25.63% is explained by the openness of the organizational and managerial process in universities.

A comparative analysis of the results showed that, compared to the USA, Russia has a greater influence of cultural differences in higher education on the inclusiveness and internationalization of universities. The reduced contribution of managing cultural differences to the inclusiveness of universities in the USA can be explained by the active development of distance learning programs that make it possible to provide culturally responsive higher education services worldwide without the need for educational tourism.

5 Discussion

The obtained results develop the scientific statements of the theory of internationalization of higher education by clarifying the specifics of the impact of different forms of cultural differences in higher education on the inclusiveness and internationalization of universities.

In contrast to (*Bischoff* et al., 2021; *Olaniyan*, 2021; *Sun* et al., 2021; *Wan Husin* et al., 2021), the authors found that internal cultural barriers to higher education do not reduce the inclusiveness (internationalization) of universities (proven by the example of the USA in 2021).

In support of (*Mao* et al., 2022; *Mbous* et al., 2022; *Popov* et al., 2022; *Zhang and You*, 2022; *Zhang* et al., 2022), it is confirmed that the cultural openness of the organizational and managerial process in universities is a universal factor supporting the inclusiveness (internationalization) of universities (proven by the example of Russia and the USA in 2021, where the correlation was 60.37% and 35.77%, respectively).

In contrast to (*Cao* et al., 2022; *Chen*, 2022; *Popkova*, 2019; *Watkins* et al., 2022), the authors substantiated that cultural neutrality of the educational process does not determine the inclusiveness (internationalization) of universities in all countries: its influence is quite strong in Russia (correlation: 25.63%) and negligible in the USA (correlation: 1.99%).

The findings on the differences in the impact of cultural differences in higher education on the inclusiveness and internationalization of universities among countries allow the authors to identify national models for managing the inclusiveness of higher education, in particular, the Russian and the American models.

6 Conclusion

The research results answered the research question (RQ). Inclusiveness and internationalization of universities determine the forms of manifestation of cultural differences in higher education (in confirmation of hypothesis H_1). The authors found significant differences in the degree to which different forms of cultural differences influence the inclusiveness of universities. In particular, internal cultural barriers to higher education were found to be a minor factor in the internationalization of universities. In general, the positive influence of overcoming cultural differences in higher education on the inclusiveness and internationalization of universities was substantiated.

It was also shown that the impact of forms of cultural differences in higher education on the inclusiveness and internationalization of universities varies among countries (in confirmation of hypothesis H_2). This points to the varying significance of overcoming cultural differences in higher education (in appropriate forms) for the inclusiveness and internationalization of universities in different countries. Thus, the most significant form of cultural inclusiveness for internationalization of higher education in the USA was cultural neutrality of the educational process (correlation: 25.63%), and in Russia, cultural openness of organizational and managerial process in universities (correlation 60.37%).

The theoretical significance of the research results is that they allowed us to rank the forms of cultural differences in higher education by the degree of their impact on the inclusiveness of universities. This strengthened the evidence base for the critical importance of culturally inclusive universities for the internationalization of higher education and highlighted an unimportant and controversial factor – internal cultural barriers to higher education – allowing future research to focus on other, more significant factors.

The practical significance of the research findings is related to the justification of the country-specific features of the impact of various forms of cultural differences in higher education on the inclusiveness of universities. This points to the need to consider country specifics when designing and implementing internationalization strategies for higher education, as well as to provide scientific and methodological support for the flexibility of these strategies. The author's conclusions are especially useful for the internationalization of higher education in Russia and the USA.

The inevitable limitation of this research is that it is conducted within the boundaries of only two countries of the world to study their practical experience in as much detail as possible. The obtained results clearly indicate the existence of country-specific differences in the influence of cultural differences on the inclusiveness of universities. The results allowed the authors to identify the outlines of the model of the USA and the Russian model. This research has provided only the beginning of the research on the issues of country-specific features of internationalization of universities on the basis of the management of cultural differences in higher education, as well as confirmed the need for this work. In further research, it is recommended to continue studying the problem with the support of the experience of other countries of the world.

References

Alt D, and Raichel N (2021) Precursors of college students' attitudes towards cross-cultural collaboration: the role of group-learning activity design and openness to diversity. *Journal of Further and Higher Education* 46(6): 737–752. DOI: 10.1080/0309877X.2021.2002280.

Ben Abdelaziz A, Melki S, Ben Hassine D, Nouira S, Chebil D, Ben Abdelaziz A, … Azzaza M (2021) Global university performance. Bibliometric analysis of the ARWU platform (2003–2020). *La Tunisie Medicale* 99(7): 693–705.

Bischoff CS, Ejrnæs A, and Rubin O (2021) A quasi-experimental study of ethnic and gender bias in university grading. *PLoS ONE* 16(7): e0254422. DOI: 10.1371/journal.pone.0254422.

Cao Q, Tan M, Xie P, and Huang J (2022) Can emerging economies take advantage of their population size to gain international academic recognition? Evidence from key universities in China. *Scientometrics* 127(2): 927–957. DOI: 10.1007/s11192-021-04218-0.

Chen L (2022) How do international faculty at Japanese universities view their integration? *Higher Education* 84: 845–862. DOI: 10.1007/s10734-021-00803-7.

Graham R (2009) The function of music education in the growth of cultural openness in the USA. *Music Education Research* 11(3): 283–302. DOI: 10.1080/14613800903144296.

Lobova SV, Bychkova SG, Yankovskaya VV, Gupanova YE, and Tkachenko TV (2021) New institutions of the educational services market in the conditions of the digital economy. In: Popkova EG, and Sergi BS (eds) *Modern global economic system: Evolutional development vs. revolutionary leap.* Cham: Switzerland, Springer, 1152–1160. DOI: 10.1007/978-3-030-69415-9_125.

Mao Y, Ji H, and Wang R (2022) Expectation and reality: International students' motivations and motivational adjustments to sustain academic journey in Chinese universities. *Frontiers in Psychology* 13: 833407. DOI: 10.3389/fpsyg.2022.833407.

Mbous YPV, Mohamed R, and Rudisill TM (2022) International students challenges during the COVID-19 pandemic in a university in the United States: A focus group study. *Current Psychology.* DOI: 10.1007/s12144-022-02776-x.

Ministry of Science and Higher Education of the Russian Federation. (2022). *Information and analytical materials on the results of monitoring the effectiveness of educational institutions of higher education in 2021.* Available (consulted 23 March 2022) at: https://monitoring.miccedu.ru/?m=vpo.

Morozova IA, Mysin MN, Gryaznov SA, and Yatsechko SS (2020) Cluster mechanism of development of educational technology in the region. In: Popkova EG (ed)

Growth poles of the global economy: Emergence, changes and future perspectives. Cham: Switzerland, Springer, 1353–1361. DOI: 10.1007/978-3-030-15160-7_138.

Nikolaichuk O, Terskaya G, and Cherednichenko L (2019). Karl Marx's heritage: "Humanization" of relationship between the natural and human world. In: Alpidovskaya ML, and Popkova EG (eds) *Marx and modernity: A political and economic analysis of social systems management.* Charlotte, NC: Information Age Publishing, 199–213.

Olaniyan F-V (2021) Paying the widening participation penalty: Racial and ethnic minority students and mental health in British universities. *Analyses of Social Issues and Public Policy* 21(1): 761–783. DOI: 10.1111/asap.12242.

Popkova EG (ed) (2019) *"Conflict-free" socio-economic systems: Perspectives and contradictions.* Bingley, UK: Emerald Publishing Limited. DOI: 10.1108/978-1-78769-993-920191041.

Popov V, Brinkman D, Fortuin KPJ, Lie R, and Li Y (2022) Challenges home and international students face in group work at a Dutch university. *European Journal of Engineering Education* 47(4): 664–678. DOI: 10.1080/03043797.2022.2044762.

QS (2022a) *World University Rankings 2021.* Available (consulted 23 March 2022) at: https://www.topuniversities.com/university-rankings/world-university-rankings/2021.

QS (2022b) *World University Rankings 2022.* Available (consulted 23 March 2022) at: https://www.topuniversities.com/university-rankings/world-university-rankings/2022.

SDG Index (2022) *Racial disparity in bachelor's degree.* Available (consulted 23 March 2022) at: https://us-inequality.sdgindex.org/map/indicators/sdg4v7_bachelors_r.

Sun X, Jong-Hwa Lee J, Rhoads, RA, and Wang X (2021) Cross-ethnic friendships among ethnic minority and Han students at a Chinese university. *Comparative Education Review* 65(2): 248–270. DOI: 10.1086/713542.

Tebbett N, Jöns H, and Hoyler M (2021) Openness towards diversity? Cultural homophily in student perceptions of teaching and learning provided by international and home academics. *Globalisation, Societies and Education* 19(5): 522–544. DOI: 10.1080/14767724.2020.1835464.

U.S. News (2022) *Most international students national universities in the 2020–2021 academic year.* Available (consulted 23 March 2022) at: https://www.usnews.com/best-colleges/rankings/national-universities/most-international.

Vodenko K, Rodionova VI, Shvachkina LA, and Tikhonovskova MP (2021) Historical memory in the management of cultural security system of Russian society. *International Journal of Sociology and Social Policy* 41(1–2): 76–84. DOI: 10.1108/IJSSP-03-2020-0072.

Wan Husin WN, Halim NA, and Zul Kernain, NF (2021) Students' perceptions on ethnic tolerance in Malaysia: A study in three public universities. *Ethnicities* 21(1): 98–119. DOI: 10.1177/1468796820951991.

Watkins S, Yielder J, Bagg W, and Curtis E (2022) The student narrative of undergoing academic difficulty and remediation in a medical programme: Indigenous Māori and Pacific Admission Scheme (MAPAS) and international student perspectives at The University of Auckland. *New Zealand Medical Journal*, 135(1551): 40–53.

WIPO (2021) *Global Innovation Index 2021: Tracking Innovation through the COVID-19 crisis*. Available (consulted 23 March 2022) at: https://www.wipo.int/global_innovation_index/en/2021/.

Zhang M, and You, Z. (2022). International branch campuses of Chinese universities in Europe: Motivations, governance and challenges. *European Journal of Education* 57(1): 78–95. DOI: 10.1111/ejed.12488.

Zhang Z, Tan S, and O'Halloran KL (2022) Managing higher education and neoliberal marketing discourses on why choose webpages for international students on Australian and British university websites. *Discourse and Communication* 16(4): 462–481. DOI: 10.1177/17504813221074076.

CHAPTER 5

Cultural Differences as Barriers to Improving Positions in the International Rankings of Universities from Less Developed Countries

Irina V. Lipchanskaya, Angela A. Bezrukova, Saida G. Dzybova and Ibragim K. Shaov

Abstract

Purpose: The purpose of the chapter is to determine the role of management of cultural differences in improving the positions of universities of developing countries in international rankings, as well as to develop recommendations for improving this management.

Design/methodology/approach: The research objects are the top 10 universities from developing countries that occupy the best positions in the QS ranking in 2022. The chapter contributes to the development of the concept of globalization of science and higher education by substantiating the key role of the factor of cultural differences and ways to overcome them in ensuring the global competitiveness of universities in developing countries.

Findings: As a result, the central place of internalization in the system of global competitiveness of universities from developing countries has been proved.

Originality/value: The theoretical significance of the results and conclusions is that they identified cultural differences as a barrier to improving positions in international rankings of universities from developing countries, and also determined prospects for overcoming this barrier – through the development of international students and international faculty. The practical significance of the research lies in developing a new approach to managing the global competitiveness of universities in developing countries through their internationalization, which enables them to overcome the lag behind universities in developed countries and compete for leading positions in international university rankings.

Keywords

cultural differences – cultural inclusiveness – internationalization of university activities – globalization of higher education – international university rankings – global competitiveness of universities – universities of developing countries

1   Introduction

The globalization of science and higher education is one of the greatest achievements of the modern model of an open society and economy implemented worldwide. This is achieved by including universities from all countries in the international university rankings. For the global community, the globalization of science and higher education provides opportunities for an international division of labor in training, improving the qualifications of university graduates, building global human potential, and reducing differences in human potential between countries (contributing to the reduction of imbalances in the world economy).

For national economic systems, the global competitiveness of their universities also creates advantages – it supports the improvement of the level of education and the development of human potential, strengthens the values of higher education and stimulates lifelong learning, helps to prevent staff shortages, and balances the labor market. For the universities themselves, the strengthening of their positions in international university rankings is associated with such advantages as the involvement of leading teachers, the possibility of establishing stricter criteria for the selection of students, the growth of investment attractiveness, etc.

The problem is that, despite the openness (openness to universities from all over the world) of international university rankings, they clearly demonstrate the inequality of countries, since universities of developing countries are in secondary positions in these rankings (*Elkanov* et al., 2021; *Gevorgyan* et al., 2021; *Katargin*, 2019; *Lobova* et al., 2021; *Osipov* et al., 2022). For example, in the QS World University Rankings in 2022, the top 10 mainly include universities from the USA and the UK, and the best position among universities from developing countries belongs to Tsinghua University (Beijing, China – Mainland, 17th place).

Based on the works of *Devlin and Warner* (2017), *Popkova* (2021), *Santamaría and Santamaría* (2017), and *Yerrick and Ridgeway* (2017), which highlight cultural barriers to the internationalization of science and higher education, this article hypothesizes that cultural differences are a barrier to improving

positions in international rankings of universities of developing countries. The purpose of this article is to determine the role of management of cultural differences in improving the positions of universities of developing countries in international rankings, as well as to develop recommendations for improving this management. The goal defined the logical structure of this chapter – it solves the following research tasks:
- The place of internalization in the system of global competitiveness of universities of developing countries is determined;
- A scenario to improve the positions of universities of developing countries in international rankings based on the management of cultural differences (internationalization) is modeled;
- A new approach to managing the global competitiveness of universities of developing countries through their internationalization is developed.

2   Literature Review

This article is based on the scientific provisions of the concept of globalization of science and higher education. The existing literature highlights the following key areas of university management in developing countries, designed to ensure the growth of their global competitiveness:
- Quality management of higher education in support of SDG 2 (*Günther* et al., 2022; *Okanović* et al., 2021);
- Managing the contribution to the sustainable development of the territory through the training of highly qualified personnel and the creation of innovations for the local economy in support of SDG 11 (*Hogan and O'Flaherty*, 2022);
- Managing labor market relations to accelerate economic growth in support of SDG 8 (*Iqbal and Piwowar-Sulej*, 2022);
- Performance management to ensure financial independence of universities in support of SDG 16 (*Severino-González* et al., 2022; *Veidemane*, 2022).

Taking into account that all the indicated directions assume the university's focus on the domestic economy, the established approach to ensuring the global competitiveness of universities in developing countries can be called internally oriented. In their works, *Erkkilä and Piironen* (2020), *Garcia-Alvarez-Coque* et al. (2021), and *Yang* et al. (2020) write about the systemic lag of universities of developing countries (from universities of developed countries) as a reason for their reduced global competitiveness – secondary positions in international university rankings.

In their publications, *Aranguren and Magro* (2020), *Hussein* et al. (2021), and *Mas-Verdu* et al. (2020) point to the need to improve the efficiency of university management in order to increase their global competitiveness – to improve their positions in international university rankings. The important role of internationalization of university activities for the globalization of science and higher education is noted in the works of *Jie and Aleksander* (2021), *Larentes da Silva* (2022), *Lee* et al. (2022), and *Nadeem* et al. (2022).

The conducted literature review showed that, despite the abundance of existing publications on the topic of globalization of science and higher education, there remains little research and uncertainty about the impact of cultural differences and ways to overcome them on the positions of universities of developing countries in international university rankings. This chapter is devoted to filling the identified gap in the literature.

3   Materials and Methods

The materials of the *QS World University Rankings* (QS, 2022) serve as the empirical basis of the study. The research objects are the top 10 universities of developing countries that occupy the best positions in the QS ranking in 2022. The sample of the study is shown in Table 5.1.

As part of the first task of this study, the method of the competitiveness polygon (graphical method of economic research) is used to determine the place of internalization in the system of global competitiveness of universities of developing countries. This method is used to determine the average level (arithmetic averages are calculated) of global competitiveness indicators: international students ratio, international faculty ratio, faculty student ratio, citations per faculty, academic reputation, and employer reputation. Also, using the variation analysis method, the spread of the values of competitiveness indicators among the sample universities is estimated.

As part of the second task of the study, the regression analysis method is used to create a scenario for improving the positions of universities of developing countries in international rankings based on the management of cultural differences (internationalization). Using this method, the regression dependence of the position of universities in developing countries (y_1, y_2) on the factors of their competitiveness (x_1-x_6) is determined. The least squares method determines the projected effects of maximizing the international students ratio and the international faculty ratio for the position of the studied universities in the QS ranking.

TABLE 5.1 The position of the top 10 universities of developing countries in the QS international University ranking in 2022

University	Geographical location of the university (city, country)	Rank	Overall score	International students ratio	International faculty ratio	Faculty student ratio	Citations per faculty	Academic reputation	Employer reputation
		y1	y2	x1	x2	x3	x4	x5	x6
Tsinghua University	Beijing, China (Mainland)	17	89.0	26.3	15.3	90.6	96.0	98.6	97.6
Peking University	Beijing, China (Mainland)	18	88.8	38.5	45.6	83.5	89.5	99.4	98.2
Fudan University	Shanghai, China (Mainland)	31	82.6	45.5	93.3	91.5	71.1	84.8	89.1
Zhejiang University	Hangzhou, China (Mainland)	45	77.4	63.0	98.5	8.0	69.0	71.2	91.5
Shanghai Jiao Tong University	Shanghai, China (Mainland)	50	75.6	36.3	25.0	55.2	9.6	83.4	86.7
Universiti Malaya (UM)	Kuala Lumpur, Malaysia	65	69.8	42.6	43.6	76.5	49.6	76.9	91.7
Lomonosov Moscow State University	Moscow, Russia	78	65.6	87.8	7.3	99.8	5.9	79.5	76.5

University	Geographical location of the university (city, country)	Rank	Overall score	International students ratio	International faculty ratio	Faculty student ratio	Citations per faculty	Academic reputation	Employer reputation
		y1	y2	x1	x2	x3	x4	x5	x6
University of Science and Technology of China	Hefei, China (Mainland)	98	60.1	6.4	8.4	83.6	99.9	52.4	14.4
Universidad Nacional Autónoma de México (UNAM)	Mexico City, Mexico	105	58.3	3.5	2.9	49.9	3.0	94.6	93.2
King Abdulaziz University (KAU)	Jeddah, Saudi Arabia	109	57.7	56.3	99.5	68.9	63.8	41.3	65.7

SOURCE: COMPILED BY THE AUTHORS BASED ON THE MATERIALS OF QS (2022)

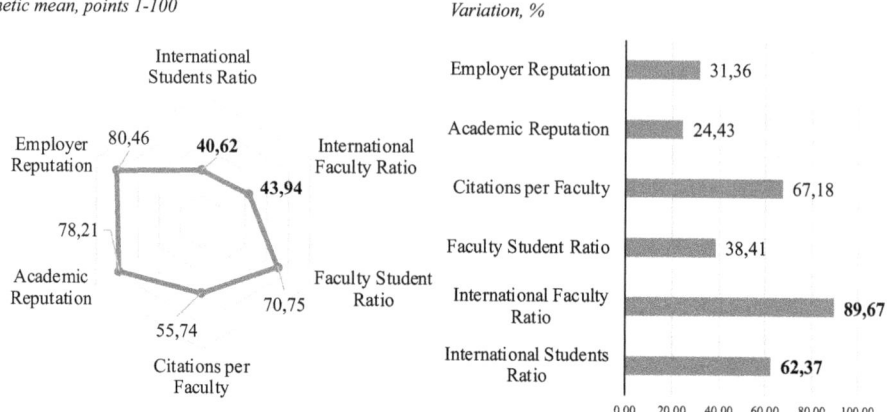

CHART 5.1 Factor analysis and analysis of the variation of competitiveness of top universities from developing countries in 2022
SOURCE: CALCULATED AND COMPILED BY THE AUTHOR

As part of the third task of the study, based on the method of expert assessments, a new approach to managing the global competitiveness of universities of developing countries through their internationalization is developed.

4 Results

4.1 The Place of Internalization in the System of Global Competitiveness of Universities from Developing Countries

As part of the first task of this study, to determine the place of internalization in the system of global competitiveness of universities from developing countries, factor analysis, and analysis of the variation in the competitiveness of top universities from developing countries in 2022 were carried out – the results obtained are shown in Chart 5.1.

The results obtained (Chart 5.1) indicate that of all the indicators (factors) of global competitiveness in universities of developing countries, the worst values are observed for the international students ratio (40.62 points) and international faculty ratio (43.94 points). According to these indicators, the greatest variation is also observed: the variation of the international students ratio is 62.37%, and the international faculty ratio is 89.67%. Consequently, cultural differences represent barriers to improving positions in the international rankings of universities in developing countries.

4.2 Scenario for Improving the Positions of Universities of Developing Countries in International Rankings Based on the Management of Cultural Differences (Internationalization)

As part of the second task of the study, the regression dependences of the position of universities of developing countries (y1, y2) on the factors of their competitiveness (x1-x6) are determined:

y1=238.88-0.50x1-0.20x2+0.10x3-0.50x4-1.84x5+0.21x6. According to the model obtained, the place of universities of developing countries in the QS World University Rankings in 2022 increases by 0.50 points with an increase in the international students ratio by one point and increases by 0.20 points with an increase in the international faculty ratio by one point. The multiple correlations in the resulting regression equation (92.69%) indicate a close relationship between the indicators;

y2=11.58+0.15x1+0.06x2-0.02x3+0.18x4+0.59x5-0.04x6. According to the model obtained, the global competitiveness of universities of developing countries according to the QS World University Rankings in 2022 increases by 0.15 points with an increase in the international students ratio by one point and increases by 0.06 points with an increase in the international faculty ratio by one point. The multiple correlations in the resulting regression equation (93.77%) indicate a close relationship between the indicators.

The least squares method based on the obtained regression equations determines the projected effects of maximizing the international students ratio and the international faculty ratio for the position of the studied universities in the QS World University Rankings. These consequences reflect the scenario of improving the positions of universities of developing countries in international rankings based on managing cultural differences (internationalization), illustrated in Chart 5.2.

The modeled scenario showed that in the absence of any additional measures, solely by increasing the international students ratio (+146.18%) and the international faculty ratio (+127.58%) to 100 points, the position of universities of developing countries in the QS World University Rankings would improve by 66.12% (from 62nd place in 2022 to 21st place), and their global competitiveness will increase by 16.97% (from 72.49 points in 2022 to 84.79 points).

4.3 A New Approach to Managing the Global Competitiveness of Universities of Developing Countries through Their Internationalization

As part of the third task of the study, a new approach to this management based on internationalization is proposed to improve the management of the global competitiveness of universities from developing countries: reducing

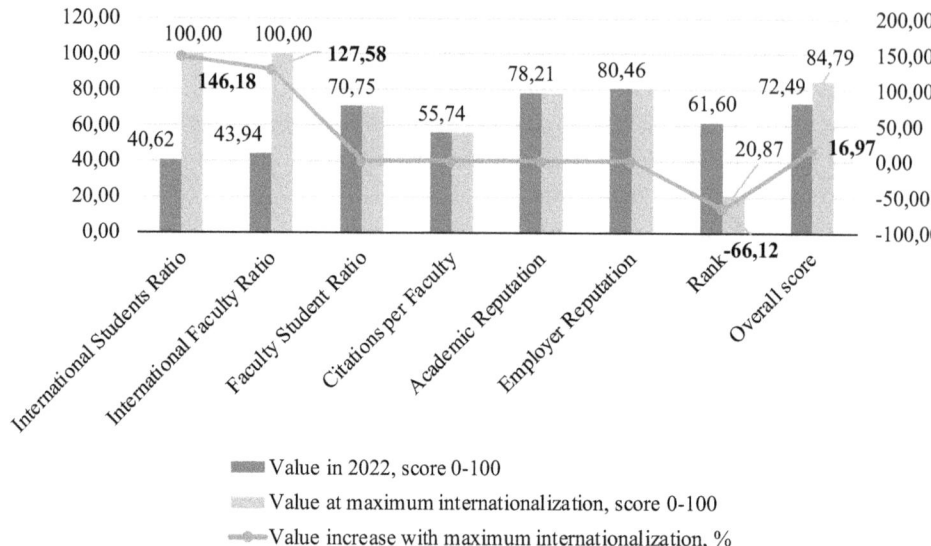

CHART 5.2 Scenario for improving the positions of universities from developing countries in international rankings based on the management of cultural differences (internationalization)
SOURCE: CALCULATED AND CONSTRUCTED BY THE AUTHORS

cultural differences and ensuring the cultural inclusiveness of universities. For the practical implementation of the authors' approach, the following management measures are proposed:

– the launch of a larger number of international educational programs that are conducted not only in the national but also in foreign languages (in English or in the languages of partner countries);
– development of a regional partnership of universities involving the exchange of students and the involvement of students from partner countries (for example, the OECD, BRICS, CIS, EU, EAEU);
– inclusion of additional courses in the study of the local (national) language in educational programs for international students;
– increasing the cultural tolerance of students and local communities.

A new approach to managing global competitiveness through internationalization provides the following advantages for universities of developing countries:

– Expansion of markets for higher education services;
– Greater prestige and transformation into international educational centers;
– Global recognition as the world's leading educational institutions;

– Prevention of stagnation of universities, exchange of knowledge and experience, timely modernization of educational programs.

5 Discussion

The chapter contributes to the development of the concept of globalization of science and higher education by substantiating the key role of the factor of cultural differences and ways to overcome them in ensuring the global competitiveness of universities of developing countries.

In contrast to *Erkkilä and Piironen* (2020), *Garcia-Alvarez-Coque* et al. (2021), and *Yang* et al. (2020), it has been found that universities of developing countries in most indicators quite correspond to the level of universities of developed countries, and the lag is observed mainly in the field of international activities (international students ratio and international faculty ratio). Consequently, only insufficient internationalization (and not systemic lag) is the reason for reduced global competitiveness – secondary positions of universities of developing countries in international university rankings.

In contrast to *Aranguren and Magro* (2020), Hussein et al. (2021), and *Mas-Verdu* et al. (2020), it has been proved that in order to increase global competitiveness – to improve the positions of universities of developing countries in international university rankings – it is necessary not to increase the efficiency of university management within the current approach to this management, but to change the approach. For this purpose, a new approach to managing the global competitiveness of universities of developing countries through their internationalization is recommended.

6 Conclusion

As a result of the conducted research, all the tasks and objectives of the work have been achieved, and the hypothesis put forward has been confirmed: it is substantiated that cultural differences are a barrier to improving positions in the international rankings of universities of developing countries. The central place of internalization in the system of global competitiveness of universities of developing countries has been proved. Of all the indicators (factors) of global competitiveness in universities of developing countries, the worst values and the greatest variation are observed in the international students ratio and international faculty ratio.

A scenario for improving the positions of universities of developing countries in international rankings based on the management of cultural differences (internationalization) has been modeled, in which the projected effects of maximizing the international students ratio and international faculty ratio are associated with an improvement in the position of universities of developing countries in the QS World University Rankings by 66.12% and an increase in their global competitiveness by 16.97%. The theoretical significance of the results and conclusions is that they identified cultural differences as a barrier to improving positions in the international rankings of universities from developing countries. They also determined prospects for overcoming this barrier – through the development of international students and international faculty.

The practical significance of the research lies in developing a new approach to managing the global competitiveness of universities in developing countries through their internationalization, which enables them to overcome the lag behind universities in developed countries and compete for leading positions in international university rankings. In the authors' approach, overcoming cultural differences (ensuring cultural inclusiveness) in support of SDG 10 and SDG 17 acts as a new key direction of university management in developing countries, designed to ensure the growth of their global competitiveness.

References

Aranguren MJ, and Magro E (2020) How can universities contribute to regional competitiveness policy-making? *Competitiveness Review* 30(2): 101–117. DOI: 10.1108/CR-11-2018-0071.

Devlin P, and Warner P (2017) Building relationships: Facilitating cultural inclusivity through Christian Service-Learning Immersion programs. *International Perspectives on Inclusive Education* 12: 175–191. DOI: 10.1108/S1479-363620170000012012.

Elkanov MD, Laipanova FH, and Kubanova MN (2021) *Information culture of personality in the conditions of artificial intelligence*. In: Popkova EG, and Ostrovskaya VN (eds) *Meta-scientific study of artificial intelligence*. Charlotte, NC: Information Age Publishing, 303–309.

Erkkilä T, and Piironen O (2020) Trapped in university rankings: Bridging global competitiveness and local innovation. *International Studies in Sociology of Education* 29(1–2): 38–60. DOI: 10.1080/09620214.2019.1634483.

Garcia-Alvarez-Coque J-M, Mas-Verdú F, and Roig-Tierno N (2021) *Life below excellence: exploring the links between top-ranked universities and regional competitiveness*. *Studies in Higher Education* 46(2): 369–384. DOI: 10.1080/03075079.2019.1637843.

Gevorgyan AA, Karapetova IN, and Kara-Kazaryan TV (2021) *IT-technologies and artificial intelligence in modern media and media education.* In: Popkova EG, and Ostrovskaya VN (eds) *Meta-scientific study of artificial intelligence.* Charlotte, NC: Information Age Publishing, 165–173.

Günther J, Overbeck AK, Muster S, Tempel BJ, Schaal S, Schaal S, ... Otto S (2022) Outcome indicator development: Defining education for sustainable development outcomes for the individual level and connecting them to the SDGs. *Global Environmental Change* 74: 102526. DOI: 10.1016/j.gloenvcha.2022.102526.

Hogan D, and O'Flaherty J (2022) Exploring the nature and culture of science as an academic discipline: Implications for the integration of education for sustainable development. *International Journal of Sustainability in Higher Education* 23(8): 120–147. DOI: 10.1108/IJSHE-06-2021-0236.

Hussein AM, Ahmed MM, and Mahmoud Khu MY (2021) *The impact of strategic planning in the university's competitiveness according to NIAS.* Academic Journal of Interdisciplinary Studies 10(5): 83–101. DOI: 10.36941/ajis-2021-0125.

Iqbal Q, and Piwowar-Sulej K (2022) Sustainable leadership in higher education institutions: social innovation as a mechanism. *International Journal of Sustainability in Higher Education* 23(8): 1–20. DOI: 10.1108/IJSHE-04-2021-0162.

Jie C, and Oleksandr R (2021) *Calculation of the competitiveness factors of international educational programs of Shanghai Transport University and Weihai Vocational College.* SIST 2021 – 2021 IEEE International Conference on Smart Information Systems and Technologies, 9465969. DOI: 10.1109/SIST50301.2021.9465969.

Katargin NV (2019) *Dynamic processes, entropy, and information in natural and social systems.* In: Alpidovskaya ML, and Popkova EG (eds) *Marx and modernity: A political and economic analysis of social systems management.* Charlotte, NC: Information Age Publishing, 269–277.

Larentes da Silva A (2022) International organizations and the technical and professional education networks in Latin America: A comparative analysis between Brazil and Mexico. *Research in Education* 112(1): 59–79. DOI: 10.1177/00345237211034881.

Lee J, Leibowitz J, and Rezek J (2022) The impact of international virtual exchange on participation in education abroad. *Journal of Studies in International Education* 26(2): 202–221. DOI: 10.1177/10283153211052777.

Lobova SV, Bogoviz AV, and Aleksashina TV (2021) The mechanism of adaptation of the educational and labor markets to the meeting of human intelligence and artificial intelligence. In: Popkova EG, and Ostrovskaya VN (eds) *Meta-scientific study of artificial intelligence.* Charlotte, NC: Information Age Publishing, 203–209.

Mas-Verdu F, Roig-Tierno N, Nieto-Aleman PA, and Garcia-Alvarez-Coque J-M (2020) Competitiveness in European regions and top-ranked universities: Do local universities matter? *Journal of Competitiveness* 12(4): 91–108. DOI: 10.7441/joc.2020.04.06.

Nadeem MU, Mohammed R, Dalib S, and Mumtaz S (2022) An investigation of factors influencing intercultural communication competence of the international students from a higher education institute in Malaysia. *Journal of Applied Research in Higher Education* 14(3): 933–945. DOI: 10.1108/JARHE-03-2021-0111.

Okanović A, Ješić J, Đaković V, Vukadinović S, and Panić AA (2021) Increasing university competitiveness through assessment of green content in curriculum and eco-labeling in higher education. *Sustainability* 13(2): 712. DOI: 10.3390/su13020712.

Osipov VS, Yankovskaya VV, Zakharov MY, and Vorozheykina TM (2022) Quality of human capital of developing countries: Measuring and management. *International Journal for Quality Research* 16(2): 461–480. DOI: 10.24874/IJQR16.02-09.

Popkova E (2021) The social management of human capital: basic principles and methodological approaches. *International Journal of Sociology and Social Policy* 41(1–2): 24–36. DOI: 10.1108/IJSSP-03-2020-0062.

Quacquarelli Symonds [QS] (2022) *QS World University Rankings 2022*. Available (consulted 10 June 2022) at: https://www.topuniversities.com/university-rankings/world-university-rankings/2022 .

Santamaría LJ, and Santamaría AP (2017) Understanding the grit and gravitas underlying culturally sustaining inclusive leadership in academy. In: Stefani L, and Blessinger P (eds) *Inclusive leadership in higher education: International perspectives and approaches*. New York, NY: Routledge, 157–172. DOI: 10.4324/9781315466095.

Severino-González P, Gallardo-Vázquez D, Ortuya-Poblete C, Romero-Argueta J, Tunjo-Buitrago E, ... Sarmiento-Peralta, G. (2022). Social responsibility: Sustainable Development Goals and COVID-19 – Perception scale of students from higher education institutions. *International Journal of Environmental Research and Public Health* 19(9): 5323. DOI: 10.3390/ijerph19095323.

Veidemane A (2022) Education for Sustainable Development in Higher Education Rankings: Challenges and Opportunities for Developing Internationally Comparable Indicators. *Sustainability* 14(9): 5102. DOI: 10.3390/su14095102.

Yang Y, Fabus M, Bae K-H, and Zhang M (2020) A diamond model based analysis for improving the sustainable competitiveness in educational exports by Chinese colleges and universities. *Entrepreneurship and Sustainability Issues* 7(3): 1858–1871. DOI: 10.9770/jesi.2020.7.3(28).

Yerrick R, and Ridgeway M (2017) Culturally responsive pedagogy, science literacy, and urban underrepresented science students. *International Perspectives on Inclusive Education* 11: 87–103. DOI: 10.1108/S1479-363620170000011007.

CHAPTER 6

Conceptual Fundamentals and Indicators of Knowledge Economy

Nataliya A. Tovma, Igor Fernández-Plazaola, Liudmila V. Popova, Rasulya R. Aetdinova and Ashirgul K. Seidildayeva

Abstract

The main research results are the clarification and systematization of the categorical apparatus of the concept of the knowledge economy. The proposed conceptual apparatus for the knowledge economy was the step for creating a single multifunctional system of statistical measurement of the knowledge economy for its full-scale monitoring, justification, and evaluation. The authors revealed distinctive features of the knowledge economy from the traditional economy. General indicators of knowledge economy include the index of knowledge, index of the knowledge economy, index of human capital, index of education, and indicators of scientific economics, health, innovation, IT technologies, and globalization. The model of economic development of knowledge is proposed.

Keywords

knowledge economy – knowledge-based economy – human capital – intellectual capital – education

1 Introduction

Knowledge becomes the foundation for all forms of production. In the knowledge economy, knowledge becomes the basis of competition.

B. Asheim (2009), S. A. Alekseeva (2010), G. S. Becker (2012), P. A. David (2003), E. Dedkova (2020), T. Eggertsson (2013), Z. Griliches (1979), A. L. Gaponenko (2022), N. V. Govorova (2006), I. Korostelkina (2020), V. N. Kostyuk (2004), A. I. Kapterev (2005), V. L. Makarov (2003), N. A. Tovma (2020a), and others worked out the problems of economic development of knowledge.

The analysis showed that there is no clear definition of the concept of the knowledge economy and its basic characteristics. Practically no research has been conducted on the distinction between the traditional economy and the knowledge economy. Indicators of the economics of knowledge are not fully disclosed. The mechanism for the development of economic knowledge is not developed.

2 Methodology

Regardless of their importance at all times, scientific knowledge, new technologies, and innovations are becoming critical factors in the economy and prosperity in today's conditions. The key resource in the pre-industrial economy was land. The capital was the key resource during the industrial economy. Nowadays, in the conditions of the knowledge economy, the key role is played by information and knowledge. Table 6.1 presents distinguishing features of the knowledge economy from the traditional economy.

In the new economy, wealth is determined by possessing human capital, although capital invested in material resources does not disappear. A significant part of knowledge is a public good. The knowledge economy has some distinctive effects that differ from all predominant types of economics – the law of increasing returns, network effects, exponential nature of growth, and positive feedback. An increase in the number of market participants and the use of production resources does not reduce the return on them after crossing the extremum.

3 Results

3.1 *Specific Interpretation of the Concept of Economy in the Results of the Literature Analysis*

The term "knowledge economy" (or knowledge-based economy) was introduced in 1962 by Fritz Mahlup (*Asheim*, 2009). A. I. Kapteev states that the practical activity of the company should include such staff units as a director of knowledge management, vice president of management of intellectual capital, manager of intellectual assets, and the director of training; group management activities should be held (*Kapterev*, 2005). According to P. A. David and D. Faure, many researchers prove that the creation of new knowledge has a real impact on the economic growth and productivity of labor (*David and Faure*, 2003). Various economists interpret the term knowledge economy differently

TABLE 6.1   Distinguished features of the economy of knowledge from the traditional economy

Distinctive features	Traditional (industrial) economy	Knowledge (postindustrial) economy
Result	A person is subject to the tasks of economic development	The economy is subject to the challenges of human development
Dominant sector in the economy	Production sector (production of products)	Non-productive sector (creation and provision of services)
Key factors	Capital and labor	Knowledge and information
Dominant stage of using knowledge	Subjective knowledge belonging to separate subjects	Objective (codified) knowledge embodied in technology and processes
Provision of resources	Restriction – the economy is limited (basic resources are depleted, limited)	Infinity – the economy of excess; knowledge is the main resource
Territorial restrictions	Transport costs. The location and geographical remoteness of a physical object have value	Insignificant. Localization of a physical object is almost not important, as long as the connection with it is provided remotely

SOURCE: DEVELOPED BY THE AUTHORS

(*Becker*, 2012). We agree with the opinion of T. Eggertsonn that the knowledge economy can be aimed at ensuring competitiveness with sustainable and economic rates of economic development (*Eggertsson*, 2013).

3.2   *Proposed Indicators of Knowledge Economy*

N. V. Govorova highlights that the knowledge economy is subdivided into three groups:
1.   Indexes and ratings that characterize the potential of the country's economy for the transition to the knowledge economy: global rating of human capital development, index of human development, and ICT development index.

TABLE 6.2   Knowledge index for 2021 by countries

Rating	Country	Significance
1	Sweden	9.38
2	Finland	9.22
3	Denmark	9.00
66	Russian Federation	6.96
73	Kazakhstan	5.40

SOURCE: COMPILED BY THE AUTHORS BASED ON (GAPONENKO, 2022)

2. Index of the knowledge economy.
3. Indices and ratings that characterize the use of knowledge economy: the rating of innovative economy, the global index of innovation, and top 100 companies of global sustainability (*Govorova*, 2006).

Different indicators affect the development of the knowledge economy. As noted by Alekseeva S. A., the determinants of economic development are knowledge: the increase of "knowledge-capacity" of various species of economic activity and the strengthening of globalization (*Alekseeva*, 2010). The main indicators of the knowledge economy are the index of knowledge, the index of the knowledge economy, the index of human capital, the level of education, indicators of scientific economics, the index of health, the index of innovation, and the globalization index.

The main indicators of the knowledge economy are as follows:

3.2.1   Knowledge Index (Table 6.2)
Kazakhstan ranks 73rd on the knowledge index.

3.2.2   Index of Economic Knowledge (Table 6.3)
Nowadays, only the USA and the EU have achieved a knowledge economy (*Alekseeva*, 2010).

3.2.3   Human Capital
Such factors as human capital also influence the development of the knowledge economy. It is impossible to develop the knowledge economy without

TABLE 6.3 Economics index for 2021 by countries

Rating	Country	Significance
1	Sweden	9.43
2	Finland	9.33
3	Denmark	9.16
66	Russian Federation	5.78
73	Kazakhstan	5.04

SOURCE: COMPILED BY THE AUTHORS BASED ON (GAPONENKO, 2022)

TABLE 6.4 Index of human development by countries for 2021

Rating	Country	Location index of human development
1	Norway	1
2	Ireland	2
3	Switzerland	3
16	Kazakhstan	51
17	Russian Federation	52

SOURCE: COMPILED BY THE AUTHORS BASED ON (GAPONENKO, 2022)

the development of human capital and new technologies. The human development index by country is presented in Table 6.4.

Norway is the leader in statistics, followed by Ireland and Switzerland. Kazakhstan surpasses the Russian Federation in this indicator by one point.

3.2.4   Education Index

The education index is calculated as an index of the adult literacy index and an index of the total share of students receiving education. Country rankings by the level of education are presented in Table 6.5.

TABLE 6.5   Country rankings according to education index for 2021

Rating	Countries	Index
1	Germany	0.943
2	Norway	0.930
3	Great Britain	0.928
35	Kazakhstan	0.830
39	Russian Federation	0.823

SOURCE: COMPILED BY THE AUTHORS BASED ON (GAPONENKO, 2022)

TABLE 6.6   Expenditures on R&D (% of GDP) for 2021

Rating	Countries	Expenditures on R&D (% of GDP)
1	South Korea	4.3
2	Israel	4.1
3	Japan	3.6
28	Russian Federation	2.8
81	Kazakhstan	0.1

SOURCE: COMPILED BY THE AUTHORS BASED ON (GAPONENKO, 2022)

3.2.5   Scientific Economy

The scientific economy includes the knowledge of humanity, innovation, culture, and society. R&D covers fundamental research, applied research, and experimental development. Let us consider the R&D expenditures (Table 6.6).

The Republic of Kazakhstan lags behind all other countries in terms of a knowledge-intensive economy.

3.2.6   Health

The possibility of creating new knowledge critically depends on the state of health (physical and mental). The country's health rating is presented in Table 6.7.

TABLE 6.7 Country rating by the level of health expenditures in 2021

Rating	Countries	Expenditures on health care in% of GDP
1	Tuvalu	17.1
2	USA	17.1
3	Marshall Island	16.4
121	Russian Federation	5.3
167	Kazakhstan	3.10

SOURCE: COMPILED BY AUTHORS BASED ON (GAPONENKO, 2022)

TABLE 6.8 Rating countries by level of innovation for 2021

Rating	Country	Index
1	Switzerland	66.1
2	Sweden	62.5
11	Russia	35.6
12	Kazakhstan	28.6

SOURCE: COMPILED BY THE AUTHORS BASED ON (GAPONENKO, 2022)

Apparently, the cost of health care in the Republic of Kazakhstan is 3.10% of GDP, which is significantly lower than in developed countries.

3.2.7   Innovations

In the innovation economy, the primary process of capital replacement is carried out in the direction of physical and natural capital. Innovative activity determines the development of an innovative economy. Table 6.8 shows the ranking of countries by the level of innovation.

The ranking of countries by the level of innovation includes 131 countries. Kazakhstan took 77th place with an index of 28.6, which is more than Kyrgyzstan but less than the EAEU countries such as Russia, Armenia, and Belarus.

TABLE 6.9 Rankings on the level of digitization in 2021 by countries

Rating	Country rating by the level of digitization	Index
1	Great Britain	5,4
2	Sweden	6,7
3	Finland	7,0
45	Russian Federation	39,3
52	Kazakhstan	49,7

SOURCE: COMPILED BY THE AUTHORS BASED ON (GAPONENKO, 2022)

3.2.8 Informatization, IT

New economic processes have become possible thanks to the spread of the Internet and the widespread use of personal computers (*Tovma* et al., 2020b). The EU has created an information service for scientific research and development "Cordis." The European Commission attaches great importance to the ICT industry (*Gaponenko*, 2022). Country rankings are presented in Table 6.9.

The knowledge economy functions in a digitalized environment. Z. Idrysheva, N. Tovma, K. Z. Abisheva, M. Murzagulova, and N. Mergenbay claim that the development of infrastructure, the reduction of the cost of processing, storage, and transfer of data will bring humanity to the threshold of a new, large-scale stage of the digital revolution, a characteristic feature of which is the merger of online and offline (*Idrysheva* et al., 2019).

The information society promotes the creative abilities of the employee in the first place. According to N. Tovma, K. Kazbekova, L. Shamina, K. Z. Abisheva, and A. Nurgalieva, employment in the digital sector provides many benefits (e.g., flexible work schedule) (*Tovma* et al., 2020a).

Norway, Sweden, and Switzerland are currently the leaders of digital countries. The top ten include the USA, the UK, Denmark, Finland, Singapore, South Korea, and Hong Kong. V. N. Kostyuk states that platforms are radically changing the business models, increasing their efficiency by eliminating intermediaries and providing optimization (*Kostyuk*, 2004).

This leads to sustainable development. As noted by I. Korostelkina, E. Dedkova, N. Varaksa, and M. Korostelkin, sustainable development is a new

TABLE 6.10 Rankings on the level of globalization in 2021 by countries

Rating	Countries	Index
1	Switzerland	91.19
2	Netherlands	90.71
3	Belgium	90.59
51	Russian Federation	72.45
84	Kazakhstan	64.45

SOURCE: COMPILED BY THE AUTHORS BASED ON (GAPONENKO, 2022)

philosophy according to which economic agents act and make any management decisions, considering socio-economic and natural factors of production (*Korostelkina* et al., 2020).

3.2.9   Globalization

Table 6.10 presents country rankings by the level of globalization.

3.2.10   Index of Creative Capital

In 2015, the most creative country was Australia, followed by the USA and New Zealand. The world's top ten creative countries also included Canada, Denmark, Finland, Sweden, Iceland, Singapore, and the Netherlands. The country ranking of creativity is presented in Table 6.11.

3.2.11   Development of a Model of Economic Development of Knowledge

The first model of economic development of knowledge was built by academician *V. L. Makarov* (2003). This model includes the budget, the Academy of Sciences, Higher Education Schools, information vectors, and the sector of scientific development.

Z. Griliches states that the number of patents issued to American companies increased by 20% per annum (*Griliches*, 1979). Thus, the model provides no direct connection between science and innovation with economic growth.

The literature notes that the model of the economy is a model that represents a system of successively interrelated basic institutions – the Institute of

TABLE 6.11 Rating of the level of creativity in 2021 by countries

Rating	Countries	Global Creativity Index
1	Australia	0.97
2	USA	0.95
3	New Zealand	0.94
38	Russian Federation	0.58
162	Kazakhstan	0.12

SOURCE: COMPILED BY THE AUTHORS BASED ON (GAPONENKO, 2022)

Knowledge Generation, the Institute of Knowledge Distribution, the Institute of Intellectual Property, and the Institute of Intelligence.

The complex model of interaction should be based on specific principles and rules that ensure its reliable functionality.

The knowledge economy is an inseparable triad of markets: knowledge market, service market, and labor market. These markets closely interact with each other (Figure 6.1).

Together with the knowledge in the economy, a new type of worker, the "Knowledge Worker," appears. This is a person who consciously uses the knowledge in their work. Knowledge workers perform repetitive operations and realize their understanding through the assigned tasks. It can be manifested in the form of critical analysis of data or innovative actions.

4 Conclusion

The knowledge economy replaces the postindustrial economy. In the knowledge economy, knowledge becomes an economic resource. "Production of knowledge" became an independent, large, and leading branch of the economy, which feeds all other branches. Knowledge of wealth is determined by the ownership of human capital. Nevertheless, capital invested in material resources does not disappear. Management of economic knowledge has specific features; for example, knowledge can uncontrollably multiply and spread. After all, the exchange always leads to the generalization of knowledge of each individual.

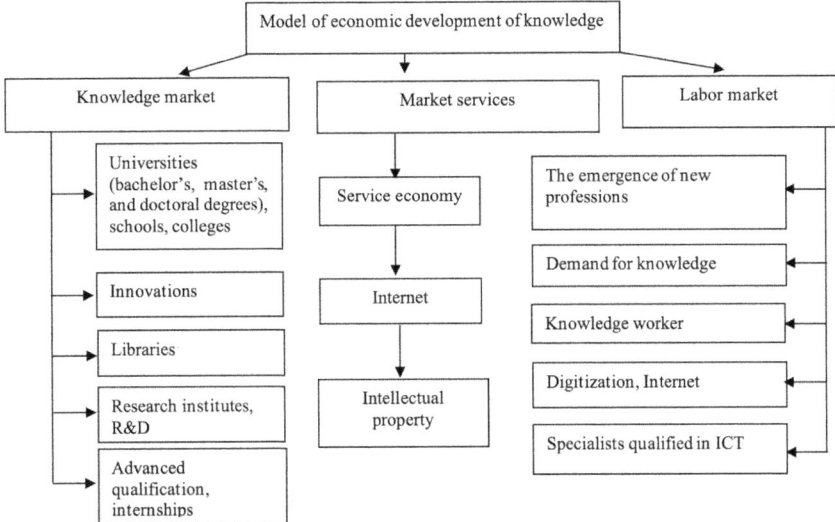

FIGURE 6.1 Model of economic development of knowledge in the Republic of Kazakhstan

The main resource of economic knowledge is scientific knowledge. The maximum achieved at a certain stage of social development and the approach to an adequate display of action in the most substantive laws is distinguished.

Acknowledgments

The article is prepared on the project: AP09057847 "Formation and development of economic knowledge in the conditions of digitalization of the Republic of Kazakhstan: conceptualization."

References

Alekseeva SA (2010) Economics of knowledge and human capital. In: *Training in foreign languages: From professionalism to professionalism: Materials of the scientific-methodical inter-university seminar*. Moscow, Russia: MGIMO University, 7–12.

Asheim B (2009) Knowledge bases, talents, and contexts: On the usefulness of the creative class approach in Sweden. *Economic Geography* 85(4): 425–442. DOI: 10.1111/j.1944-8287.2009.01051.x.

Becker GS (2012) *Economic analysis and human behavior* Moscow, Russia: HSE University.

David PA, and Faure D (2003) The economic foundations of a knowledge society. *Economic Bulletin of Rostov State University* 1(1): 29–55.

Eggertsson T (2013) *Knowledge and social progress: The role of social technologies.* Paris, France.

Gaponenko AL (2022) *Economics, based on knowledge.* Moscow, Russia: RAGS Publishing House.

Govorova NV (2006) Economics of knowledge: European realities and prospects. *Modern Europe* 4: 110–119.

Griliches Z (1979) Issues in assessing the contribution of research and development to productivity growth. *The Bell Journal of Economics* 10(1): 92–116. DOI: 10.2307/3003321.

Idrysheva Z, Tovma N, Abisheva K-Z, Murzagulova M, and Mergenbay N (2019) Marketing communications in the digital age. *E3S Web of Conferences* 135: 04044. DOI: 10.1051/e3sconf/201913504044.

Kapterev AI (2005) *Management of knowledge: From theory and technology.* Moscow, Russia: Liberea Bibinform.

Korostelkina I, Dedkova E, Varaksa N, and Korostelkin M (2020) Models of tax relations: Improving the tax culture and discipline of taxpayers in the interests of sustainable development. *E3S Web of Conferences* 159: 06014. DOI: 10.1051/e3sconf/202015906014.

Kostyuk VN (2004) Specifics of economics, based on knowledge. *Social Sciences and Contemporary World* 4: 134–144.

Makarov VL (2003) *Knowledge of economics: Lessons for Russia.* Moscow, Russia: Economics.

Tovma N, Kazbekova K, Shamina L, Abisheva K-Z, and Nurgaliyeva A (2020a) Modern trends of development of electronic trade in the conditions of digital economy *E3S Web of Conferences* 159: 04039. DOI: 10.1051/e3sconf/202015904022.

Tovma N, Ussabayev A, Baimukasheva Z, and Tyurina Y (2020b) Marketing ensuring of the competitiveness of the Republic of Kazakhstan regions in the transition to the digital economy *Management Science Letters* 10(7): 1575–1586. DOI: 10.5267/j.msl.2019.12.009.

CHAPTER 7

Cultivating a Novel Culture for Higher Education
Successes from a Social Learning Service Program

Pennee Narot and Narong Kiettikunwong

Abstract

The movement towards a digital economy has fundamentally changed business. The transition from a traditional to a contemporary economy requires a rethinking of the way of doing business to face the challenges of a volatile, uncertain, complex, and ambiguous (VUCA) world. Employees of organizations will need to learn new skills and modify old ones given the new social norms of the workplace, with more emphasis on developing an unfamiliar skill set, requiring ability, experience, and knowledge, and the ability to communicate this to others of different backgrounds and beliefs. Thai students will need to understand the context of the digital, inclusive, and egalitarian society created around us and appreciate that they need to be responsible for their education rather than wanting to be spoon-fed the same old information. Teachers need to learn to be more creative, which will be uncomfortable initially, and a continuous, critical self-evaluation of their teaching. This need for different and improved skills will pressure Higher Education Institutions (HEIs) to change the way they teach and the skills they offer to their graduates. This chapter offers a glimpse at one possible method, a student-based, team-oriented, social development project, and an analysis of how this could be one way to achieve the goals for change outlined above.

Keywords

education – social learning – higher education – knowledge culture – welfare

1 Introduction

1.1 *Diversity, Organization, and Educational Reform toward the Future*

In an era of global challenges driven by the digital economy, organizations are forced to be more fluid to transform themselves strategically and operationally. Organizations struggling to deal with the wicked problems arising from the era of volatile, uncertain, complex, and ambiguous (VUCA) contexts are most likely to go extinct. After studying management styles in many organizations, *Laloux* (2014, p. 382) came up with a proposal for a new style of the organization ready to overcome these challenges, called a "Teal organization." He saw the organization as a living system with its own life and goals. Instead of controlling its workers, this type of organization allows workers to listen to each other to understand how the organization will evolve and thus predict their future. The concept can also be applied to help traditional organizations trying to fit into the current era. Many organizations have taken on this concept to expand or even to survive. Important features of this type of organization are shown in Figure 7.1:

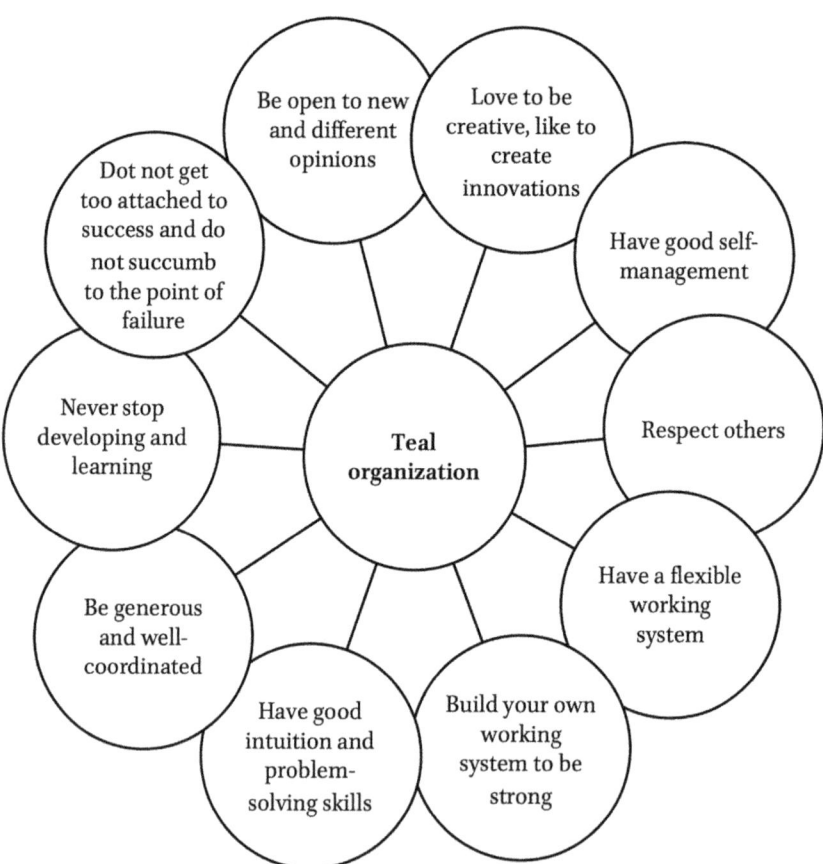

FIGURE 7.1 Key features of a Teal organization

Teal-like organizations are more likely to survive and be more competitive in the new era because they are more agile, non-hierarchical, and non-bureaucratic, which is advantageous over competitive environment factors – such as globalization or fast technological changes, and others – as compared to traditional organizations (*Kaivo-oja and Lauraeus*, 2018). Not only does the physical structure of the organization need to be adapted to survive, but its inner core-like culture must also be transformed. *Nithyanantham* et al. (2021) suggested that gender diversity is very important to the sustainable growth of any organization. Similarly, based on *Moon and Christensen's* exploration (2020) of how diversity benefits the workforce and organizations, they suggest that realizing a diverse climate in an organization can significantly impact organizational performance. Moreover, an examination of the relationship between levels of diversity-organizational performance done by *Telyani, Farmanesh, and Zargar* (2022) confirms that diversity in age and experience affects the performance of an organization and innovative culture. There is more research that gives insights in the same direction, for instance, Madera et al. (2019), *Duchek, Raetze, and Scheuch* (2020), *Yadav and Rajak* (2021), etc. Thus, it can be summarized that for an organization to stay in the game in the future, it must transform externally and internally. While the structure of future organizations must be agile, non-hierarchical, and non-bureaucratic, there must be a climate of diversity in the organization.

This view of diversity in organizations encourages HR managers in non-diverse organizations to ensure that their organization becomes more populated with non-identical members. Although "diversity" can be viewed as useful for an organization, some Thais may not agree. A Thai idiom says, "Mak khon mak khwam" (many people, many troubles), suggesting that diversity causes problems. Concerning diversity in organizations from the viewpoint of traditional organizations, a non-diverse organization would seem much easier to manage and be better. Recruitment in the former days would focus more on finding people with the same (or similar) values or culture so that the organization would be as little diversified as possible. The most common interview question was, "Where did you graduate from?" perhaps checking the applicant's cultural values. There was significant demand for graduates from notable institutions, and so less diversity. When the labor market acted this way, the higher educational institutions (HEIs), hoping to enhance their reputation for graduates entering prestigious organizations, had to continue to produce the same type of "tamed" graduates. Based on this, in the past, all programs run by HEIs were designed to ensure that students were more likely to be alike rather than different, so they were acceptable to traditional organizations.

Thus, when members of future organizations are required to be more than ordinary day-to-day workers, it is interesting to consider how well HEIs are currently preparing students, through their various courses, to work in this new era toward a digital economy worldwide. To respond to this challenge, *Nasheeda* et al. (2019) pointed out that HEIs must do much more to ensure that students can be successful in the contemporary economy, which requires the ability to manage diverse situations, rather than simply filling in positions that are already diminishing in the real world. This requires new educational structures that can help guide young adults to function in the future workplace. The skill set that students currently get is molded by the weaknesses of the people supposed to be training them and the Thai system (impossible expectations, lack of reward for success, everyone deserves the same (however good or bad they are), everyone must pass, etc.). Moreover, it is not only courses that form the character of the student but also a well-structured teaching organization, where varied student activities can be carried on out of the classroom, encouraging students to help other people, each other, society, etc., that must be embedded in the future HEIs (*Dollinger and Lodge*, 2020).

To some extent, it may be questionable as to what the diversity factor has to do with organizational reform in the future. The components listed in Figure 7.1 must be considered alongside the diversity factors in the organization. A few examples here will help realize these two topics' interconnectedness. This will be discussed in detail in the latter part of this chapter. First, there is no argument that the Teal prerequisite, "Be open to new and different opinions," involves a variety of opinions; these are more easily found in people with different backgrounds, knowledge, or beliefs. This is inevitably part of the definition of diversity. Second, the component "Love to be creative, like to create new innovations" covers the use of diverse thinking methods and perspectives. Multiple perspectives suggest diversity and the systemic and efficient management of that diversity, which can be interpreted as male/female, LGBTQ+, young/old, rich/poor, educated/uneducated, etc. Third, problem-solving skills ("Have good intuition and problem-solving skills") enable an individual (or entity) to overcome complex problems by the ability to create possible solutions. Solving a complex problem requires looking at it from different perspectives by considering opinions and having discussions in forums; hence, it requires diversity in an organization (*Moreno Romero* et al., 2020). The Teal management model focuses on relationships between members, dynamic planning, continuous diversity of values to clients, and good communications, which are the absolute opposite of the traditional Thai system. Moreover, Teal management encourages members to believe in the company mission and the deeper meaning of their work (*Rutkowska and Kaminska*, 2020). To sum up, the examples mentioned above should demonstrate that diversity is a fundamental element that is crucial for an organization to move towards becoming an organization of the future. Therefore, the next most important question to contemplate is whether HEIs have prepared their students well to tackle diversity.

1.2 Movement of Thai Higher Education Institutions towards the Future

To upgrade the role of Thai HEIs in producing graduates of the future, the Cabinet approved the budget scheme for HEIs for FY2022, amounting to $3.4 billion (117.88 billion THB), focusing on developing excellent HEIs that are up to international quality standards and can produce human resources to fill in the gaps in a new world economy that is continually evolving (*Office of National Higher Education Science Research and Innovation Policy Council*, 2021). Thus, Thai administrators also realize the urgent need for HEIs to transform themselves and prepare students for their future careers by equipping them with the life skills necessary to overcome the challenges of the 21st century after their graduation. To meet the new requirements of the labor market, it is necessary to overcome the following three major obstacles hindering higher education reform:

1. Laws and regulations that do not support reform;
2. An educational quality assurance system focusing on accuracy of reporting, often seen as a burden on the educators who must prepare reports rather than enhancing the efficiency of the education management system;
3. The lack of readiness or awareness of people in the higher education system itself.

Thus, given these challenges, the approved budget serves as a wake-up call for HEIs to begin revising their operations urgently.

To accomplish the future goals of Thai HEIs, it is necessary to revise and implement new approaches that are deemed necessary to provide students with opportunities to learn by themselves in real-life situations, with emphasis on critical thinking through the use of applied technology, and civic education with reduced emphasis on narrowly defined academic fields. Furthermore, the new teaching and learning approach must be based on specialties that cut across disciplines and incentivize students to be more focused on interdisciplinary approaches to solving complex problems and meeting social needs in addition to economic goals (*Ra-ngabtook*, 2020; *Shaules*, 2019).

1.3 Alternative Approaches to Preparing Students

Since economic trends and organizational shifts will inevitably become more active, despite their multi-faceted roles, one of HEIs' roles in aiding dynamic movement in society is to boost students' potential with a future-ready ability to fit into the labor market and organizations of the future. Thus, HEIs must ensure that their students possess the ability to solve conflicts between economic and social activities independently and be able to work well in a highly diversified environment after their graduation. However, despite the vast budgeting scheme being approved, the majority of HEIs are still offering their courses with a formal teaching method – i.e., a "chalk and talk" approach (a form of teaching that focuses on the teacher and blackboard, or now via digital mediums like ZOOM Cloud Meeting, MS TEAMS, Google Classroom, etc.) – whereas this form is becoming obsolete and replaced by other more collaborative forms of learning where students take center stage in many countries (e.g., the UK, the USA, Singapore, Australia, and New Zealand) (*Gleason*, 2018). One contemporary form of teaching and learning that could be effective in producing future-ready graduates and solutions to the current societal, economic, and climatic challenges of today and tomorrow is the social learning service program (SLSP), which is just one method that is efficient and the easiest to do. Ideally, an SLSP is a type of social learning (SL) platform offered by HEIs to their students in different shapes and forms. One form that will be thoroughly discussed in this chapter is organized as a credited course experience, in which students participate in a service activity that meets identified community needs and in which students gain a deeper understanding of the course content. Students from various disciplines (be it social sciences, science, engineering, medicine, etc.), who have undergone SLSP, are expected to have a broader view of the discipline and an enhanced sense of personal value and civic responsibility. Simultaneously, SLSP redirects the students' world view toward others by enhancing their capacity to collaborate, cooperate, and critically engage with the ideas of others in respectful ways, developing relationships with people living under different conditions to form skills and experiences, such as working with local people, the elderly, and people who have different backgrounds in different communities (*Haste and Vidur*, 2020). Ideally, students learn firsthand about "Empathy," which is the first step in design thinking (a skill that allows persons to understand and share the same feelings that others feel) and part of what future organizations need to thrive (*McCurdy* et al., 2020). Furthermore, *Alias and Rahimb's* (2019) study of SL (presumably an umbrella term for SLSP) proved that it is a highly impactful practice that has the potential to develop students' knowledge and skills. Students can also gain important experience working with diverse members of their communities and seeing how service learning can be used to connect classroom learning with societal issues (*Yusof* et al., 2019). SL provides an opportunity for students to link academic work with real situations and work with different groups of people. This kind of program aims to enable the learning of skills, demonstrating that the curriculum must go beyond content learning (*Gleason*, 2018).

Therefore, SLSP is an important mechanism that HEIs can use to prepare students for the future labor market and organizations. Another reason to use this alternative approach to produce graduates is because, under the VUCA context, graduates with traditional, outdated mindsets will be less likely to survive or have difficulty surviving, while those with more agile and pragmatic characteristics will be more prone to becoming successful (*Stein*, 2021). This requires the ability to accept more responsibility until one can manage independently. However, the real challenge is to let this trait be borne from within. Thus, HEIs must provide venues for students to link academic work with real situations and work with different groups of people, not just learn course content (*Gleason*, 2018). To enable students to learn to be able to cope with diversity and handle the complexity arising from VUCA from within (i.e., not to force them), HEIs must move toward a new phase of teaching and learning. The authors propose the "inside-out" approach as a new concept for HEIs to use SLSP as a vehicle that aligns with contemporary management concepts to stimulate diversity while cultivating a knowledge culture (Figure 7.2). The concept of knowledge culture is well-recognized in business development and concerns knowledge creation. Tacit knowledge is transformed into explicit knowledge, facilitating other knowledge management processes such as storage or dissemination of knowledge that motivate people to create, share, and utilize knowledge for the benefit and success of the organization (*Oliver and Kandadi*, 2006; *Sánchez* et al., 2013).

2 Method

2.1 *Context of the Program*

As mentioned before, the Thai government has realized the need for HEIs to change and has decided to transform the higher education system abruptly. To help students to develop their skills to be ready for the future need of the labor market to introduce diversity among graduates, the Thai Ministry of Higher Education, Science, Research, and Innovation (MHESI) has launched an SLSP pilot program called "Yu-wa-chon-arsa" (youth volunteers). The mission is to send undergraduate students in groups to apply the knowledge they have learned in class to solve "real" community problems through self-made

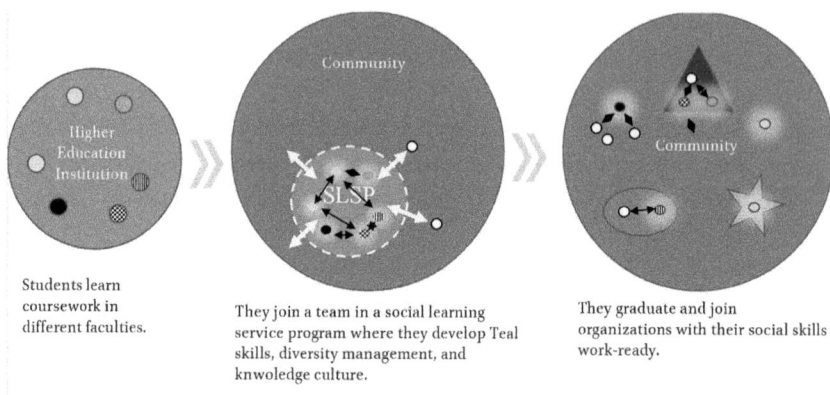

FIGURE 7.2   The proposed use of an SLSP to give students skills useful to new organizations

projects. Khon Kaen University (KKU) in the northeastern part of Thailand was selected as a host for the program, with the initial scheme being held in Kalasin province. Undergraduate students from assorted disciplines were recruited. Participation was voluntary in exchange for academic credits and a small stipend for living expenses during the project. These students were required to work with the community for one semester (approximately four months) under the supervision of a mentor (university faculty member) assigned to each group. The assessment was not based on a successfully completed project (as some projects were ongoing) but on aspects such as knowledge integration, diversity management, problem-solving, critical thinking, etc. These traits are needed for 21st-century work and organizations of the new generation (*Moreno Romero* et al., 2020).

2.2 *Participants and Procedure*

To prove the hypothesis that the use of SLSP is a legitimate way to prepare students for the future, the authors conducted an experiment. A total of 150 undergraduate students who joined the program were later subdivided into smaller groups (8–10 persons). One group was recruited to partake in the observation of their fellows. Prior to the debut of the program, each group was assigned to a different location (district) in the same province. The students were required to attend a two-day orientation to familiarize themselves with their group members, acquire fundamental knowledge concerning the community they were assigned to, and obtain general survival skills (under circumstances that they must stay overnight in the community when required).

3 Results

This SLSP certainly stresses management skills amid diversity and the ability to create a knowledge culture (gathering and recording diverse information) that students can apply to real situations when they graduate. It is a possible practical model for HEIs to consider in the adaptation of their teaching and learning processes. We wanted to assess whether the SLSP is actually a pragmatic model to prepare students for work in the future. In other words, are the key features of the SLSP aligned with those highlighted in the concept of a Teal organization? Details from the program below can illustrate this.

3.1 Be Open to New and Different Opinions

Under this program, students must work with people from different backgrounds. A community visit forces students to interact with team members and community members. To achieve the goal of their self-made project and receive a good performance evaluation from their mentor, students must familiarize themselves with people from different cultures and adjust themselves to work well with others, such as other group members, the village headman, the sub-district headman, etc. Thus, they must learn to be open to new and different opinions to get things done because a successful project only comes from the agreement of both groups of representatives – from the community and the students – about how the program's activities should proceed for the issue that has been agreed upon.

3.2 Love to Be Creative, Like to Create New Innovations

In the SLSP setting, despite each group being under the close supervision of a mentor (a university faculty member) whose key role was only monitoring and evaluation (grading the project based on creativity and innovation), the project had to originate and be implemented from the students' ideas. This pushes the students to create activities deemed necessary to themselves rather than follow their mentor's instruction. This unlocks their potential to be creative and work with people of diverse backgrounds. With this teaching and learning method, many students demonstrated that they could use knowledge from their varied course work and help develop the package they introduced to solve real problems for the community. One group that dealt with drug addiction problems in a village used their creativity to produce video clips for public relations. Another group applied the marketing knowledge they learned from a class in their sophomore year to help villagers market their outstanding craftwork as a unique selling point (USP). One of the reasons for using this UTP was that not only were they looking to increase sales, but the team also thought they wanted to project a good image of Thai villages to the outside world.

3.3 Have Good Self-management

To some people, the new generation is mistakenly known as individuals with a leisurely lifestyle. However, this was proved to be not entirely true when they were working in the field, especially with diverse groups of people (their team members, mentor, villagers, government officials, etc.) and under different conditions. The SLSP provided opportunities for the students to manage their schedules differently. Without strict instruction and a task-oriented goal, they had to learn to develop their self-management skills, or else they would not have been able to get things done within the given timeframe. When they came across some problems, such as not being able to complete their data collection from the villages as they planned, they all agreed to stay in the community for a few days more to finish the task (it should be noted that the community is not as comfortable as their dormitory, apartment, or home). When they wanted to consult the village headman, they planned their schedule and made appointments properly. The students divided their tasks, and each of them managed their time and finished their tasks completely. Even though a few free-riding students were unavoidably identified in several groups, the rest of the team members managed to cover up their unfinished assignments and reorganized their scheduling to ensure that they could still meet all deadlines.

3.4 Respect Others

Based on observation of one group of students, those with a lower academic score usually stayed quiet. However, after six weeks of working together, the team members with outstanding academic scores encouraged and motivated all members to express their opinions.

3.5 Flexible Working System

A flexible working system could be the key solution when dealing with uncertain situations in a future organization. With this in mind, students must learn to work flexibly. One example of clear evidence of the ability to work flexibly was when they faced a situation where some of the community members declined to be interviewed, saying that they would be busy with merit-making ceremonies. Instead of repeating the same approach, the next time that the villagers said they would be spending the weekend fishing for the whole community, the students went back to ask the villagers if they could join in such activities (this illustrated that the students could manage their working system flexibly). The outcome was promising because students managed to obtain all information they needed and gain the trust of the community members.

3.6   Build Their Own Working System to Be Strong

Under this program, the students were forced to think about appropriate approaches for alleviation of the problems in the community. To overcome the challenge, different techniques and working systems were employed; for instance, one team came up with the idea of working with school students to analyze the situation of drug addiction. This showed the development of deep engagement, analytical skills, and full participation even among members with weaknesses; they found a working system based on their capacity. As for other programs for the villages, such as a rubbish recycling project, the students carefully planned their work and allocated tasks for each team based on their specialties. When all tasks were put together, the villagers accepted the products well.

3.7   Good Intuition and Problem-Solving Skills

In the normal classroom setting, when a student stumbles upon a problem, he or she seeks help from a teacher. This is not the case in the real world or for this SLSP. Generally speaking, students deal with real-life situations and solve relevant problems. By making real mistakes along the way, they learn that knowledge from textbooks alone cannot make a difference. Besides, the SLSP makes them aware that a split second in real life can mean life or death, success or failure, etc. There are no teachers or people to run to (at least not constantly) for consultation at every obstacle they encounter. This makes students notice that their best friends when solving dilemmas are themselves. Thus, little by little, they learn to develop good intentions and problem-solving skills.

3.8   Generous and Well-Coordinated

One of the strong points of the SLSP was that it embraced good coordination between the groups. Notwithstanding the interdisciplinary differences between the students, when they worked, they shared concepts and supported each other very well. They picked up the strong points of their friends and made use of them so that when they developed activities as part of their project in the field, their work and activities would run seamlessly. In groups with members with special needs, the use of the buddy system was common for safety reasons, as well as to ensure that their friends would enjoy the activities together while all deadlines were well met.

3.9 Never Stop Developing, Never Stop Learning

One of the pieces of evidence that demonstrates the key characteristic of "Never stop developing, never stop learning" that the students acquired from this SLSP are the success of one group working on a project with school children (and their apparent willingness to do more for the villagers rather than simply receive a good evaluation). They were eager to learn more about the details of the problems on hand and find solutions to unravel the problems from different viewpoints. The students gathered information from all the things they had learned from classrooms and different online channels and conducted a survey to learn about the village's background to recognize its strengths, weaknesses, opportunities, and threats of the village. When the students found out about the village's strong points, they researched even more, using their digital literacy skills and meeting with their former teachers (who were not under assignment as mentors) to learn how those points could be amplified sustainably. This feature of "Never stop developing, never stop learning" is indeed reflected in the students' enthusiasm to do more for the greater good of the community, which cannot be taught in the conventional classroom setting.

3.10 Do Not Get Too Attached to Success and Do Not Succumb to the Point of Failure

In a competitive environment, the ability to "Fail Fast, Fail Forward" is like a motif employed by champion organizations worldwide. This implies that failure is an integral part of learning and getting too attached to success means starting to lower standards or walking backward. Therefore, one of the original underlying concepts of this SLSP was to encourage students to persevere with their refusal to give up. Most of the time, the students became discouraged when things did not go as planned. It was their responsibility to face up to failure; they came back with a new approach. When students succeeded, they were very happy. The next day they would get back to work with regular routines and use their best efforts again. Some students admitted that their work was less than perfect and that talking about failure was difficult. Nevertheless, these students did not feel they were stigmatized and would be willing to try again.

4 Discussion

The SLSP is a method to enhance diversity management, a future skill that cannot be taught in a normal classroom setting. Forcing students to be innovative is impossible. Rather, familiarizing them with diverse experiences so that they can adjust to real-life situations is the key for Thai education to move forward. The key concept of this SLSP is in line with the constructivism approach on which *Vygotsky and Cole* (1978) commented that learning is inherently social and embedded in particular settings, as the process of learning occurs in the real world like an apprenticeship, where the novice gets support from an expert.

Simultaneously, the diversity management process creates a knowledge culture that is valuable for students because they can conquer future dilemmas, and the knowledge created as a by-product of the process benefits other members and newcomers in the organization (*Azmee and Kassim*, 2019). This SLSP provided great opportunities for students to share knowledge and be open to new and different opinions. In this respect, students who do not perform well in the normal classroom setting can catch up with the knowledge and work procedures of their friends. The outstanding students also learn to be generous and well-coordinated. This creates learning satisfaction while nurturing respect within the group. Students learn to develop relationships with people from different backgrounds (team members and community people), which is consistent with the contemporary approach to forming skills and experiences (*Haste and Vidur*, 2020).

However, the concept of change or reform in education cannot be independent of political and economic forces. Challenges for the SLSP include:
- At the policy level, specifically, in this case, strong commitment from the MHESI and the vision of the government minister who delivers the program with financial support, university leadership, and other stakeholders;
- University staff who work along with the students and networking;
- Community leaders and other experts in the local areas.

To sum up, the SLSP works efficiently when the three following factors are present:
1. Leadership vision. There are two levels of leadership: (1) at the MHESI that launched a strategy to provide opportunities for students to learn from a social learning project based on community-based experience with full financial support; and (2) a positive attitude from teachers toward the project along with the vision to prepare students with the knowledge and understanding to facilitate the students' learning and adjust to diversity situations. The law and system of regulations must be flexible and ready;
2. Full involvement and networking of stakeholders. The project can run smoothly and securely when there is support by networking. The staff who work in the field and the students can benefit from these networks

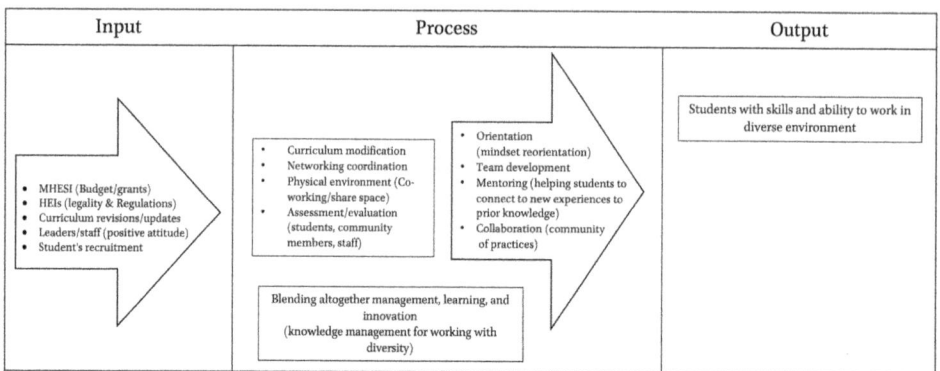

FIGURE 7.3   Development model for implementation for the SLSP to create diversity experiences

because these could provide connection or support for the students when needed;

3. Freedom and equality. Mentors must take roles as listeners, facilitators, and co-constructors of knowledge and the blending of knowledge culture to ease the development process of the students to the end of the project.

The overall framework for developing and transforming traditional HEI programs to the SLSP for knowledge culture and equipping students with a diversity-friendly and diverse management mind in higher education, which will enhance the skills required for future organizations, can be illustrated as shown in Figure 7.3:

5   Conclusion

The SLSP can be employed as a model for HEIs across Thailand to equip students with future skills for the changing world. One of the key success factors is financial resources. In this particular case, the first key success began with top management (the institutional level) based on their commitment and dedication to take responsibility for sufficient budget allocation to support the entire program. Second, in terms of sustainability, the proper legislation must be in place to support the continued transformation process, which is crucial for this type of program (*Nasheeda* et al., 2019). Third, it is necessary to ensure participation and coordination among the faculty staff members who carry out the development program and are willing to work closely with students (at the individual level). This factor is also critical to the success or failure of the implementation of the SLSP. Fourth, preparation of the students must be conducted prior to the debut of the program to supply students with an orientation about the background knowledge concerning the community and community development schemes. There is also a requirement for well-planned community coordination and a monitoring system with input from all involved parties; both of these are deemed to be very important aspects. In this SLSP, a network of alumni in the area was used. To clearly assess students' performance outputs, a competency-based assessment, formative, summative, and participative evaluation for students should be considered for this type of program.

References

Alias N, and Rahimb FA (2019) *The Impact of Service Learning on Students' Social Skill*. In: Proceedings of the Inspirational Scholar Symposium (ISS). Cetakan Pertama: Pusat Penajaran Pembela Jaran Universiti (UTLC), 55–66. Available (consulted 12 August 2022) at: https://www.utlc2021.tlgateway.edu.my/images/2021/ebook/Proceeding_ISS2019.pdf#page=67.

Azmee NN, and Kassim NA (2019) Employee empowerment, learning culture and technology in a research-based organization. *International Journal for Infonomics* 12(2): 1878–1883. Available (consulted 12 August 2022) at: https://infonomics-society.org/wp-content/uploads/Employee-Empowerment-Learning-Culture-and-Technology.pdf.

Dollinger M, and Lodge J (2020). Student-staff co-creation in higher education: An evidence-informed model to support future design and implementation. *Journal of Higher Education Policy and Management* 42(5): 532–546. DOI: 10.1080/1360080X.2019.1663681.

Duchek S, Raetze S, and Scheuch I (2020) The role of diversity in organizational resilience: A theoretical framework. *Business Research* 13(2): 387–423. DOI: 10.1007/s40685-019-0084-8.

EL Telyani A, Farmanesh P, and Zargar P (2022) An examination of the relationship between levels diversity-organizational performance: Does innovative culture matter? *SAGE Open* 12(1). DOI: 10.1177/21582440211067244.

Gleason NW (2018) Higher education in the era of the fourth industrial revolution. In: Gleason NW (ed) *Higher education in the era of the fourth industrial revolution*. Singapore: Palgrave Macmillan, 1–11.

Haste H, & Vidur C (2020) *The future of education for participation in 2050: Educating for managing an ambiguity*. Available (consulted 12 August 2022) at: https://unesdoc.unesco.org/ark:/48223/pf0000374441.

Kaivo-oja JRL, and Lauraeus IT (2018) The VUCA approach as a solution concept to corporate foresight challenges and global technological disruption. *Foresight* 20(1): 27–49. DOI: 10.1108/FS-06-2017-0022.

Laloux F (2014) *Reinventing organizations: A guide to creating organizations inspired by the next stage in human consciousness*. Brussels, Belgium: Nelson Parker.

Madera JM, Ng L, Sundermann JM, and Hebl M (2019) Top management gender diversity and organizational attraction: When and why it matters. *Archives of Scientific Psychology* 7(1): 90–101. DOI: 10.1037/arc0000060.

McCurdy RP, Nickels ML, and Bush SB (2020) Problem-based design thinking tasks: Engaging student empathy in STEM. *The Electronic Journal for Research in Science & Mathematics Education* 24(2): 22–55.

Moon KK, and Christensen RK (2020) Realizing the performance benefits of workforce diversity in the US federal government: The moderating role of diversity climate. *Public Personnel Management* 49(1): 141–165. DOI: 10.1177/0091026019848458.

Moreno Romero A, Uruburu Á, Jain AK, Acevedo Ruiz M, and Gómez Muñoz CF (2020) The path towards evolutionary – Teal organizations: A relationship trigger on collaborative platforms. *Sustainability* 12(23): 9817. DOI: 10.3390/su12239817.

Nasheeda A, Abdullah HB, Krauss SE, and Ahmed NB (2019) A narrative systematic review of life skills education: Effectiveness, research gaps and priorities. *International Journal of Adolescence and Youth* 24(3): 362–379. DOI: 10.1080/02673843.2018.1479278.

Nithyanantham V, Ogunmola GA, Venkateswaran PS, Rajest SS, and Regin R (2021) The impact of gender diversity on organizational performance in banks. *Turkish Journal of Physiotherapy and Rehabilitation* 32(3): 45453–45489.

Office of National Higher Education Science Research and Innovation Policy Council. (2021) *Cabinet approves 117.88 billion THB for FY2022 higher education budget*. Available (consulted 12 August 2022) at: https://www.nxpo.or.th/th/en/7316/.

Oliver S, and Kandadi KR (2006) How to develop knowledge culture in organizations? A multiple case study of large, distributed organizations. *Journal of Knowledge Management* 10(4): 6–24. DOI: 10.1108/13673270610679336.

Ra-ngabtook W (2020) Thai learner's key competencies in a VUCA world. *Journal of Teacher Professional Development* 1(1): 1–11.

Rutkowska M, and Kaminska AM (2020) Turquoise management model-Teal organization. In: Soliman Kh. S. (ed) *Education excellence and innovation management: A 2025 vision to sustain economic development during global challenges*. Seville, Spain: IBIMA, 11380–11387.

Sánchez JH, Sánchez YH, Collado-Ruiz D, and Cebrián-Tarrasón D (2013) Knowledge creating and sharing corporate culture framework. *Procedia-Social and Behavioral Sciences* 74: 388–397.

Shaules J (2019) *Language, culture, and the embodied mind: A developmental model of linguaculture learning*. Singapore: Springer. DOI: 10.1007/978-981-15-0587-4.

Stein S (2021) Reimagining global citizenship education for a volatile, uncertain, complex, and ambiguous (VUCA) world. *Globalisation, Societies and Education* 19(4): 482–495. DOI: 10.1080/14767724.2021.1904212.

Vygotsky LS, and Cole M (1978) *Mind in society: Development of higher psychological processes*. Cambridge, MA: Harvard University Press.

Yadav M, and Rajak R (2021) Impact of diversity management practices on learning organization and organizational performance in hotel industry. *International Journal of System Assurance Engineering and Management* 13: 81–91. DOI: 10.1007/s13198-021-01264-y.

Yusof N, Tengku RAHTF, and Ariffinc HN (2019) *Understanding impact of service learning practices in higher education*. In: Proceedings of the Inspirational Scholar Symposium (ISS). Cetakan Pertama: Pusat Penajaran Pembela Jaran Universiti (UTLC), 365–370. Available (consulted 12 August 2022) at: https://www.utlc2021.tlgateway.edu.my/images/2021/ebook/Proceeding_ISS2019.pdf#page=67.

PART 2

Inclusive Higher Education in Support of Social Mobility

CHAPTER 8

Assessment of the Level of Cultural Differences and Openness to People with Disabilities and the Impact of These Characteristics on the Inclusiveness of Russian Universities

Ludmila L. Shtofer, Nafiset Z. Daurova, Inna N. Gaidareva and Zara A. Mamisheva

Abstract

This chapter aims to assess the level of cultural differences and openness to people with disabilities and the impact of these characteristics on the inclusiveness of Russian universities. The first task of this chapter is to determine the impact of the level of cultural differences and openness to people with disabilities on the inclusiveness of Russian universities by correlation analysis. The research objects for this task are the top seven universities in Russia for people with disabilities in 2022. The second task is to identify the connection between the openness of universities and the inclusiveness of the social environment in Russia. For this purpose, the authors study the dynamics of inclusiveness in Russia from 2013 to 2020, as well as the dynamics of changes in the representation of Russian universities in the Times Higher Education ranking. The authors conducted a quantitative-qualitative study based on the method of horizontal analysis. As a result, the authors substantiate that the level of cultural differences (cultural barriers to entry and study at universities), the openness of universities to persons with disabilities, and their impact are critical to the inclusiveness of today's universities. There is also a strong correlation between the openness of universities and the inclusiveness of the social environment. The experience of Russian universities clearly demonstrates this. The theoretical significance of the research results is that the author's findings clarified the essence and cause-effect relations of inclusiveness of universities and contributed to the development of the theoretical and methodological framework for the management of inclusiveness of universities.

Keywords

cultural differences – openness to people with disabilities – inclusiveness of universities – universities of Russia – international university rankings

1 Introduction

On the one hand, the inclusiveness of universities is their openness to all persons interested. This includes passing grades (requirements for applicants), the cost of education (financial barriers), and the number and proportion of budgetary places in the university. It is also necessary to consider the transparency of the educational process, the fairness of the assessment of the knowledge, and the proximity of universities to applicants (the main universities – to large cities and their branches – to small towns and villages).

On the other hand, the attractiveness of universities is rooted in competitiveness. This includes the prestige of studying at a university, the value of its diplomas in the labor market (opportunities for employment in the profession and career building for graduates), and opportunities for return on investment in education. In today's globalized world, the most important indicators of the inclusiveness of universities are their positions in national and international university rankings.

For Russia, ensuring the inclusiveness of universities is of strategic importance for three reasons. First, high inclusiveness is a historical feature of the Russian system of science and higher education. Second, the production capacity of Russian universities is very high; it is even greater due to the new opportunities offered by the digital economy. Third, as a dynamically developing economy, Russia is interested in unlocking the potential of the system of science and higher education to serve as vectors of economic growth.

The problem is that in the context of dynamic social progress, the conditions for achieving inclusiveness in universities are subject to change. Against the backdrop of general global trends in international cooperation and the increasing openness of society to persons with disabilities, this chapter hypothesizes that they represent new conditions for the inclusiveness of universities. This chapter aims to assess the level of cultural differences and openness to people with disabilities and the impact of these characteristics on the inclusiveness of Russian universities.

2 Literature Review

This chapter draws on the scientific provision of the Theory of Inclusiveness of Universities, which has received much attention in the existing literature. *Aerts* et al. (2022) and *Toklucu* et al. (2022) note that the technical management of universities forms the basis of its inclusiveness. For example, most rankings of Russian universities focus on the availability of dormitories and sports complexes, library facilities, equipped classrooms, and other university infrastructure (*Education in Russia*, 2022).

In their works, *de Castro Peixoto* et al. (2022), *Gerhardt and Karsan* (2022), and *Gonzalez-Sanchez* et al. (2022) consider inclusiveness as an area of internal university management and a criterion for distinguishing universities. The argument is that there are significant differences in the inclusiveness of universities within the same country and even within the same territory (e.g., a region).

Bartz (2020), *Lavigne* et al. (2022), and *Mellifont* (2020) see the removal of cultural barriers and opening up to people with disabilities as two separate, unrelated areas of university governance. The issues of inclusiveness in Russian universities are covered in some detail by *Akhmetova* (2017), *Bogoviz* et al. (2018), *Burdakova* et al. (2019), *Dudukalov* et al. (2016), *Muller* (2021), *Shabaltina* et al. (2021), *Vanchukhina* et al. (2019), and *Yankovskaya* et al. (2022).

Devlin and Warner (2017), *du Toit and Forlin* (2009), *Liu and Zou* (2022), Popkova (2019), and Skoglund and Stacker (2016) note the increased role of the international activities of universities when ranking them. *Forlin* et al. (2015), *Loreman* et al. (2014), *Lui* et al. (2015), and *Sharma* et al. (2017) attach great importance to the openness of universities to people with disabilities in determining their inclusiveness.

Thus, the literature review showed that while the level of cultural difference and openness to persons with disabilities have been extensively studied in the existing literature as separate characteristics of universities, their significance for university inclusiveness has not been sufficiently developed, which is a research gap. To fill the identified gap, this chapter assesses the level of cultural differences in Russian universities and their openness to people with disabilities, as well as the impact of these characteristics on the inclusiveness of Russian universities.

3 Materials and Methods

The research goal is achieved through two research objectives. The first task involves determining the impact of the level of cultural differences and openness to people with disabilities on the inclusiveness of Russian universities. The research objects are the top seven universities in Russia for people with disabilities and disabilities (openness index) in 2022, as evaluated by the *Educational Forum "Entrance Navigator"* (2022). Using the case study method, the authors reveal the best practices of these universities for achieving openness to people with disabilities.

Using the method of correlation analysis, the authors evaluated the correlation of the rating function of these universities among the best universities of Russia RAEX-100 (as an indicator of inclusiveness (*RAEX Pro*, 2022)) with the index of openness and with indicators of cultural differences (International Students Ratio and International Faculty Ratio according to QS (2022)), as well as the share of international students and the share of foreign teachers according to MIREA – Russian technological university (*Main Information and Computing Center*, 2022). Statistical data for the study are summarized in Table 8.1.

The second objective of this research is to identify the relationship between the openness of universities and the inclusiveness of the social environment in Russia. For this purpose, we study the dynamics of inclusiveness in Russia from 2013 to 2020 and the dynamics of changes in the representation of Russian universities in the Times Higher Education rating (2022). A quantitative-qualitative study based on the method of horizontal analysis is conducted.

4 Results

4.1 The Impact of the Level of Cultural Differences and Openness to Persons with Disabilities on the Inclusiveness of Russian Universities

As part of the first task of this research, the authors used the case study method to identify the best practices for achieving openness of Russian universities in the sample (Table 8.1) for people with disabilities. At the HSE, special educational advisors assist people with disabilities. The educational process is tailored to the special needs of people with disabilities; they are provided with special social assistance, medical care, and support for further employment.

The RSUH and the RUDN have special (most loyal) conditions for admission, education, and housing for people with disabilities. The RSSU has a resource center for people with disabilities, which helps with education, career

ASSESSMENT OF THE LEVEL OF CULTURAL DIFFERENCES

TABLE 8.1 Cultural differences and inclusiveness of Russian universities that are most open to persons with disabilities in 2022

University	Openness index	Indicators of cultural differences				Indicator of inclusiveness
	PLACE IN THE TOP SEVEN UNIVERSITIES IN RUSSIA FOR PEOPLE WITH DISABILITIES	INTERNATIONAL STUDENTS RATIO ACCORDING TO QS, POINTS 1–100	INTERNATIONAL FACULTY RATIO ACCORDING TO QS, POINTS 1–100	SHARE OF INTERNATIONAL STUDENTSA, %	SHARE OF FOREIGN TEACHERSB, %	RAEX-100 RATING FUNCTIONALITY AMONG RUSSIA'S BEST UNIVERSITIES, SCORES 1–5
Higher School of Economics (HSE)	1	16.5	2.3	10.03	5.97	4.5250
Russian State University for the Humanities (RSUH)	2	5.1	1.1	5.97	1.24	2.4681
Peoples' Friendship University of Russia (RUDN)	3	93.2	3.5	26.23	8.94	3.8221
Russian State Social University (RSSU)	4	–	–	5.24	0.99	–
Moscow State University of Humanities and Economics (MSUHEU)	5	–	–	10.77	1.01	–

(cont.)

University	Openness index			Indicators of cultural differences			Indicator of inclusiveness
	PLACE IN THE TOP SEVEN UNIVERSITIES IN RUSSIA FOR PEOPLE WITH DISABILITIES	INTERNATIONAL STUDENTS RATIO ACCORDING TO QS, POINTS 1–100	INTERNATIONAL FACULTY RATIO ACCORDING TO QS, POINTS 1–100	SHARE OF INTERNATIONAL STUDENTS[a], %	SHARE OF FOREIGN TEACHERS[b], %	RAEX-100 RATING FUNCTIONALITY AMONG RUSSIA'S BEST UNIVERSITIES, SCORES 1–5
Chelyabinsk State University (ChelSU)	6	-	-	0.00	0.00	-
Novosibirsk State Technical University (NSTU)	7	51.2	1.3	11.71	0.94	2.6157

Note:
a The share of foreign students who have completed Bachelor's, Specialist's, and Master's degree programs in the total number of students (cumulative contingent)
b The share of foreign nationals among NDPs in the total number of academic staff

SOURCE: COMPILED BY THE AUTHORS BASED ON QS (2022), *MAIN INFORMATION AND COMPUTING CENTER OF THE MIREA UNIVERSITY* (2022), *EDUCATIONAL FORUM "ENTRANCE NAVIGATOR"* (2022), *RAEX PRO* (2022)

guidance, and employment. Inclusive education for students with locomotor disorders is organized at the MSUHEU. The ChelSU has the status of a resource center for training people with disabilities. The NSTU has an Inclusive Support Center for students with disabilities, providing everyone with an opportunity to study to become a social worker.

The overall level of inclusiveness in 2022 and its relationship with the index of openness and the indicators of cultural differences of the considered universities was determined using statistics from Table 8.1 and the method of correlation analysis (Chart 8.1).

According to Chart 8.1, the ratio of international students in Russian universities is relatively high and amounts to 41.50 points. According to QS, the international faculty ratio is significantly lower (2.05 points). However, it is essential to note that the sample does not include the leading Russian universities but rather the universities most open to people with disabilities.

The share of international students in the considered universities is quite high and amounts to 9.99%; the share of foreign teachers is 2.73%. The rating functionality of the considered universities among the best universities in Russia RAEX-100 (inclusiveness) is quite high and amounts to 3.36 points (out of the maximum 5).

The connection of the openness of universities to people with disabilities was negative but high (-56.69%). This suggests that improving a university's position in the openness ranking increases its inclusiveness (in fact, the relationship is positive). The correlation of the international student ratio with the

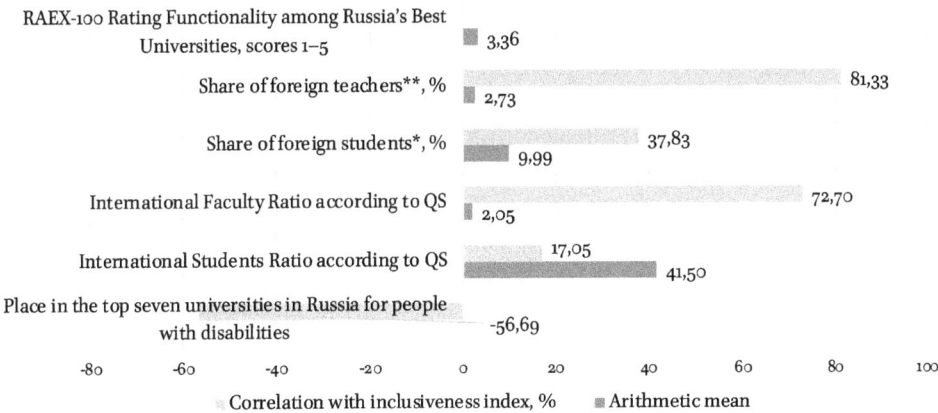

CHART 8.1   Overall level of inclusiveness and its connection with openness and cultural differences of Russian universities in 2022
SOURCE: CALCULATED AND COMPILED BY THE AUTHORS

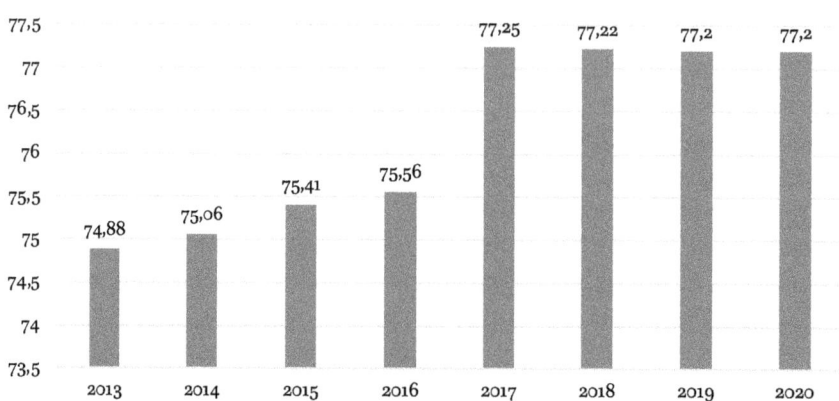

CHART 8.2 Dynamics of social inclusion in Russia in 2013–2020
SOURCE: CALCULATED AND COMPILED BY THE AUTHORS BASED ON *GLOBAL GREEN GROWTH INSTITUTE* (2022)

inclusiveness of universities was moderate (17.05%), as was the correlation of the international student ratio with the inclusiveness of universities (37.83%). The correlation of the international faculty ratio with the inclusiveness of universities was high (72.70%), as was the international faculty ratio (81.33%).

4.2 Linking the Openness of Universities with the Inclusiveness of the Social Environment in Russia

To achieve the second objective of this research, Chart 8.2 presents the dynamics of social inclusion in Russia from 2013 to 2020.

Horizontal analysis of the statistics from Chart 8.2 showed that social inclusion in Russia remained virtually unchanged (changed within 1) from 2013 to 2016. However, in 2017, this indicator saw a sharp increase of 2.24%. The analysis of the dynamics of changes in the representation of Russian universities in the *Times Higher Education* (2022) showed that only 13 Russian universities were represented in this ranking in 2016, while in 2017, their number increased sharply to 24 universities.

This indicates the existence of a link between the openness of universities and the inclusiveness of the social environment in Russia. Thus, the increase in social inclusion in Russia in 2017 may have been caused by the fact that international statistics began to consider the achievements of not only the leading universities (that have mainly technical achievements) but also regional universities (that have social achievements related to their openness to people with disabilities). The opposite effect is also possible and evident. Due to the overall growth of Russia's social inclusiveness, the presence of its universities in international university rankings has increased markedly.

5   Discussion

The chapter contributes to the literature through the development of scientific statements of the Theory of University Inclusiveness, clarifying and substantiating the significant contribution of the level of cultural differences and openness to persons with disabilities in the inclusiveness of universities (demonstrated on the example of Russian universities). In contrast to *Aerts* et al. (2022) and *Toklucu* et al. (2022), the authors reasoned that social management is as important as technical management in achieving the inclusiveness of today's universities. For example, campuses specially equipped for people with disabilities and educational programs tailored to them and international students are no less important than dormitories, sports complexes, and library facilities.

In contrast to *de Castro Peixoto* et al. (2022), *Gerhardt and Karsan* (2022), and *Gonzalez-Sanchez* et al. (2022), the authors proved that inclusiveness is rather an area of external than internal university governance. Achieving inclusive universities requires general social inclusiveness of society, which, in turn, fuels the inclusiveness of universities. Thus, it is a cyclical process. Contrary to *Bartz* (2020), Lavigne et al. (2022), and *Mellifont* (2020), the authors reasoned that removing cultural barriers and ensuring openness to people with disabilities are considered closely related areas of university governance that must be implemented systemically to achieve the best outcomes of university inclusiveness.

6   Conclusion

Thus, we can conclude that the level of cultural differences (cultural barriers to entry and study at universities) and openness to people with disabilities, as well as the impact of these indicators, are critical to the inclusiveness of today's universities. This is clearly demonstrated in the experience of Russian universities, where cultural neutrality determines inclusiveness up to 81.33% and openness to people with disabilities up to 56.69% in 2022.

There is also a strong correlation between the openness of universities and the inclusiveness of the social environment. Thanks to this connection, social inclusiveness and the presence of Russian universities in international university rankings saw a sharp increase in 2017 (shown by the example of the Times Higher Education ranking). The theoretical significance of the results is that the author's findings clarified the essence and cause-effect relations of inclusiveness of universities and contributed to the development of the theoretical and methodological framework for the management of inclusiveness of universities.

The practical significance of the author's conclusions is that they make it possible to improve the management of inclusiveness of universities. From the perspective of corporate governance, it is recommended to systemically implement measures aimed at overcoming cultural differences and ensuring the openness of universities to people with disabilities. From the perspective of public administration, it is proposed to support the inclusiveness of universities by increasing the overall level of social inclusiveness. The proposed recommendations will be useful not only for Russia but also for other countries.

References

Aerts G, Cauwelier K, Pape SD, Jacobs S, and Vanhondeghem S (2022) An inside-out perspective on stakeholder management in university technology transfer offices. *Technological Forecasting and Social Change* 175: 121291. DOI: 10.1016/j.techfore.2021.121291.

Akhmetova AV (2017) Transformation of ethnocultural development of indigenous peoples in the conditions of socialist modernization of the Far East in 1920–1970s: Problems of historiography. In: Popkova EG, Sukhova VE, Rogachev AF, Tyurina YG, Boris OA, and Parakhina VN (eds) *Integration and clustering for sustainable economic growth.* Cham, Switzerland: Springer, 553–558. DOI: 10.1007/978-3-319-45462-7_53.

Bartz J (2020) All inclusive?! Empirical insights into individual experiences of students with disabilities and mental disorders at German universities and implications for inclusive higher education. *Education Sciences* 10(9): 223. DOI: 10.3390/educsci10090223.

Bogoviz A, Averin A, and Yanovskaya V (2018). Gender analysis of local budgets in law enforcement and educational organizations of Russia. *MATEC Web of Conferences* 212: 09015. DOI: 10.1051/matecconf/201821209015.

Burdakova G, Byankin A, Usanov I, and Pankova L (2019) Smart technologies in education and formation of entrepreneurial competencies. *IOP Conference Series: Materials Science and Engineering* 497(1): 012066. DOI: 10.1088/1757-899X/497/1/012066.

de Castro Peixoto L, Barbosa RR, and de Faria AF (2022) Management of regional knowledge: Knowledge flows among university, industry, and government. *Journal of the Knowledge Economy* 13(1): 92–110. DOI: 10.1007/s13132-020-00702-9.

Devlin P, and Warner P (2017) Building relationships: Facilitating cultural inclusivity through Christian Service-Learning Immersion programs. *International Perspectives on Inclusive Education* 12: 175–191. DOI: 10.1108/S1479-363620170000012012.

du Toit P, and Forlin C (2009) Cultural transformation for inclusion, what is needed? A South African perspective. *School Psychology International* 30(6): 644–666. DOI: 10.1177/0143034309107081.

Dudukalov EV, Rodionova ND, Sivakova YE, Vyugova E, Cheryomushkina IV, and Popkova EG (2016) Global innovational networks: Sense and role in development of global economy. *Contemporary Economics* 10(4): 299–310. DOI: 10.5709/ce.1897-9254.217.

Education in Russia (2022) *University Rankings 2022*. Available (consulted 12 June 2022) at: https://russiaedu.ru/rating.

Educational Forum "Entrance Navigator" (2022). *Top 7 universities in Russia for people with disabilities in 2022*. Available (consulted 12 June 2022) at: https://propostuplenie.ru/article/vuzy-dlja-invalidov-i-ljudej-s-ovz/.

Forlin C, Kawai N, and Higuchi S (2015) Educational reform in Japan towards inclusion: Are we training teachers for success? *International Journal of Inclusive Education* 19(3): 314–331. DOI: 10.1080/13603116.2014.930519.

Gerhardt T, and Karsan S (2022) Talent management in private universities: the case of a private university in the United Kingdom. *International Journal of Educational Management* 36(4): 552–575. DOI: 10.1108/IJEM-05-2020-0222.

Global Green Growth Institute (2022) *Green growth index: Social inclusion in Russia in 2013–2020*. Available (consulted 12 June 2022) at: https://gggi-simtool-demo.herokuapp.com/SimulationDashBoard/country-profile.

Gonzalez-Sanchez MB, Gutiérrez-López C, and Barrachina Palanca M (2022) How can universities engage lecturers in knowledge transfer? Analyzing the influence of performance management systems. *Journal of Knowledge Management* 26(4): 1083–1110. DOI: 10.1108/JKM-02-2021-0131.

Lavigne E, Cowley S, and Sá CM (2022) Scholarship, management, and leadership in academic administration: The case of Canadian university presidents and provosts. *Tertiary Education and Management* 28: 121–134. DOI: 10.1007/s11233-022-09089-5.

Liu Q, and Zou N (2022) Further convergence management to build a more resilient education System for international students at Tsinghua University in COVID-19 pandemic period. *Journal of International Students* 12(S11): 83–90. DOI: 10.32674/jis.v12iS1.4609.

Loreman T, Forlin C, and Sharma U (2014) Measuring indicators of inclusive education: A systematic review of the literature. *International Perspectives on Inclusive Education* 3: 165–187. DOI: 10.1108/S1479-363620140000003024.

Lui M, Sin K-F, Yang L, Forlin C, and Ho F-C (2015). Knowledge and perceived social norm predict parents attitudes towards inclusive education. *International Journal of Inclusive Education* 19(10): 1052–1067. DOI: 10.1080/13603116.2015.1037866.

Main Information and Computing Center of the MIREA University (2022) *Information and analytical materials on the results of monitoring the activities of educational institutions of higher education in 2021.* Available (consulted 12 June 2022) at: https://monitoring.miccedu.ru/?m=vpo.

Mellifont D (2020) A critical exploration of university policy supporting the employment and career development of people with disability in the Australian academy. *Australian Journal of Career Development* 29(2): 117–126. DOI: 10.1177/1038416220919799.

Muller NV (2021) Research and modeling of industrial and social processes to improve the safety of human life. In: Shakirova OG, Bashkov OV, and Khusainov AA (eds) *Current problems and ways of industry development: Equipment and technologies.* Cham, Switzerland, Springer, 744–751. DOI: 10.1007/978-3-030-69421-0_80.

Popkova EG (2019) Classification of conflicts in socio-economic systems. In: Popkova EG (ed) *Conflict-free socio-economic systems: Perspectives and contradictions.* Bingley, UK: Emerald Publishing Limited: 21–27. DOI: 10.1108/978-1-78769-993-920191004.

QS (2022) *World University Rankings 2022.* Available (consulted 12 June 2022) at: https://www.topuniversities.com/university-rankings/world-university-rankings/2022.

RAEX Pro (2022) *RAEX-100 ranking of the best universities in Russia, 2022.* Available (consulted 12 June 2022) at: https://raex-rr.com/pro/education/russian_universities/top-100_universities/2022/.

Shabaltina LV, Karbekova AB, Milkina E, and Pushkarev IY (2021) The social impact of the downturn in business and the new context of sustainable development in the context of the 2020 economic crisis in developing countries. In: Popkova EG, and Sergi BS (eds) *Modern global economic system: Evolutional development vs. revolutionary leap.* Cham, Switzerland, Springer, 74–82. DOI: 10.1007/978-3-030-69415-9_9.

Sharma U, Forlin C, Marella M, and Jitoko F (2017) Using indicators as a catalyst for inclusive education in the Pacific Islands. *International Journal of Inclusive Education* 21(7): 730–746. DOI: 10.1080/13603116.2016.1251979.

Skoglund P, and Stacker H (2016) How can education systems support all learners? Tipping-point leadership focused on cultural change and inclusive capability. *International Perspectives on Inclusive Education* 8: 111–136. DOI: 10.1108/S1479-363620160000008008.

Times Higher Education (2022) *World University Rankings 2016–2017.* Available (consulted 12 June 2022) at: https://www.timeshighereducation.com/world-university-rankings/2017/world-ranking#!/page/0/length/25/locations/RUS/sort_by/rank/sort_order/asc/cols/stats.

Toklucu E, Silman F, Turan S, Atasoy R, and Kalkan Ü (2022) The effects of the crisis management Skills and Distance Education Practices of Universities on student satisfaction and organizational image. *Sustainability* 14(10): 5813. DOI: 10.3390/su14105813.

Vanchukhina L, Leybert T, Rogacheva A, Rudneva Yu, and Khalikova E (2019) New model of managerial education in technical university. *International Journal of Educational Management* 33(3): 511–524. DOI: 10.1108/IJEM-08-2018-0270.

Yankovskaya VV, Bulgarov MA, Gimelshtein IV, Konovalova ME, Kuzmina OY (2022) Innovative approach to educating young people in the regional education market in the context of the digital economy of the future. *Education in the Asia-Pacific Region* 65: 301–307. DOI: 10.1007/978-981-16-9069-3_33.

CHAPTER 9

The Value of Higher Education Inclusiveness for Sustainable and Innovative Development of the Knowledge Economy

Larisa V. Popova, Tatiana A. Dugina, Svetlana Yu. Shaldohina and Elena A. Nemkina

Abstract

The paper aims to determine the importance of inclusiveness of higher education for sustainable and innovative development of the knowledge economy. Using the method of regression analysis, the authors reveal the manifestations of inclusiveness of higher education, which are most significant for the sustainable and innovative development of the knowledge economy at a moderate and high level of development of higher education. Through optimization using the method of least squares, the authors determine the prospects and offer recommendations for sustainable and innovative development of the knowledge economy based on increasing inclusiveness (its most significant manifestations) of higher education, considering the established features of different levels of its development. The theoretical significance of this research lies in the provision of the paramount importance of inclusiveness as a key criterion of higher education in assessing its contribution to the sustainable and innovative development of the knowledge economy. The novelty of the research is provided by the consideration of the differences in the level of development of higher education for the most accurate and reliable assessment of its importance for sustainable and innovative development of the knowledge economy. This allows us to consider the characteristics of countries with different levels of development of higher education and offer them the most effective recommendations for managing the inclusiveness of higher education to ensure sustainable and innovative development of the knowledge economy.

Keywords

inclusiveness of higher education – sustainable development – innovative development – knowledge economy

1   Introduction

The knowledge economy is a model of the economic system, the feature of which is the central role of knowledge in its functioning and development. This feature is manifested in all areas of economic activity. In the economic sector, the value of human capital is increasing, and the success of unlocking human potential determines the competitiveness of businesses in target markets, which are becoming increasingly high-tech. The legal sector provides normative protection of intellectual property. The social sector, where knowledge is generated and diffused through higher education, plays a fundamental role (*Bogoviz* et al., 2018b; *Popkova*, 2020).

The priority for the development of the knowledge economy is sustainability. The knowledge economy focuses on a person with their interests in the market of educational services (accumulation of human potential – gaining knowledge) and in the labor market (disclosure of human potential – the practical application of accumulated knowledge to achieve high productivity, improve the results of creative work, receive increased pay, and build a career). The key Sustainable Development Goals (SDGs) that are being achieved in this process are SDG 4 (quality education with a focus on higher education), SDG 8 (with a focus on decent work), and SDG 9 (with a focus on innovation).

Another priority for the development of the knowledge economy is innovation. The knowledge economy should support social, scientific, and technological progress and provide outstripping (rather than catching up) development of the economic system, guarantee its digital competitiveness, and strengthen its position in high-tech markets. The above determines the great significance of higher education for sustainable and innovative development of the knowledge economy, noted in numerous works, including *Kichuk* (2021), *Rottleb and Kleibert* (2022).

In recognition of this, over the past decades, pursuing a knowledge economy, countries have paid close attention to improving the quality of higher education and increasing the efficiency of universities. With the adoption of the SDGs, a new criterion has emerged by which higher education is being increasingly evaluated – inclusiveness (*Sibirskaya* et al., 2019). This new criterion of higher education is particularly important for sustainable and innovative development of the knowledge economy because it determines the mass training of highly qualified personnel and their deficit-free economic system.

When inclusiveness is insufficient, higher education becomes elitist – accessible only to a narrow social category. In this case, the high quality of higher education services allows meeting the need of the knowledge economy only to some extent for highly qualified personnel who find themselves in the minority and have difficulties in team building, which reduces their productivity and innovation activity. The efficiency of universities is more of a commercial criterion that determines their profitability but plays a secondary role in the development of the knowledge economy (*Huber* et al., 2020).

Also, a lack of inclusiveness can cause the "institutional trap" of higher education, whereby certain social groups, rather than the worthiest candidates, are selected for admission to universities. Low competition for university admission can lead to low requirements for students, which causes the formality (not supported by knowledge) of diplomas and insufficiently high quality of higher education. The result could be a regression of the knowledge economy (*Frunzaru* et al., 2018).

Inclusiveness can overcome and avoid the formation of the described institutional trap of higher education. Combined with the mentioned existing criteria, the inclusiveness of higher education makes it accessible to the most deserving candidates in a highly competitive environment, both on admission and during university study. Because of this, the inclusiveness of higher education stimulates the growth of its quality and increases the informativeness and value of higher education diplomas.

Despite the high degree of elaboration of the essence and manifestations of inclusiveness of higher education, a gap in the literature lies in insufficient elaboration and uncertainty on the importance of inclusiveness of higher education for sustainable and innovative development of the knowledge economy. This raises the research question (RQ) of this paper: "What manifestations of inclusiveness of higher education are most significant for the sustainable and innovative development of the knowledge economy?" The hypothesis (H) of this research is that as higher education develops, the most significant manifestations of its inclusiveness for sustainable and innovative development of the knowledge economy change.

The research aims to define the importance of inclusiveness of higher education for sustainable and innovative development of the knowledge economy. To achieve the goal, this paper pursues a set of the following tasks:
- To identify the manifestations of inclusiveness of higher education, which are most significant for the sustainable and innovative development of the knowledge economy at a moderate level of the development of higher education;
- To identify the manifestations of inclusiveness of higher education, which are most significant for the sustainable and innovative development of the knowledge economy at a high level of the development of higher education;

– To determine the prospects and offer recommendations for sustainable and innovative development of the knowledge economy based on increasing inclusiveness (its most significant manifestations) of higher education, considering the established features of its different levels of development.

The research novelty is ensured by considering the differences in the level of development of higher education for the most accurate and reliable assessment of its importance for the sustainable and innovative development of the knowledge economy. This allows us to consider the characteristics of countries with different levels of development of higher education and offer them the most effective recommendations for managing the inclusiveness of higher education to ensure sustainable and innovative development of the knowledge economy.

2   Literature Review

This work is based on the theory of the knowledge economy. The current global community pays a great deal of attention to maintaining statistics on the knowledge economy. One of the most comprehensive and authoritative sources of statistics on the knowledge economy is the Global Knowledge Index, calculated annually by UNDP (2022) – it is chosen as the information base for this research. Relevant areas of sustainable and innovative development of the knowledge economy are the following:

– Innovative economic development (*Rodríguez* et al., 2022), an indicator of which is the "share of GERD in GDP";
– Innovation activity of private businesses (*Zhang* et al., 2022), an indicator of which is "firms that spend on R&D";
– Creating knowledge-intensive jobs (*Kim* et al., 2021), an indicator of which is "high-skilled employment";
– Bringing innovative products to market (*Héraud*, 2021), an indicator of which is "firms with a new product/service";
– High-tech economy (*Hernández* et al., 2021), an indicator of which is "the share of high-tech trade in the total structure of trade."

Al-Husseini et al. (2020), *Durazzi* (2019), *Wirba* (2021), and *Yeo and Lee* (2020) note the important role of higher education in the sustainable and innovative development of the knowledge economy while pointing to such criteria of higher education development as quality and efficiency.

This research is also based on the theory of inclusiveness of higher education. In accordance with it, inclusiveness is understood as openness and equal opportunities for representatives of different social groups to receive higher education. According to the criterion of social barriers to higher education, which are overcome through inclusiveness, we can distinguish the following manifestations of inclusiveness:

- Gender inclusiveness: gender neutrality in higher education (*Bogoviz* et al., 2018a; *Parra-Martínez* et al., 2021). Its indicator is "Gross attendance ratio for tertiary education, gender parity" (UNDP, 2022);
- Financial inclusiveness: accessibility of higher education for people of different financial status, provided through a flexible pricing policy of universities, social scholarships and grants for higher education, and budgetary places in universities (on the terms of the state order) (*Faura-Martínez and Cifuentes-Faura*, 2021). Its indicator is "Gross attendance ratio for tertiary education, wealth parity" (UNDP, 2022);
- Geographical inclusiveness: the openness of higher education to people from different geographical areas, including hard-to-reach (rural) areas provided by opening branches of universities in different territories, offering dormitories to students, and distance learning (*Kirupainayagam and Sutha*, 2021; *Ngo* et al., 2021). Its indicator is "Gross attendance ratio for tertiary education, location parity" (UNDP, 2022);
- Lifelong learning inclusiveness: the possibility of lifelong learning, expressed in a move up the higher education ladder (bachelor's, master's, and doctorate). Its indicators are "Enrolment in bachelor's or equivalent level" and "Enrolment in master's, doctoral, or equivalent" (UNDP, 2022), reflecting the gradation and continuity of higher education (*Kandiko Howson and Lall*, 2020);
- Inclusiveness for people with disabilities: equality of access to university and higher education for people with different health conditions, provided in support of people with disabilities, many of whom have outstanding human potential and are of great value to the knowledge economy (*Bartz*, 2020; *Brewer and Movahedazarhouligh*, 2021; *Sheppard-Jones* et al., 2021). Unfortunately, despite its paramount importance, the statistical record of this manifestation of inclusiveness is not systemically maintained at the international level. To avoid the incomparability of data when using national statistics from different sources in different languages and with different units of measurement, in this chapter, we will omit this criterion, recognizing its unconditional importance, which does not need proof.

Alzyoudi et al. (2021) and *Zaki and Ismail* (2021) pout out the necessity of increasing the inclusiveness of higher education in its unity of all its manifestations. The works by *Anyira and Idubor* (2020), *Baslom and Tong* (2019), *Grebski and Grebski* (2018), *Mohanty and Mishra* (2019), and *Varma* et al. (2021)

argue for increasing the inclusiveness of higher education in all its manifestations in all countries based on the universality of SDG 4, SDG 8, and SDG 9.

Within the framework of the noted theories, the fundamental and applied issues of this study have been studied in sufficient detail. Nevertheless, there is a research gap at the intersection of these theories, which is the unclear meaning of the inclusiveness of higher education for the sustainable and innovative development of the knowledge economy. The present study seeks to fill this gap.

3   Materials and Method

The hypothesis (H) of this research relies on the fact that countries with high levels of the development of higher education do not keep statistics on their gender, financial, and geographic inclusiveness (it is not given in UNDP (2022)), which is apparently very high and varies little among these countries. Nevertheless, the need for inclusiveness of higher education in these countries is also high but in another manifestation – the inclusiveness of lifelong learning.

The research strategy carried out in this work is designed to ensure that the goal is achieved and that the hypothesis (H) is tested to answer the posed research question (Table 9.1).

According to the research strategy (Table 9.1), the first task is related to the identification of manifestations of inclusiveness of higher education, which are most significant for sustainable and innovative development of the knowledge economy at a moderate level of development of higher education. This research task is achieved by using the method of regression analysis. For this purpose, we formed a sample of low-10 countries of the *UN ranking* (2022) of the results in the implementation of SDG 4 ("quality of education") in 2021.

The correlation between the influence of gender, financial, and geographical inclusiveness on the development of the knowledge economy is determined. Table 9.2 presents statistics on the equity and inclusiveness of higher education in these countries. Table 9.3 presents statistics on the sustainable and innovative development of the knowledge economy.

As shown in Table 9.2, the top-10 countries by the development of inclusiveness in 2021 keep detailed statistics on gender and financial inclusiveness of higher education. Therefore, these aspects are given great attention in the public administration of higher education in these countries.

TABLE 9.1   Research strategy

Research objectives	Research method	Research sample	Essence and logic of the research
To identify the manifestations of inclusiveness of higher education that are most significant for the sustainable and innovative development of the knowledge economy at a moderate level of the development of higher education	Method of regression analysis	Low-10 countries in the results of the *UN ranking* (2022) in SDG 4 ("quality of education") in 2021	The relationship of gender, financial, and geographic inclusiveness to the development of the knowledge economy
To identify the manifestations of inclusiveness of higher education that are most significant for the sustainable and innovative development of the knowledge economy at a high level of the development of higher education	Method of regression analysis	Top 10 countries in the results of the *UN ranking* (2022) in SDG 4 ("quality of education") in 2021	Modeling the dependence of the knowledge economy on the inclusiveness of lifelong learning
To determine the prospects and offer recommendations for sustainable and innovative development of the knowledge economy based on increasing inclusiveness (its most significant manifestations) of higher education, considering the established features of its different levels of development	Optimization by least squares method	Both samples (Low-10 and Top-10 countries of the *UN ranking* 2022) separately	Determination of the optimal ratio of manifestations (parameters) of inclusiveness for the most sustainable and innovative development of the knowledge economy, as well as the benefits of optimization

SOURCE: DEVELOPED AND COMPILED BY THE AUTHORS

The second objective of this research is to identify the manifestations of inclusiveness of higher education, which are most significant for the sustainable and innovative development of the knowledge economy at a high level of development of higher education using the method of regression analysis. For this purpose, we formed a sample of the top-10 countries of the *UN ranking* (2022) of results in the implementation of SDG 4 ("quality of education") in 2021. The dependence of the knowledge economy on the inclusiveness of lifelong learning is modeled. Table 9.4 shows the statistical basis for the study in this task.

As shown in Table 9.4, the top-10 countries by the level of the implementation of SDG 4 in 2021 keep detailed statistics on the inclusiveness of lifelong learning. Thus, this indicator receives considerable attention in the public management of higher education in these countries.

The selection of the regression analysis method is explained by the fact that it is a highly accurate and widespread (generally recognized) method of econometrics, which allows one to conduct the most profound and detailed study of the relationship of statistical indicators and eventually obtain regression models suitable for optimization. This makes it possible to support the author's applied recommendations with mathematical calculations and thus achieve their high accuracy and efficiency. The research model of this study is as follows:

$$y_{low} = a_{low} + b1_{ow1} * x_1 + b_{low2} * x_2 + b_{low3} * x_3;$$
$$y_{top} = a_{top} + b_{top4} * x_4 + b_{top5} * x_5. \quad (1)$$

The proof of the hypothesis (H) is the positive values of the coefficients b in the research model (1). The significance of manifestations of inclusiveness of higher education is defined as the sum of regression coefficients in the research model (1).

The third task of this research is to identify the prospects and offer recommendations for sustainable and innovative development of the knowledge economy based on increasing inclusiveness (its most significant manifestations) of higher education, considering the established features of its different levels of development. For this purpose, the least-squares optimization is carried out with the support of both samples (low-10 and top-10 countries) of the *UN ranking* (2022) separately. As a result of solving this task, it is expected to determine the optimal ratio of manifestations (parameters) of inclusiveness for the most sustainable and innovative development of the knowledge economy, as well as the benefits (Δy) due to optimization.

TABLE 9.2   Statistics and inclusiveness of higher education in low-10 countries by the level of its development in 2021

Country	Gross attendance ratio for tertiary education, gender parity	Gross attendance ratio for tertiary education, wealth parity	Gross attendance ratio for tertiary education, location parity
	x_1	x_2	x_3
Niger	31.8	2.4	14.3
Mali	66.9	22.4	2.6
Chad	42.6	6.3	4.5
Guinea	48.5	9.2	0
Liberia	93.2	3.4	0
Senegal	97.8	16.8	3.9
Nigeria	70.3	26.6	2.2
Mauritania	54.2	40.1	16.9
Angola	71.9	2.4	0
Sudan	90.9	29.3	8.7

SOURCE: DEVELOPED AND COMPILED BY THE AUTHORS BASED ON (UNDP, 2022)

4   Results

4.1   *The Importance of Inclusiveness of Higher Education for the Sustainable and Innovative Development of the Knowledge Economy at a Moderate Level of the Development of Higher Education*

In the first task of this research, the arithmetic mean of the data from Table 9.2 and Table 9.3 was determined to identify the manifestations of inclusiveness of higher education that are most significant for the sustainable and innovative development of the knowledge economy at a moderate level of higher education development. The results are shown in Chart 9.1.

According to Chart 9.1, in countries with moderate development of higher education, gender inclusiveness of higher education is very high (66.81 points); financial inclusiveness is much lower (15.89 points), and geographic inclusiveness is low (5.31 points). Countries of this category have achieved the most significant progress in developing the knowledge economy in the area of business, bringing new products to market (67.67%). The share of companies

TABLE 9.3 Statistics of sustainable and innovative development of the knowledge economy in low-10 countries by the level of the development of higher education in 2021

Country	GERD, % GDP	Firms that spend on R&D, %	High-skilled employment, %	Firms with new product/service, %	High-technology trade, % total trade
	y_{1low}	y_{2low}	y_{3low}	y_{4low}	y_{5low}
Niger	n/d	15.1	24.8	54.7	45.7
Mali	5.7	22.4	0	90.1	33.4
Chad	5.9	25.6	0.3	79.5	n/d
Guinea	n/d	13.3	12.5	77.7	18.0
Liberia	n/d	20.4	n/d	92.7	n/d
Senegal	11.5	16.1	4.2	66.7	32.1
Nigeria	n/d	27.5	n/d	68.6	42.6
Mauritania	0	48.8	n/d	67.2	1.1
Angola	0.4	n/d	16.2	n/d	26.0
Sudan	n/d	52.0	n/d	79.5	51.0

SOURCE: SYSTEMATIZED AND COMPILED BY THE AUTHORS BASED ON (UNDP, 2022)

that finance R&D (24.12%) and the share of high technology in foreign trade (24.99%) are also quite high. GERG in the structure of GDP is, on average, 2.35%. The share of highly qualified personnel averages 5.8%.

To determine the relationship of the impact of gender, financial, and geographic inclusiveness on the development of the knowledge economy, the authors apply the method of regression analysis to determine the dependence of the resulting variables from Table 9.3 on the factor variables from Table 9.2. The resulting regression statistics are collected in Table 9.5.

In Table 9.5, using the method of scientific experiment, the authors selected those regression models that exclude a negative relationship of indicators. The share of GERD in GDP was dependent only on gender inclusiveness; high-skilled employment was dependent only on geographic inclusiveness; firms with a new product/service were dependent only on gender and geographic inclusiveness. The other areas of sustainable and innovative development of the knowledge economy – companies that spend on R&D and high-tech

TABLE 9.4 Statistics on the knowledge economy and the inclusiveness of higher education in the top-10 countries by its development in 2021

Country	Enrolment in bachelor's or equivalent level, %	Enrolment in master's, doctoral, or equivalent, %	GERD, % GDP	Firms that spend on R&D, %	High-skilled employment, %	Firms with new product/service, %	High-technology trade, % total trade
	x_4	x_5	y_{1top}	y_{2top}	y_{3top}	y_{4top}	y_{5top}
Lithuania	43.9	62.1	18.9	2.8	n/d	55.9	52.8
Japan	34.1	22.1	66.2	n/d	67.2	n/d	70.0
Ireland	44.7	48.5	23.0	31.8	n/d	59.0	78.9
France	21.4	100.0	44.3	n/d	n/d	n/d	66.4
Russian Federation	32.4	45.6	19.7	16.8	92.4	48.3	47.9
Singapore	22.3	11.8	38.8	n/d	n/d	n/d	91.0
Switzerland	33.6	61.6	68.1	n/d	n/d	n/d	54.7
Norway	43.0	85.5	41.8	n/d	n/d	n/d	51.9
Sweden	33.4	87.4	67.0	31.2	n/d	62.8	61.3
Brunei Darussalam	13.6	12.5	5.4	n/d	70.9	n/d	29.3

SOURCE: SYSTEMATIZED AND COMPILED BY THE AUTHORS BASED ON (UNDP, 2022)

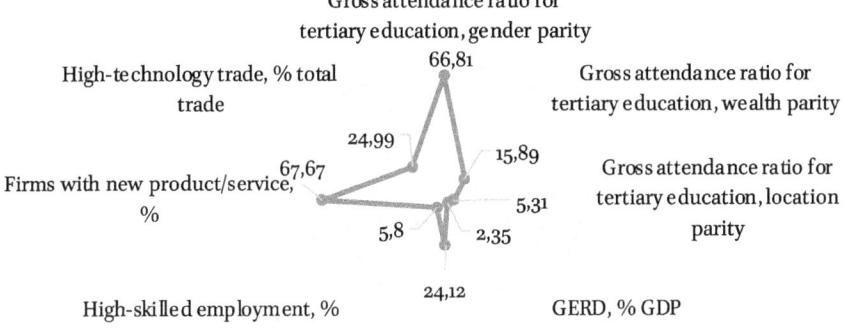

CHART 9.1   The average level of development of the knowledge economy of inclusiveness of higher education in the countries with moderate levels of its development in 2021
SOURCE: CALCULATED AND COMPILED BY THE AUTHORS

trade – depend on all three considered manifestations of the inclusiveness of higher education.

Thus, the most significant factor for the sustainable and inclusive development of the knowledge economy in countries with moderate development of higher education has proved to be geographical inclusiveness. The sum of its regression coefficients (b in Table 9.5) was the highest and equaled 1.89. The financial inclusiveness of higher education is in the second place of importance (0.80) in these countries. However, the area of its influence on the knowledge economy is relatively narrow (limited to firms that spend on R&D and high-technology trade). Gender inclusiveness of higher education is in the third place of importance in the countries of this category (0.47). However, this factor is universal enough and positively influences almost all directions of sustainable and innovative development of the knowledge economy.

4.2   The Importance of Inclusiveness of Higher Education for the Sustainable and Innovative Development of the Knowledge Economy with a High Level of Development of Higher Education

As part of the second task of this study, the authors determined the arithmetic mean of the data from Table 9.4 to identify manifestations of inclusiveness of higher education, which are most significant for the sustainable and innovative development of the knowledge economy at a high level of development of higher education. The results are presented in Chart 9.2.

According to Chart 9.2, in countries with high levels of the development of higher education, the availability of undergraduate education is moderate,

TABLE 9.5 Regression statistics on the dependence of the knowledge economy on the inclusiveness of higher education in countries with the moderate development of the knowledge economy

Regression statistics	Regression model					Significance
	y_{1low}	y_{2low}	y_{3low}	y_{4low}	y_{5low}	
Correlation, %	26.56	85.69	13.24	12.15	21.46	-
a_{low}	-0.80	0.81	4.77	55.91	10.38	-
b_{low1}	0.05	0.10	-	0.15	0.17	0.47
b_{low1}	-	0.75	-	-	0.05	0.80
b_{low1}	-	0.93	0.19	0.28	0.48	1.89

SOURCE: CALCULATED AND COMPILED BY THE AUTHORS

averaging 32.24%. The availability of master's and doctoral studies is high, averaging 53.71%. Overall, the inclusiveness of lifelong learning is quite high.

The countries in this category have made the most considerable progress in the development of the knowledge economy in the field of highly qualified personnel, whose share in the labor market is 93.05%. Businesses also actively bring new products to market (82.6%). The share of firms financing R&D (68.26%) and the share of high technology in foreign trade (60.42%) is quite large. GERG in the structure of GDP accounts for an average of 39.32%.

To identify the manifestations of inclusiveness of higher education, which are most significant for the sustainable and innovative development of the knowledge economy at a high level of development of higher education, the authors applied the method of regression analysis to model the dependence of the knowledge economy on the inclusiveness of lifelong learning based on the data from Table 9.4. The resulting regression statistics are collected in Table 9.6.

In Table 9.6, using a scientific experiment, the authors selected those regression models that exclude a negative relationship between the indicators. However, this was not achieved in every case. Firms with new products/services were only dependent on the availability of undergraduate education, while firms that spent on R&D and firms with new products/services were only positively dependent on the availability of graduate and doctoral education. The share of GERD in GDP and high-skilled employment showed a positive correlation with the openness of both levels of higher education.

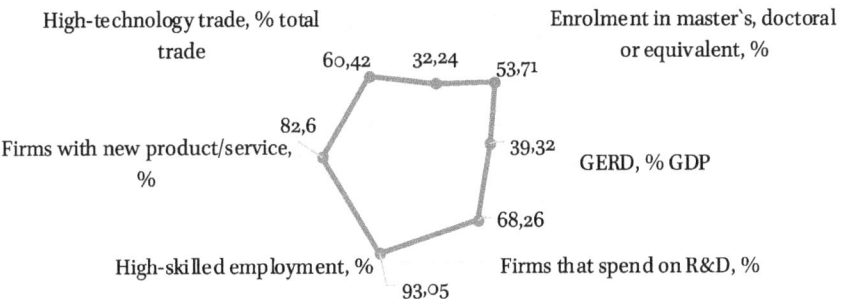

CHART 9.2 The average level of development of the "knowledge economy" of inclusiveness of higher education in the countries with high levels of its development in 2021
SOURCE: CALCULATED AND COMPILED BY THE AUTHORS

Thus, the inclusiveness of lifelong learning has proven to be a major factor in the sustainable and inclusive development of the knowledge economy. The openness of undergraduate education was more significant (0.57), although with a narrower scope of influence on the knowledge economy (limited only to GERD support for GDP, high-skilled employment, and high-technology trade). The availability of graduate and doctoral studies was more universal but slightly less significant (0.49). Simultaneously, all areas of sustainable and innovative development of the knowledge economy were positively influenced by at least one of the considered manifestations of inclusiveness of higher education.

4.3 Prospects and Recommendations for Sustainable and Innovative Development of the Knowledge Economy Based on Increasing Inclusiveness of Higher Education

As part of the third task of this research, to determine the prospects of improving the sustainability and innovativeness of the knowledge economy in the countries with a moderate level of development of higher education, based on the regression models obtained in Table 9.5 through optimization by least squares method, the authors revealed the following optimal ratio of manifestations (parameters) of inclusiveness for the most sustainable and innovative development of the knowledge economy in countries with a moderate level of the development of higher education. The resulting optimum ratio is presented in Chart 9.3.

According to the prospects for optimizing the manifestations of inclusiveness of higher education and their ratio and increase compared to 2021

TABLE 9.6 Regression statistics of the dependence of the knowledge economy on the inclusiveness of higher education in countries with a high level of its development

Regression statistics	Regression model					Significance	
	y_{1top}	y_{2top}	y_{3top}	y_{4top}	y_{5top}		
Correlation, %	0.3306	0.5305	0.6543	0.5054	0.1665	-	
a_{top}	25.45	136.45	72.86	117.71	51.51	-	
b_{top4}	0.05	-2.14	0.25	-1.12	0.28	0.57	
b_{top5}	0.23	0.02	0.23	0.02	-	0.49	

SOURCE: CALCULATED AND COMPILED BY THE AUTHORS

in countries with a moderate level of the development of higher education (Chart 9.3), the following recommendations are offered:
– Increasing gender inclusiveness of higher education by 7.75% from 66.81 points in 2021 to 71.99 points;
– Increasing financial inclusiveness of higher education by 250.09% from 15.89 points in 2021 to 55.63 points;
– Increasing geographic inclusiveness of higher education by 927.87% from 5.31 points in 2021 to 54.58 points.

The benefits of optimizing the manifestations of inclusiveness of higher education for the sustainable and innovative development of the knowledge economy in countries with moderate levels of the development of higher education are shown in Chart 9.4.

According to Chart 9.4, the benefits of optimizing the manifestations of inclusiveness of higher education for the knowledge economy in countries with the moderate development of higher education include the following:
– Increasing the share of companies that spend on R&D by 314.58% from 24.12% in 2021 to 100%;
– Increasing the share of GERD in GDP by 10.40% from 2.35% in 2021 to 2.59%;
– Increasing the share of high-skilled employment by 165.31% from 5.80% in 2021 to 15.39%;
– Increasing the share of new products/services by 21.79% from 67.67% in 2021 to 82.42%;
– Increasing the share of high-tech trade by 106.53% from 24.99% in 2021 to 51.61%.

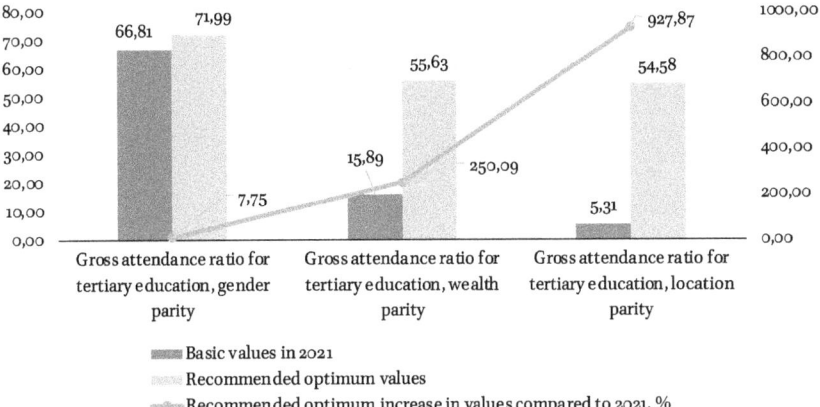

CHART 9.3   Prospects for optimizing the manifestations of inclusiveness of higher education, their ratio and increase compared to 2021 in countries with the moderate development of higher education
SOURCE: CALCULATED AND COMPILED BY THE AUTHORS

Similarly, to determine the prospects of improving the sustainability and innovativeness of the knowledge economy in countries with a high level of development of higher education, based on the regression models obtained in Table 9.6, using optimization by the method of least squares, the following optimal ratio of manifestations (parameters) of inclusiveness for the most sustainable and innovative development of the knowledge economy in countries with a high level of development of higher education was revealed.

On this basis, it is recommended to increase the availability of training in master's and doctoral studies by 86.19%, from 53.71% in 2021 to 100%. The benefits of optimizing the inclusiveness of lifelong learning for the sustainable and innovative development of the knowledge economy in countries with high levels of higher education development are demonstrated in Chart 9.5.

According to Chart 9.5, the benefits of optimizing the manifestations of inclusiveness of higher education for the knowledge economy in countries with high levels of higher education development include the following:
– Increasing the share of GERD in GDP by 27.08% from 39.32% in 2021 to 49.97%;
– Increasing the share of firms that spend on R&D by 1.06% from 68.26% in 2021 to 68.98%;
– Increasing the share of high-skilled employment by 11.31% from 93.05% in 2021 to 103.57%;

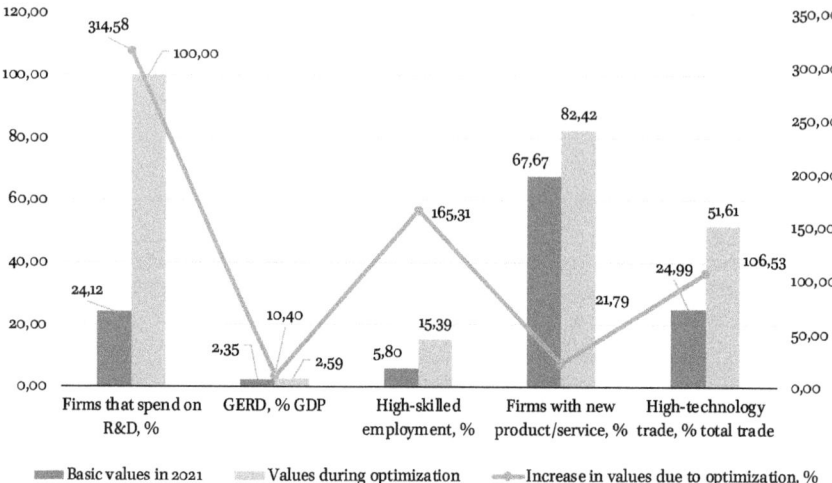

CHART 9.4 Benefits of optimizing the manifestations of inclusiveness of higher education for the knowledge economy in countries with the moderate development of higher education
SOURCE: CALCULATED AND COMPILED BY THE AUTHORS

– Increasing the share of companies with new products/services by 1.17% from 82.60% in 2021 to 83.56%.

The results of optimization revealed the serious potential for sustainable and innovative development of the knowledge economy in countries with different levels of development of higher education, the disclosure of which involves increasing the inclusiveness of higher education in reasonable key manifestations.

5 Discussion

The obtained results develop the provisions of the theory of the knowledge economy and the theory of inclusiveness of higher education. The difference between the new findings and the existing literature within the framework of these theories is indicated in Table 9.7.

As is marked in Table 9.7, in contrast to *Al-Husseini* et al. (2020), *Durazzi* (2019), *Wirba* (2021), *Yeo and Lee* (2020), the made conclusions show that stability and innovativeness of the knowledge economy are promoted not so much by the development (by quality and efficiency criterion) of higher education but by the inclusiveness of higher education. Consequently, it is expedient to estimate the contribution of higher education to the sustainable

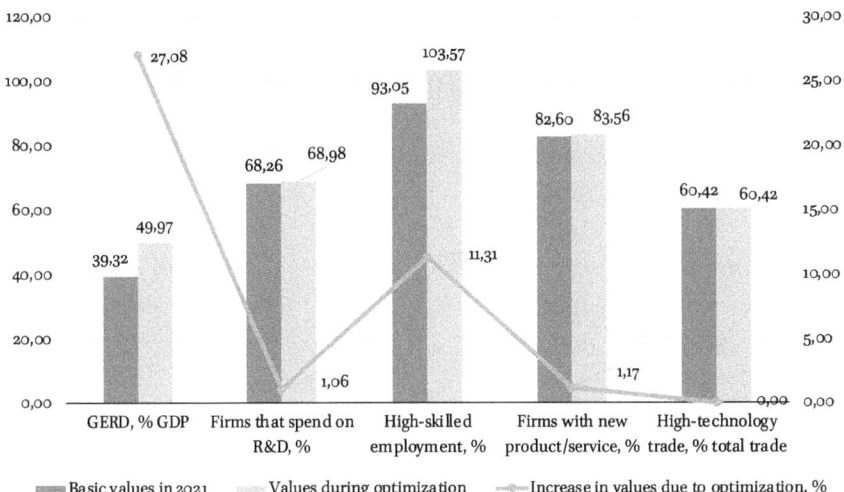

CHART 9.5   The benefits of optimizing the manifestations of inclusiveness of higher education for the knowledge economy in countries with a high level of the development of higher education
SOURCE: CALCULATED AND COMPILED BY THE AUTHORS

and innovative development of the knowledge economy using the criterion of inclusiveness.

In contrast to *Alzyoudi* et al. (2021) and *Zaki and Ismail* (2021), the results show that despite the universality of SDG 4, SDG 8, and SDG 9, the importance of inclusiveness of higher education for the sustainable and innovative development of the knowledge economy is fundamentally different in countries with different levels of the development of higher education.

In contrast to *Anyira and Idubor* (2020), *Baslom and Tong* (2019), *Grebski and Grebski* (2018), *Mohanty and Mishra* (2019), and *Varma* et al. (2021), the author's conclusions showed that the specifics of countries with different levels of development of higher education must be considered when managing its inclusiveness of the interests of sustainability and inclusiveness of the knowledge economy. In countries with moderate levels of the development of higher education, geographic inclusiveness is the most important, less significant, and less universal, but financial and gender inclusiveness are also important. In countries with a high level of the development of higher education, the inclusiveness of lifelong learning is most significant.

The contribution of the research to the literature lies in accurately quantifying and modeling the contribution of manifestations of inclusiveness of higher education to the sustainable and innovative development of the knowledge

TABLE 9.7   Contribution of the research results to the increase in scientific knowledge

Theoretical provision	Existing literature		New findings from this work
	Existing scientific provisions	Literature sources	
Criteria for evaluating the contribution of higher education to the development of the knowledge economy	quality and efficiency of higher education		Inclusiveness of higher education
An approach to increasing the inclusiveness of higher education	in the unity of all its manifestations		Countries with different levels of the development of higher education have the most significant different manifestations of inclusiveness of higher education; optimization also contributes to the realization of SDG 10
The need for more inclusive higher education	Equally high in all countries due to the universality of SDG 4, SDG 8, and SDG 9		

SOURCE: DEVELOPED AND COMPILED BY THE AUTHORS

economy in countries with different levels of higher education development. The resulting models better explain and clarify the cause-effect relations of the development of the knowledge economy based on higher education.

6   Conclusion

According to the research results, the hypothesis (H) is proven, and the research question (RQ) is answered. It is proved that as higher education develops, the most significant manifestations of its inclusiveness for sustainable and innovative development of the knowledge economy change. For the sustainable and innovative development of the knowledge economy in countries with a moderate level of the development of higher education, geographic, financial, and gender inclusiveness are the most significant (the manifestations are listed in decreasing order of importance). For the sustainable and innovative development of the knowledge economy in countries with a high level of the development of higher education, the inclusiveness of lifelong learning is most important.

The contribution of the research to the literature is the development of the theory of the knowledge economy and the theory of inclusiveness of higher education. The proof of the significance of differences between countries with different levels of the development of higher education has opened a new wide field for future (in-depth and case study) studies of the countries of the highlighted categories separately. The theoretical significance of the research is also that it proved the paramount importance of inclusiveness as a key criterion of higher education in assessing its contribution to sustainable and innovative development of the knowledge economy.

The empirical significance of the research results is that the consideration of the characteristics of countries with different levels of development of higher education allows for offering more focused (precise) recommendations for the management of its inclusiveness for sustainable and innovative development of the knowledge economy. This laid the foundation for a more practice-oriented and, therefore, more effective approach to implementing SDG 4, SDG 8, and SDG 9.

The social implications of the research results are that the author's conclusions and recommendations revealed significant prospects and paved the way for overcoming imbalances in the sustainability and balance in the development of the knowledge economy among the countries – overcoming the gap between the countries of the highlighted categories. This can make the balanced development of the knowledge economy in the world economy possible and accessible, which will contribute to the practical implementation of SDG 10 (overcoming the inequalities of countries).

Nevertheless, it should be noted that the lack of official international statistics does not allow us to fully fill all the body of accumulated knowledge gaps at the intersection of the theory of the knowledge economy and the theory of inclusiveness of higher education. In particular, the lack of data on the gender, financial, and geographic inclusiveness of higher education in highly developed countries leaves open the question of what the significance of these manifestations of inclusiveness is in these countries.

The inclusion of people with disabilities and its relevance to the knowledge economy also remains understudied. Filling this gap requires further studies (perhaps case studies) based on alternative data or national statistics. The inclusion of people with disabilities may prove to be a universal manifestation of inclusiveness of higher education, most significant in all countries regardless of the level of development of higher education systems.

In this regard, the obtained results have laid the foundation and made a successful start. However, they determine the need for further and more detailed study of the importance of inclusiveness of higher education for sustainable and innovative development of the knowledge economy. It is proposed to devote future scientific research to this.

References

Al-Husseini SJK, Hussein AU, and Almohamme BNM (2020) The role of the knowledge economy in harmonising the outcomes of higher education with the needs of the labour market. *International Journal of Innovation, Creativity and Change* 13(1): 702–719.

Alzyoudi M, Opoku MP, and Moustafa A (2021) Inclusive higher education in United Arab Emirates: Will perceived knowledge of inclusion impact positively on university students' attitudes towards learning with peers with disabilities? *Frontiers in Education* 6: 793086. DOI: 10.3389/feduc.2021.793086.

Anyira IE, and Idubor I (2020) Role of education and libraries in developing Nigeria's knowledge economy. *Library Philosophy and Practice* 2020: 1–17.

Bartz J (2020) All inclusive?! empirical insights into individual experiences of students with disabilities and mental disorders at German universities and implications for inclusive higher education. *Education Sciences* 10(9): 223. DOI: 10.3390/educsci10090223.

Baslom MMM, and Tong S (2019) Knowledge management (KM) practices in education and learning: Establishing a knowledge economy in Saudi Arabia. *Humanities and Social Sciences Letters* 7(1): 1–9. DOI: 10.18488/journal.73.2019.71.1.9.

Bogoviz A, Averin A, and Yanovskaya V (2018a) Gender analysis of local budgets in law enforcement and educational organizations of Russia. *MATEC Web of Conferences* 212: 09015. DOI: 10.1051/matecconf/201821209015.

Bogoviz A, Lobova S, and Popkova E (2018b) Transformational leadership as a factor in the success of knowledge-intensive companies. *MATEC Web of Conferences* 212: 10001. DOI: 10.1051/matecconf/201821210001.

Brewer R, and Movahedazarhouligh S (2021) Students with intellectual and developmental disabilities in inclusive higher education: Perceptions of stakeholders in a first-year experience. *International Journal of Inclusive Education* 25(9): 993–1009. DOI: 10.1080/13603116.2019.1597184.

Durazzi N (2019) The political economy of high skills: Higher education in knowledge-based labour markets. *Journal of European Public Policy* 26(12): 1799–1817. DOI: 10.1080/13501763.2018.1551415.

Faura-Martínez Ú, and Cifuentes-Faura J (2021) Building a dynamic indicator on inclusive education in higher education. *European Journal of Special Needs Education* DOI: 10.1080/08856257.2021.1929237.

Frunzaru V, Vătămănescu EM, Gazzola P, and Bolisani E (2018) Challenges to higher education in the knowledge economy: Anti-intellectualism, materialism and employability. *Knowledge Management Research and Practice* 16(3): 388–401. DOI: 10.1080/14778238.2018.1493368.

Grebski W, and Grebski M (2018) Keeping higher education aligned with the requirements and expectations of the knowledge-based economy. *Production Engineering Archives* 21(21): 3–7.

Héraud J-A (2021) A new approach of innovation: From the knowledge economy to the theory of creativity applied to territorial development. *Journal of the Knowledge Economy* 12(1): 201–217. DOI: 10.1007/s13132-016-0393-5.

Hernández V, Nieto MJ, and Rodríguez A (2021) Product and process innovations and the institutional context of transition economies: The effects of external knowledge. In: Verbeke A, van Tulder R, Rose EL, and Wei Y (eds) *The multiple dimensions of institutional complexity in international business research*. Bingley, UK: Emerald Publishing Limited, 155–170. DOI: 10.1108/S1745-886220210000015010.

Huber E, Gunderson J, and Stephens JD (2020) Private education and inequality in the knowledge economy. *Policy and Society* 39(2): 171–188. DOI: 10.1080/14494035.2019.1636603.

Kandiko Howson C, and Lall M (2020) Higher education reform in Myanmar: Neoliberalism versus an inclusive developmental agenda. *Globalisation, Societies and Education* 18(2): 109–124. DOI: 10.1080/14767724.2019.1689488.

Kichuk Y, Kunchenko-Kharchenko V, Hrushchynska N, Zhukova Y, and Yarish O (2021) Intellectual capital of institutions of higher education in the knowledge economy. *Journal of Optimization in Industrial Engineering* 14(1): 183–190. DOI: 10.22094/JOIE.2020.677844.

Kim CY, Seo E-H, Booranabanyat C, and Kim K (2021) Effects of emerging-economy firms' knowledge acquisition from an advanced international joint venture partner on their financial performance based on the open innovation perspective. *Journal of Open Innovation: Technology, Market, and Complexity* 7(1): 67. DOI: 10.3390/joitmc7010067.

Kirupainayagam DS, and Sutha J (2021) Technology facilitation on inclusive learning; higher education institutions in Sri Lanka. *International Journal of Educational Management* 36(4): 441–469. DOI: 10.1108/IJEM-02-2020-0048.

Mohanty S, and Mishra PC (2019) Bologna education reforms: Lessons for Indian knowledge economy. *Espacios* 40(44): 21. Available (consulted 27 February 2022) at: https://www.revistaespacios.com/a19v40n44/a19v40n44p21.pdf.

Ngo Q-T, Tran HA, and Tran HTT (2021) The impact of green finance and COVID-19 on economic development: Capital formation and educational expenditure of ASEAN economies. *China Finance Review International* 12(2): 261–279. DOI: 10.1108/CFRI-05-2021-0087.

Parra-Martínez J, Gutiérrez-Mozo M-E, and Gilsanz-Díaz A (2021) Inclusive higher education and the built environment. A research and teaching agenda for gender mainstreaming in architecture studies. *Sustainability* 13(5): 2565. DOI: 10.3390/su13052565.

Popkova EG (2020) A new treatment of quality of goods and services in the conditions of the knowledge economy: Opposition of traditions and innovations. *International Journal for Quality Research* 14(2): 329–346. DOI: 10.24874/IJQR14.02-01.

Rodríguez A, Hernández V, and Nieto MJ (2022) International and domestic external knowledge in the innovation performance of firms from transition economies: The role of institutions. *Technological Forecasting and Social Change* 176: 121442. DOI: 10.1016/j.techfore.2021.121442.

Rottleb T, and Kleibert JM (2022) Circulation and containment in the knowledge-based economy: Transnational education zones in Dubai and Qatar. *Environment and Planning A: Economy and Space.* DOI: 10.1177/0308518X221077105.

Sheppard-Jones K, Moseley E, Kleinert H, Collett J, and Rumrill P (2021) The Inclusive higher education imperative: Promoting long-term postsecondary success for students with intellectual disabilities in the COVID-19 era. *Journal of Rehabilitation* 87(1): 48–54. Available (consulted 27 February 2022) at: https://worksupport.com/research/documents/pdf/InclusiveHigherEducationImperative.pdf .

Sibirskaya E, Popkova E, Oveshnikova L, and Tarasova I (2019) Remote education vs traditional education based on effectiveness at the micro level and its connection to the level of development of macro-economic systems. *International Journal of Educational Management* 33(3): 533–543. DOI: 10.1108/IJEM-08-2018-0248.

UN (2022) *Sustainable Development Report 2021.* Available (consulted 27 February 2022) at: https://dashboards.sdgindex.org/.

UNDP (2022) *Global Knowledge Index 2021.* Available (consulted 27 February 2022) at: https://www.undp.org/publications/global-knowledge-index-2021.

Varma A, Patel P, Prikshat V, Hota D, and Pereira V (2021) India's new education policy: A case of indigenous ingenuity contributing to the global knowledge economy? *Journal of Knowledge Management* 25(10): 2385–2395. DOI: 10.1108/JKM-11-2020-0840.

Wirba AV (2021) Transforming Cameroon into Knowledge-Based Economy (KBE): The role of education, especially higher education. *Journal of the Knowledge Economy* 13: 1542–1572. DOI: 10.1007/s13132-021-00776-z.

Yeo Y, and Lee J-D (2020) Revitalizing the race between technology and education: Investigating the growth strategy for the knowledge-based economy based on a CGE analysis. *Technology in Society* 62: 101295. DOI: 10.1016/j.techsoc.2020.101295.

Zaki NHM, and Ismail Z (2021) Towards inclusive education for special need students in higher education from the perspective of faculty members: A systematic literature review. *Asian Journal of University Education* 17(4): 201–211. DOI: 10.24191/ajue.v17i4.16189.

Zhang F, Lyu C, and Zhu L (2022) Organizational unlearning, knowledge generation strategies and radical innovation performance: Evidence from a transitional economy. *European Journal of Marketing* 56(1): 133–158. DOI: 10.1108/EJM-10-2019-0756.

CHAPTER 10

The Concept of Inclusive Higher Education and Approach to Its Implementation Based on Openness to Persons with Disabilities

Svetlana A. Popova, Elena Kzh. Pilivanova, Evgeny A. Likholetov and Galina N. Zvereva

Abstract

The paper aims to develop an approach to implementing the concept of inclusiveness in higher education based on openness to persons with disabilities through the justification of key factors and the prospects of increasing inclusiveness based on their optimization. For this purpose, using the method of regression analysis, the authors carry out a factor analysis of the inclusiveness of higher education and select key factors contributing to the openness of universities towards persons with disabilities. The authors develop an approach to the implementation of the concept of inclusive higher education based on openness towards persons with disabilities and justify the prospects of its implementation through the optimized management of selected key factors of inclusiveness. The research novelty lies in the fact that it clarifies the essence of the influence of the main factors on the inclusiveness of higher education and provides a transition from a qualitative to a quantitative study of these factors. The author's conclusions and recommendations allow for improving the effectiveness of managing the inclusiveness of higher education through targeted management of its openness to persons with disabilities, precisely focused on the selected key factors. The uniqueness and novelty of the author's approach to the implementation of the concept of inclusive higher education lie in the isolated consideration of the influence of the main (generally accepted) factors on the openness of higher education to persons with disabilities.

Keywords

inclusive higher education – university openness – people with disabilities

1   Introduction

An environment conducive to life and human flourishing is the basic idea of an inclusive society that gave rise to the concept. Persons with disabilities are particularly vulnerable and sensitive to the slightest manifestation of inequality. Therefore, it is especially important to maintain an open social environment for them and provide them with social support. Moreover, many people with disabilities are naturally gifted with unique talents, the development and practical application of which is beneficial to them and the economy.

Cruz-Morato et al. (2021) and *Schloemer-Jarvis* et al. (2022) write about the outstanding innovative potential of people with disabilities. An unconventional view of the world makes people with disabilities indispensable personnel in the relevant professions, as well as in the development and implementation of strategies and programs of corporate social responsibility and social protection of the population. This points to the need to ensure the accessibility of higher education for persons with disabilities.

Nevertheless, there are objective reasons for the reduced accessibility of higher education for persons with disabilities. First, many of them are less mobile than other university students. Even if the university building is appropriately equipped (e.g., with ramps), the urban infrastructure necessary for the daily transportation of people with disabilities to the university should be unavailable (*Pov*, 2021). If individuals with disabilities require special care (involving social workers and special accommodations), they are homebound and can only study at a university remotely (*Green and Bingham*, 2017; *Jenkin* et al., 2019).

Second, the standard educational program does not apply to many people with disabilities. Some may have difficulty socializing for their own (internal) reasons, even though other students are open to communication (*Chambers and Forlin*, 2021). Others may show reduced performance in the student population, fail to meet accepted timelines, or experience difficulty in mastering certain educational programs (*Correia* et al., 2021). Therefore, in many cases, individuals with disabilities require an individualized approach to higher education (*Forlin and Chambers*, 2020).

Thus, an urgent scientific and practical problem is the determination of factors and conditions favorable to the involvement of persons with disabilities in the process of obtaining higher education. The existing literature devotes a great deal of attention to this problem, which *Aldehami* (2022) and *Meeks* et al. (2022) propose to address by increasing the inclusiveness of higher education.

The basic principles and other fundamentals of this concept are laid out in the available works by *Han* et al. (2022) and *Papadakaki* et al. (2022) and are commonly known. However, the empirical experience and prospects for the practical achievement of openness in higher education for persons with disabilities remain poorly understood and constitute a research gap.

In this regard, this paper poses a research question (RQ): How (by what approach) can the concept of inclusive higher education be realized based on openness to persons with disabilities? To answer the RQ, this paper hypothesizes that commonly known factors that increase the inclusiveness of higher education have varying and even contradictory effects on the accessibility of university education for people with disabilities.

This research aims to develop an approach to implementing the concept of inclusiveness in higher education based on openness to persons with disabilities through the justification of key factors and the prospects for increasing inclusiveness based on their optimization. The set research goal is achieved through the sequential solution of the following tasks:

- To conduct a factor analysis of the inclusiveness of higher education and select key factors that contribute to the openness of universities to persons with disabilities;
- To develop an approach to the implementation of the concept of inclusive higher education based on openness to persons with disabilities and justify the prospects of its implementation through the optimization of management of the selected key factors of inclusiveness.

The research novelty lies in the fact that it clarifies the essence of the influence of the main factors on the inclusiveness of higher education and provides a transition from a qualitative to a quantitative study of these factors. The author's conclusions and recommendations allow for improving the effectiveness of managing the inclusiveness of higher education through targeted management of its openness to persons with disabilities, precisely focused on the selected key factors.

The uniqueness and novelty of the author's approach to the implementation of the concept of inclusive higher education lie in the isolated consideration of the influence of the main (generally accepted) factors on the openness of higher education for persons with disabilities. The transition from a broad (generalized) interpretation of inclusiveness in the unity of its manifestations (e.g., gender neutrality, cultural openness, combating ageism, elimination of geographical and financial barriers to education in universities, etc.) to a narrow interpretation of inclusiveness (with a focus on the opening of universities to persons with disabilities) allows us to draw more accurate conclusions and offer more effective recommendations in this area of management of inclusiveness in higher education.

2   Literature Review

This research is based on the concept of inclusive higher education, which interprets inclusiveness as the openness of universities to all people, regardless of their difference. This concept embodies and supports the practical implementation of SDG 10, "Reducing Inequality," as articulated and encouraged by the UN. The works by *Bartz* (2020), *Lopez-Gavira* et al. (2021), *Yadav* et al. (2020), and others present the approach to implementing this concept based on increasing the overall openness of universities to ensure equality of higher education opportunities for all people.

The literature identifies four main (generally recognized) factors of inclusiveness in higher education. The first facto is the inclusiveness of society. This factor is social in nature and characterizes the general commitment of most people to tolerance towards each other and openness to communication and joint economic activity, regardless of the characteristics of those around them. Society's inclusiveness is determined by culture, historical heritage, and society's receptivity to change (propensity to innovate) because inclusiveness is a relatively new trend for ancient cultures.

The inclusiveness of society is considered fundamental because it determines the influence of other factors. The inclusiveness of society helps people with disabilities to socialize, join the student body, and feel a part of it. A comfortable social environment helps individuals with disabilities discover their talents and supports their learning, competency acquisition, and talent development (*Gebhardt* et al., 2022; *Wang*, 2021).

The second factor is digitalization. This factor is of a technological nature. It characterizes the new technical possibilities of social communications and economic activity. The technological factor has traditionally influenced the inclusiveness of society, but digital technology took shape as a new factor under the influence of the Fourth Industrial Revolution (*Cheng*, 2021; *Popkova* et al., 2021; *Sibirskaya* et al., 2019; *Wending*, 2022).

Digital technologies in higher education increase the flexibility of the educational process, increasing the possibilities of distance and individual learning. This allows universities to diversify their educational offerings and tailor the most appropriate educational approaches for people with disabilities on a case-by-case basis. Under the influence of this factor, the inclusiveness of universities toward people with disabilities becomes massively accessible.

The third factor is the progressiveness of universities. This factor relates to corporate governance and characterizes the contribution of universities to the inclusiveness of their internal social environment and the openness of the educational process for people with disabilities. It is assumed that the more competitive the national higher education system, the greater the willingness of universities to change – to become more open to people with disabilities. International university rankings (e.g., QS and THE) pay increasing attention to issues of inclusiveness, including relevant criteria in the system of evaluating the competitiveness of universities. However, the emphasis is so far placed on the internationalization (cultural inclusiveness) of higher education. This factor reflects the willingness and determination of the universities to open their doors to people with disabilities (*Happ and Bolla*, 2022; *Muyor-Rodríguez et al.*, 2021; *Strnadová et al.*, 2015).

The fourth factor is the effectiveness of institutions. This factor belongs to the field of public administration and characterizes the effectiveness of state regulation of higher education. It should be noted that the considered factor is determined by the factors described above because institutions embody and reinforce practices that already exist in society. The effectiveness of institutions includes state norms and standards of higher education services for persons with disabilities, as well as the availability of special quotas (in the state order to universities) for persons with disabilities (*Ashman*, 2010; *Lee and Taylor*, 2022).

The described factors simultaneously and comprehensively influence the inclusiveness of higher education. According to the provisions of the established approach, the totality of these factors determines the openness of universities to persons with disabilities. The undoubted advantage of the current approach lies in the most comprehensive coverage of all forms and manifestations of inequality and their eradication in the higher education system. Simultaneously, the limitations of this approach lie in its generalization and lack of attention to each area of university inclusiveness individually.

A gap in the literature is the scarcity of empirical research in certain areas of university inclusiveness management and, in particular, the uncertainty of the impact of commonly known factors of inclusiveness on the accessibility of higher education for persons with disabilities. The identified gap is filled in this research through an in-depth empirical study of the influence of generally accepted factors on the openness of universities for persons with disabilities, allowing us to consider the features of this direction of managing the inclusiveness of higher education.

3   Materials and Methods

The logic of the hypothesis (H) is that, despite the priority of achieving absolute inclusiveness (in the unity of all its manifestations), there tends to be an imbalance in the implementation of various directions of inclusiveness. For example, if a university has achieved a high degree of gender neutrality, it does not mean that its doors are wide open to people with disabilities. This disproportion in the implementation of the directions of inclusiveness unfortunately persists. However, there are good reasons to expect that, with the support of the UN, absolute inclusiveness in higher education will be achieved in the coming years (perhaps by 2030).

The verification of the hypothesis (H) and the answer to the research question (RQ) is based on the following research strategy (Table 10.1).

According to the strategy of this research shown in Table 10.1, its first task is to conduct a factor analysis of the inclusiveness of higher education and select key factors that contribute to the openness of universities to people with disabilities. This task is achieved by using the method of regression analysis. The essence of this task is to model the dependence of tertiary educational attainment by persons with disabilities (y) on inclusiveness factors (x_1–x_4). The research model is as follows:

$$y = a + b_1 * x_1 + b_2 * x_2 + b_3 * x_3 + b_4 * x_4 \tag{1}$$

where:

x_1 – Government effectiveness, reflecting the effectiveness of institutions, based on statistics from the *World Bank* (2022);

x_2 – (Level of development of the) tertiary education, reflecting the progressivity factor of universities, based on statistics from the *World Bank* (2022);

x_3 – Social inclusiveness, reflecting the inclusiveness of society, based on statistics from the *Global Green Growth Institute* (2022);

x_4 – Digital competitiveness, reflecting the digitalization factor based on statistics from *IMD* (2022);

y – Tertiary educational attainment by persons with disabilities, reflecting the target result (inclusiveness of higher education) based on statistics from *Eurostat* (2022).

The positive influence of factors (x_1–x_4) on the target result (y) in the model (1) is indicated by positive values of regression coefficients b_1-b_4. The reliability of the results of econometric modeling is evaluated by the significance of F – only reliable regression models are selected.

Since full-scale international statistics on the inclusiveness of higher education for persons with disabilities, covering most countries from different regions of the world, has not yet been formed, this study selected statistics of the EU countries, calculated by *Eurostat* (2022), as an empirical basis. For the

TABLE 10.1 Research strategy

Research objective	Research method	Indicators for the study (common to both research objectives)			Essence and logic of the research
			ECONOMETRIC MEANING OF THE VARIABLE	INCLUSIVENESS INDICATOR	
To conduct a factor analysis and select key factors that contribute to the openness of universities to people with disabilities	Method of regression analysis	Factors	Effectiveness of institutions Progressiveness of universities Inclusiveness of society Digitalization	Government effectiveness (x_1) (Level of development of the) tertiary education (x_2) Social inclusiveness (x_3) Digital competitiveness (x_4)	Modeling the dependence of tertiary educational attainment by persons with disabilities (y) on inclusiveness factors (x_1–x_4)
To develop an approach to the implementation of the concept of inclusive higher education based on openness to persons with disabilities and justify the prospects for its implementation	Optimization by the least-squares method	Target result		Tertiary educational attainment by persons with disabilities (y)	Determining the optimal balance of factors for the greatest openness of universities to people with disabilities, as well as the benefits of optimization

SOURCE: DEVELOPED BY THE AUTHORS

research, the authors form a sample of 17 EU countries for which a complete set of data is available (there are no gaps in statistical records).

The statistics on tertiary educational attainment by persons with disabilities by disability status, reflecting the target outcome, are collected in Table 10.2. As noted in *Eurostat* (2022) materials, these statistics were originally collected in 2011 and then updated – the last update was in 2019–2020. Given that major changes in inclusiveness are only achievable in the medium (or even long-term) time horizon, the available data can be considered relevant for 2021.

The factors for the inclusiveness of higher education in 2021 are compiled in Table 10.3.

The advantage of the selected factor variables is that they all have the same units of measurement. This allows the authors to reliably compare them with each other and accurately measure the differences in their impact on the inclusiveness of higher education for persons with disabilities.

The second objective of this research is to develop an approach to the implementation of the concept of inclusive higher education based on openness to persons with disabilities and justify the prospects of its implementation through the optimization of management of selected key factors of inclusiveness. To solve this problem, the authors carried out optimization by the method of least squares. The essence of this problem is to determine the optimal ratio of factors for the greatest openness of universities for persons with disabilities, as well as the benefits of optimization.

4 Results

4.1 Factor Analysis of the Inclusiveness of Higher Education from the Perspective of the Openness of Universities to Persons with Disabilities

In the first task of this research, the authors carried out a factor analysis of the inclusiveness of higher education using regression analysis to select key factors that contribute to the openness of universities to people with disabilities, relying on the statistics from Table 10.2 and Table 10.3. The results of modeling the dependence of tertiary educational attainment by persons with disabilities (y) on inclusiveness factors (x_1–x_4) are shown in Tables 10.4–10.7.

In Table 10.4, the significance of F (0.11338) is too high for the regression model to be considered reliable. This indicates that the openness of higher education to persons with disabilities having difficulty in basic activities does not consistently depend on factors of inclusiveness.

TABLE 10.2 Tertiary educational attainment (age group 30–34), by disability status, by country, in %

Country	Having difficulty in basic activities	Having no difficulty in basic activities	Having a work limitation caused by a LHPAD	Having no work limitation caused by a LHPAD
	y_1	y_2	y_3	y_4
Belgium	19.5	47.0	17.8	47.0
Czech Republic	10.7	24.2	11.3	24.4
Denmark	19.1	43.3	21.7	43.3
Ireland	27.5	50.6	20.3	51.3
Estonia	34.8	43.0	35.3	43.1
France	32.6	48.1	33.6	47.6
Italy	8.8	20.2	11.2	20.0
Luxembourg	37.3	49.8	32.1	49.2
Netherlands	23.3	43.1	22.1	43.2
Austria	25.5	24.6	17.5	25.2
Poland	17.0	37.6	13.2	37.6
Portugal	22.3	24.7	18.0	25.2
Slovenia	20.6	38.4	25.2	38.5
Finland	36.7	49.6	33.0	49.8
Sweden	29.7	51.4	34.0	51.2
UK	30.4	47.1	25.4	47.2
Switzerland	22.3	44.9	32.5	44.2

SOURCE: COMPILED BY THE AUTHORS BASED ON (EUROSTAT, 2022)

With the support of the research model (1) and based on the results from Table 10.5, the authors can make the following regression model:

$$y_2 = 144.05 + 0.54^* x_1 - 0.93^* x_2 - 1.57^* x_3 + 0.44^* x_4 \qquad (2)$$

The resulting model (2) shows that only factors x_1 and x_4 have a positive effect on the target result. For example, a one-point increase in government

TABLE 10.3 Factors of inclusiveness in higher education in 2021, score 0–100

Country	Government effectiveness	(Level of development of the) Tertiary education	Social inclusiveness	Digital competitiveness
	x_1	x_2	x_3	x_4
Belgium	73.6	36.6	90.48	75.255
Czech Republic	70.3	44.5	87.35	65.224
Denmark	93.7	43.3	92.33	95.158
Ireland	79.1	43.7	85.01	79.156
Estonia	76.8	45.9	88.66	75.421
France	81.4	42.0	89.31	75.656
Italy	60.9	37.9	87.30	61.767
Luxembourg	89.2	35.8	90.27	77.358
Netherlands	90.6	40.1	92.51	93.309
Austria	83.8	58.8	89.31	80.877
Poland	64.0	35.1	89.29	60.943
Portugal	76.3	43.8	89.87	65.178
Slovenia	74.7	44.3	88.53	64.965
Finland	93.5	51.1	91.21	90.134
Sweden	91.3	43.9	94.06	95.189
UK	82.6	47.1	90.07	85.827
Switzerland	94.0	45.1	90.93	94.939

SOURCE: COMPILED BY THE AUTHORS BASED ON (GLOBAL GREEN GROWTH INSTITUTE, 2022; IMD, 2022; WORLD BANK, 2022)

effectiveness provides a 0.54% increase in tertiary educational attainment for individuals with disabilities who have no difficulty in basic activities. A one-point increase in digital competitiveness achieved a 0.44% increase in tertiary educational attainment for people with disabilities who had no difficulty in basic activities.

The obtained value of the multiple R indicates a high correlation of variables: the change in tertiary educational attainment by persons with disabilities having no difficulty in basic activities by 76.35% is explained by the influence

TABLE 10.4 Regression statistics on the dependence of the openness of higher education for people with a disability experiencing difficulties in basic activities on inclusiveness factors

Regression statistics

Multiple R	0.6625
R-square	0.4389
Normalized R-square	0.25187
Standard error	7.26809
Observations	17

Variance analysis

	df	SS	MS	F	Significance of F		
Regression	4	495.847	123.962	2.34664	0.11338		
Balance	12	633.902	52.8252				
Total	16	1129.75					
	Coefficients b	Standard error	t-statistics	P-value	Lower 95%	Upper 95%	
Constant (a)	36.5222	102.632	0.35586	0.72813	-187.09	260.139	
x_1	0.98572	0.45654	2.15912	0.05179	-0.009	1.98043	
x_2	0.02197	0.35849	0.06128	0.95215	-0.7591	0.80306	
x_3	-0.7054	1.23595	-0.5708	0.5787	-3.3983	1.98748	
x_4	-0.3729	0.38178	-0.9768	0.34796	-1.2047	0.45891	

SOURCE: CALCULATED AND COMPILED BY THE AUTHORS

of inclusiveness factors in higher education. The reliability of the model (2) is evidenced by the obtained significance of F (0.02368) – the model is reliable at a significance level of 0.05.

With the support of the research model (1) and based on the results from Table 10.6, the authors can make the following regression model:

$$y_2 = -7.36 + 0.85^* x_1 - 0.13^* x_2 - 0.15^* x_3 - 0.23^* x_4 \qquad (3)$$

The resulting model (3) shows that only factor x_1 positively affects the target result. Thus, a one-point increase in government effectiveness achieves a 0.85% increase in tertiary educational attainment for individuals with a work disability caused by a LHPAD.

TABLE 10.5 Regression statistics on the dependence of the openness of higher education for persons with disabilities experiencing no difficulty in basic activities on inclusiveness factors

Regression statistics

Multiple R	0.76347
R-square	0.58289
Normalized R-square	0.44386
Standard error	7.8368
Observations	17

Variance analysis

	df	SS	MS	F	Significance of F
Regression	4	1029.92	257.479	4.19241	0.02368
Balance	12	736.986	61.4155		
Total	16	1766.9			

	Coefficients b	Standard error	t-statistics	P-value	Lower 95%	Upper 95%
Constant (a)	144.047	110.663	1.30167	0.21746	-97.067	385.161
x_1	0.53665	0.49226	1.09018	0.29704	-0.5359	1.60919
x_2	-0.9309	0.38654	-2.4084	0.03301	-1.7731	-0.0887
x_3	-1.5709	1.33266	-1.1788	0.26132	-4.4746	1.33268
x_4	0.43886	0.41165	1.0661	0.30736	-0.458	1.33576

SOURCE: CALCULATED AND COMPILED BY THE AUTHORS

The resulting multiple R value indicates a high correlation of the variables: the 69.46% change in tertiary educational attainment by individuals with a work limitation caused by a LHPAD is explained by the influence of inclusiveness factors in higher education. The reliability of the model (3) is evidenced by the obtained significance of F (0.07487) – the model is reliable at a significance level of 0.1.

With the support of the research model (1) and based on the results from Table 10.7, the authors can make the following regression model:

$$y_2 = 146.26 + 0.52^* x_1 - 0.89^* x_2 - 1.60^* x_3 + 0.44^* x_4 \qquad (4)$$

TABLE 10.6 Regression statistics on the dependence of the openness of higher education for people with a work disability caused by a LHPAD on inclusiveness factors

Regression statistics

Multiple R	0.69457
R-square	0.48242
Normalized R-square	0.3099
Standard error	6.95751
Observations	17

Variance analysis

	df	SS	MS	F	Significance of F	
Regression	4	541.427	135.357	2.79622	0.07487	
Balance	12	580.884	48.407			
Total	16	1122.31				

	Coefficients b	Standard error	t-statistics	P-value	Lower 95%	Upper 95%
Constant (a)	-7.3624	98.2466	-0.0749	0.9415	-221.42	206.699
x_1	0.84648	0.43703	1.9369	0.07666	-0.1057	1.79868
x_2	-0.128	0.34317	-0.3731	0.71556	-0.8758	0.61967
x_3	-0.1513	1.18314	-0.1279	0.90038	-2.7291	2.42656
x_4	-0.2317	0.36546	-0.6341	0.53792	-1.028	0.56454

SOURCE: CALCULATED AND COMPILED BY THE AUTHORS

The resulting model (4) shows that only factors x_1 and x_4 have a positive effect on the target result. For example, a one-point increase in government effectiveness results in a 0.52% increase in tertiary educational attainment for individuals with no work limitations caused by a LHPAD. A one-point increase in digital competitiveness achieved a 0.44% increase in tertiary educational attainment for persons with no work limitations caused by a LHPAD.

The resulting multiple R value indicates a high correlation of variables: the change in tertiary educational attainment by persons with disabilities having no work limitations caused by a LHPAD by 75.69% is explained by the influence of factors of inclusiveness in higher education. The reliability of the model (4) is evidenced by the obtained significance of F (0.02715) – the model is reliable at a significance level of 0.05.

Thus, the results revealed that the factors of inclusiveness determine (1) openness of higher education to persons with disabilities having no difficulty in basic activities; (2) openness of higher education to persons with disabilities having a work limitation caused by a LHPAD; and (3) openness of higher education to persons with disabilities, having no work limitation caused by a LHPAD. The key factors of inclusiveness are the effectiveness of institutions (a universal factor) and digitalization (only positively affects the openness of higher education for persons with disabilities, having no difficulty in basic activities, and having no work limitation caused by a LHPAD).

4.2 Approach to the Implementation of the Concept of Inclusive Higher Education Based on Openness to Persons with Disabilities

As part of the second task of this research, the results of econometric modeling (models (2), (3), and (4)) were used to develop an approach to the implementation of the concept of inclusive higher education based on openness to persons with disabilities. The resulting approach is illustrated in Figure 10.1.

As shown in Figure 10.1, managing inclusiveness in higher education for people with disabilities involves a set of measures. The proposed approach is implemented at the micro-level (at the level of universities). In this approach, the management subject is the university administration with the support of the relevant state regulators. The first measure is to increase emphasis on inclusiveness in regulating higher education. This measure seeks to improve the effectiveness of institutions through norms, standards, and quotas for persons with disabilities.

The second measure is to support the digitalization of universities. This measure is designed to stimulate the digitalization of society in general and higher education in particular through the development of distance and individualized learning for people with disabilities. It is also necessary to develop a third measure (special management measures) designed to increase the openness of higher education for persons with disabilities who have difficulty in basic activities through targeted support for inclusiveness, considering the characteristics of this category of persons with disabilities.

To justify the prospects of its implementation through the optimization of the management of selected key factors of inclusiveness with the support of models (2), (3), and (4), the authors performed the optimization by least squares. Given the contradictory influence of the digitalization factor, two optimal ratios of factors for the greatest openness of universities for persons with disabilities were identified – two optimization scenarios.

TABLE 10.7 Regression statistics on the dependence of the openness of higher education to persons with no work limitations caused by a LHPAD on inclusiveness factors

Regression statistics

Multiple R	0.75648
R-square	0.57226
Normalized R-square	0.42968
Standard error	7.84478
Observations	17

Variance analysis

	df	SS	MS	F	Significance of F		
Regression	4	987.989	246.997	4.01357	0.02715		
Balance	12	738.486	61.5405				
Total	16	1726.48					
	Coefficients b	Standard error	t-statistics	P-value	Lower 95%	Upper 95%
Constant (a)	146.264	110.776	1.32037	0.21134	-95.095	387.624
x_1	0.51904	0.49276	1.05333	0.31294	-0.5546	1.59267
x_2	-0.892	0.38694	-2.3054	0.03981	-1.7351	-0.049
x_3	-1.6033	1.33402	-1.2018	0.25261	-4.5098	1.30331
x_4	0.44449	0.41207	1.07868	0.30194	-0.4533	1.3423

SOURCE: CALCULATED AND COMPILED BY THE AUTHORS

The first scenario assumes reliance on a universal factor – maximizing the efficiency of institutions. The second scenario is associated with a more even optimization and assumes managing the contradictory factor – digitalization. The benchmark values of inclusiveness factors in both scenarios compared with the baseline values of these indicators are shown in Chart 10.1.

As shown in Chart 10.1, the optimization according to the first scenario assumes an increase of 23.56%: from 80.93 points in 2021 to 100 points. The optimization according to the second scenario additionally assumes an increase by 27.21%, from 78.61 points in 2021 to 100 points. The benefits of

THE CONCEPT OF INCLUSIVE HIGHER EDUCATION AND APPROACH 159

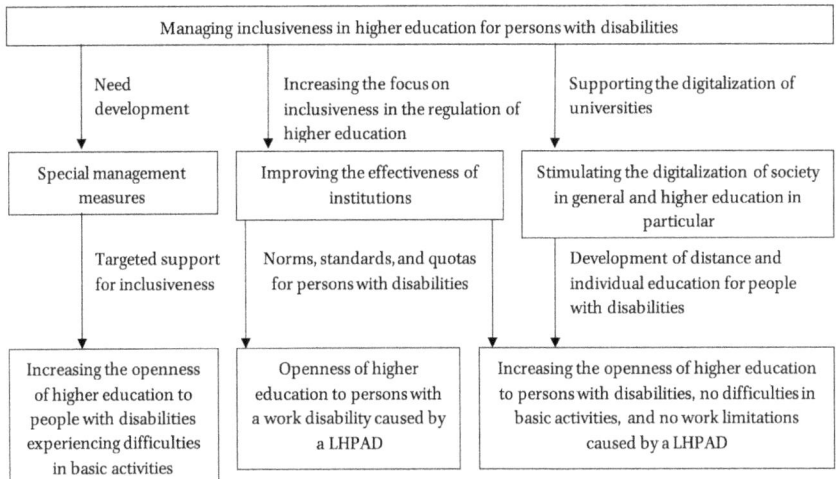

FIGURE 10.1 An approach to implementing the concept of inclusive higher education based on openness to persons with disabilities

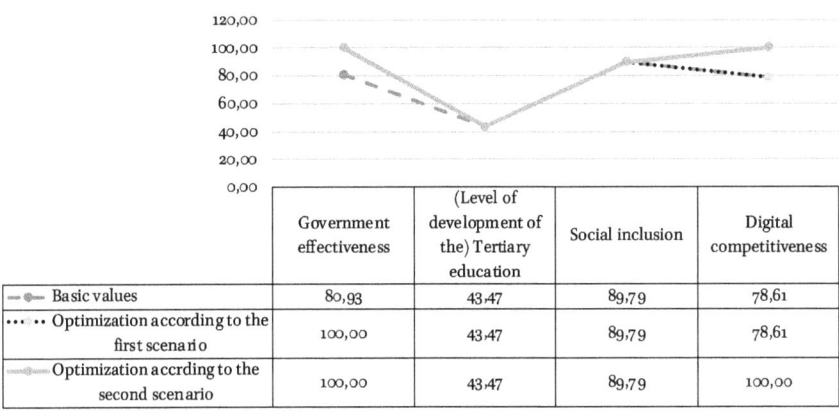

CHART 10.1 Benchmark values of the inclusiveness factors in both scenarios compared to the baseline values of these indicators
SOURCE: CALCULATED AND COMPILED BY THE AUTHORS

optimization under the first scenario are shown in Chart 10.2, and under the second scenario – in Chart 10.3.

According to Chart 10.2, the benefits of optimization for increasing inclusiveness in higher education for people with disabilities in the first scenario include the following:

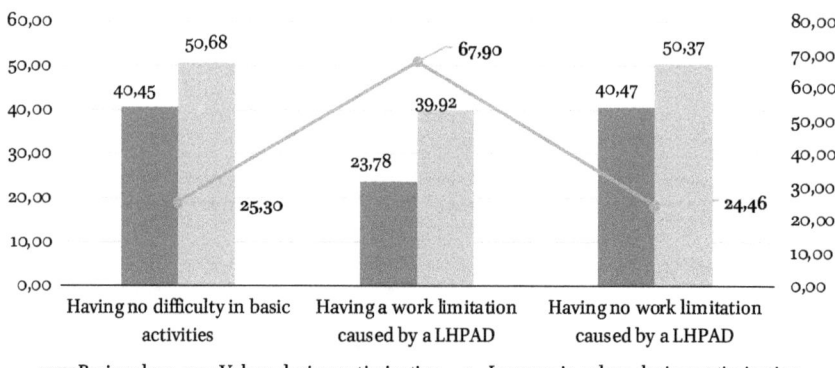

CHART 10.2 The benefits of optimization to increase inclusiveness in higher education for people with disabilities in the first scenario
SOURCE: CALCULATED AND COMPILED BY THE AUTHORS

– Increasing the openness of higher education to people with disabilities who have no difficulty in basic activities by 25.30%, from 40.45% to 50.68%;
– Increasing the openness of higher education to persons with a work disability caused by a LHPAD by 67.90%, from 23.78% to 39.92%;
– Increasing the openness of higher education to persons with no work limitations caused by a LHPAD by 24.46%, from 40.47% to 50.37%.

According to Chart 10.3, the benefits of optimization for increasing inclusiveness in higher education for people with disabilities in the second scenario include the following:

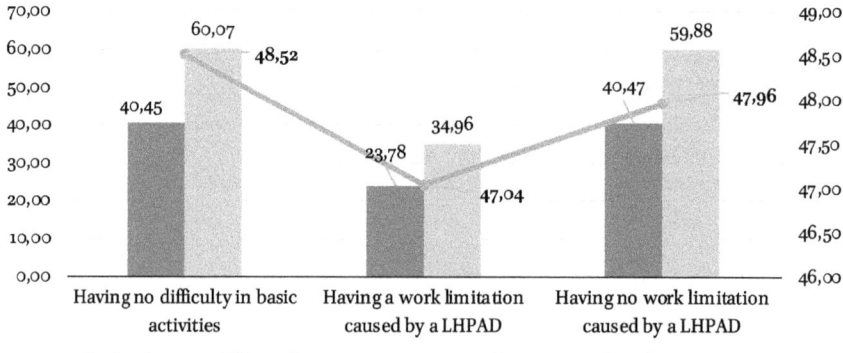

CHART 10.3 The benefits of optimization to increase inclusiveness in higher education for people with disabilities in the second scenario
SOURCE: CALCULATED AND COMPILED BY THE AUTHORS

- Increasing the openness of higher education to people with disabilities who have no difficulty in basic activities by 48.52%, from 40.45% to 60.07%;
- Increasing the openness of higher education to persons with a work disability caused by a LHPAD by 47.04%, from 23.78% to 34.96%;
- Increasing the openness of higher education to persons with no work limitations caused by a LHPAD by 47.96%, from 40.47% to 59.88%.

5 Discussion

The obtained results develop and complement the scientific provisions of the concept of inclusive higher education (Table 10.8).

As described in Table 10.8, the new research findings showed that, unlike (*Gebhardt* et al., 2022; *Wang*, 2021), institutional effectiveness is not a secondary (determinant of other factors) but a primary, key (determinant of other factors) factor of inclusiveness in higher education, making it open to persons with disabilities, having no difficulty in basic activities, having a work limitation caused by a LHPAD, and having no work limitation caused by a LHPAD. In contrast to (*Cheng*, 2021; *Popkova* et al., 2021; *Sibirskaya* et al., 2019; *Wending*, 2022), a factor such as the progressiveness of universities has not been shown to make a clearly positive contribution to the openness of higher education to individuals with disabilities.

In contrast to (*Happ and Bolla*, 2022; *Muyor-Rodríguez* et al., 2021; *Strnadová* et al., 2015), it is substantiated that such a factor as the inclusiveness of society does not clearly contribute positively to the openness of higher education to persons with disabilities. In contrast to (*Ashman*, 2010; *Lee and Taylor*, 2022), it has been found that digitalization is another key factor in the inclusiveness of higher education, ensuring its openness to people with disabilities, having no difficulty in basic activities, and having no work limitation caused by a LHPAD.

The particular findings allow the authors to draw a systemic conclusion that the well-known factors that increase the inclusiveness of higher education have a pronounced varying and even contradictory impact on the accessibility of education at universities for persons with disabilities, proving the hypothesis (H). Based on the findings, the authors developed a new approach to the implementation of the concept of inclusive higher education based on openness to persons with disabilities, which relies on the management of selected key factors – the effectiveness of institutions and digitalization.

The alternative approach (outlined in *Bartz*, 2020; *Lopez-Gavira* et al., 2021; *Yadav* et al., 2020) based on increasing the overall openness of universities to ensure equality of higher education opportunities for all people

TABLE 10.8 Contribution of the research results to the increase in scientific knowledge

A widely recognized factor in the inclusiveness of higher education	Existing literature		Conclusions on the research results	
	EXISTING SCIENTIFIC PROVISIONS	SOURCES OF LITERATURE	PARTIAL CONCLUSIONS	GENERAL (SYSTEM) OUTPUT
Effectiveness of Institutions	State norms and standards of higher education services for persons with disabilities, as well as the availability of special quotas – determined by other factors	(Gebhardt et al., 2022; Wang, 2021).	Contribution to the openness of higher education to persons with disabilities, having no difficulty in basic activities, having a work limitation caused by a LHPAD, and having no work limitation caused by a LHPAD	Commonly known factors that increase the inclusiveness of higher education have a pronounced in varying degrees and even contradictory impact on the accessibility of university education for persons with disabilities; hypothesis (H) is proved
Progressiveness of universities	Open door policy based on CSR and, striving to improve positions in university rankings	(Cheng, 2021; Popkova et al., 2021; Sibirskaya et al., 2019; Wending, 2022).	Lack of an explicit positive contribution to the openness of higher education to persons with disabilities	

A widely recognized factor in the inclusiveness of higher education	Existing literature		Conclusions on the research results	
	EXISTING SCIENTIFIC PROVISIONS	SOURCES OF LITERATURE	PARTIAL CONCLUSIONS	GENERAL (SYSTEM) OUTPUT
Inclusiveness of society	Foundational factor, support of socialization	(Happ and Bolla, 2022; Muyor-Rodríguez et al., 2021; Strnadová et al., 2015).		
Digitalization	Development of distance learning, increasing the availability of higher education	(Ashman, 2010; Lee and Taylor, 2022).	Contribution to the openness of higher education to persons with disabilities, having no difficulty in basic activities and no work limitations caused by a LHPAD	

SOURCE: DEVELOPED BY THE AUTHORS

is correct. Nevertheless, the application of this approach is appropriate at a higher (national, macro) level, while separate approaches should be combined (implemented in parallel) at the university level (micro-level) to manage inclusiveness in each of its individual forms.

In particular, the openness of universities to people with disabilities definitely needs a stand-alone approach that considers the peculiarities of this area. This is the contribution of the findings to the literature – the substantiation of the need and development of scientific and methodological recommendations for implementing a special approach to the implementation of the concept of inclusive higher education based on openness to persons with disabilities.

6   Conclusion

Thus, both tasks have been solved according to the research results. The factor analysis of inclusiveness in higher education carried out in the first task allowed the authors to select the key factors that contribute to the openness of universities to persons with disabilities – the effectiveness of institutions and digitalization.

The approach to the implementation of the concept of inclusive higher education based on openness to persons with disabilities, developed in the second task, relies on the management of selected factors. The prospects (advantages) of its implementation include an increase in the openness of higher education:
– For people with disabilities, having no difficulty in basic activities by 25.30%–48.52%;
– For persons with a work limitation caused by a LHPAD by 47.04%–67.90%;
– For persons with disabilities, having no work limitation caused by a LHPAD by 24.46%–47.96%.

The theoretical significance of the findings and conclusions consists in the development of scientific provisions of the concept of inclusive higher education by outlining the range of key factors for the openness of universities for persons with disabilities. The practical significance of the author's developments is related to the fact that the proposed new approach allows one to effectively combine state and corporate (at the level of universities) management of inclusiveness in higher education and guarantees more pronounced results in the field of openness of universities to persons with disabilities. The author's approach supports the practical implementation of SDG 10 in higher education in relation to persons with disabilities.

Speaking about the limitations of the research, it should be noted that its approach to the implementation of the concept of inclusive higher education is focused only on one of the many areas of inclusiveness management (the direction of ensuring the openness of universities for persons with disabilities).

The obtained evidence that this direction requires a specific approach to its practical implementation suggests that each of the other directions (gender neutrality, cultural openness, combating ageism, elimination of geographical and financial barriers to university education, etc.) similarly needs its own narrowly focused approach at the micro-level (implemented by universities) of management. In this regard, it is recommended that future research be devoted to identifying the specifics of the influence of various factors on the success of the practical implementation of each area of inclusiveness in higher education separately, as well as the development of specific approaches for each area.

There is also a worrying signal that there is no consistent correlation between the openness of higher education to persons with disabilities, having difficulty in basic activities, and the factors of inclusiveness. Special measures are required for this category of persons with disabilities. The development of these measures is envisaged by the proposed management approach. It is also proposed that future research be devoted to the development of these measures.

References

Aldehami S (2022) Saudi Arabia special education teachers' attitudes toward assistive technology use for students with intellectual disability. *Contemporary Educational Technology* 14(2): ep353. DOI: 10.30935/cedtech/11541.

Ashman A (2010) Modelling inclusive practices in postgraduate tertiary education courses. *International Journal of Inclusive Education* 14(7): 667–680. DOI: 10.1080/13603111003778429.

Bartz J (2020) All inclusive?! empirical insights into individual experiences of students with disabilities and mental disorders at German universities and implications for inclusive higher education. *Education Sciences* 10(9): 223. DOI: 10.3390/educsci10090223.

Chambers D, and Forlin C (2021) A historical ethnography of the enactment of Rawl's theory of justice as applied to the education of learners with disability in Western Australia. *International Journal of Inclusive Education*. DOI: 10.1080/13603116.2021.1941322.

Cheng S (2021) The change of Chinese university students with hearing impairment in thinking styles: Implications for Inclusive/Mainstreaming Higher Education.

International Journal of Disability, Development and Education. DOI: 10.1080/1034912X.2021.1921125.

Correia A, Teixeira V, and Forlin C (2021) Home-school collaboration in assessment, placement, and individual education plan development for children with special education needs in Macao: The views of parents: The views of parents. *School Community Journal, 31*(1), 205–231. Available (consulted 21 March 2022) at: https://www.adi.org/journal/2021ss/CorreiaEtAlSS21.pdf.

Cruz-Morato MA, García-Mestanza J, and Dueñas-Zambrana C (2021) Special employment centres, time factor and sustainable human resources management in Spanish hotel industry: Can corporate social marketing improve the Labour situation of people with disabilities? *Sustainability* 13(19): 10710. DOI: 10.3390/su131910710.

Eurostat (2022) *Archive: Disability statistics – Access to education and training.* Available (consulted 21 March 2022) at: https://ec.europa.eu/eurostat/statistics-explained/index.php?title=Archive:Disability_statistics_-_access_to_education_and_training&oldid=413588.

Forlin C, and Chambers D (2020) Diversity and inclusion and special education. In: Sharma U, and Salend SJ (eds) *Oxford encyclopedia of inclusive and special education.* Oxford, UK: Oxford University Press. DOI: 10.1093/acrefore/9780190264093.013.1214.

Gebhardt M, Schurig M, Suggate S, Scheer D, and Capovilla D (2022) Social, systemic, individual-medical or cultural? *Questionnaire on the Concepts of Disability Among Teacher Education Students. Frontiers in Education* 6: 701987. DOI: 10.3389/feduc.2021.701987.

Global Green Growth Institute (2022) *Green growth index 2020. GGGI Technical Report No. 16 Measuring performance in achieving SDG target.* Available (consulted 21 March 2022) at: https://greengrowthindex.gggi.org/wp-content/uploads/2021/01/2020-Green-Growth-Index.pdf.

Green SE, and Bingham SC (2017) "I could have so easily been excluded": Exploring narratives of inclusion and exclusion in the lives of professional performers with disabilities. *International Perspectives on Inclusive Education* 10: 11–29. DOI: 10.1108/S1479-363620170000010006.

Han C, Cumming TM, and Strnadová I (2022) The education of students with disabilities in remote or rural areas of China. *Intervention in School and Clinic* 57(4): 268–273. DOI: 10.1177/10534512211024940.

Happ É, and Bolla V (2022) A theoretical model for the implementation of social sustainability in the synthesis of tourism, disability studies, and special-needs education. *Sustainability* 14(3): 1700. DOI: 10.3390/su14031700.

IMD (2022) *World Digital Competitiveness Ranking, 2021.* Available (consulted 21 March 2022) at: https://www.imd.org/centers/world-competitiveness-center/rankings/world-digital-competitiveness/.

Jenkin E, Wilson E, Clarke M, and Campain R (2019) Bridging the local-universal divide of human rights research: Voices of children with disability in developing countries. *International Perspectives on Inclusive Education* 13: 121–137. DOI: 10.1108/S1479-363620190000013010.

Lee CE, and Taylor JL (2022) A review of the benefits and barriers to postsecondary education for students with intellectual and developmental disabilities. *Journal of Special Education* 55(4): 234–245. DOI: 10.1177/00224669211013354.

Lopez-Gavira R, Moriña A, and Morgado B (2021) Challenges to inclusive education at the university: the perspective of students and disability support service staff. *Innovation: The European Journal of Social Science Research* 34(3): 292–304. DOI: 10.1080/13511610.2019.1578198.

Meeks LM, Stergiopoulos E, and Petersen KH (2022) Institutional accountability for students with disabilities: A call for liaison committee on medical education action. *Academic Medicine* 97(3): 341–345. DOI: 10.1097/ACM.0000000000004471.

Muyor-Rodríguez J, Fuentes-Gutiérrez V, De la Fuente-Robles YM, and Amezcua-Aguilar T (2021) Inclusive university education in Bolivia: The actors and their discourses. *Sustainability* 13(19): 10818. DOI: 10.3390/su131910818.

Papadakaki M, Maraki A, Bitsakos N, and Chliaoutakis J (2022) Perceived knowledge and attitudes of faculty members towards inclusive education for students with disabilities: Evidence from a Greek university. *International Journal of Environmental Research and Public Health* 19(4): 2151. DOI: 10.3390/ijerph19042151.

Popkova EG, Bogoviz AV., and Sergi BS (2021) Towards digital society management and 'capitalism 4.0' in contemporary Russia. *Humanities and Social Sciences Communications* 8(1): 77. DOI: 10.1057/s41599-021-00743-8.

Pov S (2021) Education of children with disabilities in Cambodia: Trends, collaborations, and challenges. *International Perspectives on Inclusive Education* 17: 139–150. DOI: 10.1108/S1479-363620210000017014.

Schloemer-Jarvis A, Bader B, and Böhm SA (2022) The role of human resource practices for including persons with disabilities in the workforce: A systematic literature review. *International Journal of Human Resource Management* 33(1): 45–98. DOI: 10.1080/09585192.2021.1996433.

Sibirskaya E, Popkova E, Oveshnikova L, and Tarasova I (2019) Remote education vs traditional education based on effectiveness at the micro level and its connection to the level of development of macro-economic systems. *International Journal of Educational Management* 33(3): 533–543. DOI: 10.1108/IJEM-08-2018-0248.

Strnadová I, Hájková V, and Květoňová L (2015) Voices of university students with disabilities: Inclusive education on the tertiary level – A reality or a distant dream? *International Journal of Inclusive Education* 19(10): 1080–1095. DOI: 10.1080/13603116.2015.1037868.

Wang L (2021) Tertiary dance education in inclusive settings: Teachers' intercultural sensitivity for teaching international students. *Research in Dance Education* 22(3): 287–305. DOI: 10.1080/14647893.2020.1766008.

Wending L (2022) Implementing the hybrid neuro-fuzzy system to model specific learning disability in special university education Programs. *Journal of Mathematics* 2022: 6540542. DOI: 10.1155/2022/6540542.

World Bank (2022) *Explore the interactive database of the WIPO Global Innovation Index 2021 indicators*. Available (consulted 21 March 2022) at: https://www.globalinnovationindex.org/analysis-indicator.

Yadav J, Sachdeva M, and Rai R (2020) A comparative study of inclusive education system in government and private universities of Lucknow city. *International Journal of Scientific and Technology Research* 9(4): 2922–2924. Available (consulted 21 March 2022) at: http://www.ijstr.org/final-print/apr2020/A-Comparative-Study-Of-Inclusive-Education-System-In-Government-And-Private-Universities-Of-Lucknow-City.pdf.

CHAPTER 11

Best Practices for Inclusiveness by Top Universities and Their Openness to Persons with Disabilities in the More Developed Countries

Elena S. Akopova, Daria O. Zabaznova, Irina A. Tarasova and Marietta A. Bolokova

Abstract

The paper aims to explore and systematize the best practices of inclusiveness and openness for persons with disabilities in top universities in developed countries and determine the prospects for translating these practices into developing countries. For this purpose, the authors conduct a quantitative-qualitative empirical study of international experience in ensuring inclusiveness and openness for persons with disabilities. The research is based on the example of the top ten countries for digital accessibility implementation and outcomes for people with disabilities. The authors also systematize the best practices of inclusiveness and openness to people with disabilities in top universities in developed countries. The novelty of this research is that it rethinks global inequality from the perspective of the inclusiveness of universities in developed and developing countries for people with disabilities. Therefore, this paper clarifies the non-commercial nature of global inequality, strengthening the theoretical and methodological basis for implementing SDG 10. The theoretical significance of the research lies in the disclosure of cause-and-effect relationships of global inequalities in the inclusiveness of higher education for persons with disabilities and the prospects for overcoming them. The practical significance of the findings and conclusions is that they offer new opportunities for overcoming global inequalities by making universities in developing countries more inclusive for persons with disabilities in support of SDG 10. The proposed author's recommendations will also improve university management practices in developed and developing countries and increase their results in terms of opening up to people with disabilities to support inclusiveness in higher education.

Keywords

best practices – inclusiveness – top universities – openness to people with disabilities – developed countries – developing countries – reducing global inequality – SDG 10

1 Introduction

This paper focuses on the openness to persons with disabilities as one of the most important forms of university inclusiveness, detailed in the works of *Chambers and Forlin* (2021), *Kuok* et al. (2020), and *Sharma* et al. (2018). The relevance of the chosen topic lies in the fact that the philosophy of inclusiveness is unevenly supported in the global community.

The problem of global inequality is clearly evident when we consider this philosophy on the scale of the world economic system. In the Global North (developed countries), societies are more progressive, inclined, and receptive to change (*Popkova* et al., 2021; *Sibirskaya* et al., 2019). The philosophy of inclusiveness is supported by and deeply rooted in the culture of these countries (*Bogoviz* et al., 2018; *Yanckovsckaya*, 2016). In contrast, societies in the Global South (developing countries) are more traditional and, correspondingly, less progressive (*Bobyshev and Akhmetova*, 2020; *Burdakova* et al., 2019). Historically, the complex social stratification of these countries has been reinforced by culture-social institutions and, therefore, is difficult to change (*Shabaltina* et al., 2021; *Vanchukhina* et al., 2018; *Vanchukhina* et al., 2022).

The research question (RQ) for this chapter is: "How do leading universities from developed countries become inclusive, and can their successful experiences be used by universities from developing countries?" To find an answer to the posed RQ, this chapter conducts an empirical study aimed at reviewing The Times Higher Education World University Ranking. The authors analyze and summarize best practices for inclusiveness and openness to persons with disabilities by top universities from developed countries and assess the replicability and usefulness of these practices to developing countries.

This research aims to explore and systematize the best practices of inclusiveness and openness for persons with disabilities in top universities in developed countries and determine the prospects for translating these practices into developing countries. The novelty of this research is that it rethinks global inequality from the perspective of the inclusiveness of universities in developed and developing countries for people with disabilities. This chapter clarifies the non-profit nature of global inequality, strengthening the theoretical and methodological basis for implementing SDG 10.

2 Literature Review

This research is based on the concept of inclusive higher education from the perspective of its openness to persons with disabilities. The works of *Maebara* et al. (2022), *Papadakaki* et al. (2022), *Villouta and Villarreal* (2022), and *Yerbury* et al. (2022) noted that universities in developed countries receive more funding (due to their greater investment attractiveness and higher tuition costs), in particular, due to their better positions in international university rankings. Moreover, these universities have more advanced technology and a more significant number of other resources and opportunities for the development of practices of inclusive higher education. In this regard, inadequate resources act as a barrier to the global transfer of the experience of universities in developed countries in providing inclusive education and implementing their best practices in developing countries.

Galleli et al. (2022), *Kaidesoja* (2022), and *Wut* et al. (2022) point out that international university rankings stimulate the growth of inclusiveness in higher education. However, it remains unclear why, despite increased resources and a strategic focus on improving positions in international university rankings, universities in developing countries cannot achieve the same high results in the inclusiveness of persons with disabilities as those in developed countries.

Thus, according to *Statista* (2022), the expenditure on higher education in the USA (the world leader) accounts for a total of 2.5% of GDP (public expenditure accounts for 0.9% and private expenditure for 1.6%). In turn, Chile, a developing country, is in second place with 2.4% of GDP (1% for public expenditure and 1.4% for private expenditure), ahead of other developed countries. According to the IMD World Competitiveness Center (2022), such a developing country as China is the world leader in robots in education and R&D in 2021 (1st place).

Uncertainty about the cause-and-effect relationship of global inequalities in inclusiveness in higher education for persons with disabilities and the prospects for overcoming them is a gap in the literature. The identified gap is filled in this research through an in-depth quantitative-qualitative study of international experience in ensuring inclusiveness in higher education for persons with disabilities.

3 Materials and Methods

To fill an identified gap in the literature and find an answer to the posed RQ, this chapter conducts a quantitative-qualitative empirical study of international experiences of inclusiveness and openness for persons with disabilities. First, the authors review the best practices for inclusiveness and openness for people with disabilities at top universities in developed countries through a case study of the top five universities in the *Times Higher Education* ranking in 2022 (*THE*, 2022).

Then, using the method of correlation analysis, the authors assess the relationship of the DARE index for persons with disabilities with the position in *THE ranking* (2022) on the example of the top ten countries for digital accessibility implementation and outcomes for persons with disabilities (based on *Global Initiative for Inclusive Information and Communication Technologies*, 2020). The empirical basis of this research is shown in Table 11.1.

The authors apply critical analysis to assess the applicability of best practices from universities in developed countries to developing countries. The obtained results are used to develop recommendations for the global translation of best practices for inclusiveness of universities in relation to persons with disabilities.

TABLE 11.1 Dare index and the position in THE rating in the top ten countries for digital accessibility implementation and outcomes for persons with disabilities

Category of countries	Country	Total dare index score (0–100)	Position in the times higher education (THE) world university rankings 2022	
			The top-ranked university in the country	Overall score (0–100)
Developing countries	Qatar	39	Qatar University	46.1–48.0
	South Africa	28	University if Cape Town	54.9
	Brazil	27	University of São Paulo	50.4–54.9
Developed countries	Israel	34	Tel Aviv University	50.4–53.9
	Australia	30	University of Melbourne	77.8
	France	30	Paris Sciences et Lettres – PSL Research University Paris	74.1
	UK	29	University of Oxford	95.7
	USA	29	Harvard University	95.0
	Italy	28	University of Bologna	55.8
	Malta	28	University of Malta	27.2–31.9

SOURCE: COMPILED BY THE AUTHORS BASED ON (*GLOBAL INITIATIVE FOR INCLUSIVE INFORMATION AND COMMUNICATION TECHNOLOGIES*, 2020; *THE*, 2022)

4 Results

4.1 International Experience in Ensuring Inclusiveness and Openness of Universities for Persons with Disabilities

Using the top five universities in the Times Higher Education ranking in 2022 (*THE*, 2022) as an example, the authors conducted a case-study review of best practices for inclusiveness and openness to persons with disabilities by top universities from developed countries. The results of this cases-study are systematized in Table 11.2.

As shown by the best practices of top universities in developed countries, the following measures of inclusiveness and openness to persons with disabilities are implemented (in decreasing order of prevalence):
- Implementation of a special initiative to make the university open to people with disabilities (from an annual conference to a special program);
- Availability of a special department to manage the university's openness to people with disabilities;
- Adjusting the educational program to support the adaptation of persons with disabilities (officially stated only at the University of Oxford).

Based on the statistics in Table 11.1, using correlation analysis on the example of the top ten countries for digital accessibility implementation and outcomes for persons with disabilities, the authors revealed no clear relationship DARE index for persons with disabilities with the position in *THE ranking* (2022). The correlation of these indicators was negative. Consequently, openness for people with disabilities does not improve the position of universities in international university rankings.

4.2 Recommendations for the Global Broadcasting of Best Practices for Inclusiveness in Universities for Persons with Disabilities

A critical analysis found that the best practices of universities from developed countries can be implemented in developing countries. The authors identified no complex measures that are not available for implementation (requiring large-scale funding, technology, and other resources). To ensure the global translation of best practices in the inclusiveness of universities toward persons with disabilities, universities in developing countries are encouraged to do the following:
- Develop and launch a special initiative to make the university open to people with disabilities, considering the characteristics of the university and its students with disabilities;
- Allocation of a special department in the university's organizational structure to manage the university's openness to persons with disabilities;

TABLE 11.2 Best practices for inclusion and openness to persons with disabilities by top universities from developed countries

Country	The top-ranked university in the country	Availability of a special department to manage the university's openness to people with disabilities	Special initiative to make the university open to people with disabilities	Adjusting the educational program to support the adaptation of persons with disabilities
UK	University of Oxford (1st place)	Yes (The Disability Advisory Service)	Yes (The Student Support Plan)	Yes (Inclusive educational practices, inclusive teaching methods)
USA	Harvard University (2nd place)	Yes (Office for Equity, Diversity, Inclusion, and Belonging)	Yes (Community space coffee chat – people withdisabilities; Disability inclusion workshop for students in the arts, and others)	No
Switzerland	ETH Zurich (15th place)	No	Yes (The Rehab Initiative)	No
Canada	University of Toronto (18th place)	No	Yes (Strengthening Accessibility & Inclusion within Professional Programs)	No

(cont.)

Country	The top-ranked university in the country	Availability of a special department to manage the university's openness to people with disabilities	Special initiative to make the university open to people with disabilities	Adjusting the educational program to support the adaptation of persons with disabilities
Singapore	National University of Singapore (21st place)	Yes (The Student Accessibility Unit (SAU), previously known as Disability Support Office)	No	No

SOURCE: SYSTEMATIZED AND COMPILED BY THE AUTHORS BASED ON (*JOHANNSSEN AND MÄRKI*, 2022; *HARVARD UNIVERSITY*, 2021; *NATIONAL UNIVERSITY OF SINGAPORE*, 2022; *UNIVERSITY OF OXFORD*, 2022; *UNIVERSITY OF TORONTO*, 2022)

– Using distance learning opportunities for flexible adjustment of educational programs and an individual approach to support the adaptation of persons with disabilities.

The authors also propose the following long-term (strategic) measures (requiring extra funding and other resources) to increase inclusion for persons with disabilities in developed and developing countries:

– Modernization of university campuses to make them more comfortable for people with disabilities;
– Systemic improvement of the university and local urban space to create a comprehensive environment conducive to living and learning for people with disabilities;
– Supporting the employment of graduates with disabilities through cooperation between universities and local employers.

5 Discussion

This paper contributes to the literature through the development of scientific provisions of the concept of inclusive higher education, revealing and systematizing the best international practices of ensuring its openness to persons with disabilities, justifying the applicability of this experience in developing countries, and outlining the prospects for global translation of best practices. The theoretical significance of this research lies in the disclosure of cause-and-effect relationships of global inequalities in the inclusiveness of higher education for persons with disabilities and the prospects for overcoming them.

In contrast to *Maebara* et al. (2022), *Papadakaki* et al. (2022), *Villouta and Villarreal* (2022), and *Yerbury* et al. (2022), the authors have shown that the measures implemented by leading universities in developed countries to make them open to people with disabilities do not require significant funding, technology, or other resources. This has shaped the scientific argument that the experience of developed countries can and should be translated globally and adopted by developing countries.

In contrast to *Galleli* et al. (2022), *Kaidesoja* (2022), and *Wut* et al. (2022), the authors have substantiated that international university rankings do not sufficiently support the openness of universities to people with disabilities. For example, *THE ranking* (2022) considers and promotes only the gender neutrality and internationality of universities. In this regard, the inclusion of appropriate indicators and the revision of the methodology of international university rankings are recommended to institutionalize the practices of increasing the openness of universities to people with disabilities.

6 Conclusion

Thus, the research answered the research question and revealed that the inclusiveness of leading universities from developed countries is achieved mainly by implementing special initiatives to make the university open for people with disabilities and has a special department to manage the openness of the university for people with disabilities, in rare cases – by adjusting the educational program to support the adaptation of people with disabilities. The successful experiences of developed countries can and should be used by universities in developing countries.

The practical significance of the findings and conclusions is that they offer new opportunities for overcoming global inequalities by making universities in developing countries more inclusive for persons with disabilities in support of

SDG 10. The proposed author's recommendations will also improve university management practices in developed and developing countries and increase their results in terms of opening up to people with disabilities to support inclusiveness in higher education.

References

Bobyshev SV, and Akhmetova AV (2020) The health care system as a mechanism for the integration of indigenous peoples of the Khabarovsk Territory into soviet society (the second half of the 1940s–the first half of the 1980s). In: Solovev DB, Savaley VV, Bekker AT, and Petukhov VI (eds) *Proceeding of the International Science and Technology Conference "FarEastCon 2019".* Singapore: Springer, 139–146. DOI: 10.1007/978-981-15-2244-4_11.

Bogoviz A, Averin A, and Yanovskaya V (2018) Gender analysis of local budgets in law enforcement and educational organizations of Russia. *MATEC Web of Conferences* 212: 09015. DOI: 10.1051/matecconf/201821209015.

Burdakova G, Byankin A, Usanov I, and Pankova L (2019) Smart technologies in education and formation of entrepreneurial competencies. *IOP Conference Series: Materials Science and Engineering* 497: 012066. DOI: 10.1088/1757-899X/497/1/012066.

Chambers D, and Forlin C (2021) An historical ethnography of the enactment of Rawl's Theory of Justice as applied to the education of learners with disability in Western Australia. *International Journal of Inclusive Education.* DOI: 10.1080/13603116.2021.1941322.

Galleli B, Teles NEB, Santos JAR, Freitas-Martins MS, and Hourneaux Jr F (2022) Sustainability university rankings: A comparative analysis of UI green metric and the times higher education world university rankings. *International Journal of Sustainability in Higher Education* 23(2): 404–425. DOI: 10.1108/IJSHE-12-2020-0475.

Global Initiative for Inclusive Information and Communication Technologies (2020) Top ten countries for digital accessibility implementation and outcomes for persons with disabilities. In *DARE index 2020: Top performing countries*. Available (consulted 4 June 2022) at: https://g3ict.org/upload/accessible_DARE-Index-2020-Top-Performing-Countries-ENGLISH-1.pdf.

Harvard University (2021) *Ability/Disability*. Available (consulted 4 June 2022) at: https://edib.harvard.edu/theme/abilitydisability.

IMD World Competitiveness Center (2022) *World digital competitiveness ranking – 2021.* Available (consulted 4 June 2022) at: https://www.imd.org/centers/world-competitiveness-center/rankings/world-digital-competitiveness/.

Johanssen C, and Märki M (2022) We take rehabilitation to also mean inclusion. *ETH Zurich*. Available (consulted 4 June 2022) at: https://ethz.ch/en/news-and-events/eth-news/news/2020/03/we-take-rehabilitation-to-also-mean-inclusion.html.

Kaidesoja T (2022) A theoretical framework for explaining the paradox of university rankings. *Social Science Information* 61(1): 128–153. DOI: 10.1177/05390184221079470.

Kuok ACH, Teixeira V, Forlin C, Monteiro E, and Correia A (2020) The effect of self-efficacy and role understanding on teachers' emotional exhaustion and work engagement in inclusive education in Macao (SAR). *International Journal of Disability, Development and Education*. DOI: 10.1080/1034912X.2020.1808949.

Maebara K, Fujii Y, Tanimura K, Suzuki T, and Takeda A (2022) A study of lifelong education for persons with intellectual disabilities at the university level. *Journal of Intellectual Disability – Diagnosis and Treatment* 10(2): 70–77. DOI: 10.6000/2292-2598.2022.10.02.1.

National University of Singapore (2022) *Student accessibility unit*. Available (consulted 4 June 2022) at: https://nus.edu.sg/osa/student-services/student-accessibility-unit.

Papadakaki M, Maraki A, Bitsakos N, and Chliaoutakis J (2022) Perceived Knowledge and attitudes of faculty members towards inclusive education for students with disabilities: Evidence from a Greek university. *International Journal of Environmental Research and Public Health* 19(4): 2151. DOI: 10.3390/ijerph19042151.

Popkova EG, Inshakova AO, and Sergi BS (2021) Venture capital and Industry 4.0: The G7's versus BRICS' experience. *Thunderbird International Business Review* 63(6): 765–777. DOI: 10.1002/tie.22235.

Shabaltina LV, Karbekova AB, Milkina E, and Pushkarev IY (2021) The social impact of the downturn in business and the new context of sustainable development in the context of the 2020 economic crisis in developing countries. In: Popkova EG, and Sergi BS (eds) *Modern global economic system: Evolutional development vs. revolutionary leap*. Cham: Springer, 74–82. DOI: 10.1007/978-3-030-69415-9_9.

Sharma U, Jitoko F, Macanawai SS, and Forlin C (2018) How do we measure implementation of inclusive education in the pacific islands? A process for developing and validating disability-inclusive Indicators. *International Journal of Disability, Development and Education* 65(6): 614–630. DOI: 10.1080/1034912X.2018.1430751.

Sibirskaya E, Popkova E, Oveshnikova L, and Tarasova I (2019) Remote education vs traditional education based on effectiveness at the micro level and its connection to the level of development of macro-economic systems. *International Journal of Educational Management* 33(3): 533–543. DOI: 10.1108/IJEM-08-2018-0248.

Statista (2022) *Expenditure on higher education as a share of GDP in selected countries worldwide in 2018*. Retrieved from https://www.statista.com/statistics/707557/higher-education-spending-share-gdp/ (Accessed 4 June 2022).

Times Higher Education (THE) (2022) *World University Rankings 2022*. Available (consulted 4 June 2022) at: https://www.timeshighereducation.com/world-university-rankings/2022#!/page/0/length/25/sort_by/rank/sort_order/asc/cols/scores.

University of Oxford (2022) *Accessible and inclusive teaching*. Available (consulted 4 June 2022) at: https://academic.admin.ox.ac.uk/accessible-and-inclusive-teaching#collapse1751816.

University of Toronto (2022) Strengthening accessibility & inclusion within professional programs. Available (consulted 4 June 2022) at: https://studentlife.utoronto.ca/program/strengthening-accessibility-inclusion-within-professional-programs/.

Vanchukhina LI, Leybert TB, Ergasheva ST, Khalikova EA, and Khanafieva IR (2022) Integration of the higher education systems of Russia and the Republic of Uzbekistan in training for the digital economy. In: Popkova EG, and Sergi BS (eds) *Digital education in Russia and Central Asia*. Singapore: Springer, 3–13. DOI: 10.1007/978-981-16-9069-3_1.

Vanchukhina LI, Leybert TB, Khalikova EA, and Khalmetov AR (2018) New approaches to formation of innovational human capital as an element of institutional environment. In: Popkova EG (ed) *The impact of information on modern humans*. Cham, Switzerland: Springer, 343–352. DOI: 10.1007/978-3-319-75383-6_44.

Villouta EV, and Villarreal ET (2022) University access policies for persons with disabilities: Lessons from two Chilean universities. *International Journal of Educational Development* 91: 102577. DOI: 10.1016/j.ijedudev.2022.102577.

Wut T-M, Xu J, and Lee SW (2022). Does university ranking matter? Choosing a university in the digital era. *Education Sciences* 12(4): 229. DOI: 10.3390/educsci12040229.

Yanckovsckaya VV (2016) Creation of permanent institutional monitoring mechanism of modern educational technology market significant for nanoindustry. *Mathematics Education* 11(6): 1545–1556. Available (consulted 4 June 2022) at: https://www.iejme.com/download/creation-of-permanent-institutional-monitoring-mechanism-of-modern-educational-technology-market.pdf.

Yerbury H, Darcy S, Burridge N, and Almond B (2022) Bringing order or creating exclusion: Systems for managing disability in a university. *Journal of Documentation* 78(3): 529–545. DOI: 10.1108/JD-12-2020-0208.

CHAPTER 12

Progressive Practices for Achieving Inclusiveness and Openness for People with Disabilities by Top Universities in Less Developed Countries

Aminat Sh. Khuazheva, Elena A. Buller, Larisa T. Tlekhurai-Berzegova and Svetlana K. Chinazirova

Abstract

Purpose: The purpose of the chapter is to study progressive practices in ensuring inclusivity and openness for people with disabilities in top universities in developing countries.

Design/methodology/approach: To achieve the indicated research purpose, the authors evaluated the contribution of distance learning to inclusiveness and openness for people with disabilities at top universities in developing countries using the Difference in Differences (DiD) method. Progressive practices of achieving inclusivity and openness for people with disabilities by top universities from developing countries are investigated by the case study method.

Findings: As a result of the conducted research, it was revealed that the inclusiveness of leading universities in developing countries is achieved through progressive practices of achieving openness for people with disabilities: distance learning, inclusive social environment, as well as inclusive higher education systems. The experience of top universities in developing countries is successful, but it is fundamentally different and, therefore, not comparable with the experience of universities from developed countries.

Originality/value: The theoretical significance of the results obtained in this chapter lies in the fact that they revealed the features of the institutions of the "knowledge economy," thanks to which the inclusiveness of leading universities in developing countries is achieved. The practical significance of the findings is that they revealed the prospects for increasing inclusiveness and openness for people with disabilities in developing countries.

Keywords

progressive practices – inclusiveness – openness for people with disabilities – top universities – developing countries – "knowledge economy" – institutional environment

1 Introduction

The foundations of inclusiveness of higher education are laid by the "knowledge economy," the concept and institutions of which took shape at the beginning of the XXI century and continue to evolve. The "knowledge economy" has identified usefulness and provided opportunities, government support, and market incentives for lifelong learning (*Abu-Alghayth*, 2021; *Suhendri*, 2021). In the "knowledge economy," education acts as a key mechanism for socio-economic growth and development; in this regard, mass, universal education is encouraged (*Agbenyega and Tamakloe*, 2021; *Popkova*, 2020; *Popkova* et al., 2022).

Thanks to this new philosophy, as well as institutions of inclusiveness, persons with disabilities have become fully integrated into social and labor economic relations and practices (have become an integral and significant part of them). The problem is that the institutional environment varies greatly among the countries of the world. One of the frequently noted (*Kalinina* et al., 2022; *Pashentsev and Antonova*, 2022; *Petrovskaya* et al., 2022) characteristics of developing countries is the reduced (compared to developed countries) effectiveness of institutions. Insufficient effectiveness of institutions can act as a barrier to developing the "knowledge economy" and ensuring the inclusiveness of higher education (*Chambers and Forlin*, 2021; *Correia* et al., 2022; *Monteiro and Forlin*, 2021).

The research question (RQ) of this chapter is as follows: How is the inclusiveness of leading universities in developing countries achieved, and is their experience as successful as that of universities in developed countries? The chapter aims to study progressive practices of achieving inclusivity and openness for people with disabilities in top universities in developing countries. To achieve this goal, this article solves the following two research tasks:
– Contribution of distance learning to inclusiveness and openness for people with disabilities in top universities from developing countries;
– A case study of progressive practices for achieving inclusiveness and openness for people with disabilities by top universities of developing countries.

2   Literature Review

Developing countries are an extensive category, in the study of which generalization (ignoring the features of sub-categories) countries may misrepresent the results when studying the "knowledge economy." The dichotomous classification of the countries of the Global North and the Global South is too simple (because it distinguishes only two categories of countries and excludes the transition of countries to another category), and the classification of the World Bank is too complex (because it identifies many categories of countries, but does not take into account the role of education in determining their borders).

To overcome their shortcomings, the authors' classification of countries is proposed according to the criterion of their current position in the international rankings of the "knowledge economy" (e.g., in the IMD and WIPO rankings) and the dynamics of changes in this position. In accordance with the authors' classification, it is proposed to distinguish:

- Developed countries leading in the international rankings of the "knowledge economy" (OECD countries – countries of the Global North);
- Developing countries immediately following developed countries (marginally lagging behind them) in the international rankings of the "knowledge economy" and improving their positions (in this regard, they can also be called dynamically developing; the term "transitional economies" was previously common) (e.g., BRICS countries, EAEU countries, CIS countries and etc.);
- Lagging countries that occupy a peripheral position in the international rankings of the "knowledge economy" and do not demonstrate clear success in improving their positions (in this regard, they can also be called moderately developing and attributed to the countries of the Global South) (e.g., a number of African countries).

The (dynamically) developing countries are chosen as the object of research in this article since their experience and example provide opportunities for a complete study of the dynamics of the development of the "knowledge economy." In the existing literature, *Adepoju and Aigbavboa* (2021), *Mohamed* et al. (2022), *Phale* et al. (2021), and *Thalgi* (2020) indicate that in developing countries, the institutions of the "knowledge economy" are less progressive than in developed countries. In turn, *Ijadunola* et al. (2022), *Lau* et al. (2016), *Maebara* et al. (2022), and *Villouta and Villarreal* (2022) consider it necessary to accelerate the development of institutions of the "knowledge economy" to increase the inclusiveness and openness of universities for people with disabilities.

The literature review has shown that the peculiarities of developing countries are poorly studied in existing publications; moreover, they are mainly considered through the prism of the experience of developed countries. This causes uncertainty about how the inclusiveness of leading universities from developing countries is achieved, which is a gap in the literature. In addition, despite the existing assumptions, it remains unclear what is the level of inclusiveness and openness of universities in developing countries for people with disabilities, including in comparison with developed countries – this also acts as a gap in the literature.

To fill the identified gaps, this article examines the progressive practices of achieving inclusiveness and openness for people with disabilities by top universities from developing countries and also compares them with the experience of developed countries.

3   Materials and Method

To determine how developing countries achieve openness and inclusiveness (especially in relation to persons with disabilities) in higher education, this chapter examines the experience of developing countries from different regions of the world, respectively representing different cultures, and conducts a comparative analysis of them. Brazil, Turkey, Chile, Russia, and Mexico were selected for the study, for which e-learning index statistics are available in 2021 (*Preply*, 2022).

The empirical study aimed at reviewing the *Times Higher Education* (2022) World University Rankings analyzes and summarizes best practices for ensuring inclusiveness and openness for people with disabilities in top universities in developing countries and also evaluates its success in comparison with the experience of developed countries.

The features of achieving inclusiveness and openness for people with disabilities by top universities from developing countries (as opposed to universities from developed countries) are revealed. The influence of advanced digital technologies on inclusiveness and openness for people with disabilities in top universities is determined. The isolated influence of the distance learning development factor on inclusivity (according to the *Global Institute for Green Growth*, 2022) and on the positions of leading universities from developing countries in the *Times Higher Education* (2022) World University Ranking based on statistical data from Table 12.1 is determined using the Difference in Differences (DiD) method.

After the quantitative analysis, a qualitative case study analysis is carried out, aimed at revealing the essence of progressive practices of achieving

TABLE 12.1 Distance learning, social inclusiveness and the position of the top universities from developing countries in the THE rankings in 2020 (by the end of 2019)-2021 (by the end of 2020), points 1–100

Country category	Country	E-learning index		Position in the times higher education (THE) world university rankings			Social inclusiveness	
		2020	2021	LEADING UNIVERSITY	2020	2021	2020	2021
Developing countries	Brazil	-	54.4	University of São Paulo	46.9–50.0	50.6–54.2	72.28	72.28
	Turkey	4.3	59.3	Cankaya University	32.8–42.3	39.8–43.5	76.92	76.92
	Chile	21.2	38.4	University of Desarrollo	38.8–42.3	39.8–43.5	74.70	74.71
	Russia	-	34.7	Lomonosov Moscow State University	54.3	55.9	77.20	77.20
	Mexico	0.0	17.5	Metropolitan Autonomous University	28.3–35.2	30.2–36.3	78.79	78.81
Developed countries	Denmark	99.4	100.0	University of Copenhagen	62.1	63.8	91.19	91.19
	USA	61.1	83.0	Stanford University	94.3	94.9	83.64	83.64
	Great Britain	51.9	80.1	University of Oxford	95.4	95.6	90.49	90.32
	France	57.3	71.4	Paris Sciences et Lettres – PSL Research University Paris	73.2	73.6	91.03	91.00
	Sweden	79.0	64.4	Karolinska Institute	74.7	76.0	94.94	94.94

SOURCE: COMPILED BY THE AUTHORS BASED ON MATERIALS FROM THE *GLOBAL INSTITUTE FOR GREEN GROWTH* (2022), *PREPLY* (2022), *TIMES HIGHER EDUCATION* (2022)

TABLE 12.2 Contribution of distance learning to inclusiveness for people with disabilities top universities in developing countries

Scope of changes	Period	Developing countries	Developed countries	Difference
Position in the Times Higher Education (THE) World University Ranking	2020	44.82	79.94	-35.12
	2021	46.68	80.78	-34.1
	Change	1.86	0.84	1.02
Social inclusiveness	2020	75.978	90.258	-14.28
	2021	75.984	90.218	-14.234
	Change	0.006	-0.04	0.046

SOURCE: CALCULATED AND COMPILED BY THE AUTHORS

inclusiveness and openness for people with disabilities by top universities from developing countries.

4 Results

4.1 *Contribution of Distance Learning to Inclusiveness and Openness for People with Disabilities in Top Universities from Developing Countries*

Further, it is reasonable to determine how actively this practice is being implemented by top universities from developing countries. To this end, it is necessary to evaluate the contribution of distance learning to inclusiveness and openness for people with disabilities in top universities in developing countries based on statistics from Table 12.1 using the Difference in Differences (DiD) method in Table 12.2.

The results obtained in Table 12.2 revealed a significant contribution of distance learning to inclusivity for people with disabilities in top universities from developing countries. The level of development of distance learning (arithmetic mean e-learning index) in developing countries in 2021 increased by more than eight times compared to 2020, while in developed countries, the level of development of distance learning increased by less than two times. Consequently, the breakthrough development of distance learning can be considered the difference between universities in developing countries and developed countries.

Using the Difference in Differences (DiD) method, it was found that due to the breakthrough development of distance learning in developing countries, the following has been achieved:
- an improvement in the position in the Times Higher Education World University Ranking by 1.02 points: (79.94-44.82)-(80.78-46.68)=1.02;
- increase in overall social inclusivity by 0.046 points: (90.258-75.978)-(90.218-75.984)=0.046.

Consequently, the breakthrough development of distance learning is a common progressive practice of achieving inclusiveness and openness for people with disabilities by top universities from developing countries.

4.2 Case Study of Progressive Practices for Achieving Inclusiveness and Openness for People with Disabilities by Top Universities in Developing Countries

As a result of the survey of top universities from developing countries (Table 12.1), it has been revealed that most of them do not implement special practices for special training of persons with disabilities. However, this does not mean that universities from developing countries are not sufficiently open to people with disabilities – their inclusivity is achieved differently.

For example, in Turkey, support for the social adaptation of persons with disabilities is conducted at the level of municipalities as a whole (and not individual universities) and includes barrier-free roads, barrier-free education, barrier-free prep school, audio library, and other measures (Cankaya Municipality, 2022). *Cankaya University* (2022) supports all these measures in its activities, which does not require it to take special measures of its own. Nevertheless, its structure includes the Cankaya University Psychological Counseling and Guidance Center, among the activities of which are psychological support for adaptation to learning for people with disabilities.

In Russia, *Lomonosov Moscow State University* (2022) also supports nationwide measures to support the education of people with disabilities. It also provides an inclusive infrastructure of campuses, dormitories, faculties, an inclusive canteen, and its own polyclinic, in which a special set of medical services is provided for people with disabilities. For each category of disabilities (e.g., vision, hearing, motor activity), a special set of university inclusion measures is provided.

5   Discussion

Thus, the article contributes to the development of literature in the field of university inclusiveness by clarifying the specifics of ensuring the openness of universities for people with disabilities in developing countries. Unlike *Adepoju and Aigbavboa* (2021), *Mohamed* et al. (2022), *Phale* et al. (2021), and *Thalgo* (2020), it is proved that it is incorrect to compare universities in developed and developing countries directly by the criterion of their openness to people with disabilities since they rely on fundamentally different institutions of the "knowledge economy."

Thus, in developed countries, special practices are implemented at universities, and in developing countries, the inclusiveness of higher education is achieved systematically – at the level of the state and municipalities with the direct support of universities. Therefore, unlike *Ijadunola* et al. (2022), *Lau* et al. (2016), *Maebara* et al. (2022), and *Villota and Villarreal* (2022), universities in developing countries should not develop along the path of the experience of developed countries in order to increase inclusiveness and openness for people with disabilities. The progress of the institutions of the "knowledge economy" of developing countries lies in their own, unique direction, taking into account their own particularities.

6   Conclusion

So, the article successfully implemented research tasks that made it possible to achieve the goal and answer the set RQ. As a result of the conducted research, it was revealed that the inclusiveness of leading universities from developing countries is achieved with the help of progressive practices to ensure openness for people with disabilities: distance learning, inclusive social environment, as well as inclusive higher education systems. The experience of top universities in developing countries is successful, but it is fundamentally different and, therefore, not comparable with the experience of universities in developed countries.

The theoretical significance of the results obtained in this chapter lies in the fact that they revealed the features of the institutions of the "knowledge economy," thanks to which the inclusiveness of leading universities in developing countries is achieved. The practical significance of the conclusions is that they revealed the prospects for increasing inclusiveness and openness for people with disabilities in developing countries – through the development of distance learning, through increasing the overall inclusiveness of the social environment, as well as through increasing the inclusiveness of higher education systems.

References

Abu-Alghayth KM (2021) Instructional collaboration in Saudi inclusive and mainstream education. *International Perspectives on Inclusive Education* 17: 41–54. DOI: 10.1108/S1479-363620210000017006.

Adepoju OO, and Aigbavboa CO (2021) Assessing knowledge and skills gap for construction 4.0 in a developing economy. *Journal of Public Affairs* 21(3): e2264. DOI: 10.1002/pa.2264.

Agbenyega JS, and Tamakloe D (2021) Using collaborative instructional approaches to prepare competent inclusive education student teachers. *International Perspectives on Inclusive Education* 17: 23–39. DOI: 10.1108/S1479-363620210000017004.

Cancaya Municipality (2022) *Our services for persons with disabilities.* Available (consulted 8 June 2022) at: https://en.cankaya.bel.tr/Services/Social/Services-For-Persons-With-Disabilities.

Cankaya University (2022) *Çankaya University Psychological Counseling and Guidance Center.* Available (consulted 8 June 2022) at: https://pdrm.cankaya.edu.tr/hakkimizda/.

Chambers D, and Forlin C (2021) An historical ethnography of the enactment of Rawl's Theory of Justice as applied to the education of learners with disability in Western Australia. *International Journal of Inclusive Education* DOI: 10.1080/13603116.2021.1941322.

Correia AM, Forlin C, and Sio E (2022). Exploring the participation and agency of students with special education needs in a Macau-Chinese secondary school. *Journal of Research in Special Educational Needs* DOI: 10.1111/1471-3802.12566.

Global Green Growth Institute (2022) *Green Growth Index – Simulation tool evidence library.* Available (consulted 8 June 2022) at: https://gggi-simtool-demo.herokuapp.com/SimulationDashBoard/country-profile.

Ijadunola M, Akinyemi P, Olowookere O, Olotu O, Goodman O, Ogundiran A, ... Ijadunola K (2022) *Addressing Inclusiveness in Tertiary Co-education: Attitude of Undergraduate and Academic Staff Towards Students with Disabilities in a South-West Nigerian University. International Journal of Disability, Development and Education* 69(1): 47–60. DOI: 10.1080/1034912X.2021.2016658.

Kalinina AE, Inshakova AO, and Elkhina IA (2022) *Analyzing structural shifts and assessing structural differences in economies of developed and developing countries.* In: Inshakova AO, and Frolova EE (eds) *The transformation of social relationships in*

Industry 4.0: Economic security and legal prevention. Charlotte, NC: Information Age Publishing, 51–63.

Lau WK, Ho DCW, and Yau Y (2016) Assessing the disability inclusiveness of university buildings in Hong Kong. *International Journal of Strategic Property Management* 20(2): 184–197. DOI: 10.3846/1648715X.2015.1107653.

Lomonosov Moscow State University (2022) *Available environment. Education of persons with disabilities.* Available (consulted 8 June 2022) at: http://www.journ.msu.ru/about/svedeniya-o-nalichii-prisposoblennykh-dlya-ispolzovaniya-invalidami.php.

Maebara K, Fujii Y, Tanimura K, Suzuki T, and Takeda A (2022) A study of lifelong education for persons with intellectual disabilities at the university level. *Journal of Intellectual Disability – Diagnosis and Treatment* 10(2): 70–77. DOI: 10.6000/2292-2598.2022.10.02.1.

Mohamed MMA, Liu P, and Nie G (2022) Do knowledge economy indicators affect economic growth? Evidence from developing countries. *Sustainability* 14(8): 4774. DOI: 10.3390/su14084774.

Monteiro E, and Forlin C (2021) Enhancing teacher education by utilizing a revised PGDE curriculum as a fundamental resource for inclusive practices in Macao. *International Perspectives on Inclusive Education* 15: 147–164. DOI: 10.1108/S1479-363620210000015012.

Pashentsev DA, and Antonova NV (2022) *Ensuring economical resilience in the conditions of developing penetrative (digital) technologies: Mechanisms for Protecting Rights and Legitimate Interests of Economic Subjects.* In: Inshakova AO, and Frolova EE (eds) *The transformation of social relationships in Industry 4.0: Economic security and legal prevention.* Charlotte, NC: Information Age Publishing, 75–84.

Petrovskaya MV, Chaplyuk VZ, Alam RMK, Hossain MN, and Al Humssi AS (2022) COVID-19 and Global Economic Outlook. In: Popkova EG, and Andronova IV (eds) *Current problems of the world economy and international trade.* Bingley, UK: Emerald Publishing Limited, 127–139. DOI: 10.1108/S0190-128120220000042013.

Phale K, Fanglin L, Mensah IA, Omari-Sasu AY, and Musah M (2021) Knowledge-based economy capacity building for developing countries: A panel analysis in southern African development community. *Sustainability* 13(5): 2890. DOI: 10.3390/su13052890.

Popkova EG (2020) A new treatment of quality of goods and services in the conditions of the knowledge economy: Opposition of traditions and innovations. *International Journal for Quality Research* 14(2): 329–346. DOI: 10.24874/IJQR14.02-01.

Popkova EG, De Bernardi P, Tyurina YG, and Sergi BS (2022) A theory of digital technology advancement to address the grand challenges of sustainable development. *Technology in Society* 68: 101831. DOI: 10.1016/j.techsoc.2021.101831.

Preply (2022) *E-Learning Index 2020–2021: The Best & Worst Countries for Digital Education*. Available (consulted 8 June 2022) at: https://preply.com/en/d/e-learning-index/.

Suhendri (2021) Inclusive education in Indonesia: Collaboration among stakeholders. *International Perspectives on Inclusive Education* 17: 151–166. DOI: 10.1108/S1479-363620210000017015.

Thalgi MJ (2020) The university's role in developing the skills of the knowledge economy from the perspective of students of Yarmouk University's faculty of Shari'a and Islamic studies. *Journal of the Knowledge Economy* 11(4): 1529–1537. DOI: 10.1007/s13132-019-00620-5.

Times Higher Education (2022) *World University Rankings 2022*. Available (consulted 8 June 2022) at: https://www.timeshighereducation.com/world-university-rankings/2022#!/page/0/length/25/sort_by/rank/sort_order/asc/cols/scores.

Villouta EV, and Villarreal ET (2022) University access policies for persons with disabilities: Lessons from two Chilean universities. *International Journal of Educational Development* 91: 102577. DOI: 10.1016/j.ijedudev.2022.102577.

CHAPTER 13

Inclusiveness of Universities as the Basis for Achieving Strategic Academic Leadership in Russia

Konstantin V. Vodenko, Margarita A. Meretukova, Irina B. Khakonova and Marina G. Shadzhe

Abstract

Purpose: The purpose of the chapter is to study the inclusiveness of universities as a basis for achieving strategic academic leadership in Russia.

Design/methodology/approach: The objects for study in this article are the top 10 Russian universities that occupy the best positions in the Times Higher Education rankings in 2022. The results have proved that the cultural inclusiveness of universities is the basis for achieving strategic academic leadership in Russia.

Findings: The high level and important place of internationalization in the system of global competitiveness of Russian universities is substantiated. The forecast scenario of improving the positions of Russian universities in international rankings based on the management of cultural differences (internationalization) is modeled, which allows them to achieve leadership positions in THE World University Rankings solely due to the increase in international activity.

Originality/value: The article contributes to the literature by clarifying the features and revealing the unique experience of the internationalization of universities in modern Russia. The practical significance of the chapter is connected with the fact that the proposed authors' recommendations on managing cultural differences (internationalization) allow for improving the positions of Russian universities in international rankings and ensuring successful and accelerated practical implementation of the Priority 2030 program. The social significance of the article is that it has strengthened the scientific and methodological basis for the practical implementation of SDG 4 and SDG 9 in Russia.

Keywords

inclusiveness of universities – international education – strategic academic leadership – Russia – Priority 2030 – global competitiveness of universities – management of cultural differences in higher education

1   Introduction

At the beginning of the world-famous and supported (including in Russia) UN proclaimed "Decade of Action" in Russia, first (in 2021) the "Year of Science and Technology" was held, then (in 2022) the "Decade of Science and Technology" was announced (*Presidential Executive Office*, 2022). This provided increased strategic importance for the implementation of SDG 4 and SDG 9 in Russia in the period up to 2030 (inclusive, that is, until 2031). Against this background, the importance of implementing the Priority 2030 program, designed to provide Russia with strategic academic leadership, has increased even more (*Ministry of Science and Higher Education of the Russian Federation*, 2022).

Strategic academic leadership means not only technological sovereignty and breakthrough development of science and technology (which is traditionally successfully achieved in Russia) but also the leading positions of Russian universities in international university rankings. The insufficient pace of achieving high results in university rankings is an urgent scientific and practical problem (*Karpunina* et al., 2022; *Sozinova and Meteleva*, 2022). The difficulty in implementing the Priority 2030 program lies in the fundamental difference between the Russian university rankings (which Russian universities are used to focusing on) from international ratings (which need to be reoriented in the coming years).

It should be noted that significant progress has been made by Russian universities in strengthening their positions in international university rankings. For example, in 2011–2012, only two Russian universities were in the Times Higher Education rankings (2022): Lomonosov Moscow State University (276–300 place) and Saint Petersburg State University (350–400 place). Over the past ten years, the situation has changed radically – in 2022. 100 Russian universities are already included in this rating, and Lomonosov Moscow State University, the leader among universities representing Russia in the rating under consideration, has improved its position to 158 place (i.e., by two times).

Given the increased importance of internationalization of universities in determining their global competitiveness (assigning them positions in international university rankings), noted in the works of *Bennett* et al. (2021), *Ghedin*

(2021), *Maconi* et al. (2019), *Sharma and Vlcek* (2021), it is advisable to pay special and more depth attention to management practice cultural differences in Russian universities in order to make the most reliable picture about the prospects for the practical implementation of the Priority 2030 program. In this regard, the purpose of this article is defined as a study of the inclusiveness of universities as a basis for achieving strategic academic leadership in Russia.

2 Literature Review

In the existing literature, such authors as *Burdakov* et al. (2019), *Popkova* et al. (2018), *Shabalina* et al. (2021), *Sibirskaya* et al. (2019), *Vanchukhina* et al. (2019), *Vodenko* et al. (2016), *Vodenko* et al. (2019), *Yankovskaya* et al. (2021) note the high cultural inclusiveness of Russia as a historical multicultural society. At the same time, taking into account the focus of the Soviet model of science and higher education in the region of Eastern Europe and Central Asia, in the works of *Algozhina* et al. (2022), *Lei* (2021), *Schneijderberg* et al. (2021) indicates the limited (historically focused on this region) international activities of Russian universities. That is, despite the openness of Russian society to representatives of all cultures (the absence of cultural barriers), the internally-oriented policy of the state and corporate governance of Russian universities hinders their globalization, in particular, the influx of students and teachers from foreign countries.

In the works of *Abdul-Rahman* et al. (2022), *Hong and Xiao* (2022), and *Nuphanudin* et al. (2022), it is also noted that Russian universities, when managing competitiveness, focus not so much on the internationalization of their activities as on the high quality of higher education services provided, as well as on the high effectiveness of their activities and support for sustainable development of local communities, unlocking human potential and acceleration of the growth rate of the Russian economy.

The literature review revealed that the applied issues of internationalization (management of cultural differences) of Russian universities are insufficiently developed. Most of the existing publications on this topic are based on historical experience and do not sufficiently take into account modern realities and the recent experience of Russian universities. The uncertainty of the current level of inclusiveness (expressed in the degree of internationalization) of modern Russian universities and its contribution to the achievement of Russia's strategic academic leadership (from the standpoint of the position of Russian universities in international university rankings) acts as a research gap filled in this article.

3 Materials and Method

The objects for study in this article are the top 10 Russian universities that occupy the best positions in the *Times Higher Education* rankings (2022) in 2022 according to the criterion of support for SDG 10 "Reduced inequalities," and for which the values of the main indicators are available (from the base rating for 2022). The factual base of this study is collected in Table 13.1.

To achieve this goal, at the first stage of the study, the place of internalization in the system of global competitiveness of Russian universities is determined. For this purpose, methods of comparative analysis and analysis of variation are used. Using these methods, arithmetic averages and coefficients of variation of sub-indicators of global competitiveness of the studied universities are calculated. The differences in the overall level and in the spread of values between the indicators of internationalization (international outlook and support for SDG10 "Reduces inequalities") and other indicators taken into account in THE World University Rankings (teaching, research, citations, and industry income) are determined.

In the second stage of the study, a scenario for improving the positions of Russian universities in international rankings based on the management of cultural differences (internationalization) is modeled. To do this, a regression analysis method is used to quantify the contribution of university inclusiveness (international outlook and support for SDG 10 "Reduced inequalities") to their position in THE World University Rankings (rank and overall score) in 2022.

Based on the obtained regression dependencies, a change in the position of Russian universities in THE World University Rankings is predicted as they further internationalize. As a result, the authors' recommendations are proposed to improve the positions of Russian universities in international rankings according to the scenario of managing cultural differences (internationalization).

4 Results

4.1 *The place of Internalization in the System of Global Competitiveness of Russian Universities*

The place of internalization in the system of global competitiveness of Russian universities is defined in Chart 13.1 based on statistics from Table 13.1.

The results presented in Chart 13.1 indicate that internalization occupies an important place in the system of global competitiveness of Russian universities in 2022. Thus, according to the indicators of internationalization, one of the highest values is observed (43.62 points for international outlook and 55.69 points for support of SDG 10 "Reduced inequalities"), and at the same time, the smallest variation of these values (39.72% for international outlook and 28.94% for the support of SDG 10 "Reduced inequalities").

Consequently, a high level of internationalization (successful management of cultural differences) acts as a global competitive advantage for Russian universities, helping them to strengthen their positions in international university rankings.

4.2 Scenario for Improving the Positions of Russian Universities in International Rankings Based on the Management of Cultural Differences (Internationalization)

The contribution of university inclusiveness (international outlook and support for SDG 10 "Reduced inequalities") to their position in THE World University Rankings (rank and overall score) in 2022 was quantified based on data from Table 13.1 using the regression analysis method in Tables 13.2–13.3.

According to the results obtained in Table 13.2, with an increase in international outlook by 1 point, the position of Russian universities in THE World University Rankings in 2022 improves by 9.39 places. With an increase in support for SDG 10 "Reduced inequalities" by 1 point, the position of Russian universities in THE World University Rankings in 2022 improves by 9.96 places. Multiple correlation (78%) indicates a close relationship between the studied indicators. The model is reliable at a significance level of 0.05.

According to the results obtained in Table 13.3, with an increase in international outlook by 1 point, the overall score of Russian universities in THE World University Rankings in 2022 improves by 0.22 points. With an increase in support for SDG 10 "Reduced inequalities" by 1 point, the overall score of Russian universities in the THE World University Rankings in 2022 improves by 0.42 points. Multiple correlation (73%) indicates a close relationship of the studied indicators. The model is reliable at a significance level of 0.1.

Based on the obtained regression dependencies, a forecast scenario of changes in the position of Russian universities in the THE World University Rankings as they further internationalize is compiled (Chart 13.2).

According to the modeled scenario, in order to achieve strategic academic leadership (1st place in the THE World University Rankings), Russian universities do not even have to reach the maximum (100 points) values of internationalization indicators – for this, it is enough to increase international outlook to 97.24 points (by 122.91% compared to 43.62 points in 2022), as well as to increase support for SDG 10 "Reduced inequalities" to 97.07 points (by 74.31%

TABLE 13.1 The position of the top 10 Russian universities in the Times Higher Education ranking in 2022

University	Rank (y1)	Overall THE score (y2)	Teaching	Research	Citations	Industry income	International outlook (x1)	Support for SDG 10 "Reduces inequalities" (x2)
Far Eastern Federal University	1201+	10.6 (10.6–22.3)	20.5	11.8	16.8	41.6	51.7	35.5 (5.2–35.5)
Immanuel Kant Baltic Federal University	1201+	22.3 (10.6–22.3)	22.6	10.7	12.8	38.3	43.6	62.4 (55.1–62.4)
Ivanovo State University of Chemistry and Technology	1201+	22.3 (10.6–22.3)	15.9	10.4	0.7	34.8	21.1	35.5 (5.2–35.5)
National Research Nuclear University MEPhI	500(401–500)	44.0 (40.9–44.0)	42.8	40.5	29.6	100.0	69.7	62.4 (55.1–62.4)
Perm National Research Polytechnic University	1201+	22.3 (10.6–22.3)	20.5	10.4	4.2	57.4	18.2	62.4 (55.1–62.4)
Peter the Great St Petersburg Polytechnic University	350(301–350)	48.0 (46.1–48.0)	27.8	18.4	87.1	77.7	56.9	62.4 (55.1–62.4)
Plekhanov Russian University of Economics	600(501–600)	40.8 (38.1–40.8)	23.3	11.0	81.5	37.4	36.0	72.5 (62.5–72.5)

INCLUSIVENESS OF UNIVERSITIES AS THE BASIS 197

University	Rank (y1)	Overall THE score (y2)	Teaching	Research	Citations	Industry income	International outlook (x1)	Support for SDG 10 "Reduces inequalities" (x2)
RUDN University	800 (601–800)	37.9 (32.0–37.9)	37.6	19.2	33.0	40.4	62.8	72.6
South Ural State University	1200 (1001–1200)	27.1 (22.4–27.1)	17.3	11.8	46.2	40.6	32.6	35.5 (5.2–35.5)
Voronezh State University	1201+	22.3 (10.6–22.3)	19.3	9.7	3.9	35.9	34.2	35.5 (5.2–35.5)

SOURCE: COMPILED BY THE AUTHORS BASED ON THE MATERIALS OF *TIMES HIGHER EDUCATION* (2022)

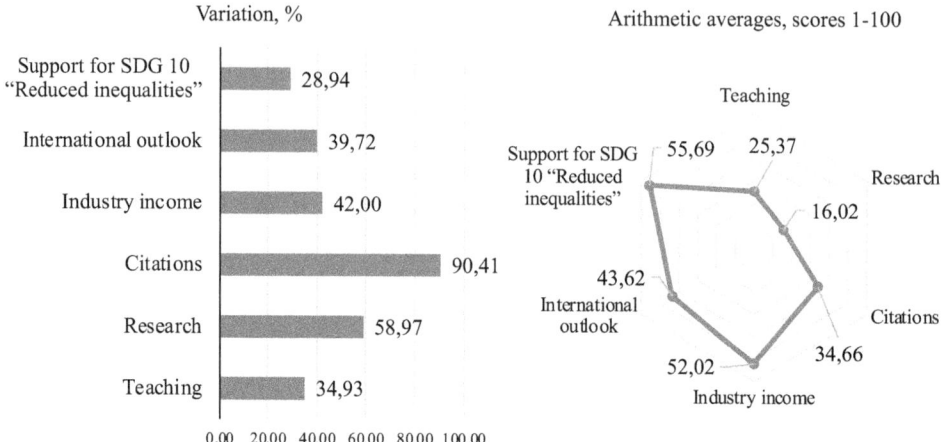

CHART 13.1 The place of internalization in the system of global competitiveness of Russian universities in 2022
SOURCE: CALCULATED AND CONSTRUCTED BY THE AUTHORS

compared to 55.69 points in 2022). This will increase the overall score to 59.58 points (by 94.76% compared to 30.59 points in 2022).

To improve the positions of Russian universities in international rankings according to the described scenario of management of cultural differences (internationalization), the following authors' recommendations are proposed:
– Further strengthening of international partnerships with the countries of Central Asia and Eastern Europe;
– Development of international cooperation with non-CIS countries, where there is a potentially high demand for studying at Russian universities. As an example, we can cite the successful long-term experience of Russian-Chinese student exchange and training of international students.

Any special management measures to overcome cultural differences are not required since Russian universities are characterized by a high level of cultural inclusiveness.

5 Discussion

Thus, the article contributes to the literature by clarifying the features and revealing the unique experience of internationalization of universities in modern Russia. Unlike *Algozhina* et al. (2022), *Lei* (2021), and *Schneijderberg* et al. (2021), it has been proved that the international activities of Russian universities are not restrained, but on the contrary – very active and serve as a global

TABLE 13.2 Regression analysis of the dependence of rank on the indicators of internationalization of Russian universities in 2022

Regression statistics

Multiple R	0.78
R-Square	0.60
Adjusted R-Square	0.49
Standard Error	248.51
Observations	10

ANOVA

	df	ss	MS	F	Significance F
Regression	2	652485.77	326242.89	5.28	0.04
Residual	7	432316.73	61759.53		
Total	9	1084802.50			

	Coefficients	Standard error	t-Stat	P-Value	Lower 95%	Upper 95%
Constant	1880.71	305.52	6.16	0.00	1158.27	2603.15
International outlook (x_1)	-9.39	5.19	-1.81	0.11	-21.66	2.87
Support for SDG 10 "Reduces inequalities" (x_2)	-9.96	5.58	-1.79	0.12	-23.14	3.23

SOURCE: CALCULATED AND COMPILED BY THE AUTHORS

TABLE 13.3   Regression analysis of the dependence of the overall score on the indicators of internationalization of Russian universities in 2022

Regression statistics

Multiple R	0.73
R-Square	0.53
Adjusted R-Square	0.40
Standard Error	9.38
Observations	10

ANOVA

	df	SS	MS	F	Significance F
Regression	2	705.06	352.53	4.01	0.07
Residual	7	615.35	87.91		
Total	9	1320.40			

	Coefficients	Standard error	t-Stat	P-Value	Lower 95%	Upper 95%
Constant	-1.77	11.53	-0.15	0.88	-29.02	25.49
International outlook (x_1)	0.22	0.20	1.10	0.31	-0.25	0.68
Support for SDG 10 "Reduces inequalities" (x_2)	0.42	0.21	1.98	0.09	-0.08	0.91

SOURCE: CALCULATED AND COMPILED BY THE AUTHORS

competitive advantage. This indicates the fundamental difference between the development model of modern Russian universities (externally oriented) and the Soviet (internally oriented) model.

In contrast to *Abdul-Rahaman* et al. (2022), *Hong and Xiao* (2022), and *Nuphanudin* et al. (2022), it has been proved that the internationalization of the activities of Russian universities makes a great contribution to their global competitiveness. In this regard, for the practical implementation of the Priority 2030 program, a revision of university development strategies by focusing on international activities is necessary.

6 Conclusion

So, the results obtained in his chapter prove that the cultural inclusiveness of universities is the basis for achieving strategic academic leadership in Russia. The high level (on average, 43.62 points in international outlook and 55.69 points in support of SDG 10 "Reduced inequalities") and the important place of internationalization in the system of global competitiveness of Russian universities have been justified (international activity determines the place in the rating by 78% and the overall score by 73% in this rating in 2022).

The forecast scenario has been modeled for improving the positions of Russian universities in international rankings based on the management of cultural differences (internationalization), which allows, solely due to the increase in international activity, to increase the overall score to 59.58 points (by 94.76% compared to 2022) and achieve leadership positions (1st place) in the THE World University Rankings.

The theoretical significance of this chapter is that the results obtained and the conclusions drawn clarified the current (high) level of inclusiveness (expressed in the degree of internationalization) of modern Russian universities and justified its significant contribution to achieving strategic academic leadership in Russia (from the position of Russian universities in international university rankings).

The practical significance of the chapter is connected with the fact that the proposed authors' recommendations on managing cultural differences

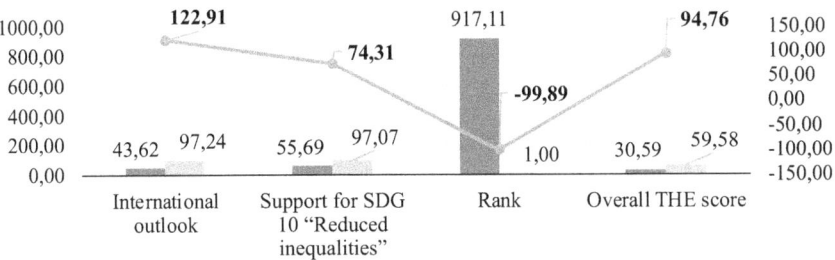

CHART 13.2 Scenario for improving the positions of Russian universities in international rankings based on the management of cultural differences (internationalization)
SOURCE: CALCULATED AND CONSTRUCTED BY THE AUTHORS

(internationalization) allow for improving the positions of Russian universities in international rankings and ensuring successful and accelerated practical implementation of the Priority 2030 program. The social significance of the article is that it has strengthened the scientific and methodological basis for the practical implementation of SDG 4 and SDG 9 in Russia.

Acknowledgments

The research was performed within the grant of the President of the Russian Federation for state support for the leading scientific schools of the Russian Federation (NSh-239.2022.2) "Academic leadership in the space of development of transprofessional identity and formation of the new economy market in the conditions of digitalization and regionalization of higher education."

References

Presidential Executive Office (2022) *Decree "On the announcement of the Decade of Science and Technology in the Russian Federation"* (April 25, 2022 No. 231). Moscow, Russia. Available (consulted 11 June 2022) at: http://kremlin.ru/acts/news/68278.

Abdul-Rahaman N, Terentev E, and Arkorful VE (2022) COVID-19 and distance learning: International doctoral students' satisfaction with the general quality of learning and aspects of university support in Russia. *Public Organization Review* DOI: 10.1007/s11115-022-00608-x.

Algozhina A, Sabirova R, Alimbayeva R, Kapbasova G, and Sarmantayev A (2022) Cross-cultural study of the qualitative aspects of higher education teachers' emotional intelligence: Kazakhstan and Russia. *Journal of Applied Research in Higher Education* 14(3): 1099–1113. DOI: 10.1108/JARHE-03-2021-0102.

Bennett S, Gallagher TL, Somma M, White R, and Wlodarczyk K (2021) Transitioning from segregation to inclusion: An effective and sustainable model to promote inclusion, through internal staffing adjustments, and role redefinition. *International Perspectives on Inclusive Education* 15: 103–116. DOI: 10.1108/S1479-363620210000015009.

Burdakova G, Byankin A, Usanov I, and Pankova L (2019) Smart technologies in education and formation of entrepreneurial competencies. *IOP Conference Series: Materials Science and Engineering* 497(1): 012066. DOI: 10.1088/1757-899X/497/1/012066.

Ghedin E (2021) Social innovation through collaboration for enabling educational inclusive ecosystems: Following Italy's lead. *International Perspectives on Inclusive Education* 17: 71–96. DOI: 10.1108/S1479-363620210000017008.

Hong M, and Xiao Y (2022) Strategies and challenges to University Internationalization in Russia: A case study of S University. *Policy Futures in Education.* DOI: 10.1177/14782103221089470.

Karpunina EK, Moskovtceva LV, Zabelina OV, Zubareva NN, and Tsykora AV (2022) *Socio-economic impact of the COVID-19 pandemic on OECD countries.* In: Popkova EG, and Andronova IV (eds) *Current problems of the world economy and international trade.* Bingley, UK: Emerald Publishing Limited, 103–114. DOI: 10.1108/S0190-128120220000042011.

Lei S (2021) Experience and Prospects of Cooperation between Beijing Institute of Technology and Russia in Higher Education. *Vestnik Sankt-Peterburgskogo Universiteta, Istoriya* 66(1): 114–131. DOI: 10.21638/11701/SPBU02.2021.107.

Maconi ML, Green SE, and Bingham SC (2019) It's not all about coursework: Narratives of inclusion and exclusion among university students receiving disability accommodations. *International Perspectives on Inclusive Education* 13: 181–194. DOI: 10.1108/S1479-363620190000013014.

Ministry of Science and Higher Education of the Russian Federation (2022) *Priority 2030: Leaders are Made, Not Born.* Available (consulted 11 June 2022) at: https://priority2030.ru/en.

Nuphanudin, Komariah A, Shvetsova T., Gardanova Z, Podzorova M, Achmad Kurniady O, ... Kosov M (2022) Effectiveness of students' motivation factors in the competency-based approach: A case study of universities in Russia and Indonesia. *Emerging Science Journal* 6(3): 578–602. DOI: 10.28991/ESJ-2022-06-03-012.

Popkova EG, Popova EV, and Sergi BS (2018) *Clusters and innovational networks toward sustainable growth.* In: Sergi BS (ed) *Exploring the future of Russia's economy and markets: Towards sustainable economic development.* Bingley, UK: Emerald Publishing Limited, 107–124. DOI: 10.1108/978-1-78769-397-520181006.

Schneijderberg C, Götze N, Jones GA, Bilyalov D, Panova A, Stephenson GK, ... Yudkevich M (2021) Does vertical university stratification foster or hinder academics' societal engagement? Findings from Canada, Germany, Kazakhstan, and Russia. *Higher Education Policy* 34(1): 66–87. DOI: 10.1057/s41307-020-00219-5.

Shabaltina LV, Karbekova AB, Milkina E, and Pushkarev IY (2021) *The social impact of the downturn in business and the new context of sustainable development in the context of the 2020 economic crisis in developing countries.* In: Popkova EG, and Sergi BS (eds) *Modern global economic system: Evolutional development vs. revolutionary leap.* Cham, Switzerland: Springer, 74–82. DOI: 10.1007/978-3-030-69415-9_9.

Sharma U, and Vlcek S (2021) Global trends in the funding of inclusive education: A narrative review. *International Perspectives on Inclusive Education* 15: 51–65. DOI: 10.1108/S1479-363620210000015006.

Sibirskaya E, Popkova E, Oveshnikova L, and Tarasova I (2019) Remote education vs traditional education based on effectiveness at the micro level and its connection to the level of development of macro-economic systems. *International Journal of Educational Management* 33(3): 533–543. DOI: 10.1108/IJEM-08-2018-0248.

Sozinova AA, and Meteleva OA (2022) Sites of states with a dynamically developing socio-political structure and economy: Analyzing forms and methods of obtaining competitive advantages of transnational (global) companies. In: Popkova EG, and Andronova IV (eds) *Current problems of the world economy and international trade.* Bingley, UK: Emerald Publishing Limited, 233–242. DOI: 10.1108/S0190-128120220000042022.

Times Higher Education (2022) *World University Rankings 2022.* Available (consulted 11 June 2022) at: https://www.timeshighereducation.com/world-university-rankings/2022#!/page/0/length/25/locations/RUS/sort_by/rank/sort_order/asc/cols/stats .

Vanchukhina L, Leybert T, Rogacheva A, Rudneva Y, and Khalikova E (2019) *New model of managerial education in technical university. International Journal of Educational Management* 33(3): 511–524.

Vodenko KV, Bokachev IA, Levchenko NA, Rodionova VI, and Shvachkina LA (2016) The specific features of a government control over higher education, considering the interests of parties to the social and labour relations. *Social Sciences (Pakistan)* 11(21): 5241–5246. DOI: 10.3923/sscience.2016.5241.5246.

Vodenko KV, Komissarova MA, and Kulikov MM (2019) Modernization of the standards of education and personnel training due to development of industry 4.0 in the conditions of knowledge economy's formation. In: Popkova E, Ragulina Y, and Bogoviz A (eds) *Industry 4.0: Industrial revolution of the 21st century.* Cham, Switzerland: Springer, 183–192. DOI: 10.1007/978-3-319-94310-7_18.

Yankovskaya VV, Osipov VS, Zeldner AG, Panova TV, and Mishchenko VV (2021) Institutional matrix of social management in region's economy: Stability and sustainability vs innovations and digitalization. *International Journal of Sociology and Social Policy* 41(1–2): 178–191. DOI: 10.1108/IJSSP-03-2020-0088.

CHAPTER 14

Differences in Approaches to Achieving Inclusiveness between Leading and Regional Universities in Russia

Legal Aspects

Olesya P. Kazachenok, Aziza B. Karbekova, Zuriet A. Zhade and Azamat M. Shadzhe

Abstract

This chapter aims to explore the legal dimension of the differences in approaches to achieving inclusiveness between the leading and regional universities in Russia. The research results reveal the essence and specificity of approaches to achieving inclusiveness in leading and regional universities in Russia. The compiled institutional model for ensuring the inclusiveness of universities in Russia reveals the legal aspect of this process, which consists of the regulatory and legal consolidation of different forms of inclusiveness in higher education and science and different requirements for universities, depending on their target forms of inclusiveness. The chapter contributes to the development of scientific provisions of the Theory of Inclusiveness of Universities through the disclosure of the legal aspect of managing the inclusiveness of universities (using the strategic academic leadership program "Priority 2030" in Russia as an example) and through clarifying the classification of universities by the criterion of approach to achieving inclusiveness with the separation of leading and regional universities. The theoretical significance of this chapter is that it has clarified the causal links of the achievement of inclusiveness by universities, showing how universities can and should meet today's requirements for inclusiveness. The novelty of this chapter is that it substantiates the central role of regulators in ensuring the inclusiveness of public universities in developing countries. The practical significance of this chapter lies in the fact that the author's conclusions have strengthened the scientific and methodological support of the "Priority 2030" program and can be used to accelerate and most effectively achieve Russia's strategic academic leadership.

Keywords

inclusiveness – strategic academic leadership – "Priority 2030" – leading universities – regional universities – Russia – normative and legal regulation – institutes – legal aspect

1   Introduction

Inclusiveness of universities is a major focus at the university, national (strategies for inclusiveness are adopted in state regulation of science and higher education), and international levels (in particular, in international university rankings). The problem lies in the contradiction between the capabilities of universities and the requirements for inclusiveness (*Perera* et al., 2021).

For example, in recent years, international university rankings have increasingly focused on the cultural (attracting international students and international faculty) and gender (increasing the proportion of women and achieving gender balance in the academic community) inclusiveness of universities (*Chambers and Forlin*, 2021). However, regional universities have traditionally focused on local culture and the provision of higher education services to local residents with low geographic mobility (*Sharma* et al., 2017). Although regional universities significantly contribute to the development of the knowledge economy (social progress, human development) in the regions, they do not meet the criteria and are not included in university rankings (*Popkova* et al., 2022; *Sibirskaya* et al., 2019).

In another example, leading technical universities are inherently more attractive to male students and teaching staff. Assessing the inclusiveness of leading technical universities from a gender-neutral perspective puts them at a disadvantage over liberal arts universities, although technical universities are driving industrial revolutions and creating breakthrough innovations (*Abu-Alghayth*, 2021). In another example, the government is interested in increasing the publication activity and citation rate of teaching staff. Nevertheless, some universities specialize in providing higher education services while R&D is secondary. Despite the outstanding quality of education, these universities do not meet the formal criteria for inclusiveness and do not qualify for university rankings (*Semon* et al., 2021).

These examples demonstrate the institutional trap of university rankings (both national and international), which impose exaggerated requirements that are unattainable by universities on a large scale. Created by relying on the unique characteristics of leading universities, rankings have become increasingly elitist, closed, and inaccessible to the broad participation of universities (*Sharma* et al., 2015; *Suhendri*, 2021).

Russia has launched the "Priority 2030" program, designed to overcome the described "institutional trap" by improving the legal and regulatory framework for managing the inclusiveness of universities. This is accomplished through the regulatory and legal recognition of differences in approaches to achieving inclusiveness between the leading and regional universities in Russia. This chapter aims to explore the legal aspect of the differences in approaches to achieving inclusiveness between the leading and regional universities in Russia.

2   Literature Review

This research is based on the Theory of Inclusiveness of Universities, which treats inclusiveness as a tool to achieve the competitiveness of the university and the implementation of the functions of the system of science and higher education. *Bogoviz* et al. (2018), *Burdakova* et al. (2019), *Makhamatova* et al. (2019), *Timchenko* et al. (2021), *Vinnikova* et al. (2021), and *Yankovskaya* et al. (2022) note that while inclusiveness can take many forms, it is a general concept that reflects openness, social justice (equity), flexibility, and transparency in the university.

Bodhi et al. (2022), *Edwards* (2022), *Nazarova and Lobanova* (2022), and *Solis-Grant* et al. (2022) note that the approach to university inclusiveness is universal and involves removing any barriers to potential and current participants in the academic community. Based on the experience of private universities from developed countries, *Afacan* et al. (2021), *Espada-Chavarria* et al. (2021), *Ward* et al. (2022), and *Warren* et al. (2021) argue that the growth of inclusiveness in today's universities is dictated by the market.

The literature review showed that although the existing publications form a clear idea of the requirements for the inclusiveness of today's universities, it remains unclear how exactly the university can and should meet these requirements. Based on current practice, it is difficult or even impossible for any university to meet all of its requirements at once. This is the research gap that this chapter fills.

3   Materials and Methods

In this chapter, the study is conducted in two consecutive stages. The first stage is a quantitative study. The authors apply the method of correlation analysis to determine the relationship of indicators of various manifestations of inclusiveness (financial – the number of FTE Students and the number of students per staff; cultural – the number of international students; gender – Female: Male ratio based on the materials of *Times Higher Education* (2022) for 2022) with the overall indicator of competitiveness score as a reflection of the general inclusiveness of universities. This reveals the differences in approaches to achieving inclusiveness between the leading and regional universities in Russia. The top ten universities from Russia and the top ten regional universities from Russia in 2022, as ranked by Times Higher Education rating (Table 14.1), are chosen as the research objects.

The second stage involves qualitative research. Based on the methodology of neo-institutionalism, the authors developed an institutional model of university inclusiveness in Russia. The normative-legal support for the development of science and higher education in Russia is reconsidered from the perspective of influencing the management of the inclusiveness of Russian universities. The legal aspect of ensuring the inclusiveness of universities in Russia in implementing the "Priority 2030" program is disclosed.

4   Results

4.1   *Approaches to Achieving Inclusiveness by Leading and Regional Universities in Russia*

Using the method of correlation analysis based on the statistics from Table 14.1, the authors determined the average level and relationship of indicators of various manifestations of inclusiveness with the overall score as a reflection of the general inclusiveness of universities (Chart 14.1).

As shown in Chart 14.1, the approach to managing inclusiveness in the leading universities of Russia is based on financial (by increasing the number of students at the expense of budgetary places: the average number of FTE Students is 13.65; their correlation with the overall score is 16.02%) and cultural inclusiveness (by attracting international students, whose share averages 23.40%; their correlation with the overall score is 35.50%). Gender inclusiveness is secondary or even of little importance to leading universities (correlation with the overall score is -2.98%).

TABLE 14.1 Indicators of inclusiveness of Russia's leading and regional universities in 2022

Category	University	Overall score, score 1–100	No. of FTE students	No. of students per teaching staff	International students, %	Female: Male ratio (share of women), %
Leading universities	Lomonosov Moscow State University	56.8	29,118	9.1	36	54
	Moscow Institute of Physics and Technology (MIPT)	53.9 (50.4–53.9)	5,920	11.6	18	26
	Peter the Great St Petersburg Polytechnic University	48.0 (46.1–48.0)	16,550	9.6	32	39
	National Research Nuclear University MEPhI	44.0 (40.9–44.0)	5,162	9.5	30	38
	Saint-Petersburg Mining University	44.0 (40.9–44.0)	7,753	11.5	11	43
	Plekhanov Russian University of Economics	40.8 (38.1–40.8)	14,450	8.8	13	61
	ITMO University	37.9 (32.0–37.9)	11,089	16.4	20	36
	National University of Science and Technology (MISiS)	37.9 (32.0–37.9)	7,207	10.9	27	40
	RUDN University	37.9 (32.0–37.9)	21,203	13.3	34	58
	Bauman Moscow State Technical University	31.9 (27.2–31.9)	18,011	6.5	13	34

(cont.)

Category	University	Overall score, score 1–100	No. of FTE students	No. of students per teaching staff	International students, %	Female: Male ratio (share of women), %
Regional universities	Kazan Federal University	31.9 (27.2–31.9)	22,587	10.2	30	75
	Tomsk Polytechnic University	31.9 (27.2–31.9)	8,794	9.2	28	32
	Siberian Federal University	27.1 (22.4–27.1)	10,168	19.3	12	35
	South Ural State University	27.1 (22.4–27.1)	20,326	14.2	9	41
	Ural Federal University	27.1 (22.4–27.1)	27,099	13.0	16	49
	Volgograd State Technical University	27.1 (22.4–27.1)	13,307	14.1	8	31
	Bashkir State University	22.3 (10.6–22.3)	14,605	13.4	3	60
	Belgorod State National Research University	22.3 (10.6–22.3)	13,290	14.8	18	63
	Immanuel Kant Baltic Federal University	22.3 (10.6–22.3)	7,306	9.3	12	62
	Irkutsk State University	22.3 (10.6–22.3)	13,039	13.5	5	68

SOURCE: COMPILED BY THE AUTHORS BASED ON *TIMES HIGHER EDUCATION* (2022)

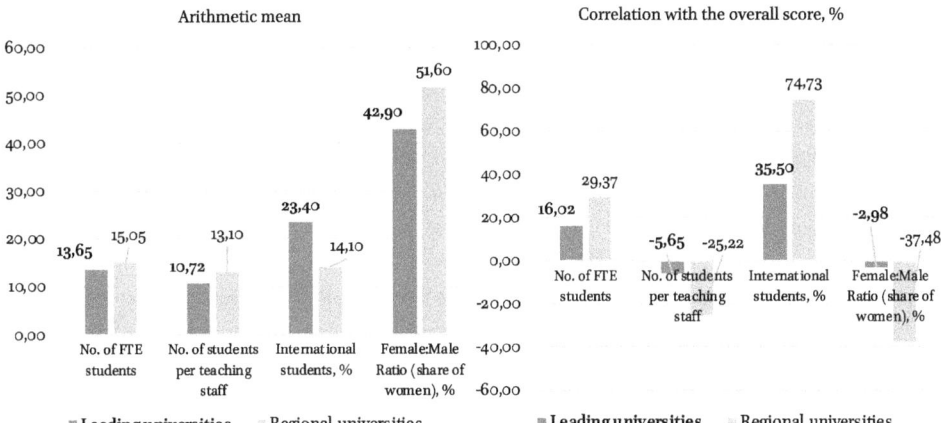

CHART 14.1 Relation of inclusiveness indicators to the competitiveness of Russian universities in 2022
SOURCE: CALCULATED AND COMPILED BY THE AUTHORS

In contrast to leading universities, the approach to managing inclusiveness in regional universities of Russia is based on ensuring financial inclusiveness but not so much on attracting students (although this is also important: the average number of students per teaching staff is 15.05, which is even higher than in the leading universities; correlation with the overall score is 29.37%).

The approach of regional universities suggests a significant role of faculty in optimizing the ratio of the number of students per staff (on average, 10.72%, which is even more than in the leading universities; the correlation with the overall score is -25.22%). Cultural inclusiveness is also important (correlation with the overall score is 74.73%; however, this correlation is secondary: the share of international students averages 14.10%). Gender inclusiveness is not required for regional universities (correlation with the overall score is -37.48%).

Thus, the authors revealed differences in approaches to achieving inclusiveness by the leading and regional universities in Russia. Leading universities in Russia increase their inclusiveness by increasing the impact of research and internationalizing their activities. Regional universities in Russia increase inclusiveness by improving the quality and accessibility of higher education in the regions.

4.2 Institutional Model and Legal Aspects of Ensuring the Inclusiveness of Universities in Russia

The identified differences in approaches to achieving inclusiveness between the leading and regional universities lie in the peculiarities of state regulation of the system of science and higher education in Russia. These features are reflected in the institutional model of inclusiveness of universities in Russia, presented in Figure 14.1.

As shown in Figure 14.1, the "Priority 2030" program proclaims university inclusiveness as a strategic goal for Russia, but universities from different categories focus on different forms of inclusiveness. Thus, when selecting participants for the "Priority 2030" program, the Government of the Russian Federation and the *Ministry of Science and Higher Education* (2022a, 2022b) held two separate competitions.

The first competition was held in the area of research leadership, the goal of which was set for national research universities (NRU) and national flagship universities (NFU). At the launch of the "Priority 2030" program, the *Ministry of Science and Higher Education* of the Russian Federation (2022a) established performance indicators of leading universities (NRU and NFU), including significant revenues from R&D, the number of protection documents for intellectual property issued by patent offices of OECD countries, and a significant share of international students and international teachers.

The second competition was held in the area of territorial leadership and industry leadership, the tasks of which were set for regional universities (federal universities and regional flagship universities). When the *Ministry of Science and Higher Education* (2022a) launched the "Priority 2030" program, it established performance indicators for regional universities, including extensive experience of administrative and managerial staff, the qualifications and

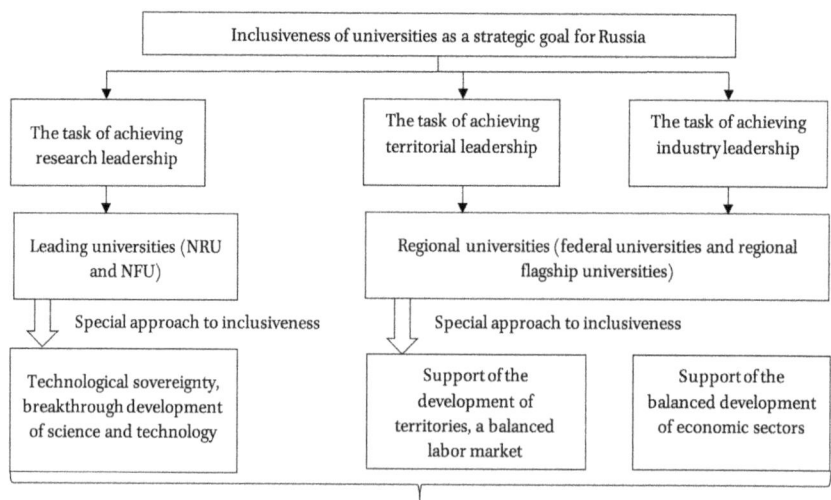

FIGURE 14.1 The institutional model of inclusiveness of Universities in Russia

experience of teaching staff, and internships and professional development of teaching staff.

As a result, the leading universities ensure technological sovereignty and breakthrough development of science and technology in Russia. Regional universities provide support for the development of territories, a balanced labor market, and support for the balanced development of sectors of the economy. All universities have a common goal of entering the top 500 institutional or subject rankings ARWU, QS, and THE, as well as increasing the number of publications in the top 1% of the most cited in scientific journals indexed by the Web of Science Core Collection (Highly Cited Papers) and Scopus. This provides a systemic result – strategic academic leadership for Russia.

5 Discussion

The chapter contributes to the development of scientific positions of the Theory of Inclusiveness of Universities through the disclosure of the legal aspect of managing the inclusiveness of universities (on the example of the "Priority 2030" program in Russia) and through clarification of the classification of universities by the criterion of approach to achieve inclusiveness with separation of leading and regional universities. In contrast to *Bogoviz* et al. (2018), *Burdakova* et al. (2019), *Makhamatova* et al. (2019), *Timchenko* et al. (2021), *Vinnikova* et al. (2021), and *Yankovskaya* et al. (2022), this chapter reasoned that inclusiveness is highly differentiated. The chapter demonstrated that each university focuses and achieves the best results in the unique (different from other universities) forms of inclusiveness it has chosen.

In contrast to *Bodhi* et al. (2022), *Edwards* (2022), *Nazarova and Lobanova* (2022), and *Solis-Grant* et al. (2022), the authors proved that universities take different approaches to ensuring their inclusiveness by removing some barriers to potential and current participants in the academic community. In contrast to *Afacan* et al. (2021), *Espada-Chavarria* et al. (2021), *Ward* et al. (2022), and *Warren* et al. (2021), it has been argued that in developing countries dominated by public universities, the growth of their inclusiveness is largely determined by regulatory enforcement and government regulation (and not just and not so much by the market).

6 Conclusion

Thus, we can conclude that the conducted research has revealed the legal aspect of the differences in approaches to achieving inclusiveness between the leading and regional universities in Russia. The essence and peculiarities of approaches to achieving inclusiveness by leading and regional universities in Russia are revealed. The approach to increasing the inclusiveness of leading universities is based on increasing research output and internationalization. The approach to increasing the inclusiveness of regional universities involves improving the quality and accessibility of higher education services in the regions.

The compiled institutional model for ensuring the inclusiveness of universities in Russia revealed the legal aspect of this process, which consists in the regulatory and legal consolidation of different forms of inclusiveness in higher education and science, as well as different requirements for universities, depending on their target forms of inclusiveness. In Russia, the "Priority 2030" program has set a task for the leading universities to ensure technological sovereignty and breakthrough development of science and technology in Russia. Regional universities are tasked with supporting the development of territories, a balanced labor market, and the balanced development of sectors of the economy.

The theoretical significance of the research is that it has clarified the causal links of the achievement of inclusiveness by universities by showing how universities can and should meet today's requirements for inclusiveness. The novelty of this chapter lies in its justification of the central role of regulators in making public universities inclusive in developing countries. The practical significance of the research lies in the fact that the author's conclusions have strengthened the scientific and methodological support of the "Priority 2030" program and can be used to accelerate and most effectively achieve Russia's strategic academic leadership.

The compiled institutional model clearly demonstrated the powers and responsibilities of state regulators and universities in ensuring the inclusiveness of science and higher education in Russia. Thus, it can be used to improve the effectiveness of managing inclusiveness in Russian universities. The experience of Russia will be useful to other developing countries because it can serve as a successful example of regulatory support for inclusive public universities.

Nevertheless, the focus on the Russian experience is a limitation of this chapter. Future studies should explore the legal aspects of inclusiveness in public universities in other developing countries to clarify the specifics of their institutional models for achieving openness in national systems of higher education and science.

References

Abu-Alghayth KM (2021) Instructional collaboration in Saudi inclusive and mainstream education. *International Perspectives on Inclusive Education* 17: 41–54. DOI: 10.1108/S1479-363620210000017006.

Afacan K., Bal A, Artiles AJ, Cakir HI, Ko D, Mawene D, ... Kim H (2021) Inclusive knowledge production at an elementary school through family-school-university partnerships: A formative intervention study. *Learning, Culture and Social Interaction* 31(Part A): 100569. DOI: 10.1016/j.lcsi.2021.100569.

Bodhi R, Singh T, Joshi Y, and Sangroya D (2022) Impact of psychological factors, university environment and sustainable behaviour on teachers' intention to incorporate inclusive education in higher education. *International Journal of Educational Management* 36(4): 381–396. DOI: 10.1108/IJEM-02-2020-0113.

Bogoviz A, Averin A, and Yanovskaya V (2018) Gender analysis of local budgets in law enforcement and educational organizations of Russia. *MATEC Web of Conferences* 212: 09015. DOI: 10.1051/matecconf/201821209015.

Burdakova G, Byankin A, Usanov I, and Pankova L (2019) Smart technologies in education and formation of entrepreneurial competencies. *IOP Conference Series: Materials Science and Engineering* 497(1): 012066. DOI: 10.1088/1757-899X/497/1/012066.

Chambers D, and Forlin C (2021) An historical ethnography of the enactment of Rawl's Theory of Justice as applied to the education of learners with disability in Western Australia. *International Journal of Inclusive Education.* DOI: 10.1080/13603116.2021.1941322.

Edwards M (2022) Inclusive learning and teaching for Australian online university students with disability: A literature review. *International Journal of Inclusive Education* 26(5): 510–525. DOI: 10.1080/13603116.2019.1698066.

Espada-Chavarria R, Diaz-Vega M, and González-Montesino RH (2021) Open innovation for an inclusive labor market for university students with disabilities. *Journal of Open Innovation: Technology, Market, and Complexity* 7(4): 217. DOI: 10.3390/joitmc7040217.

Makhamatova ST, Makhamatov TM, and Makhamatov TT (2019) Dialectics of equality and justice in the economic theory of Karl Marx. In: Alpidovskaya ML, and Popkova EG (eds) *Marx and Modernity: A political and economic analysis of social systems management.* Charlotte, NC: Information Age Publishing, 215–224.

Ministry of Science and Higher Education (2022a) *Selection of participants in the "Priority 2030" program*. Available (consulted 14 June 2022) at: https://priority2 030.ru/upload/medialibrary/629/3mhkzikbyq4471gtyy83i19lxgzo2r3n/Otbor-ucha stnikov-v-programmu.pdf.

Ministry of Science and Higher Education (2022b) *Strategic Academic Leadership Program*. Available (consulted 14 June 2022) at: https://fgosvo.ru/uploadfiles/met hod/Program_strategyc_leadership.pdf.

Nazarova OL, and Lobanova EE (2022) Contemporary Conditions of Efficient Implementation of Inclusive Education at the University. *Journal of Higher Education Theory and Practice* 22(3): 142–149. DOI: 10.33423/jhetp.v22i3.5089.

Perera VH, Moriña A, Sánchez-díaz N, and Spínola-elias Y (2021) Technological platforms for inclusive practice at university: A qualitative analysis from the perspective of Spanish faculty members. *Sustainability* 13(9): 4755. DOI: 10.3390/su13094755.

Popkova EG, Bogoviz AV, Lobova SV, Chililov AM, Sozinova AA, and Sergi BS (2022) Changing entrepreneurial attitudes for mitigating the global pandemic's social drama. *Humanities and Social Sciences Communications* 9(1): 141. DOI: 10.1057/ s41599-022-01151-2.

Semon S, Lane D, and Jones P (2021) Mapping collaboration across international inclusive educational contexts. *International Perspectives on Inclusive Education* 17: 1–6. DOI: 10.1108/S1479-363620210000017002.

Sharma U, Forlin C, Marella M, and Jitoko F (2017) Using indicators as a catalyst for inclusive education in the Pacific Islands. *International Journal of Inclusive Education* 21(7): 730–746. DOI: 10.1080/13603116.2016.1251979.

Sharma U, Simi J, and Forlin C (2015) Preparedness of pre-service teachers for inclusive education in the Solomon Islands. *Australian Journal of Teacher Education* 40(5): 103–116. DOI: 10.14221/ajte.2015v40n5.6.

Sibirskaya E, Popkova E, Oveshnikova L, and Tarasova I (2019) Remote education vs traditional education based on effectiveness at the micro level and its connection to the level of development of macro-economic systems. *International Journal of Educational Management* 33(3): 533–543. DOI: 10.1108/IJEM-08-2018-0248.

Solis-Grant MJ, Espinoza-Parçet C, Sepúlveda-Carrasco C, Pérez-Villalobos C, Rodríguez-Núñez I, Pincheira-Martínez C, … Aránguiz-Ibarra D (2022) Inclusion at universities: Psychometric properties of an inclusive management scale as perceived by students. *PLoS ONE* 17(1): e0262011. DOI: 10.1371/journal.pone.0262011.

Suhendri (2021) Inclusive education in Indonesia: Collaboration among stakeholders. *International Perspectives on Inclusive Education* 17: 151–166. DOI: 10.1108/ S1479-363620210000017015.

Timchenko OV, Timchenko AB, Abakumova SI, Mansurova AA, and Suyunova GB (2021) Tools of intellectual systems in the context of problems of organization of open education. In: Popkova EG, and Ostrovskaya VN (eds) *Meta-scientific study of artificial intelligence*. Charlotte, NC: Information Age Publishing, 271–278.

Times Higher Education (2022) *World University Rankings 2022*. Available (consulted 12 June 2022) at: https://www.timeshighereducation.com/world-university-rankings/2022#!/page/0/length/50/locations/RUS/sort_by/rank/sort_order/asc/cols/stats.

Vinnikova IS, Egorova AO, Kuznetsova EA, Kuryleva OI, and Lavrentyeva LV (2021) The experience of organization of educational space and increasing the financial literacy of all layers at Minin University. In: Popkova EG, and Ostrovskaya VN (eds) *Meta-scientific study of artificial intelligence*. Charlotte, NC: Information Age Publishing, 319–325.

Ward C, Topham T, Dixon H, Peterson, A, Rieder J, Duffin B, … Coburn J (2022) Culturally inclusive STEM Learning: Mentored internships for Native American undergraduates at a tribal college and a university. *Journal of Diversity in Higher Education*. DOI: 10.1037/dhe0000413.

Warren SR, Martinez RS, and Pacino MA (2021) Accepting educational responsibility for an inclusive university campus: The impact of the diversity ambassador program. *Journal of Higher Education Theory and Practice* 21(8): 131–143. DOI: 10.33423/JHETP.V21I8.4510.

Yankovskaya VV, Zakharov MY, Abramov AN, Dianova VY, and Dvoretskaya VV (2022) Innovative development of education in the digital economy of the future for young people: Distance learning versus smart technologies in education. In: Popkova EG, and Sergi BS (eds) *Digital education in Russia and Central Asia*. Singapore: Springer, 295–300. DOI: 10.1007/978-981-16-9069-3_32.

CHAPTER 15

Enroute towards Inclusive Technical and Vocational Education and Training Colleges

South African Case

Selina Kungwane and Anneline Korf-Taljaard

Abstract

This chapter investigates the work done by the Department of Higher Education and Training (DHET) in South Africa (SA) since its inception towards creating an inclusive post-school education and training (PSET) sector, with a specific focus and emphasis on the development of inclusive education in the technical and vocational education and training (TVET) colleges as the area of investigation. The authors considered various policies, legislations, and strategies responding to the ratified United Nations (UN) conventions, declarations, treaties, and agreements in the country. Strategies for improving inclusive TVET colleges, their implementation, and the challenges associated with them were identified. The authors proposed strategies to improve the inclusion of persons with disabilities (PwDs) in the TVET sector. Moreover, the authors recommended future research avenues to understand barriers to inclusion.

Keywords

disabilities – inclusion – inclusive – students – support

1   Introduction

Democracy brought transformation changes to the landscapes of South Africa's (SA) education sector (*Kungwane and Boaduo*, 2021). During the apartheid era, education was focused on the development and empowerment of the minority, and institutions were discriminative and had inequalities embedded in them (*Lemon*, 2004; *Soudien*, 2010). There was separation according to communities, races, and social and economic status (*Pather*, 2011). Most African students did not have access to post-school education, and if they did have access at all, they were by default deprived of the support they needed to succeed.

Democracy provided SA with an opportunity to be incorporated into the decisions of the United Nations (UN) to create a better world for all, including persons with disabilities (PwDs), by co-signing various international conventions, declarations, treaties, and agreements.

The Constitution of South Africa, Act 109 of 1996, mandates that all citizens of the country, including PwDs, have access to education, and the state has the responsibility to make it accessible (*Republic of South Africa*, 1996; *Heymann et al.*, 2014; *Howell*, 2006). The transformation agenda tried to address the imbalances of the past and work towards responding to global demands while being influenced by those demands. During the transformation of education, the Council on Higher Education (CHE) was established to focus on the issues of higher education to create a unified system for coordinating all educational matters. This formed the foundation of the later formalization of different higher education institutions: universities, universities of technology, technical and vocational education and training (TVET) colleges, and community colleges (*Mzangwa*, 2019).

The Global Education Monitoring report indicates that SA has made much progress (*UNESCO*, 2014), but there are still challenges in accessing the education sector. The TVET sector is not immune to the challenges, especially pertaining to students with disabilities (SwDs).

Therefore, it is imperative to evaluate developments toward inclusive TVET colleges.

It is necessary to clarify two concepts:

1. Inclusive education in the SA context refers to a learning environment that promotes the full personal, academic, and professional development of all learners irrespective of race, class, gender, disability, religion, culture, sexual preference, learning styles, and language (*Mpu and Ado*, 2021).
2. Disability refers to a loss or exclusion of opportunities to participate equitably in community activities. It includes various impairments that may be permanent, temporary, or episodic, causing limitations and restrictions in participating within mainstream society. The barriers may be influenced by economic, physical/structural, social, attitudinal, or cultural factors (*Department of Higher Education and Training*, 2018).

2   Method

The authors consulted various legislations, policies, reports, and literature to gather information on the progress toward inclusive education in the TVET sector. This research focused on the response of SA to international treaties and declarations as a member state of the UN. Issues related to implementing policies, legislation, and strategies were explored by looking at their development, implementation, successes, and challenges. The following three research questions guided this study:

1. What policies and strategies are in place to promote an inclusive TVET sector?
2. Does SA have progress in creating an inclusive TVET sector?
3. What can be done to improve the inclusion of SwDs in the TVET sector?

The first two research questions identify gaps in creating inclusive TVET colleges for SwDs. The last question focuses on what may be done to improve inclusion.

The findings are discussed, and the strategies for improving the creation of inclusive TVET colleges are proposed. The authors provide recommendations in line with the inclusion of SwDs and their support.

3 Discussion

Transformation into an inclusive educational environment should be done based on the top-down approach. The new SA government developed several legislative and policy documents to act as guiding directives to address the imbalances of the past, one of which led to the split of the Department of Education (DoE) into the Department of Basic Education (DBE) and the Department of Higher Education and Training (DHET) in 2009. The DBE focuses on school-going learners, while the DHET focuses on post-school-level students.

The DHET was established according to the recommendations of the Council on Higher Education (CHE). Its mandate is derived from the constitution of education at all levels of tertiary education as a functional area of national and provincial legislative competence. The Higher Education Act (Act No 101 of 1991), as amended, promotes access to higher education institutions inclusive for SwDs (*Council on Higher Education*, 1998; *Department of Education*, 1997; *Republic of South Africa*, 1998). These institutions include universities, universities of technology, technical and vocational education and training (TVET) colleges (private and public), and community colleges. The sector is responsible for improving accessibility and quality of education while providing a knowledgeable and skilled labor force needed for the country's economic development.

To execute this responsibility, the DHET identified the need for a socially inclusive post-school education and training (PSET) system that cuts across state boundaries, regardless of racial, ethnic, gender, disability, class and socio-economic status, and national and religious identities to achieve a united human race based on human dignity (*Department of Higher Education and Training*, 2018). Moreover, those who neither work nor study in educational institutions are covered by community colleges.

3.1 Transformation of the Former Further Education and Training (FET) Colleges

Political history influenced vocational education (*Bisschoff and Nkoe*, 2005), where training for specific vocations was only reserved for a specific race or cultural group. *Powell* (2014) described the transformation from previously white training centers to institutions that could be fully inclusive and cater to the labor needs in SA.

Larger or macro institutions were formed (*Bisschoff and Nkoe*, 2005) by merging 153 technical colleges and skills training centers into 50 further education and training (FET) colleges across the country for accessibility. The new FET Colleges were guided by the FET Act 98 of 1998 (*Republic of South Africa*, 1998) (replaced with the FET Act 16 of 2006) and were better managed and coordinated.

Merging the technical colleges brought benefits like campuses specializing in specific programs. This improved cost-effectiveness, quality program delivery, and standardization of operations.

The inherited infrastructures differed across campuses. Funding for improving and upgrading buildings was availed by DHET. The unavailability of students' residential areas at some campuses became a barrier to studying programs of choice (*Van Wyk*, 2010). Student accommodation is still a challenge.

3.2 Changing the Name from FET to TVET

The term "TVET" was created at the 1999 UNESCO International Congress on Technical and Vocational Education. TVET became an international concept to improve awareness and provision of training programs and was adopted by the SA government (*South African Government News Agency*, 2012). Subsequently, the FET Act 16 of 2006 was replaced by the Continuing Education and Training (CET) Act, intended to regulate the provision of education and training for students in TVET colleges.

Academic access to the TVET programs has different entry points (*Department of Higher Education and Training*, 2019a). The minimum school qualification for entry is a grade 9 or a General Education Certificate (GEC);

students with a National Senior Certificate (NSC) could gain access to qualifications for a national higher diploma (*Delubom* et al., 2020).

The Policy Framework for Administration and Management of Student Admissions in TVET Colleges guide all TVET College Councils in developing student admission policies for their respective colleges (*Department of Higher Education and Training*, 2019b).

3.3 Challenges

SwDs face various challenges in accessing TVET colleges for various reasons; if they access colleges at all, they face barriers to success. Lack of support to participate in academic and non-academic activities leads to demoralization and dropouts (*Mutanga*, 2017). Colleges try to manage support on all campuses. Thus, at least one Student Support Officer at each campus offers holistic support to all students. The latter is a challenge on its own because of diverse disabilities requiring various types of support that need academic and non-academic expertise, which the sector does not have.

The diverse challenges require the sector to develop strategies and mechanisms to transform the sector toward inclusion and the provision of quality education as expected by the signed UN conventions, declarations, treaties, and agreements. Diversified disabilities impose curricular challenges. Curricula and assessment tools should be adapted to accommodate diverse disabilities and needs. Learners from some special schools have limited opportunities to continue learning since their grading levels do not comply with the minimum requirements to transit into colleges. Therefore, recognition of prior learning needs must be disclosed to improve enrollment in the sector since the theory is a minimal part of curricula in special schools.

Despite the progress achieved by the government in making education accessible, SwDs still seem to be unable to access the TVET sector due to various reasons, including infrastructure, financial support, technological support, human support, perceptions, inabilities of college in offering support (academic and non-academic), college curriculum, the attitude of society and officials, lack of capacity of key stakeholders, the invisibility of disability in community, poverty, lack of acceptance, lack of interest, gender discrimination, lack of awareness, poor physical access, un/availability of various support systems, and poor socioeconomic status and government policies focusing on the education of SwDs in colleges.

Policies in place are ambiguous for implementing inclusivity in colleges. They are too silent or have gaps in addressing issues of access, admissions, teaching, and learning of SwDs. There is a need for various expertise in clearing the grey areas and gaps for ease of interpretation, implementation, and monitoring. The Strategic Policy Framework on Disability for the PSET sector could not be interpreted and implemented by all colleges with ease. Therefore, the DHET developed a Framework and Guidelines to Accommodate SwDs in TVET colleges (*Department of Higher Education and Training*, 2021a) to guide colleges to support SwDs. The inability of management and staff to interpret and implement policies correctly affects all students, including SwDs. This impacts the accessibility of the sector, throughput, and dropout rates because creating inclusive classrooms is still a challenge.

Policies like Screening, Identification, Assessment, and Support (SIAS) are lacking in the TVET sector. They should be developed to provide a framework to standardize the procedures to identify, assess, and provide programs for all learners to be included in colleges (*Matolo and Rambuda*, 2022).

The lecturers are challenged because they find themselves in the same classroom with students with various capabilities, levels of education, age, and disabilities; some claim to have been unprepared to teach SwDs (*Delubom* et al., 2020). The vast diversity of disabilities present in one classroom should also be considered. Disabilities could include, for example, a student with low vision that would need an enlarged font, a deaf student who uses a sign language interpreter, a student with attention-deficit/hyperactivity disorder (ADHD), or a student with dyslexia; not even to mention students with stress and anxiety disorders, depression, or even schizophrenia (mental health disorders), not forgetting the gifted. Therefore, it is necessary to have the necessary skills and knowledge to educate SwDs or the gifted in one classroom.

Various researchers indicate the challenges of accessibility of infrastructure in colleges. *Delubom* et al. (2020) allude to ancient infrastructures' inaccessibility. *Van Wyk* (2010) adds that the responsibility for addressing challenges of accessibility and provision of support to SwDs lies with management.

The DHET trained TVET colleges on national infrastructure asset management standards and maintenance planning. Beyond that, they are expected to submit work package applications to DHET for approval before expenditure is incurred. Upon approval of the maintenance plan, the college may utilize the funds according to the approvals to avoid mismanagement. The DHET approves the spending of the funds in line with the approved costed maintenance plans (*Parliamentary Monitoring Group*, 2019a, 2019b). Therefore, colleges may access funding to improve their infrastructure to be inclusive according to the Universal Design Principles of Buildings.

Student support services (SSS) is not a fully funded mandate. Thus, in respect of the provision of these services, colleges are at different levels and resourced differently. The college councils should consider using the college funds or external sponsorships and donations to enhance the provision of

SSS and the relevant infrastructure, such as fully-equipped student resource centers across all campuses.

Staffing of disability support units (DSUs) by professional staff with expertise is still fragmented, and colleges do as they see fit and depend on the budget available to afford specialists. Even though some colleges afford to attract these specialists, most of them are at entry-level, and as soon as they acquire some form of experience, they leave the sector for better opportunities. Therefore, the sector struggles to retain experienced professionals.

4   Results

The findings are presented as (i) policies and legislations for inclusivity; (ii) promotion of student support services, (iii) promotion, advocacy, and protection of the rights of PwDs in the TVET sector and lessons learned from universities, (iv) status quo of inclusive education in the TVET Colleges, and (v) number of students with disabilities in TVET Colleges.

4.1   Policies and Legislations Implementation for Inclusivity

The Constitution of South Africa, Act 109 of 1996 addresses unfair discrimination and includes disability in section 9(3) (*Gray and Vawda*, 2020, p. 36), resulting in the development of policies, legislations, guidelines, and strategies to ensure that SwDs are not fairly or unfairly discriminated against because of their disability.

White paper 6: Special Needs Education, Building an Inclusive Education and Training System (*Department of Education*, 2001) and The Education White Paper 3 (*Department of Education*, 1997) advocate for an increased and broadened participation in higher education, promotion of equal access and fair opportunities to all who wish to realize their capabilities while removing all barriers and forms of discrimination. There was a need to empower those who were discriminated against to balance accessing educational opportunities in a fair and just manner (*Leibowitz and Bozalek*, 2014). In addition, White Paper 3 outlines the framework for change towards a planned, governed, and funded single national coordinated higher education system, which will overcome the previous imbalances, inequalities, and inefficiencies (*Department of Education*, 1997).

4.2   Promotion of Student Support Services in Colleges

The Student Support Services (SSS) framework and the manual were developed to enable FET Colleges to establish effective and efficient student support services. There was no official and organized support for students, including SwDs. Colleges offered support according to their own discretion, affordability, and understanding (*Department of Education*, 2009a, 2009b).

The SSS manual proposed a phase-in model to provide support services on pre-registration, course, and exit and offered guidelines to support students in various areas for accessibility and academic success. These guidelines did not specify how to support SwDs, but the FET Colleges Act No 16 of 2006 states that the responsibility lies with the College councils to ensure that colleges have disability policies providing adequate access and support structures for SwDs. Furthermore, no students should be discriminated against based on their disability. The manual did, however, also offer a plan for academic "catch-up" intervention programs for "high-risk" students.

The period 2000–2010 was characterized mainly by under-resourced student support units. Some brave colleges attempted to train SwDs, but the challenges that students faced were so vast that SwDs often dropped out because of a lack of support (*Maharaj*, 2018).

SSS managers were appointed and were much involved with operational support (e.g., marketing and registration and administration of NSFAS bursary applications). Although the SSS manual addresses the necessity of career advice, colleges could not offer specialist services such as career or personal counseling and often refer to external service providers. *Maharaj* (2018) warned that finding employment is challenging and career guidance for SwDs is imperative before starting studies to enable integration into the world of work. Other functions were filled by appointed staff members, and the range of general support services to students increased dramatically. As the need for emotional support was recognized, most colleges appointed counselors or social workers. Some colleges also appointed other occupation-related specialists, such as psychometrists or career development practitioners, educational psychologists, occupational therapists, librarians, and sports coordinators.

Awareness of SwDs and requests from DHET to provide statistics have now indicated that students with a wide variety of disabilities are registered at the colleges (*Department of Higher Education and Training*, 2021d, p. 35).

4.3 Promotion, Advocacy, and Protection of the Rights of PwDs in the TVET Sector and Lessons Learned from Universities

In 2009, Disability Rights Units (DRU) from universities in SA formed an advocacy and rights-based non-profit organization, Higher and Further Education Disability Services Association (HEDSA). The constitution (*Higher and Further Education Disability South Africa*, 2012) states the following objectives of HEDSA:

- To ensure equal opportunities for all students with disabilities by stimulating and facilitating dialogue and critical reflection; promoting equity, diversity, and inclusivity within all institutions of HE and TVET; networking and cooperating with national bodies, such as Universities South Africa, CHE, DHET, and Non-Governmental Organizations (NGOs); facilitating collaboration at a national level and promoting the creation of an inclusive environment in all HEDSA activities.
- To assist institutions of higher education and TVET colleges by supporting them in advocacy and disability-related areas of change management; identifying current issues and areas of need, with specific reference to SwDs in institutions of higher education and TVET; undertaking various projects or programs that are achievable, affordable, and appropriate; encouraging research, collaboration, and development.

The transformation of the PSET led to HEDSA extending membership to TVET colleges. Collaborative events provide networking opportunities that strengthen relationships among the disability support staff members in the sector. Because most universities have well-established disability rights units, colleges have access to this wealth of knowledge and experience through shared best practice models.

4.4 Status Quo of Inclusive Education in TVET Colleges

In 2021, the DHET (Chief Directorate: Programmes and Qualifications) published a report on an investigation of support services offered to SwDs in TVET colleges (*Department of Higher Education and Training*, 2021b). Colleges responded to a number of questions, including policies, staff members, accessibility of buildings and facilities, etc. It is reported that 44% of the respondents have approved disability policies, and 32% indicated that the SwDs have access to a DSU (an established structure fully equipped with resources such as financial and human resources) or a disability support desk (DSD) (officials who offer or are assigned the responsibility to offer support to SwDs). The accessibility to facilities varied by college and type of disabilities. The report further mentions that, in general, buildings are inaccessible and recommends that infrastructure audits should be done to inform decisions to improve them to be aligned with Universal Principles of Buildings.

4.5 Enrolments of SwDs in Colleges

The DBE reported to a Parliamentary Monitoring Group on Inclusive Education that the total number of learners with disabilities in all grades of special schools, as well as in ordinary public schools, in 2018 was not less than 215160 (*Department of Basic Education*, 2017, 2019).

Contrary to these numbers, data from the TVET College sector indicates that a total number of 2537 SwDs were registered in 2019. This is less than 1% of the overall 673490 registered students (*Department of Higher Education and Training*, 2021d).

The number of SwDs in the TVET sector thus seems to be very low. This observation is supported by the White Paper on Rights of People with Disabilities (*Department of Social Development*, 2015), which reports that most young people between the ages of 20–24 were not attending any higher education institution.

One could argue that statistics might not be a true reflection of the number of SwDs in the TVET colleges. Reasons for non-disclosure of disability status might include the following:

1. Emotional barriers (*Pearson and Boskovich*, 2019), administrative barriers, and misunderstandings such as that students are expected to declare their disabilities to enable the institutions to give them the necessary support;
2. Lack of uniform classification definitions used amongst different institutions.

Access to support in TVET colleges depends on the student's self-disclosure, unlike in basic education, where policies such as SIAS are in place. Therefore, students have significant responsibilities to decide when it is appropriate or necessary to disclose or not (*Pearson and Boskovich*, 2019).

4.6 Proposed Strategies and Role Players toward Advancing Inclusive TVET Colleges

White Paper 6 is more focused on addressing the issues of inclusiveness in schools than in the PSET sector. The PSET sector deals more with adults who, according to the SA Constitution, can make decisions for themselves without parental or guardian consent. Therefore, implementing this White Paper in the PSET is challenging.

Additionally, the DoE developed the SSS Framework and Manual to assist TVET colleges with implementing student support, without mentioning how SwDs should be supported. Since development, the documents have not been reviewed to be aligned with the current demands and influences of the international agreements that outline accessibility of quality technical and vocational education by PwDs for sustainable livelihood.

The DHET has the responsibility to respond to the implementation of the White Paper on the Rights of People with Disabilities (WPRPD) (*Department of Social Development*, 2015). One of the objectives of the WPRPD is to outline the responsibilities and accountabilities of the involvement of various stakeholders (in this case, the DHET) in offering SwDs a barrier-free, appropriate, effective, efficient, and coordinated inclusive service (*Department of Higher Education and Training*, 2013). The White Paper on PSET System addresses the shortcomings of White Paper 6 and the SSS Framework. TVET Colleges must admit learners of all ages that are seeking education and training, provide quality vocational learning opportunities, and offer the necessary support to all students regardless of their disabilities.

The TVET Branch within the DHET is also responsible for monitoring the implementation of the policy framework in TVET colleges. Two recently developed and adopted documents are (i) a classification model for disabilities and (ii) a Strategic Policy and Framework on Disabilities for the Post-School System, which the colleges have to implement while the DHET monitors progress.

Drawn upon lessons of the past, the following strategies are therefore recommended to expedite the inclusion of SwDs in TVET colleges:

– *Strategy 1.* The implementation of the Strategic Policy Framework on disability for the PSET to guide the PSET sector towards accommodation of SwDs and ensure mainstreaming of SwD. The Framework and guidelines should guide colleges to accommodate SwDs in TVET colleges.
– *Strategy 2.* The implementation of the new classification model adopted from the Washington Disability Classification Model to address issues of disability categories disability in the PSET sector. Furthermore, it is necessary to assist with the planning (projections for the following years, budgets, reasonable accommodation needs, an accessible environment consistent with the Universal Design Principles of Buildings, and provision of holistic support for SwDs without discrimination).
– *Strategy 3.* Addressing the issues of access to inclusive teaching and learning, which makes it difficult for SwDs not to progress or even drop out. All barriers to accommodating learners should be removed, including curriculum adaptation (*Ntombela*, 2019), infrastructural barriers, retraining or empowering lecturers, and assessment methods.
– *Strategy 4.* Maximizing the use of current funding to improve the accessibility of colleges to SwDs, focusing on funding for students (special needs education funding and national student financial aid scheme (NSFAS)), College Improvements Expenditure Grant, Sector Education and Training Associations (SETAS) funding, and donor-funded lecturer development programs. Colleges need to be capacitated and supported to utilize the funds allocated efficiently.

– *Strategy 5*. The establishment of DSUs with financial resources, human support (including specialists according to the needs of students), and other resources to efficiently service SwDs with the necessary support.

5 Conclusion

This chapter explored the development of inclusive education in TVET colleges since the democracy and establishment of the DHET. Despite the legislative and documentary strides made at different levels of governmental and institutional management to create inclusive colleges, there are still challenges. SwDs are still discriminated against, fairly or unfairly, for various reasons not limited to infrastructure, funding, curriculum, stigma, and lecture development issues. The latter needs to be attended to for the sector to be inclusive. Furthermore, it is necessary to train SwDs with the necessary knowledge and skills to enable them to advocate for their rights.

After investigating various legislations, policies, reports, and literature, the authors identified some challenges and suggested five strategies to expedite the ambitious task of developing inclusive TVET Colleges.

The issues influencing discrimination against SwDs should be investigated more to understand why there is a lack of progress toward total inclusion. Additionally, strategies and mechanisms should be developed to include them in accessing and qualifying successfully within the sector.

Further research should investigate the following:

1. Why SwDs do not articulate to TVET colleges? An argument that SwDs need more financial support was pre-empted, and the DHET has ring-fenced special funds to support these students. Nevertheless, it does not seem as if the numbers have increased drastically (*Department of Higher Education and Training*, 2021c).
2. Investigate factors that support retention and throughput of SwDs, as well as the reasons for dropouts. To facilitate changes for the inclusion of SwDs, it is necessary to consider issues of the abilities, retention, access, equity, citizenship, and diversity of SwDs (*South African Government News Agency*, 2012).

References

Bisschoff TC and Nkoe MN (2005) The merging of further education and training colleges: Challenging factors in three provinces of South Africa. *South African Journal of Higher Education* 19: 203–217. DOI: 10.4314/SAJHE.V19I3.25514.

Council on Higher Education (1998) *Legislative and Policy Mandate*. Available (consulted 24 August 2022) at: https://www.che.ac.za/about-us/legislative-and-policy-mandate.

Delubom NE, Newlin M and Mqondiso AB (2020) Managers' challenges on implementing inclusive education: Technical vocational education and training colleges. *Cypriot Journal of Educational Sciences* 15(6): 1508–1518. Available (consulted 14 April 2022) at: https://un-pub.eu/ojs/index.php/cjes/article/view/5294.

Department of Basic Education (2017) *Inclusive education and special education: DBE progress report; with deputy minister* [Meeting minutes]. Available (consulted 18 April 2022) at: https://pmg.org.za/committee-meeting/24505/.

Department of Basic Education (2019, October 30) *Inclusive education: Status update* [Meeting minutes]. Available (consulted 18 April 2022) at: https://pmg.org.za/committee-meeting/29205/.

Department of Education (1997) *Education White Paper 3: A Programme for the Transformation of Higher Education*. Available (consulted 18 April 2022) at: https://www.gov.za/documents/programme-transformation-higher-education-education-white-paper-3-0.

Department of Education (2001) *White Paper 6: Special Needs Education, Building an Inclusive Education and Training System* [White Paper]. Available (consulted 25 May 2022) at: https://www.gov.za/sites/default/files/gcis_document/201409/educ61.pdf.

Department of Education (2009a) *Student support services framework for further education and training colleges*. Department of Education.

Department of Education (2009b) *Student support services manual for further education and training colleges*. Department of Education.

Department of Higher Education and Training (2013) *White Paper for Post School Education and Training*. Available (consulted 18 April 2022) at: https://www.dhet.gov.za/SiteAssets/Latest%20News/White%20paper%20for%20post-school%20education%20and%20training.pdf.

Department of Higher Education and Training (2018) *Strategic Policy Framework on Disability for the Post School Education and Training System*. Available (consulted 18 April 2022) at: https://www.dhet.gov.za/SiteAssets/Gazettes/Approved%20Strategic%20Disability%20Policy%20Framework%20Layout220518.pdf.

Department of Higher Education and Training (2019a) *Continuing Education and Training Act, 2006 (Act no. 16 of 2006)* [Policy Framework for Administration and

Management of Student Admission in Technical and Vocational Education and Training Colleges].

Department of Higher Education and Training (2019b) *Policy Framework for Administration and Management of Student Admissions in Technical and Vocational Education and Training College* [Policy]. Available (consulted 18 April 2022) at: https://www.dhet.gov.za/SiteAssets/Policy%20framework%20on%20Administration%20and%20Management%20of%20Student%20admissions.pdf.

Department of Higher Education and Training (2021a) *A Draft Framework and Guidelines to Accommodate Students with Disabilities in Technical and Vocational Education and Training Colleges*. Available (consulted 16 April 2022) at: https://www.dhet.gov.za/SiteAssets/DRAFT%20FRAMEWORK%20AND%20GUIDELINES%20TO%20ACCOMMODATE%20STUDENTS%20WITH%20DISABILITIES%20IN%20TVET.pdf.

Department of Higher Education and Training (2021b) *A report on the investigations of services offered to students with disabilities in technical and vocational education and training colleges*. Available (consulted 16 April 2022) at: https://www.dhet.gov.za/SiteAssets/A%20REPORT%20ON%20THE%20INVESTIGATION%20OF%20SERVICES%20OFFERED%20TO%20STUDENTS%20WITH%20DISABILITIES%20IN%20TVET%20COLLEGES.pdf.

Department of Higher Education and Training (2021c) *Statistics on post-school education and training in South Africa: 2017* [Report]. Available (consulted 18 April 2022) at: https://www.dhet.gov.za/PSET%20Statistics/Statistics%20on%20Post-School%20Education%20and%20Training%20in%20South%20Africa%202019.pdf.

Department of Higher Education and Training (2021d) *Statistics on post-school education and training in South Africa: 2019* [Report]. Available (consulted 16 April 2022) at: https://www.dhet.gov.za/DHET%20Statistics%20Publication/Statistics%20on%20Post-School%20Education%20and%20Training%20in%20South%20Africa%202019.pdf.

Department of Social Development (2015) *White Paper on Rights of People with Disabilities* [White Paper]. Available (consulted 18 April 2022) at: https://www.gov.za/sites/default/files/gcis_document/201603/39792gon230.pdf.

Gray A and Vawda Y (2020) *Health legislation and policy: A focus on disability*. Available (consulted 11 August 2022) at: https://journals.co.za/doi/pdf/10.10520/ejc-healthr-v2020-n1-a7.

Heymann J, Raub A and Cassola A (2014) Constitutional rights to education and their relationship to national policy and school enrolment. *International Journal of Educational Development* 39. DOI: 10.1016/j.ijedudev.2014.08.005.

Higher and Further Education Disability South Africa (2012) *Constitution of the Higher and Further Education Disability Services Association*. HEDSA. Available (consulted 19 April 2022) at: https://www.hedsa.org.za.

Howell C (2006) Disabled students and higher education in South Africa. In: Watermayer B, Swartz L, Lorenzo T, Schneider M and Priestley M (eds) *Disability and social change* (pp. 164–178). Cape Town, South Africa: Human Sciences Research Council Press. Available (consulted 11 August 2022) at: https://open.uct.ac.za/bitstream/item/3988/Disability_SocialChange_eBook.pdf?sequence=1#page=176.

Kungwane S and Boaduo M (2021) The collaborative partnership between teachers and occupational therapists in public special schools in South Africa. In: Semon SR, Lane D and Jones P (ed) *Instructional Collaboration in International Inclusive Education Contexts*. Bingley, UK: Emerald Publishing Limited, 115–126. DOI: 10.1108/S1479-363620210000017011.

Leibowitz B and Bozalek V (2014) Access to higher education in South Africa. *Widening Participation and Lifelong Learning* 16(1): 91–109. DOI: 10.5456/WPLL.16.1.91.

Lemon A (2004) Redressing school inequalities in the Eastern Cape, South Africa. *Journal of Southern African Studies* 30(2): 269–290. DOI: 10.1080/0305707042000215392.

Maharaj R (2018) *An investigation into the retention and dropout of mechanical engineering students at a FET College* (Unpublished Master's Thesis). Durban, South Africa: University of KwaZulu-Natal.

Matolo MF and Rambuda AM (2022) Evaluation of the application of an inclusive education policy on screening, identification, assessment and support of the learners at schools in South Africa. *International Journal of Education and Practice* 10(1): 11–24. DOI: 10.18488/61.v10i1.2274.

Mpu Y and Ado EO (2021) The challenges of inclusive education and its implementation in schools: The South African perspective. *Perspectives in Education* 39(2): 225–238. DOI: 10.18820/2519593X/pie.v39.i2.16.

Mutanga O (2017) Students with disabilities experience in South African higher education – A synthesis of literature. *South African Journal of Higher Education* 31(1): 135–154.

Mzangwa ST (2019) The effects of higher education policy on transformation in post-apartheid South Africa. *Cogent Education* 6(1): 1592737. DOI: 10.1080/2331186X.2019.1592737.

Ntombela GN (2019) *The dynamics of inclusive education in further education and training in South Africa: A case study of two technical and vocational education and training colleges in Pietermaritzburg* (Unpublished Doctorate Thesis). Durban, South Africa: University of KwaZulu-Natal.

Parliamentary Monitoring Group (2019a, October 30) *Inclusive education: Status update, basic education* [Minutes of a meeting of the Basic Education committee]. Available (consulted 18 April 2022) at: https://pmg.org.za/committee-meeting/29205/.

Parliamentary Monitoring Group. (2019b). *Overview of the TVET sector with respect to governance, management, teaching, learning & new campuses higher education, science and innovation* [Meeting Summary]. Available (consulted 18 April 2022) at: https://pmg.org.za/committee-meeting/28817/.

Pather S (2011) Evidence on inclusion and support for learners with disabilities in mainstream schools in South Africa: Off the policy radar? *International Journal of Inclusive Education* 15(10): 1103–1117. DOI: 10.1080/13603116.2011.555075.

Pearson H and Boskovich L (2019, February 28) Problematizing disability disclosure in higher education: Shifting towards a liberating humanizing intersectional framework. *Disability Studies Quarterly* 39(1). DOI: 10.18061/dsq.v39i1.6001.

Powell L (2014) *Reimagining the purpose of vocational education and training: The perspectives of further education and training college students in South Africa* (Unpublished Doctorate Thesis). Nottingham, UK: University of Nottingham.

Republic of South Africa (1996, December 18) *The Constitution of the Republic of South Africa Act 108 of 1996*. Available (consulted 13 April 2022) at: https://www.gov.za/documents/constitution/constitution-republic-south-africa-1996-1.

Republic of South Africa (1998) *Further Education and Training Act No. 98 of 1998*. Cape Town, South Africa. Available (consulted 18 April 2022) at: https://www.dhet.gov.za/Private%20FET%20Colleges/Further%20Education%20and%20Training%20Act%20No.98%20of%201998.pdf.

Soudien C (2010) *Some issues in affirmative action in higher education in South Africa*. Available (consulted 13 April 2022) at: https://journals.co.za/doi/epdf/10.10520/EJC37609.

South African Government News Agency (2012, March 14) *Vocational education needed to make NGP a reality*. Available (consulted 11 August 2022) at: https://www.sanews.gov.za/south-africa/vocational-education-needed-make-ngp-reality.

UNESCO. (2014). *Teaching and learning: Achieving quality for all; EFA global monitoring report, 2013–2014*. Available (consulted 11 August 2022) at: https://unesdoc.unesco.org/ark:/48223/pf0000225660.

Van Wyk AE (2010) *Challenges faced by a rural FET college: A case study of a FET college in northern KwaZulu-Natal* (Unpublished Master's Thesis). Durban, South Africa: University of KwaZulu-Natal.

PART 3

Digital Technology in Higher Education and Its Importance for Increasing Social Mobility

∵

CHAPTER 16

Key Factors to Increase Attractiveness of Digital Socio-oriented Clusters in Pandemic Conditions

Views of Generation Z Students

Mikhail V. Vinichenko, Marina V. Rybakova, Oksana L. Chulanova, Sergey A. Barkov and Sergey A. Makushkin

Abstract

The paper aims to identify the main factors for increasing the attractiveness of digital socially-oriented clusters in a pandemic for students of Generation Z. The work used general scientific and special research methods, including a questionnaire survey, in-depth interviews, and a focus group in a remote format. The empirical base was made up of students of Generation Z (n=806 people) from 27 Russian universities. The research revealed a high degree of readiness of Generation Z students to participate in digital socially-oriented clusters in the pandemic. The authors identified the most important factors for increasing attractiveness, including gaining work experience in a large digital socially-oriented cluster, good wages, interest in communicating with various people, and the opportunity to make a career. The paper clarifies the categorical-conceptual apparatus on the research subject. The factors contributing to the participation of young people in digital socially-oriented clusters in the context of the pandemic include difficulties in entering the labor market, exacerbated by pandemic restrictions, and discrimination against young people, especially in small and medium-sized businesses and public service. The results obtained can be used to improve the planning system and provide digital socially-oriented clusters with human resources based on young people with developed digital competencies and high motivation.

Keywords

social economy – Generation Z – digital socially-oriented cluster – social values – attractiveness factors – human potential – COVID-19 pandemic

1 Introduction

The development of the economy in recent years is increasingly associated with the implementation of large socially-oriented projects. Some of them are focused on the construction of roads, social housing, and water supply (*Garay* et al., 2021; *Hetemi* et al., 2020; *Liu* et al., 2021). To implement megaprojects, it is necessary to correctly predict the expected socio-economic and environmental effects of their implementation, create an effective management system, and think over financing (*Gao* et al., 2021; *Larumbe* et al., 2021; *Sampath* et al., 2021). This should contribute to achieving the sustainable development goals (SDGs) (*Kramarenko* et al., 2020).

However, large companies, along with the fight against COVID-19, sometimes implement projects with a negative impact on the social and environmental environment (*Crimmins* et al., 2021; *Schulte*, 2021; *Ushakov* et al., 2018). As practice shows, non-professional risk assessment of projects (clusters) can also lead to negative consequences for the living conditions of local residents and infrastructure and cause environmental risks and problems (*Aung* et al., 2021; *Fang* et al., 2021; *Korytarova and Hromadka*, 2021; *Rybakova* et al., 2019). Digital projects based on artificial intelligence pose risks to the very existence of humanity (*Wang* et al., 2021).

The success of implementing socially-oriented projects (clusters) lies in the plane of attracting highly qualified specialists and competent involvement of young people, especially university graduates, in the labor activity. It should be noted that the struggle for talented specialists by smart employers begins with first-year university students. It is important to create favorable working conditions and synchronize the existing career model for young professionals and university graduates. Simultaneously, a flexible and promising model of motivation should become the center of work with young, talented employees (*Chulanova* et al., 2018; *Rogach* et al., 2016).

Current conditions require the continuous development of digital competencies and digital culture (*Libin*, 2020). In this issue, all participants in the labor market should work in the same coordinate system. It is necessary to minimize the risks to young people from introducing artificial intelligence into business processes (*Shi*, 2019). It is especially important to involve specialized personnel companies that use the potential of artificial intelligence in this process.

The high need for active, talented, and well-motivated personnel to implement digital socially-oriented projects (clusters) rests on the difficulty of attracting promising young professionals with sufficient digital competencies. It is also important for organizers and investors to understand what the positive factor is for young people, contributing to involvement in large projects, and what scares Generation Z. This study was conducted among students of Generation Z to identify factors that increase the attractiveness of digital social clusters in the COVID-19 pandemic. This work is an element of solving the problem of involving young people in digital socially-oriented clusters.

2 Materials and Method

2.1 *Scientific and Methodological Foundations and Hypothesis*

This study is an integral part of the scientific works of the authors to identify the opinions of students of Generation Z regarding the digitalization of society and the use of artificial intelligence. The article formed the scientific and methodological apparatus, including the goal, scientific tasks, hypothesis, approaches, and research methods. The categorical-conceptual apparatus was also clarified.

The purpose of the study is to identify the main factors for increasing the attractiveness of digital socially-oriented clusters in the COVID-19 pandemic for students of Generation Z. To achieve the goal of the research, the following *scientific tasks* were identified:
1. To identify the degree of readiness of students of Generation Z for participating in digital socially-oriented clusters in the COVID-19 pandemic.
2. To determine the degree of influence of specific factors and identify the most important factors in the system of influence on students of Generation Z in the COVID-19 pandemic.
3. To clarify the categorical and conceptual apparatus of the subject area.

The authors put forward the following *hypothesis*:

H_1. The degree of readiness of Generation Z students to participate in digital socially-oriented clusters depends on the working conditions created and a set of factors that determine the attractiveness of these projects.

Factors for increasing the attractiveness of a digital social cluster are understood as the most important factors that provide a favorable opinion of Generation Z from the standpoint of possible participation in social clusters in the COVID-19 pandemic.

The research was organized and conducted in Russian universities from August 25 to October 10, 2021. Generation Z students (n=806 people) from 27 Russian universities took part in the sociological survey (the Lomonosov Moscow State University, Bauman Moscow State Technical University, MGIMO, RSSU, FEFU, KFU, etc.) with a general population of n= 1.200.000 people. The sampling error was 4.75%, with a confidence level of 95%. The main quota

TABLE 16.1 Socio-demographic characteristics of respondents, %

Characteristics of respondents		Participation share
Gender	Male	31%
	Female	69%
Age	14 to 18 years old	59%
	19 to 25 years old	41%
Education	Higher	10%
	Incomplete higher	33%
	Specialized secondary	17%
	Secondary	39%
	Initial	1%
Work experience	1 year	71%
	1–3 years	20%
	4–5 years	6%
	6–10 years	1%
	More than 10 years	2%
The nature of work	Supervisor	3%
	Specialist	12%
	State employee	4%
	Worker	7%
	Self-employed	7%
	Unemployed	4%
	Student	63%

SOURCE: COMPILED BY THE AUTHORS

features in the selection of respondents were determined: gender, age, education, as well as work experience. An analysis of the data in Table 16.1 allowed the authors to establish that the gender structure of the respondents turned out to be in favor of women – 69% versus 31% of men.

Most respondents have secondary and incomplete higher education, with no more than a year of work experience, and come from a purely student environment, which does not combine work and study very well.

2.2   *Methods*

The work used an interdisciplinary approach with general scientific and special research methods. These included such empirical methods as a sociological survey, in-depth interviews, and focus groups. The questionnaire for the sociological survey was formed based on the Likert scale (scaling from 1 point to 5). On the eve of the survey, the questionnaire was tested on a sample of Generation Z students from three Moscow universities. Attractiveness factors were determined by the expert group by ranking based on the analysis of the respondents, which was obtained during the test survey using the method of a matrix of pairwise comparisons. The respondents' involvement in the sociological survey was carried out using the "snowball" method. In the first stage, a group of 67 people (students from several universities) was identified with the task of attracting acquaintances, former classmates – students of other universities of generation Z. As a result, 806 respondents took part in the survey.

Due to pandemic restrictions, the survey was conducted remotely using the Google Forms platform. In-depth interviews and focus groups were conducted using the Skype VoIP service.

Respondents were involved in the in-depth interview by random selection. As a result, 17 people took part in the in-depth interview. During in-depth interviews, causal relationships were clarified in the decision to accept (not accept) participation in a socially-oriented cluster by respondents and assessment of attractiveness factors.

The focus group consisted of eight experts and analyzed the most problematic issues based on the survey results and in-depth interviews.

3   Results

The categorical-conceptual apparatus was specified in the work. The article understands the socially-oriented cluster as a set of entities, the activities of which are united by a single goal of intensive sustainable socio-economic development of the territory. The concept of a socially-oriented cluster has a certain semantic identity with the concept of a megaproject, which involves the unification of various projects in terms of tasks, time, and place to ensure sustainable socio-economic development of territories. A digital socially-oriented cluster involves the complete or partial digitalization of public life in the framework of achieving the goal (*Vinichenko* et al., 2021).

The analysis of the data in Chart 16.1 showed that the majority of Generation Z students (77%) are ready to participate in digital socially-oriented clusters. This opinion was expressed in the context of two years of restrictions related to the COVID-19 pandemic.

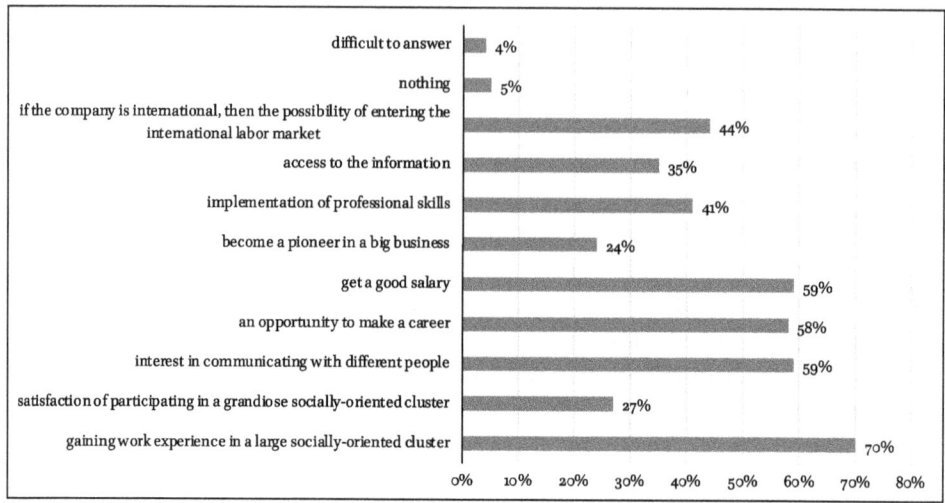

CHART 16.1 Options for answering the question: "What attracts you the most in digital socially-oriented cluster?"
SOURCE: COMPILED BY THE AUTHORS

Less demanded was the possibility of a confident entry into the international labor market in an international company (44%), implementation of professional competencies (41%), and access to the information (35%).

The factors of low attractiveness for participation in a digital socially-oriented cluster (less than 30%) include becoming a pioneer in a big business (24%) and satisfaction from participating in a grand socially-oriented cluster (27%).

Thus, during the sociological survey, it was possible to establish the degree of readiness of Generation Z students to participate in a digital socially-oriented cluster. The ranking of attractiveness factors allowed identifying the four most important factors for making a decision in favor of the participation of Generation Z students in a digital socially-oriented cluster.

4   Discussion

During the survey, it was possible to establish that the degree of readiness of Generation Z students to participate in the digital socially-oriented cluster is quite high. The vast majority of Generation Z students are willing to participate to varying degrees. Only a small part of respondents has a categorically negative attitude toward the idea of participation in a cluster (6%). This attitude is based on the relative ease of changing places at a young age and the desire of first-year students to get into large international projects that provide further reliable prospects. During the in-depth interview, it was revealed that the desire to get into the digital socially-oriented cluster also comes from the hope of seeing a lot of young people in it. A comfortable youth atmosphere adapted to digital communications will contribute to the disclosure of creative potential. Focus group experts noted that the majority of Generation Z students do not have sufficient work experience (71% – 1 year), which could serve as a deterrent and contributor to active participation in the labor market, especially if there is an opportunity to prove oneself in a large project. The freedom, which has appeared in the social environment, is also affected by high school graduation, the entry into the student environment, and a large separation from parental control.

During in-depth interviews, it was possible to establish that gaining work experience in a large digital socially-oriented cluster has become a leading factor for young people due to the difficulty of entering the labor market and adapting to multi-age and multi-ethnic teams. The obtained minimum work experience demonstrated that in most companies and government agencies, young workers are not taken seriously enough; superior employees often consider them as an ancillary and temporary workforce. Young people feel discrimination, especially in small and medium-sized businesses and public service. This does not allow them to make a good breakthrough at the start of their career. Thus, the desire for a high salary and the opportunity to make a career, in this case, is more of a dreamlike (desirable) character.

A special place was occupied by interest in communication with various people. This factor has become one of the leading factors in the COVID-19 pandemic when the number of contacts and communications has significantly decreased. Pandemic restrictions have already exacerbated existing socio-ethnic and religious problems (*Nikiporets-Takigawa*, 2018; *Oseev* et al., 2018). This negatively impacted the possibility of expanding business ties, developing creative potential, joining an effective team, and building a multi-vector career path. These conclusions correlate to some extent with some studies (*Matraeva* et al., 2020).

In the focus group, the experts noted that the block of the most important factors for increasing attractiveness has formed logically and testifies to the established priorities in the further development of Generation Z students. Entry into large socially-oriented clusters formed on a digital basis has become especially relevant during the pandemic. They can expand the scope of communication and make a career with a good salary. This correlates with studies of several scientists, who note the desire of young professionals for career growth and high wages (*Chulanova* et al., 2018). Additionally, these factors contribute to the improvement of the social status of young people. Simultaneously, experts focused on the need to create favorable conditions for the integrated and effective use of these factors (*Britto* et al., 2020).

Some experts expressed the opinion that more and more young people are striving to enter the international labor market by developing digital competencies. An important aspect was the need to have the necessary information, especially in the digital sector and artificial intelligence (*Demchenko* et al., 2017).

The low indicator of the factor to become a pioneer in big business (24%) is generally natural. This is due to two reasons. First, people who are convinced in practice that it is very difficult to build a career in large companies with extensive experience and powerful brands are striving to become pioneers in developing new business areas. Much effort, time, and health with the dubious result can be spent. Therefore, young people are not too eager to spend their energy on a "dim" future. Along with this, startups provide more opportunities to move forward on the career ladder quickly. Second, first-year students have not yet felt the strength and confidence to achieve global goals defined in digital socially-oriented clusters.

5   Conclusion

The study found that the degree of readiness of Generation Z students to participate in digital socially-oriented clusters in the pandemic is quite high. The majority of Generation Z students (77%) are ready to participate in such projects. The analysis of sociological survey data allowed the authors to determine the degree of influence of specific factors on the attractiveness of digital socially-oriented clusters from the perspective of Generation Z students. The most important and less significant factors were determined by the ranking method. The block of the most important factors for increasing attractiveness included gaining work experience in a large digital socially-oriented cluster, good wages, interest in communicating with various people, and the opportunity to make a career. During in-depth interviews and focus groups, the authors clarified cause-and-effect relationships in choosing priorities in determining factors for increasing attractiveness. The factors contributing to the participation of young people in digital socially-oriented clusters in the context of the pandemic include difficulties in entering the labor market, exacerbated by pandemic restrictions, and discrimination against young people, especially in small and medium-sized businesses and public service. Generation Z students are not very eager to become business pioneers in digital social clusters. Their goals are more mundane, mercantile, and tangible. Additionally, there is a certain uncertainty and fear of responsibility in the process of taking high positions in digital socially-oriented clusters. This research clarifies the categorical-conceptual apparatus on the research subject.

The hypothesis was confirmed – the degree of readiness of Generation Z students to participate in digital socially-oriented clusters depends on the created working conditions and set of factors determining the attractiveness of these projects.

The results obtained during the research can be used to improve the planning system and provide digital socially-oriented clusters with human resources based on young people with developed digital competencies and high motivation.

References

Aung TS, Fischer TB, and Azmi AS (2021) Social impacts of large-scale hydropower project in Myanmar: A social life cycle assessment of Shweli hydropower dam 1. *International Journal of Life Cycle Assessment* 26(2): 417–433. DOI: 10.1007/s11367-021-01868-3.

Britto R, Smite D, Damm L-O, and Borstler J (2020) Evaluating and strategizing the onboarding of software developers in large-scale globally distributed projects. *Journal of Systems and Software* 169: 110699. DOI: 10.1016/j.jss.2020.110699.

Chulanova OL, Ryngach OL, Vinichenko MV, Kaurova OV, Demchenko MV, and Demchenko TS (2018) Increase of staff loyalty by improving the motivation (stimulation) system in enterprises oil and gas complex of the Khanty-Mansiy Autonomous District-Ugra. *Modern Journal of Language Teaching Methods* 8(7): 303–314.

Crimmins TM, Posthumus E, Schaffer S, and Prudic KL (2021) COVID-19 impacts on participation in large scale biodiversity-themed community science projects in the United States. *Biological Conservation* 256: 109017. DOI: 10.1016/j.biocon.2021.109017.

Demchenko TS, Karácsony P, Ilina IY, Vinichenko MV, and Melnichuk AV (2017) Self-marketing of graduates of high schools and young specialists in the system of personnel policy of the organization. *Modern Journal of Language Teaching Methods* 7(9): 58–65.

Fang JM, Huang DC, and Xu JR (2021) Social Risk early warning of environmental damage of large-scale construction projects in China based on network governance and LSTM model. *Complexity* 8863997. DOI: 10.1155/2020/8863997.

Gao JW, Guo FJ, Ma ZY, and Huang X (2021) Multi-criteria decision-making framework for large-scale rooftop photovoltaic project site selection based on intuitionistic fuzzy sets. *Applied Soft Computing* 102: 107098. DOI: 10.1016/j.asoc.2021.107098.

Garay A, Ruiz A, and Guevara J (2021) Dynamic evaluation of thermal comfort scenarios in a Colombian large-scale social housing project. *Engineering Construction and Architectural Management* DOI: 10.1108/ECAM-09-2020-0684.

Hetemi E, Gemunden HG, and Mere JO (2020) Embeddedness and actors' behaviors in large-scale project life cycle: Lessons learned from a high-speed rail project in Spain. *Journal of Management in Engineering* 36(6): 05020014. DOI: 10.1061/(ASCE)ME.1943-5479.0000849.

Korytarova J, and Hromadka V (2021) Risk assessment of large-scale infrastructure projects-assumptions and context. *Applied Sciences-Basel* 11(1): 109. DOI: 10.3390/app11010109.

Kramarenko AV, Manaenkov KL, Melnichuk AV, Makushkin SA, and Vinichenko MV (2020) Sustainable development of construction in the context of mitigating environmental pollution. *Revista Inclusiones* 7(s1): 579–590.

Larumbe J, Garcia-Barruetabena J, and Lopez-de-Ipina D (2021) Methodology for the implementation of configuration management on large scale projects. *DYNA* 96(1). DOI: 10.6036/9806.

Libin E (2020) Future competencies for digitally aligned specialties: Coping intelligently with global challenges. In: Proceedings of HEAd'20: *6th International Conference on Higher Education Advances*. Valencia, Spain: Technical University of Valencia, 1119–1125. DOI: 10.4995/HEAd20.2020.11210.

Liu M, Wang SH, Wang TC, Duan MY, Su YQ, Lin XF, ... Li ZH (2021) Application of microfiltration-nanofiltration combined technology for drinking water advanced treatment in a large-scale engineering project. *Aqua-Water Infrastructure Ecosystems and Society* DOI: 10.2166/aqua.2021.020.

Matraeva AD, Rybakova MV, Vinichenko MV, Oseev AA, and Ljapunova NV (2020) Development of creativity of students in higher educational institutions: Assessment of students and experts. *Universal Journal of Educational Research* 8(1): 8–16. DOI: 10.13189/ujer.2020.080102.

Nikiporets-Takigawa G (2018) Youth and youth policy in the UK: Post-BREXIT view. *Sovremennaya Evropa* 1(80): 47–58. DOI: 10.15211/soveurope120184758.

Oseev AA, Dudueva FA, Karácsony P, Vinichenko MV, and Makushkin SA (2018) The peculiarity of the ethno-social conflicts in the Russian labor market: Comparative analysis of Russia, Great Britain and Germany. *Revista Espacios* 39(22): 12. Available (consulted 18 February 2022) at: https://www.revistaespacios.com/a18v39n22/a18v39n22p12.pdf.

Rogach OV, Frolova EV, Kirillov AV, Bondaletov VV, and Vinichenko MV (2016) Development of favorable learning environment and labor protection in the context of harmonization of social interaction of educational system objects. *IEJME – Mathematics Education* 11(7): 2547–2558.

Rybakova MV, Vinichenko MV, Ushakova YS, Chulanova OL, Barkov SA, Malyshev MA, ... Makushkin SA (2019) Ecological problems of Russian cities on the views of young people. *Ekoloji* 28(107): 5019–5026.

Sampath S, Gel ES, Kempf KG, and Fowler JW (2021) A generalized decision support framework for large-scale project portfolio decisions. *Decision Sciences*. DOI: 10.1111/deci.12507.

Schulte K (2021) Large-scale Project Corona Vaccination. *INTERNIST* 61(12): 1268–1269.

Shi Y (2019) Impact of artificial intelligence on the accounting industry. In: Xu Z, Choo KK, Dehghantanha A, Parizi R, and Hammoudeh M (eds) *Cyber security intelligence and analytics*. Cham, Springer: Switzerland, 971–978. DOI: 10.1007/978-3-030-15235-2_129.

Ushakov D, Vinichenko M, and Frolova E (2018) Environmental capital in national economy stimulation: Limitations of rationality. *Journal of Computational and Theoretical Nanoscience* 24(9): 6290–6292. DOI: 10.1166/asl.2018.13032.

Vinichenko MV, Frolova EV, Nikiporets-Takigawa GYu, and Karácsony P (2021) Interpretation of the views of east European Catholics on the impact of artificial intelligence on the social environment. *European Journal of Science and Theology* 17(1): 11–23.

Wang ZL, Nixon R, Erwin A, and Ma Z (2021) Assessing the impacts of large-scale water transfer projects on communities: Lessons learned from a systematic literature review. *Society & Natural Resources* 34(6): 822–843. DOI: 10.1080/08941920.2020.1859029.

CHAPTER 17

Education Platforms in Pandemic Conditions

Liliya V. Samosudova, Nadezhda V. Eremkina, Irina I. Kondrashkina and Sergey M. Imyarekov

Abstract

Purpose: The paper aims to describe some educational platforms that were used during the COVID-19 pandemic and analyze their advantages and disadvantages.

Methodology: In the research, the authors applied the analysis and generalization of scientific literature on the research topic, processing and interpretation of the information obtained, and the method of system analysis. Educational electronic platforms were used as the research object, developed by foreign and Russian specialists.

Findings: It is determined that the necessity of distance learning is urgently growing due to the conditions of COVID-19, which has spread worldwide. The universities have to isolate students and teachers and continue the learning process, which could be reached using various education platforms.

Originality/values: Based on the conducted analysis of the advantages and disadvantages of e-learning and studying on different platforms, the authors can admit that it is possible to continue the educational process and achieve some positive results even at the time of forced isolation.

Keywords

educational platform – learning process – pandemic – e-Learning – distance learning – blended learning

1   Introduction

The educational process and its organization have undergone significant changes over the past few years. With the advent of e-learning, various educational platforms have emerged that have made their own adjustments to traditional education. Education began to be conducted remotely and on digital platforms. The electronic publishing house FinancesOnline informs that there are more than 1000 different online platforms for distance learning in the world.

Let us find out what an online platform in distance education is.

The idea of creating distance learning did not appear yesterday. In the beginning, there was a necessity due to the growing number of students and lack of schooling capacity to provide them with the required materials. The COVID-19 pandemic gave a powerful impetus to the transition to a new education format. COVID-19 first appeared in China in December 2019 and then spread worldwide. The virus is spreading fast enough, and the only way to stem the pandemic's growth is through social distancing, staying at home, and isolation. In this regard, the use of distance methods has become relevant and necessary, especially among educational institutions.

The digital platform, or LMS, is a learning management system that allows learners to access learning materials and study remotely. In the Russian Federation, such platforms are called the SDL – system of distance learning (*Kameneva*, 2016).

Remote platforms are used not only in education. Large companies tend to use them for corporate training of employees. These platforms are also used by tutors, trainers, and coaches who launch online projects.

To start with, let us consider distance education in general. It began its development abroad in the middle of the 19th century. The founder of distance learning is Isaac Pitman, who taught stenography in the UK. He used to send letters to his students by mail; since then, there have been distance learning courses. Since the founding of the University of London, which allowed students from other cities to take exams on the condition that they attend accredited higher education institutions, the tendency turned out to be in demand and quickly gained popularity.

In many European countries, there were a lot of institutions and colleges carrying out training classes by mail according to the university curriculum.

In the USA, distance learning also was applied by different educational organizations. This work was done not only by post but using the media where the materials necessary for studying were published. Such publications have become very popular. In a fairly short period, the distance learning system has got in many countries (*Maslakova*, 2015).

The present stage of e-learning is associated with the active development of information technology. This includes various means of communication: e-mail, teleconferencing, graphics, and multimedia. In other words, the interaction between a teacher and a student is arranged with the assistance of electronic means and technologies.

In Russia, the development of distance education dates back to 1917. It was primarily based on consultations that teachers gave their students during the so-called sessions. The learning process was arranged on the opportunity of combining the work with studies held at correspondence departments at a university. These departments allowed students to independently learn the material (that was described and provided) during a specified period and then come to the sessions to pass the exams. This system was actively developed and later transferred into distance learning.

At the beginning of the 2000s, many e-learning projects were launched, and they were used not only at educational institutions. Large companies started to use distance learning opportunities for training their staff, improving their qualifications, etc.

Until recently, the system of distance learning in Russia has been developing in accordance with international standards and has already become a significant part of education programs. About 40% of universities provide distance learning opportunities on various educational platforms.

What is an educational platform, and how can it aid in organizing the learning process?

Essentially, educational platforms are online teaching tools used for blended learning. This is a combination of in-person and online learning. We find them frequently used in higher education because it is a tool that allows learning to continue even after students have left the classroom.

Educational tools like these are used for uploading and downloading resources like lessons, notes, and assignments. Most educational platforms offer discussion boards where multiple users can interact with each other. They also offer at least basic testing features, where students can complete assessments online and submit them for grading (*Kukushkina and Samosudova*, 2019).

Some learning platforms even allow for video and audio uploading. However, the vast majority do not seamlessly support features like live lesson streaming, video conferencing, or integration with other online tools.

The new way of teaching allows one to communicate more effectively with learners through groups of chats, video calling, voting, and document exchange.

A critical review of the literature on the use of educational platforms in distance learning shows that the opinions of researchers differ when discussing this issue. In their studies, the debate is mainly on the question of whether distance learning can be considered as an alternative to the existing system of distance education and the traditional form of education in general, how to carry out in modern conditions the transition from the established educational traditions to new forms and methods laid down in distance learning.

2 Materials and Methods

During the research, the authors applied the analysis and generalization of scientific literature on the research topic, processing and interpretation of the information obtained, and the method of system analysis. For the research, the authors used electronic educational platforms developed by foreign and Russian specialists.

3 Results

Even before COVID-19, there was already a strong rise in digital education technology. However, these days, using different platforms is becoming more urgent. These platforms can be ranked variously; each organization can choose whatever it needs and likes. Therefore, the authors decided to compile their own list of services, dividing them into two areas: (1) top platforms for distance learning that can be used for free and (2) top paid platforms for organizing distance learning.

As a result of the COVID 19 pandemic, universities started to use distance learning technologies actively. Most of them use the Moodle platform as an information and educational environment for basic or additional education.

It is one of the most popular digital educational platforms for distance learning used in Russia (*Verkhotin*, 2019). The higher educational institutions in Russia most often choose Moodle. In 2020, Moodle became the leader among distance learning platforms in terms of the number of users – there are more than 118 million of them.

The first site based on this platform was created in 2001. Nowadays, the number of sites on Moodle has exceeded one million worldwide. The system supports over 120 languages, including Russian. This platform is well suited for the tasks of educational institutions. With its help, the university can maintain a reporting system and monitor the progress of students, and this requires minimal functionality; that is, setting up will not take much time and resources.

Let us take a look at the advantages and disadvantages of Moodle.

As a system of interaction between teachers and students, Moodle can solve the following tasks:
- Creation and management of a distance course;
- Differentiated access for members of the educational portal;
- Tracking the implementation of educational elements by teachers and students;

- Placement of educational materials of various formats: graphics, texts, audio, and video;
- Receiving notifications about course events (messages, passed tests, etc.);
- Content download.

The most important advantage that potential users immediately notice is the free Moodle software. The system allows uploading simple (e.g., files and folders) or more complex schemes (e.g., Wiki sections, glossaries (students can fill in), assignments, and various forms of testing). It is an open-source system that provides the following benefits:
- It allows one to create additional modules and extensions;
- Convenient built-in editors for creating courses and filling them;
- Different training formats: audio, video, and testing;
- Lectures with feedback;
- Opportunities for project-based learning;
- Access to the mobile application;
- Analytics and reporting;
- Opportunities for differentiated teaching of students;
- More than 100 languages, including Russian.

For all its versatility, Moodle has several disadvantages, including the following:
- Installation requires certain knowledge in the field of software; to organize training and create full-fledged courses, the system must be installed. If one does not have the necessary knowledge and experience, it will be necessary to hire an IT specialist. As a result, setting up the service becomes an expensive task;
- It is necessary to buy a server or hosting for storing software. Moodle is demanding on the server. Free services of providing resources for hosting sites allow one to install only old versions of the system; the service uses considerable resources, which may entail additional costs;
- Moodle is a large system with an abundance of functions, some of which are not used;
- One needs additional customization of the interface and revision of programs;
- If one does not have minimal experience in managing the distance education system, then Moodle will require a long and serious study. One will not be able to quickly figure out the abundance of sections, attachments, and forms.

The Moodle learning management system is optimal for universities in terms of a set of functions and a free distribution scheme. With its help, teachers can keep records and monitor student progress, plan tests several months in advance, and organize group work. However, the system is not suitable for rapid implementation. It will take time for untrained users to master it.

Along with the Moodle platform, the distance learning platform developed by Google has gained widespread use. This platform is designed to help teachers and students organize effective distance learning during the COVID-19 pandemic and forced self-isolation. It is based on Google cloud services and applications, adapted for use in the academic environment, considering the recommendations of the UNESCO Institute for Information Technologies in Education. The Internet giant Google has always had many tools that help learn successfully. Google Classroom has become a kind of center that combines all the service's capabilities. It is not a classic educational distance learning platform but rather a set of collaboration tools. The main advantages of the platform include simple registration and the Russian language of the interface.

The Google platform allows each teacher to create a microsite for their subject area and upload class schedules, teaching materials, and a list of recommended reading to it. To communicate with students, video conferencing and messaging facilities are provided using Hangouts Chat. Integration with Google Docs allows one to check assignments in real-time and create online tests.

Google Forms is an online service for creating feedback forms, online tests, and surveys. The tool is popular; the whole range of its possibilities is wide enough. Using Google Class, it is possible to upload educational material, set tasks, monitor its implementation, and systematize the work of students without leaving home. Google Meet allows one to conduct lectures, seminars, and workshops online. It is possible to record a video meeting and post this recording in Classroom, which allows students to watch it to review the proposed material. For example, this educational technology is widely applied in the Saransk Cooperative Institute for conducting distance classes. In our opinion, the platform has proven itself only on the positive side and can be used even when learning in real-time, offline (*Samosudova*, 2020).

Another popular educational platform used for teaching is Edmodo, a cloud-based educational platform for distance learning. This means that this platform does not need to be installed anywhere. The creators of Edmodo position it not as an educational platform but as a social network for learning, comparing it to Facebook. Indeed, they have a lot in common: registration, creating groups, private chats, and a calendar of events.

This platform was created for participants in the educational process: teachers, students, and their parents. Using this resource is very simple. Without unnecessary conventions, one can register as a teacher, create a class, and indicate the registration code to the students and parents. Edmodo allows instructors to attach files to posted assignments. It only takes one click to do this.

Students and teachers can create digital libraries using hyperlinks. Access to files is provided from any computer connected to the Internet. Students can ask questions to each other and the teacher. Teachers can also send messages to all students with assignments and announcements.

Teachers can create classes and groups of their students in accordance with the courses they teach or create temporary groups of students working on one collective task or project. It is possible to organize student polls, create and conduct quizzes, and communicate with other teachers.

The main advantages of this platform include the fact that it is not necessary to download and install it; one needs to go through an easy registration. Edmodo can be accessed through any mobile device. Thus, all Edmodo resources are always at the disposal of learners with smartphones.

The disadvantages of the platform include the lack of an interface in Russian. Moreover, the groups do not unite with each other, which means that the student will have to learn not only educational materials but also remember the links. Additionally, the list of educational tools is rather limited.

Among the paid platforms for distance learning, there are both new and long-established options. The authors consider those that most often fall at the top of various ratings, allowing users to create interesting training programs and learn well: iSpring Learn and Yo-Study.

iSpring Learn is considered to be one of the best distance learning educational platforms. One does not need to download it; it is just necessary to register for the service, download the necessary materials, and start working. iSpring Learn allows one to quickly start training and store large amounts of data in the cloud. This online distance learning platform is more commonly used by businesses and companies for staff training.

It is a cloud-based LMS with a simple and up-to-date interface that allows one to run remote training and testing of employees within one day.

Key features of iSpring Learn LMS are as follows:
– Download and store tutorials, presentations, quizzes, and interactive dialogues created with iSpring products, as well as documents in SCORM 1.2 and 2004 formats (all versions), video (.FLV), audio (.MP3), reference documents (.PDF, .DOC, .XLS), presentations (.PPT), and flash files (.SWF).
– Create and edit courses and learning paths;
– Add users, combine them into groups, and provide them with access to training materials;
– Motivate users to learn using gamification elements;
– Conduct training via a mobile application in offline mode;
– Sell e-learning courses online;

– Conduct and record webinars;
– Generate detailed reports on courses, users, and events.

A joint solution may be primarily of interest to companies that need to quickly and inexpensively conduct mobile training and certification of a large number of employees. It should be especially interesting for those who plan to create training courses and tests with the help of in-house experts without resorting to the help of external developers.

iSpring Learn is used by PwC, Lamoda, Re:Store, SCA Hygiene Products, Kcell, AGC Glass Russia, Medi Rus, Egis, Alfa Capital, Vostochny Bank, United Europe Holding, Rusagro Group, Honeywell, Johnson & Johnson, Unilever, and Modul Bank.

The platform's main advantages include unlimited storage for materials and the ability to study not only on a computer but also through smartphones and tablets. When using the platform, it is possible to keep 23 reporting forms. It is easy to use and manage content and users. Online meetings and webinars can be held. All videos are also saved to the cloud. There is a trial period (14 days). There is a 40% discount for educational institutions.

The disadvantage of the platform is primarily its cost: on average, using the platform costs 90 rubles per user per month, the minimum cost of an annual subscription is 56000 rubles; the minimum number of users is 50 people.

Yo-Study is a Russian platform for distance learning. The service allows one to create workspaces that store educational material, assignments, presentations, and videos, as well as easily manage processes. It is great for colleges, universities, and additional vocational education. It has tools to support face-to-face and distance learning. It can also be used in organizations for briefing and testing personnel.

The platform has powerful tools for conducting practical work with students online. In Yo-Stage, one can create assignments of various types: with file upload, test, discussion, as well as classes without an assignment. The system has a convenient mechanism for importing tests from documents, thanks to which one does not have to put each question into the system separately. One can also import a list of disciplines or a list of students.

For small educational organizations, Yo-Study is perhaps an alternative to the Moodle system. Simultaneously, Yo-Study works in the cloud and does not require a full-time system administrator. The system can be used from a mobile phone.

The main advantages of the platform are the possibility to import ready-made tests, automatic generation of the grade book, analytics and reporting, setting up notifications for students and teachers, and the possibility of group discussions on the forum.

Disadvantages of the platform include additional payment for video material if its duration is more than an hour. There is no opportunity for webinars and no video communication. Only the desktop version is available. The Yo-Study platform offers four tariffs, among which there is a free one – their cost depends on the number of course users.

4 Discussions

Working in a remote format, we involuntarily assess what is happening and try to predict the future. Realizing the possibility of a repetition of a current or a similar situation, it is necessary to be prepared and prepare students for such a turn of events. Therefore, university teachers are faced with a number of tasks that can be grouped in two directions. The first direction is the modernization of their teaching activities, carried out in a distance format (improving oneself as a teacher). The second direction is the introduction of the necessary changes dictated by distance learning into the programs of the courses taught.

Among the tasks, the solution of which can improve the work of a university teacher in a distance format and adjust educational activities, the authors designate the preparation and placement on the platforms selected for distance learning:
- Strictly structured lecture materials accompanied by a number of control questions of different levels of complexity;
- Illustrative, audio, and video materials that can clearly explain the proposed text and supplement it;
- Materials of practical and laboratory classes that do not require constant supervision of the teacher and can influence the level of formation of the declared competencies;
- Test tasks that perform diagnostic and training functions;
- Materials of pedagogical practices, fully explaining the structure, sequence of work performed, assessment criteria, sample reports, etc.

Nevertheless, even with a strictly built algorithm for passing each specific procedure, much depends on the functioning of the platform on which the work is carried out, the functioning of the computer equipment with which the student works, as well as the functioning of the Internet. Only with the well-coordinated work of all components will we be able to get a decent process for conducting intermediate certification in a remote format.

5 Conclusion

For a long time, e-learning has been perceived as complementary to traditional classroom instruction because it has long been the preferred choice. As a result of the COVID-19 pandemic, users have begun to get used to its scalability and overall success. The increase in the number of users of e-learning resources proves that there is an increased appreciation of this type of learning among individuals and groups worldwide.

Nowadays, the Internet system and universal (as it is believed) computerization have significantly expanded the possibilities of distance learning, and the COVID-19 pandemic that overtook humanity made this form vital.

References

Kameneva NA (2016) Features of distance learning foreign languages in a non-linguistic university. *Philological sciences. Questions of Theory and Practice* 3(57): 201–216.

Kukushkina EA, and Samosudova LV (2019) Innovative methods in teaching a foreign language. In: Khairov RR, and Kuznetsova EG (eds) A*ctual problems of socio-economic development of society: Proceedings of scientific conference.* Saransk, Russia: RUC, 52–57.

Maslakova ES (2015) The history of the development of distance learning in Russia. In: Theory and practice of education in the modern world. St. Petersburg, Russia, 29–32. Available (consulted 26 September 2021) at: https://moluch.ru/conf/ped/archive/185/9249/.

Samosudova LV (2020) The realities of distance learning: Advantages and disadvantages. In: Khairov RR (ed) *Scientific research in the socio-economic development of society: Proceedings of scientific conference.* Saransk, Russia: RUC, 185–187.

Verkhotin DG (2019) The distance learning in the Moodle system as a means of teaching students. *Bulletin of Science and Education* 2–2(56): 78–80. Available (consulted 26 September 2021) at: https://cyberleninka.ru/article/n/distantsionnoe-obuchenie-v-sisteme-moodle-kak-sredstvo-obucheniya-shkolnikov.

CHAPTER 18

Using VR and AR Technologies for the Sustainable Social Development of Intercultural and Interlanguage Exchange in the Area of Education in the Conditions of International Cooperation

Julia Yu. Rybasova, Flera L. Mazitova, Asiya G. Nizamieva, Zarema M. Zaripova and Elmira N. Uteeva

Abstract

In today's conditions, the importance of training professionals and specialists is once again relevant to the use of interactive forms in teaching the disciplines of the humanities cycle. One of the leading trends in the educational process is the development and application of augmented and virtual reality technologies. High interest in VR and AR technologies is demonstrated by teachers and especially by students. The advantage of these technologies in the framework of the educational process is the ability to connect the real space with the virtual world. For example, when students listen to the information in a foreign language class or participate in practical seminars in the humanities, the effect of a binaural beat appears. With it, the direction to the source of rhythmic sound is determined. The rhythm of the sound becomes voluminous, and immersion in virtual reality becomes more natural for the student. The paper emphasizes that using various innovative visualization techniques is a powerful tool in solving intercultural communication issues and teaching a foreign language based on VR and AR technologies. As a form of creating virtual reality for learning foreign languages and intercultural communication, complex information system and the principle of building the educational process as part of the work on the immersion method with ClassVR are described. VR and AR technologies expand the cognitive side of a student's future profession. These technologies are developed and implemented in the educational process to solve a specific problem and find the most optimal ways to improve it. It is also important to note that AR and VR are assistants for students with disabilities. Their educational and social development requires the development of VR and AR technology programs. These technologies will enable them to infiltrate the world of VR and not let themselves feel lonely in it.

Keywords

virtual reality – VR and AR technology – visualization – network infrastructure – tablet computers – binaural sound rhythm

1   Introduction

The relevance of the research topic lies in the fact that the main direction in the current educational environment is the introduction of VR and AR technologies as universal information tools for improving the intercultural and interlingual knowledge of students (*Kuznetsov* et al., 2019)

The research aims to improve intercultural and interlingual knowledge exchange using VR and AR technologies in the educational process as part of the social development of the student's personality and in international cooperation.

The research objectives are as follows:
1. To analyze the interaction of the presentation of educational material through the use of VR and AR technologies in the framework of the exchange of knowledge of intercultural and interlingual learning;
2. To apply VR and AR technologies to improve the quality of delivery of educational programs for more sustainable social development of students;
3. To implement augmented and virtual reality technologies as an exchange of skills and abilities in the context of international cooperation (*Kumicheva*, 2019)

In current social conditions and the global problem of COVID-19, there is a need for changes in the area of education. The project "Digital Technologies" is being implemented within the framework of the national project "Digital Economy of the Russian Federation." One of the tasks of this program indicates the importance of introducing virtual and augmented reality into the educational process (*Sergienko and Seraya*, 2020)

In the Decree "On national goals and strategic objectives of the development of the Russian Federation for the period up to 2024," the President of the Russian Federation sets the following educational goals for the Government of the Russian Federation. Rising a harmoniously developed and socially responsible person based on the spiritual and moral values of the peoples of Russia and the historical past, it is necessary to improve the native language and be sure to remember and not forget about national and cultural traditions. To achieve this goal, within the framework of education, it is necessary to create an advanced and safe digital educational environment that can provide high quality and accessibility of education at all levels of training (*Presidential Executive Office*, 2018)

2 Materials and Method

From the point of view of foreign and Russian researchers, even more intensive development of education is expected, in which there will be an opportunity to implement projects using VR and AR technologies. They will allow developing and improving the quality of students' knowledge in their professional activities (*Ivanova*, 2018).

Current educational technology focuses on an individualized approach to learning. The world does not stand still; education needs constant improvement. Thus, it became necessary to apply virtual (VR) and augmented (AR) technologies in the development of the education system. Practice shows that today's students perceive the complexity of the scientific language very poorly. It is possible to get out of this situation by introducing technologies with AR and VR into educational disciplines, which will simplify the educational process of explaining complex concepts, making it interactive.

To improve the educational process at the university, it is valuable to determine the trajectory of the educational movement and make a sample of training with the aim of sustainable social development of intercultural and interlingual exchange in the process of studying the disciplines of the humanitarian cycle. VR can help make the learning process exciting (*Izosina and Semerkova*, 2017). The use of interactive technologies in the educational process with the help of VR and AR is the student's interaction with the surrounding world of the studied subject. They aim to implement the cognitive and creative activity of students, provide an opportunity to improve the quality of education, and correctly allocate time for educational activities.

The advantage of VR and AR technologies for the teacher lies not in the possibility of explaining the material "really simple" but in the creation of animated material. In other words, three-dimensional graphics allow visually stimulating the educational process with the necessary detail (*Andrushko*, 2018).

3 Results

The learning process can be organized in the form of a game, a tour of historical sites and eras can also be conducted, and students can hear the language of the peoples who lived in those distant times. For example, as part of the study of the discipline "International Cultural Exchange and Business Communications," we can reveal the topic "The problem of historical and cultural typology in the studies of the Russian philosopher Danilevsky," where teachers and students discuss cultural and historical types using the example of 12 civilizations.

Nowadays, the Google EarthVR educational program is used in the international educational space. This program allows one to see the world's attractions from all sides virtually. Returning to this discipline and the main topic of this research, the authors can also delve into the mysteries of the twelve civilizations and virtually trace their birth, rise, and fall. Additionally, they discuss the work of Danilevsky, transform him into a living image, and discuss the relevance of the problems noted by the scientist.

Another educational program "The VR Museum of Fine Art" allows students to visit a virtual museum. For example, we can introduce students to Egyptian exhibits, the first creators of the alphabet – the Phoenicians. They can virtually visit the Roman Forum and meet the great orator Cicero and the strategist and tactician Caesar. This program allows walking in the streets of Athens and talking with Socrates, Plato, and Aristotle, taking part in the Battle of Pavia, and looking into the Coliseum. "The VR Museum of Fine Art" also allows students and teachers to collect additional educational material and visit libraries and music and audio libraries (*Stoyanov and Marychev*, 2020).

Fast and high-quality learning of foreign languages always remains relevant. Many methods and technologies have been introduced and tested in the educational environment over the past decades. Unfortunately, the expected effect – quality and speed of mastering a foreign language in the required volume – is rarely achieved. The rapid development of innovative technologies and methods does not prevent teachers from further searching for the most optimal ways to learn foreign languages and implement them as soon as possible in the educational process. The virtual educational environment is subject to a great discussion, including by linguists, in the case of VR and AR technologies. Despite the existing disagreements, most linguists talk about the positive aspects of these innovations for the educational process as a whole, such as the effect of presence, overstimulation of the senses, visibility, involvement, focusing, safety, and many others. Using these technologies, a teacher can immerse students in a virtual environment where they can communicate with virtual program participants, recognize their speech, get acquainted with the culture and traditions of the country of the studied language, and study its history. Students can determine where and in what situations they want to be and develop communication skills. This is relevant not only for foreign languages.

A student can get acquainted with the lexical minimum in the form of mini-lessons on selected topics.

Using AR and VR, the interaction of touching and hearing information occurs in the form of the binaural beat effect, which allows students to feel the connection between the real and the virtual space. The binaural sound rhythm will add volume, and immersion in virtual reality will become a natural environment for students and teachers (*Maslov and Khaminova*, 2016).

Thus, in the process of teaching a foreign language, it is possible to create a situation in the far abroad, for example, intercultural and interlingual exchange in the area of education at the international level (conferences, symposiums, and business meetings). VR and AR are technologies that provide a special information space where students receive information and interact with it. They have an opportunity to implement various projects and apply elements of scientific and educational activities in student scientific forums, scientific seminars, and Russian and international competitions (*Kotenko*, 2020).

The use of a new type of blended learning is expected with the advent of courses based on traditional learning and learning with VR elements. In today's conditions, where online learning is becoming inevitable for the educational environment, VR tools, properly integrated into the system (e.g., online language courses), can be useful for students who prefer or are forced to learn languages online.

Putting on a virtual reality helmet and downloading the VR Learn English application, students find themselves in a virtual situation (*Antoniadi and Grubich*, 2020)

The program must have many locations, for example, hotel, office, shop, city walk, airport, a museum, etc. The lists of virtual spaces which can help improve language and intercultural communication skills must be wide and include topics that provide knowledge in these two closely related disciplines.

In foreign language classes, using social networks, the authors offer to create their own virtual images, which will present students' personalities or some events in the form of interesting illustrated stories. Living a small fragment of computer life, students enter into the game of linguistic and cultural realities and social statuses (*Koshetarova and Losinskaya*, 2019)

VR and AR technologies also help students with various forms of disability to overcome obstacles. The authors propose to organize a virtual trip to the historical places of the student's native city in the process of passing the topic: "Intercultural contacts and connections of the peoples of Tatarstan." Wearing VR glasses, a young person with disabilities will be able to move freely to any part of the city, communicate with people, and overcome the fear of loneliness. He or she will have an incentive to find an additional source of fiction or journalistic literature to take a fresh look at native spaces and overcome the language barrier.

Foreign language teachers can offer a number of tasks to overcome the complexities of international languages. This will provide an opportunity to independently acquire knowledge, skills to work with a large amount of information, information analysis skills, creative thinking, and incentive to improve a foreign language. Such tasks aim to train communication skills and make a person feel confident in similar situations in real life. This is also important for people with autism (*Dyakonova*, 2020).

The authors also recommend introducing animation tools that will more accurately simulate the process of presenting educational material in the form of a motion schedule, for example, in interior design or any ceremonial part (*Gritsevich*, 2017).

4 Conclusion

VR and AR technologies allow for creating an environment in which a person perceives all material through the senses. VR and AR technologies simulate comfortable conditions for obtaining new knowledge. No one thinks for students, they are looking for virtual ways out of difficult learning situations by themselves (*Butov and Grigoriev*, 2018).

The importance of using VR and AR technologies in the development of the education system lies in the quality of the presentation and acquisition of knowledge for students. Many scientific and practical materials are devoted to scientific practices in Russia and abroad.

The ability to properly organize the learning process using VR and AR technologies is the result that contributes to the activation of students' creative attitude to society, themselves, and their profession.

The educational environment of Kazan universities, in particular the Kazan Cooperative Institute (Russian University of Cooperation), creates various scientific platforms for intercultural and interlingual exchange, where VR and AR technologies are used to improve the development and training of personnel in various areas of activity. The knowledge offered by teachers of higher educational institutions meets the requirements of Russian and international quality of student training.

References

Presidential Executive Office (2018) *Decree "On national goals and strategic objectives of the development of the Russian Federation for the period up to 2024"* (No. 204 of May 7, 2018, with amendments and additions). Moscow, Russia. Available (consulted 10 October 2021) at: https://base.garant.ru/71937200/.

Andrushko DYu (2018) Application of virtual and augmented reality technologies in the educational process: Problems and prospects. *Scientific Review. Pedagogical Sciences* 6: 5–10. Available (consulted 10 October 2021) at: https://science-pedagogy.ru/ru/article/view?id=1779.

Antoniadi KS, and Grubich TYu (2020) Application of VR and AR technologies in education. In: Emelyanov NV (ed) *New impulses for development: Research issues.* Belgorod, Russia: Dobrosvet, 26–29. Available (consulted 10 October 2021) at: https://cyberleninka.ru/article/n/primenenie-vr-i-ar-tehnologiy-v-obrazovanii.

Butov RA, and Grigoriev IS (2018, April 24) *Virtual and augmented reality technologies for education.* Available (consulted 10 October 2021) at: https://prodod.moscow/archives/6428.

Dyakonova EA (2020) Project: "Let's travel together": VR-technologies for social rehabilitation. *Scientific works of the Free Economic Society of Russia* 224(4): 453–463. Available (consulted 10 October 2021) at: https://cyberleninka.ru/article/n/proekt-davayte-puteshestvovat-vmeste-vr-tehnologii-dlya-sotsialnoy-reabilitatsii.

Gritsevich LV (2017) Transformation of types and principles of design in the contemporary world. *Economic and Social-Humanitarian Studies* 4(16): 13–17. Available (consulted 10 October 2021) at: https://cyberleninka.ru/article/n/transformatsiya-vidov-i-printsipov-dizayna-v-sovre.

Ivanova AV (2018) VR & AR technologies: Opportunities and application obstacles. *Strategic Decisions and Risk Management* 3(106): 88–107. DOI: 10.17747/2078-8886-2018-3-88-107.

Izosina EV, and Semerkova LN (2017) Strategic appeal evaluation of the virtual and augmented reality market in Russia. *University Proceedings. Volga Region. Social Sciences* 3(43): 193–202. DOI: 10.21685/2072-3016-2017-3-21.

Koshetarova LN, and Losinskaya AYu (2019) Fluctuations of virtuality: Models of virtual reality in the context of cultural dynamics. *Values and Meaning* 1(59): 62–77. Available (consulted 10 October 2021) at: https://cyberleninka.ru/article/n/fluktuatsii-virtualnosti-modeli-virtualnoy-realnosti-v-kontekste-kulturnoy-dinamiki.

Kotenko VV (2020) Challenges and opportunities of application of augmented and virtual reality technologies in teaching the foreign language. *Scientific Notes of the University named after P.F. Lesgaft* 3(181): 252–257. DOI: 10.34835/issn.2308-1961.2020.3.p252-258.

Kumicheva DA (2019) Prospects of Russian it companies in the world market of VR and AR technologies. *Bulletin of Science and Education* 12–1(66): 73–76. Available (consulted 10 October 2021) at: https://cyberleninka.ru/article/n/perspektivy-ros siyskih-it-kompaniy-na-mirovom-rynke-vr-i-ar-tehnologiy.

Kuznetsov VA, Russu VG, and Kupriyanovskiy VP (2019) On the use of virtual and augmented reality. *International Journal of Open Information Technologies* 7(4): 75–84. Available (consulted 10 October 2021) at: https://cyberleninka.ru/article/n/ob-ispol zovanii-virtualnoy-i-dopolnennoy-realnosti.

Maslov EA, and Khaminova AA (2016) Implementation of new technologies of virtual and augmented reality in the creative industries: Trends and problems. *Humanitarian Informatics* 10: 35–46. DOI: 10.17223/23046082/10/4.

Sergienko AYu, and Seraya AS (2020) *Augmented and virtual reality technologies: Applications*. Available (consulted 10 October 2021) at: https://scienceforum.ru /2020/article/2018019913.

Stoyanov SS, and Marychev SN (2020) *VR and AR technologies in the modern world*. Available (consulted 10 October 2021) at: https://scienceforum.ru/2020/article/201 8022163.

CHAPTER 19

Digitalization of Education
Student Assessments and Factors of Its Formation in a Pandemic

Elena V. Frolova, Olga V. Rogach and Natalia V. Medvedeva

Abstract

The vector of state policy, which is aimed at intensifying the processes of digitalization of higher education, as well as the risks of the COVID-19 pandemic, actualizes the importance of research on this topic. During the work on the article, the authors used qualitative and quantitative research methods. Quantitative methods include a questionnaire survey of Russian university students (N=1553 people) conducted in February-April 2020 based on the Google platform. The authors also conducted focus groups with the participation of full-time and part-time students. Additionally, the methods of correlation analysis were applied during the research.

The most optimistic assessments of students relate to the issues of organizing training and assessing knowledge in the context of digitalization: 74.1% believe that more understandable requirements for the work performed are provided, and 72.9% believe that the control system is becoming clearer.

Aspects related to interactions with teachers are rated somewhat lower: only 61.6% believe that in the context of digitalization, the presentation of the material becomes more understandable, and 49.6% of respondents believe that "communication with teacher becomes more accessible." The third part of the respondents (30.2%) believes that digital technologies contribute to the overload of students in the learning process. Among students with a low level of digital literacy, the proportion of such respondents increases (38.8%), which is 8.6% higher than the average values for the sample. During the focus groups, it was noted that only a small number of students had direct experience of interaction with teachers using advanced digital technologies (Mentimeter, Kahoot, Quizizz, Socrative, and Padlet) in the educational process to increase its intensification and interactivity. Today's youth have a superficial understanding of digitalization processes, replacing its content with the primary attributes of informatization: online teaching of disciplines, electronic personal account of students, and electronic educational materials. Digitalization assessments are primarily based on subjective factors – understanding their experience of remote learning during the COVID-19 pandemic. Correlation analysis has presented the existence of a relationship between the level of digital literacy of students and the perception of the digitalization processes of education.

Keywords

digitalization – digital competencies – digital literacy – education – higher education institution – pandemic

1   Introduction

The relevance of studying the issues of digitalization of education has increased significantly in the context of the epidemiological crisis. Universities worldwide are increasingly digitizing their activities. The COVID-19 pandemic has led to increased digitalization of the education sector: the development of "e-pedagogics" (*Komljenovic*, 2020) and new forms of knowledge assessment, as well as modification of consulting practices (*Jiang* et al., 2021).

The emergency transition to remote format was accompanied by many mistakes that caused a negative perception of the introduction of digital technologies in the educational process by students and teachers. Research results have shown an increase in stress in the context of online learning and in the study load (*Marek* et al., 2021). Negative trends are a decrease in the level of development of students' cognitive competencies and their communication skills, as well as the loss of the fundamental nature of education (*Strekalova*, 2019). The total transition to the virtual space in the context of the COVID-19 pandemic has actualized the importance of technological solutions to compensate for the lack of practices of direct interactions between key subjects of the educational process (*Roig-Vila* et al., 2021). Russian scientists also highlight such problems as a significant increase in the amount of information, dependence on electronic devices, cognitive distortions, reduced information memorization skills, lack of disciplinary control, and poor health (*Manikovskaya*, 2019; *Mikhailov and Denisova*, 2020). Additionally, in the context of digitalization, the focus of attention of teachers is more concentrated on the technological aspects of the educational process, while interpersonal communication and creativity fade into the background (*Cladis*, 2018). Another significant negative consequence of digitalization is the growing digital inequality. Research shows that students from families with a low level of education have fewer opportunities to use digital technologies (*Perez-Lopez* et al., 2021). The closure of schools and universities during the COVID-19 pandemic exacerbated the digital inequality and exposed the vulnerable position of young people with insufficient digital literacy and students whose financial resources did not allow them to solve technical problems for comprehensive inclusion in online learning (*Espinosa*, 2021). In this regard, it seems reasonable to conclude that the introduction of online learning must be accompanied by monitoring the level of readiness of students and teachers for its implementation (*Belyakova*, 2020).

In contrast to the analysis of the negative consequences of digitalization, many scientific papers consider its advantages. In particular, in the conditions of a high rhythm of life, such parameters as the opportunity to receive education in a convenient mode and schedule and regardless of the place of residence become of great importance (*Boychenko and Smirnova*, 2019). The digitalization of education provides the opportunity for active learning, freedom to choose an educational trajectory, and overcoming spatial and temporal boundaries (*Karabelskaya*, 2017). Additional benefits of using digital technologies in the educational process are the development of students' creativity and improvement of their learning ability (*Paul and Lal*, 2018), the possibility of building flexible individual educational trajectories (*Kohtz* et al., 2012), increasing the intensification of the educational process and interest in it on the part of students (*Frolova* et al., 2020).

Considering the dilatability of the issue of the advantages and negative trends of digitalization of education, it is quite natural *to analyze the factors that determine the boundaries of variability in the perception of its parameters and consequences.* Material and technical (access to the Internet, availability of necessary devices and programs) and personal factors (motivation, self-organization, self-discipline) are of primary importance. The personal motivation of students determines their readiness to use digital technologies in the educational process and the effectiveness of the remote learning process (*Aleshkovsky* et al., 2020). The requirements of digitalization update the importance of the methodological, technological, and informational work of educational organizations (*Narbut* et al., 2020). The issues of the digital competence of teachers and their readiness to use digital technologies in the educational process are also of particular importance (*Frolova* et al., 2019). The effectiveness of these practices is associated with the moral and material motivation of teachers, as well as optimization of the teaching load (*Lobova and Ponkina*, 2021). The condition for ensuring the effectiveness of education in the context of digitalization is the development of information and communication infrastructure, the reduction of technological and competence digital inequality, and the formation of integrated educational resources and high-quality digital content (*Nazarov* et al., 2021). Subjective assessments of the process of digitalization of education, the perception of its advantages, and limitations are associated with the level of organizational support for digital innovations in an educational organization (*Al-Maroof* et al., 2021; *Rogach* et al., 2017).

2   Materials and Method

This article is based on the research findings that found partial coverage in the publication "The specifics of students' perception of the digitalization of education: understanding the experience of online learning in a pandemic" (*Frolova and Rogach*, 2021).

The research toolkit included qualitative and quantitative methods. The key method was a questionnaire survey of students of Russian universities (N=1553 people), conducted in February-April 2020. The questionnaire was posted on the Google platform,[1] link to the survey was distributed through virtual student communities. The limitation of this study lies in the possible shift in the representation of certain socio-demographic groups of students, which is due to the use of a spontaneous sample of respondents. Qualitative research methods included focus group interviews. Two focus groups were held with the participation of full-time and part-time students in January-February 2021. The number of participants in each focus group was 12 people. The study results showed that the key factors in the effectiveness of digitalization in higher education are its material and technical base and the level of digital competence of students and teachers (*Frolova and Rogach*, 2021). The analysis of the obtained results required an understanding of the conclusions regarding the use of pedagogical technologies that consider the specifics of online learning and the expansion of theoretical conclusions on the negative and positive consequences of digitalization for young people. In September 2021, an additional focus group was held (N=11).

Focus groups were conducted online through the Skype platform. The use of the online format imposed certain restrictions, reducing the level of communicative activity of the respondents.

The research uses the results of correlation analysis of the data obtained during the survey, which allowed forming a deeper understanding of the significance of several factors affecting the perception of digitalization.

The purpose of the article is to analyze the processes of digitalization of education in Russian universities and the stereotypes of its perception among

---

1   Questionnaire survey of students of Russian universities. Available (consulted 19 February 2021) at: https://docs.google.com/forms/d/1K-83c0CqLCDB9l26uzFGDPB42foIKgfpsq9hJ3iw uqo/edit.

young people, as well as to study its negative and positive consequences for today's youth. The research hypothesis was the assumption of the dominant influence of subjective factors on students' perception of the specifics of the digitalization of education. Subjective factors include the level of digital literacy and the experience of remote learning during the COVID-19 pandemic.

Separate components of the problem studied in this research are analyzed by such authors as *Matsiola* et al. (2019).

3   Results

The research results demonstrated that less than a third of respondents are not familiar with the concept of "digitalization of education"; 65.3% of respondents have given a positive answer to this question. It should also be noted that students have a superficial perception of digitalization processes. Thus, during a questionnaire survey, respondents were asked to express what associations the digitalization of education evokes in them. The following statements prevailed in the answers: "electronic environment," "distance education," "online learning," "Internet," "computer," etc. Only a small part of the respondents chose such associations as: "virtual environment," "interactive learning," "virtual reality," "network education," and "digital technologies." During the focus groups, students have also noted that they strongly associate digitalization with the primary attributes of informatization: an electronic personal account of a student, electronic educational materials, etc.

The respondents' answers, which illustrate the students' self-assessment of the level of development of digital literacy, are also of great interest. According to the data obtained, the respondents rated their skills quite highly: 36.6% and 25.8% gave marks of 4 and 5 points, respectively. Almost a third of the respondents (27.8%) rated their skills in using information and communication technologies as satisfactory. There remains only a small proportion of respondents who, in the context of widespread digitalization of education, believe that their level of digital literacy is significantly below the average level: 2.8% and 7% of respondents gave their skills in using information and communication technologies a score of 1 and 2 points.

Similar to the results of the questionnaire survey, students in the focus group highly rated their level of digital literacy. While specifying their digital skills and abilities, respondents described the following set of skills for working in an electronic environment: working with the software used for communication (Skype, Zoom, WhatsApp, Teams, etc.) and preparation of infographics using Canva and Microsoft PowerPoint platforms. Students noted that such a set of digital competencies is quite enough to organize their educational process. The students did not experience difficulties in preparing for practical classes.

The focus group revealed an interesting phenomenon. Some students in the remote work environment interacted with teachers who actively applied additional digital tools to maintain interest in learning. In particular, they talked about digital tools for engaging the group in work (Mentimeter, Kahoot, Quizizz, Socrative, and Padlet) and platforms for organizing and conducting online training (Webinar.ru and Discord). The students highly appreciated the new practices of using digital technologies that ensure the interactivity of the educational process and offer a different look at traditional teaching. A small number of students had such an experience of getting acquainted with advanced digital technologies in education, but they demonstrate the growing need for improving digital literacy. They believe that digitalization will enrich the educational process and increase involvement and interest in learning.

It can be assumed that higher education teachers can become a driver for updating the digital needs of young people and ensuring the introduction of digital technologies in the educational process. Respondents' answers are dominated by the opinion (67.1%) that the success of education in the context of digitalization depends on the competence of teachers.

Students of Russian universities were also asked to evaluate the "character" of the digitalization of education as a contemporary phenomenon (Chart 19.1). According to the data obtained, despite the presence of a number of problems and dysfunctions, which have manifested themselves in the conditions of distance learning, the majority of respondents consider the digitalization of education as a "positive phenomenon."

During the analysis of the results of the focus group, the following pattern was revealed: students who positively assess the experience of distance learning and positively perceive the consequences of digitalization are generally less inclined to highlight its negative trends. However, those who assess the quality of remote education as relatively low express more concerns about the digitalization of education. They are also pessimistic about its consequences for Russian higher education.

From the point of view of the research objectives, it is also of interest to analyze the relationship between the perception of digitalization processes and assessments of the level of digital literacy (Table 19.1).

The number of degrees of freedom is four. The value of the χ^2 criterion is 70.926. The critical value of χ^2 at significance level $p=0.01$ is 13.277. The relationship between the factor and resultant signs is statistically significant at a significance level of $p<0.01$. The significance level is $p<0.001$. Thus, the research

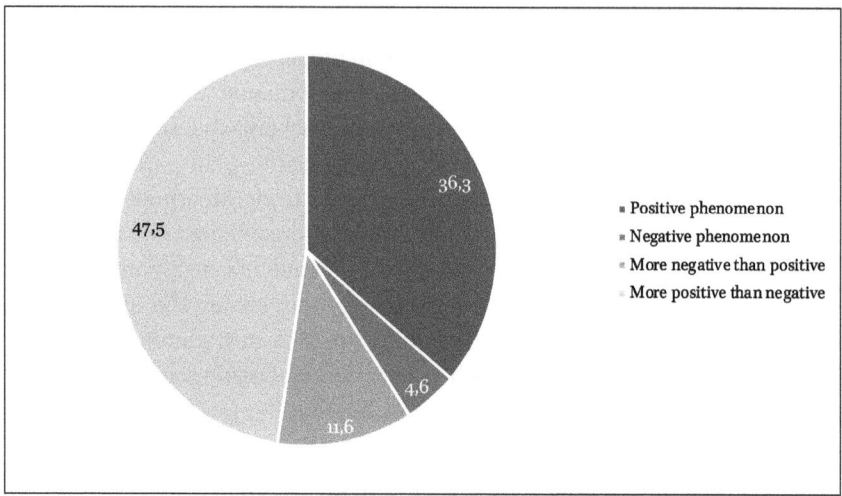

CHART 19.1 Distribution of answers to the question: "What do you think the digitalization of education in general is ...?" %
SOURCE: COMPILED BY THE AUTHORS BASED ON THE RESULTS OF THE STUDY

TABLE 19.1 Correlation analysis of the impact of assessments of the level of digital literacy of students on the perception of digitalization processes, person

Digital literacy assessments	Perception of digitalization processes		Sum
	Positive and rather positive	Negative and rather negative	
5	355	45	*400*
4	495	74	*569*
3	358	74	*432*
2	72	37	*109*
1	22	21	*43*
Total	*1302*	*251*	*1553*

SOURCE: COMPILED BY THE AUTHORS BASED ON THE RESULTS OF THE STUDY

results show that the level of digital literacy determines the perception of digitalization.

Despite the fact that the research results demonstrate a positive attitude of students towards the digitalization of education, only 14.9% of respondents believe that it does have no negative consequences. The majority of students (58.3%) see the deterioration of interpersonal communication skills as a key threat. These risks are associated with a decrease in the time for classroom work and live communication with the teacher, which is the second most important problem in the rating of negative consequences of digitalization (this answer was chosen by 49.3% of the students surveyed). Every third student (33.4%) is concerned about the development of social inequality due to uneven access to digital technologies. The decrease in the level of knowledge of students in the context of digitalization is a significant problem for 37.3% of respondents.

Assessing the characteristics of the educational process in the context of digitalization, students mostly give positive assessments. Only a third of respondents believe that students are not ready to introduce digital technologies in education. Optimistic expectations of students are centered on the plane of organization and control of educational activities. Thus, more than two-thirds of the respondents agree with the statement that digitalization makes the control system clearer (72.9%) and the requirements for the work performed more understandable (74.1%). Optimism is more cautious regarding communication with teachers. Only 61.6% believe that in the context of digitalization, the presentation of the material becomes more understandable. Opinions were divided on the statement "communication with teachers becomes more accessible," 49.6% agreed with this, and 50.4% did not agree.

A third of respondents (30.2%) believe that digital technologies contribute to the overload of students in the learning process, 48% do not agree with this statement, and 21.8% found it difficult to answer. Let us consider whether the level of digital literacy affects the perception of students' overload in the context of digitalization (Table 19.2).

The number of degrees of freedom is eight. The value of the χ^2 criterion is 28.727. The critical value of χ^2 at the significance level $p=0.01$ is 20.09. The relationship between the factor and resultant signs is statistically significant at a significance level of $p<0.01$.

The questionnaire survey showed that 62% of the students surveyed had noted the lack of time to communicate with the teacher in the context of digitalization. During the discussion of this issue in the focus group, the respondents emphasized that, despite the growing possibilities of digital technologies in terms of achieving a level of visibility and expressiveness of educational

TABLE 19.2 Correlation analysis of answers to the questions "Assess the level of your digital literacy" and "Do you agree with the statement that the use of digital technologies causes overload of students?," person

Digital literacy assessments	The consequence of the use of digital technologies is an overload of trainees			Sum
	Yes	No	Difficult to answer	
5	132	210	58	400
4	154	278	137	569
3	125	202	105	432
2	42	43	24	109
1	17	12	14	43
Total	470	745	338	1553

SOURCE: COMPILED BY THE AUTHORS BASED ON THE RESULTS OF THE STUDY

materials, reducing the time of communication with teachers becomes a more significant problem that reduces the quality of education.

In the final part of the study, students were asked questions regarding their motivational attitude and their relationship with digital technologies applied in the educational process. According to more than half of the respondents (54.9%), digital technologies increase motivation and interest in learning. However, a quarter of the respondents (25.9%) did not agree with this statement, and 19.1% found it difficult to answer.

According to the results of the focus group, the positive relationship between motivation and the introduction of digital technologies in the educational process has no objective basis. Most of the respondents, who stated that digital technologies increase interest in learning and motivation to acquire new knowledge, could not give examples from personal experience. These answers are based on well-established positive stereotypes. Many participants referred to the foreign practice and future expectations. Only a small part of the students could tell how they were motivated by a teacher interested in applying new digital tools.

4 Discussion

The results of the questionnaire survey demonstrated a high level of self-assessment of students' digital literacy. The findings generally correlate with independent studies. In particular, the joint analytical report of the All-Russian Center for the Study of Public Opinion and the Social Business Group gives the following figures: Russians were divided into four groups in terms of the level of digital competencies – with a high level of proficiency (30%), above average (32%), below average (18%), and low proficiency (20%). Simultaneously, most respondents are satisfied with their level of digital competencies (60%) (*VCIOM*, 2020).

It is really interesting that digital literacy is perceived by students in a simplified form; the respondents of the focus groups attributed the basic skills of preparing presentations and using software for communication on the Internet to their digital skills. In this regard, of particular interest is the study by Noh, where digital literacy is understood more broadly as a complex phenomenon that includes technical literacy, information literacy (search, recognition, editing, information processing), and virtual community literacy (*Noh*, 2017).

Additionally, we can conclude that respondents replace the concept of digitalization with informatization and the development of computer technologies. In this context, the authors agree with the opinion of Nikulina and Starichenko, who emphasize that the informatization of education provides only the basis for a qualitative transition to its digitalization. The authors rightly believe that digital technologies impose new requirements on the participants in the educational space: changes in learning models, the transformation of mentality, and modernization of pedagogical tools and forms of work (*Nikulina and Starichenko*, 2018). Developing this idea, Vinichenko insists on the need to use the capabilities of artificial intelligence in the education management system, activate the teacher's position in the context of digitalization, and introduce gamification methods into the educational process. These findings are consistent with the results of this research (*Vinichenko* et al., 2020, 2021). Thus, students focus their expectations on the digital skills of teachers and their readiness to use digital technologies to increase interest in learning. These perspectives are factors in the positive attitude of students towards digitalization, while personal experience does not allow fully speaking about the expected level of use of digital technologies in the educational process. There are only individual cases of the active position of a teacher who fully involves students in the educational process through digital technologies. The authors agree with the opinion of Kumar that in today's conditions, special attention must be paid to the training of teaching staff and the formation of their motivation to use digital technologies (*Kumar* et al., 2019). The study established the significant role of teachers with a high level of digital competence and readiness to use advanced digital technologies in the educational process. This position of a teacher allows for actualizing the educational needs of students and involving young people in the educational process as much as possible.

The research results (questionnaire and focus groups) illustrate the high relevance of the problems of effective communication between teachers and students. This issue is included in the zone of high risks when analyzing the negative consequences of digitalization. The authors agree with the opinion of Van den Beemt, Thurlings, and Willems, who indicate that the lack of communication, the exchange of students' experiences with each other, and the practices of "direct interaction" between teachers and students are serious challenges of digitalization (*Van den Beemt* et al., 2019).

The results of the correlation analysis showed that the level of digital literacy is one of the key factors in the perception of the digitalization of education and assessment of its negative and positive consequences. Despite the dominant point of view in scientific research about the "information overload" of students in the context of digitalization (*Dobrinskaya and Martynenko*, 2019), the questionnaire survey found that not all respondents share this position. Moreover, the results of the correlation analysis have demonstrated that the higher the level of self-assessment of digital literacy, the less students fear information overload. This conclusion can be confirmed by studies conducted under the direction of Atoy in the Philippines. It has been concluded that digital literacy is the most significant factor in students' media competence, providing more successful strategies for finding information in the virtual space (*Atoy* et al., 2020).

Thus, the obtained data complement the results of Russian and international studies in terms of analyzing the role of digital literacy in the perception of the processes of digitalization of education, reducing its negative consequences such as cognitive distortions and information overload. The conclusions made in the research provide an increase in empirical data on the problems of interactions between key actors in the educational space in the context of digitalization.

5   Conclusion

Students tend to have a simplified understanding of the processes of digitalization of education; its content is often replaced by the characteristics of informatization, its basic elements: the student's electronic account and electronic educational materials. The research found confirmation of the hypothesis about the dominant role of subjective factors in assessing the consequences of digitalization on the development of higher education. In particular, the subjective experience of distance learning has a significant impact on the perception of the problems and consequences of the digitalization of education. Students tend to have high expectations of promising changes in the education system under the influence of digitalization in terms of increasing interest in learning and introducing innovations. These expectations are not backed up by real learning practices using digital technologies in Russian universities. There are separate examples of pedagogical practices that are not supported so much by the university administration as by the initiative of teachers with a high level of digital competence. The active "digital position" of a teacher allows for actualizing the digital needs of students and increasing their level of motivation and interest in learning. The level of digital literacy of a student is a determining factor in assessing the processes of digitalization and the number of its negative consequences.

The results obtained may have practical significance for the development of compensators for key dysfunctions of the digitalization of education, for determining the directions for increasing the digital competence of teachers, and for searching for promising mechanisms for increasing students' interest in learning in the context of digitalization.

References

Al-Maroof RS, Alhumaid K, and Salloum S (2021) The continuous intention to use e-learning, from two different perspectives. *Education Sciences* 11(1): 6. DOI: 10.3390/educsci11010006.

Aleshkovsky IA, Gasparishvili AT, Krukhmaleva OV, Narbut NP, and Savina NE (2020) Russian university students about distance learning: Assessments and opportunities. *Higher Education in Russia* 29(10): 86–100. DOI: 10.31992/0869-3617-2020-29-10-86-100.

Atoy MB, Garcia FRO, Cadungog RR, Cua JDO, Mangunay SC, and de Guzman AB (2020) Linking digital literacy and online information searching strategies of Philippine university students: The moderating role of mindfulness. *Journal of Librarianship and Information Science* 52(4): 1015–1027. DOI: 10.1177/0961000619898213.

Belyakova EG (2020) Online learning: In statu nascendi. *Vocational Education and Labor Market* 2: 45–47. DOI: 10.24411/2307-4264-2020-10207.

Boychenko OV, and Smirnova OYu (2019) Information-communication and digital technologies in education. *Problems of Modern Teacher Education* 64–2: 29–33.

Cladis AE (2018) A shifting paradigm: An evaluation of the pervasive effects of digital technologies on language expression, creativity, critical thinking, political discourse, and interactive processes of human communications. *E-Learning and Digital Media* 17(5): 341–364. DOI: 10.1177/2042753017752583.

Dobrinskaya DE, and Martynenko TS (2019) Perspectives of the Russian information society: Digital divide levels. *RUDN Journal of Sociology* 19(1): 108–120. DOI: 10.22363/2313-2272-2019-19-1-108-120.

Espinosa MA (2021) COVID-19, education and children's rights in Spain. *Revista Internacional de Educacion para la Justicia Social* 9(3): 245–258. DOI: 10.15366/riejs2020.9.3.013.

Frolova EV, and Rogach OV (2021) Particularities of students' perceptions of the digitalization of education: Comprehending the experience of online learning in a pandemic environment. *Perspectives of Science and Education* 3(51): 43–54. DOI: 10.32744/pse.2021.3.3.

Frolova EV, Rogach OV, and Ryabova TM (2020) Digitalization of education in modern scientific discourse: New trends and risks analysis. *European Journal of Contemporary Education* 9(2): 331–336. DOI: 10.13187/ejced.2020.2.313.

Frolova EV, Ryabova TM, and Rogach OV (2019) Digital technologies in education: Problems and prospects for "Moscow Electronic School" project implementation. *European Journal of Contemporary Education* 8(4): 779–789. DOI: 10.13187/ejced.2019.4.779.

Jiang ZH, Wu HB, Cheng HQ, Wang WM, Xie AN, and Fitzgerald SR (2021) Twelve tips for teaching medical students online under COVID-19. *Medical Education Online* 26(1): 1854066 DOI: 10.1080/10872981.2020.1854066.

Karabelskaya IV (2017) The use of digital technologies in the educational process of higher education. *Bulletin of Ufa State Petroleum Technological University, Series: Economics* 1(19): 127–131.

Kohtz C, Gowda C, Stockert P, White J, and Kennel L (2012) The use of Web 2.0 technologies. *Nurse Educator* 37(4): 162–167. DOI: 10.1097/NNE.0b013e31825a87b3.

Komljenovic J (2020) The future of value in digitalised higher education: why data privacy should not be our biggest concern. *Higher Education* 83: 119–135. DOI: 10.1007/s10734-020-00639-7.

Kumar S, Martin F, Budhrani K, and Ritzhaupt A (2019) Award-Winning Faculty Online Teaching Practices: Elements of Award-Winning Courses. *Online learning* 23(4): 160–180. DOI: 10.24059/olj.v23i4.2077.

Lobova SV, and Ponkina EV (2021) Online courses: To accept impossible to ignore. *Higher Education in Russia* 30(1): 23–28. DOI: 10.31992/0869-3617-2021-30-1-23-35.

Manikovskaya MA (2019) Digitalization of education: Challenges to traditional norms and moral principles. *Power and Management in the East of Russia* 2(87): 100–106.

Marek MW, Chew CS, and Wu WCV (2021) Teacher experiences in converting classes to distance learning in the COVID-19 pandemic. *International Journal of Distance Education Technologies* 19(1): 40–60. DOI: 10.4018/IJDET.20210101.oa3.

Matsiola M, Spiliopoulos P, Kotsakis R, Nicolaou C, and Podara A (2019) Technology-enhanced learning in audiovisual education: The case of radio journalism course design. *Education Sciences* 9(1): 62. DOI: 10.3390/educsci9010062.

Mikhailov OV, and Denisova YaV (2020) Distance learning at Russian universities: Step forward, two steps back? *Higher Education in Russia* 29(10): 65–76. DOI: 10.31992/0869-3617-2020-29-10-65-76.

Narbut NP, Aleshkovsky IA, Gasparishvili AT, and Krukhmaleva OV (2020) Forced shift to distance learning as an impetus to technological changes in the Russian higher education. *RUDN Journal of Sociology* 20(3): 611–621. DOI: 10.22363/2313-2272-2020-20-3-611-621.

Nazarov VL, Zherdev DV, and Averbukh NV (2021) Shock digitalisation of education: The perception of participants of the educational process. *Education and Science* 23(1): 156–201. DOI: 10.17853/1994-5639-2021-1-156-201.

Nikulina TV, and Starichenko EB (2018) Informatization and digitalization of education: Concepts, technologies, management. *Pedagogical Education in Russia* 8: 107–113. DOI: 10.26170/po18-08-15.

Noh Y (2017) A study on the effect of digital literacy on information use behavior. *Journal of Librarianship and Information Science* 49(1): 26–56. DOI: 10.1177/0961000615624527.

Paul S, and Lal K (2018) Adoption of digital technologies in tertiary education: Evidence from India. *Journal of Educational Technology Systems* 47(1): 128–147. DOI: 10.1177/0047239518768513.

Perez-Lopez E, Atochero AV, and Rivero SC (2021) Distance Education in COVID-19's period: An analysis from the perspective of university students. *Ried-revista Iberoamericana de Educacion a Distancia* 24(1): 331–350. DOI: 10.5944/ried.24.1.27855.

Rogach OV, Frolova EV, and Ryabova TM (2017) Academic competition: Rating race. *European Journal of Contemporary Education* 6(2): 297–307. DOI: 10.13187/ejced.2017.2.297.

Roig-Vila R, Urrea-Solano M, and Merma-Molina G (2021) Communication at university classrooms in the context of COVID-19 by means of videoconferencing with Google Meet. *Ried-revista Iberoamericana de Educacion a Distancia* 24(1): 197–220. DOI: 10.5944/ried.24.1.27510.

Russian Public Opinion Research Center [VCIOM] (2020, May 15) Digital literacy and remote working in a pandemic: Analytical report. Available (consulted 19 February

2021) at: https://wciom.ru/analytical-reports/analiticheskii-doklad/czifrovaya-gramotnost-i-udalennaya-rabota-v-usloviyakh-pandemii.

Strekalova NB (2019) Risks of implementation of digital technologies into education. *Bulletin of Samara University. History, Pedagogy, Philology* 25(2): 84–88. DOI: 10.18287/2542-0445-2019-25-2-84-88.

Van den Beemt A, Thurlings M, and Willems M (2019) Towards an understanding of social media use in the classroom: A literature review. *Technology Pedagogy and Education* 29(1): 35–55. DOI: 10.1080/1475939X.2019.1695657.

Vinichenko MV, Melnichuk AV, and Karácsony P (2020) Technologies of improving the university efficiency by using artificial intelligence: Motivational aspect. *Entrepreneurship and Sustainability Issues* 7(4): 2696–2714. DOI: 10.9770/jesi.2020.7.4(9).

Vinichenko MV, Rybakova MV, Chulanova OL, Makushkin SA, and Karacsony P (2021) Views on working with information in a semi-digital society: Its possibility to develop as open innovation culture. *Journal of Open Innovation: Technology, Market, and Complexity* 7(2): 160. DOI: 10.3390/joitmc7020160.

CHAPTER 20

Education for Sustainable Development in Modern Conditions of Digitalization

Elvira K. Samerkhanova, Olga V. Smyshliaeva, Irina V. Panova, Lyudmila N. Bahtiyarova and Alexander V. Ponachugin

Abstract

The purpose of the article is to substantiate the tools for the formation of skills and competencies necessary for sustainable development through the disciplines of the field "Artificial Intelligence."

The article considers the possibilities of developing skills to achieve the goals of sustainable development in the disciplines of artificial intelligence and the possibilities of artificial intelligence technologies for education for sustainable development.

When writing the article, the authors used the following methods: praximetric (study of regulatory documentation); theoretical (analysis of domestic and foreign literature, generalization, comparison, forecasting, and pedagogical modeling).

Approaches to the role of education in achieving sustainable development goals are analyzed. The possibilities of artificial intelligence technologies for education for sustainable development are considered.

The theoretical significance of the work is a generalization of the experience of integrating vendor courses into the educational process.

The practical significance of the work lies in presenting the experience of developing skills for sustainable development through the disciplines of the field of "Artificial Intelligence," implemented in the engineering and pedagogical areas of study at the Minin Nizhny Novgorod State Pedagogical University (Minin University), as well as in the framework of additional education at Minin University.

The results of the study are updating the educational programs of engineering and pedagogical specialties and the inclusion of educational content for the formation of digital competencies.

Keywords

sustainable development – sustainable development goals – education – educational program – artificial intelligence – digitalization of education

1   Introduction

The concept of sustainable development was developed at the end of the 20th century to find solutions to global problems associated with human activities and the development of technologies that threaten the existence of humanity.

Sustainable development is a concept that puts the human being at the center of problems and decision-making. The three directions that define it correspond to three aspects of human activity: our environment, our way of life, and our standard of living. Three aspects of sustainable development form a single whole and cannot be considered separately (*UN Documents*, 1987).

Since then, the concept of sustainable development has gone through several stages in its development, adapting to modern problems associated with the large-scale development of technologies, but the fundamental principles have not changed much. They are reflected in the document "Sustainable Development Goals." As part of the 2030 Agenda for Sustainable Development, 17 goals for sustainable development have been adopted by the Member States of the United Nations. The present time is called "a decade of action and accomplishments in the name of sustainable development" and provides for an increase in the efficiency of processes at the national level.

Education plays a special role in achieving these goals. It allows us to accelerate the solution of many problems that are identified in the formulation of sustainable development goals (SDGs) (*UN*, n.d.). In 1992, at the United Nations World Conference on Environment and Development, education was called "a decisive factor for change" (*UN Documents*, 1987). By receiving a quality education, a person expands his capabilities and moves toward a more conscious, healthy, and stable life. Today, the young generation receives education and is responsible for the future of the country and the world as a whole (*Malinin* et al., 2022).

The task of the study is to analyze the possibilities of education to achieve the goals of sustainable development, identified by experts in foreign and domestic sources. Analyze the possibilities of artificial intelligence (AI) in education to achieve the SDGs. The scientific and practical task is to show the possibilities of forming competencies to achieve sustainable development goals in the process of studying artificial intelligence disciplines and the use of artificial intelligence tools in education, as well as within the framework of additional education at Minin University.

2   Materials and Method

Education plays an important role in the SDGs because issue 4 is all about this topic. This means that quality education has been set as a goal to be achieved at the global level and has a number of goals to be met. In fact, in recent years, UNESCO has published various papers that show the importance of education:

The Incheon Education 2030 Declaration, developed in 2015, is a reference document outlining global education priorities for the next 15 years.

Rethinking Education, written in 2015, which addresses the purpose of education and the organization of learning.

However, SDG 4 is not the only one that takes this direction into account, as most of them talk about education either directly, included in one of its goals, or implicitly. Moreover, the report Education for Sustainable Development: Learning Challenges shows how all of the SDGs can be applied in the school curriculum, given the skills being worked on.

The fact that education is present in different SDGs means that this is a very important area for sustainable development and achievement of the set goals. As stated at the beginning, this is one of the most important management tools that society has, and this is confirmed. Through education, we can educate citizens, develop a critical spirit, and provide guidance on finding and comparing information. In this way, he will become an engine of change to achieve a positive future that is more respectful for us and the planet (*UN Documents*, 1987).

ESD is a lifelong learning process and an integral part of quality education. It improves the cognitive, social, emotional, and behavioral aspects of learning. It is holistic and transformative and embraces learning content and outcomes, pedagogy, and the learning environment.

ESD is recognized as key to achieving all the Sustainable Development Goals and achieves its goal by transforming society. ESD empowers people of all genders, ages, and current and future generations while respecting cultural diversity (*UNECE*, 2005).

In 2012, 8 Russian universities, along with universities from other countries, committed to assisting in achieving sustainable development goals. Universities have been working on developing a methodology for including educational material that contributes to the formation of knowledge, skills, and abilities in the field of sustainable development, as well as holding conferences and other events that help draw attention to this area. Researchers refer to ESD in Russia as a gradual shift in emphasis from the greening of education to the study and modeling of the future.

The active development of technologies of the fourth industrial revolution, such as artificial intelligence, big data, and new computing technologies, opens up great opportunities for economic development and solving social and environmental problems (*Sedykh* et al., 2022). Nevertheless, at the same time, there are new risks of the adverse impact of these technologies on the environment and society both in the short and long term, in particular, very high energy costs and carbon footprint. Studies have been conducted to assess the impact these technologies will have on the achievement of the Sustainable Development Goals. In The Role of Artificial Intelligence in Achieving the Sustainable Development Goals, researchers look at how artificial intelligence can either help or hinder the achievement of the SDGs. This study shows that AI can contribute to the achievement of 79% of the goals for all SDGs, as a rule, due to technological improvement, but in 35% (relative to all SDGs), the negative impact of the development of artificial intelligence is possible (*Vinuesa* et al., 2020).

Among the sustainable development goals, the achievement of which could be positively affected by the use of technologies based on artificial intelligence, the article cites the SDG "Ensure inclusive and equitable quality education and promote lifelong learning opportunities for all."

In the field of education, new solutions for teaching and learning are being created around the world with the help of artificial intelligence technologies. Artificial intelligence, on the one hand, is seen as a means to improve learning outcomes and the equity and quality of education. On the other hand, educational programs in many countries include elements of artificial intelligence as a subject area, which is associated with an increase in the use of artificial intelligence in all aspects of human activity and the need to prepare students for the new realities of professional life.

The UNESCO document "Artificial intelligence in education: challenges and opportunities for sustainable development," published in 2019, examines the role of artificial intelligence in education in achieving the Sustainable Development Goals. The document's purpose is to define the tasks of educational policy in this direction. The document analyzes examples of the introduction of artificial intelligence in education worldwide. There are three main areas:

Using AI to Achieve Equity and Quality in Education: Personalize and Improve Learning Outcomes; intelligent learning systems to support teachers; data analysis in education management information systems (opportunities for managing educational systems by increasing the amount of data on schools and learning).

Introducing students to AI systems and technologies to "thrive in an AI-rich future": Redesigning curricula and incorporating learning content to build digital competencies ("Agenda for a digital and AI-enabled world"); development of advanced training programs and retraining programs in the direction of "Artificial Intelligence."

Problems in the implementation of AI in education and ways to solve them.

In February 2020, a draft document "Key directions for the development of Russian education to achieve the Goals and objectives of sustainable development in the education system" until 2035 was published.

The document discusses the relationship between the priorities in the educational policy of the Russian Federation and the goals of sustainable development in the field of education. In particular, among the SDG targets by 2030:
- guarantee equal access for men and women to quality education;
- provide X% of the population with the opportunity to have the skills necessary for employment and doing business;
- all students will receive knowledge and skills that contribute to sustainable development (*"Draft document ...,"* 2020).

Next, we will consider examples of the implementation of AI in education around the world, published in a UNESCO document and presented by the Roscongress Foundation at panel discussions of the business program of international events held by the Roscongress Foundation (*Roscongress*, 2020).

Artificial intelligence technologies are used to ensure equal and inclusive access to education.

In the context of an AI-enabled near-future society, it is important to develop new skills to create and decode digital technologies (*Khlap*, 2022).

Companies tend to be quick to adopt AI-based solutions. This means a growing demand for new types of jobs and skills related to the use of AI in the industry. Thus, the education sector urgently needs to respond that curricula need to be redesigned and policies reformulated. However, no country in the world is ready for intelligent automation. However, countries worldwide are doing exemplary work to ensure that their education systems contribute to acquiring competencies required by an artificial intelligence society.

New programs are being introduced at different levels of education – in elementary schools, universities, and additional courses. For example, in Singapore, too, they start developing AI skills among students early. In 2016, the PlayMaker program was launched, which introduced robots to 160 preschools to develop appetite and competence in robotics, programming, and computer science in very young students through play (*Business Portal TAdviser*, 2022).

In January 2022, GoStudent presented research data on how the access and use of various learning methods, such as artificial intelligence, is spreading across Europe.

According to the company, the amount of time spent on online learning is greater for the children of high-income working parents. According to the

European average, 9 out of 10 children studied online during the last school year, and in 2021 almost half of their time spent studying was spent online.

Adaptive learning is more suitable for high-income urban families whose parents have a high level of education. The penetration of adaptive learning/ AI-based learning increases as the rural population grows: while less than 15% of children living in rural areas, 17% of children in small towns have access to such innovative learning methods, 39% of children attending school in suburbs of large cities and large cities, can use adaptive learning methods. The willingness to promote innovative teaching methods in children's schools is higher among parents with a master's or PhD degree (21%) than among parents belonging to another level of education (16%–18%).

The most open to updated learning technologies are working parents with high incomes, higher education, and living in large cities.

If we talk about Russia, then the pace of the introduction of AI in the field of education can be considered quite fast. The Moscow Government is implementing the Moscow E-School project, within which various digital educational materials and services for interactive learning are available.

LANIT Group, a major software developer in Russia, uses machine learning to personalize training courses: each student receives their own educational track, which cuts their learning time in half while contributing to the development of the material, the company reports. In addition, the company is working on using machine learning to check the correctness of the wording in texts, generate questions based on educational materials, and recognize answers given by students in free form, for example, in essays.

However, the inertia of the educational system, the slow mastering of AI tools by teachers, and the lack of equipping regional schools with computers are still obstacles to the rapid introduction of AI technologies in Russian education (*Samerkhanova* et al., 2022).

Next, we will consider an example of the formation of skills and competencies necessary to achieve sustainable development goals in studying artificial intelligence disciplines and the use of artificial intelligence tools in education, as well as within the framework of additional education at Minin University.

3 Results

In accordance with the National Strategy for the Development of Artificial Intelligence for the Period up to 2030, we have carried out work to include modules in the educational programs of engineering and pedagogical areas aimed at studying artificial intelligence technologies and systems. The educational program in the direction of training 09.03.03 "Applied Informatics in Management" (AIM) includes the module K.M.02 "Systems and Technologies of Artificial Intelligence," which contains the disciplines: "Programming in Python" (3 Credits) and "intellect" (4 Credits). The module is studied in the first year and included in the training from September 1, 2021. The educational program of the pedagogical direction with two profiles 44.03.05 "Computer science and technology" includes the module K.M.12 "Modern digital technologies and industry 4.0" with the disciplines: "Artificial intelligence and machine learning" (3 Credits), "Reality" (3 Credits), "Big Data Processing Methods" (3 Credits). Disciplines are studied in the fourth and fifth years. In the educational program of the training direction 09.03.02 "Information Systems and Technologies" (IST), the work program of the discipline "Intelligent Systems and Technologies" from the module K.M.09 "Fundamentals of Systems Theory" was modernized. The changes included the inclusion of modern approaches to the implementation of machine learning and the construction of neural networks using the Python language.

When teaching the above disciplines that study artificial intelligence, the method of projects is used, among other things. As a learning outcome, students present a project using elements of artificial intelligence. When getting acquainted with projects in the field of AI and discussing work at the stage of setting the task, students are invited to get acquainted with the Sustainable Development Goals, analyze what problems are typical for the region where they live and whether it is possible to solve the chosen problem using artificial intelligence. Thus, students learn to formulate socially significant topics for projects and see the possibilities of artificial intelligence for solving sustainable development problems. Examples of real tasks and projects have a great motivational effect. For example, in November 2021, at the AI Journey international conference on AI, the leitmotif of the event was unleashing the power of AI for ESG and sustainability challenges. Representatives of many successful foreign and Russian companies spoke about the importance of developing technologies in accordance with the objectives of sustainable development and presented their AI solutions in this direction. These projects are considered by students in the first lesson as examples of the use of artificial intelligence technologies to solve socially significant problems.

In accordance with the "National Strategy for the Development of Artificial Intelligence for the Period until 2030," it is necessary to include educational modules that form competencies that contribute to the development of artificial intelligence at all levels of education (*Presidential Executive Office*, 2019). This is due to the growing demand for new types of work and skills related to the use of artificial intelligence in professional activities. Future teachers also need to understand the potential of artificial intelligence technologies for education. First, it is the personalization of learning, the construction of individual trajectories. To date, there are already adaptive learning platforms that adjust to the individual characteristics of students. Another direction is the intellectual analysis of educational data for more efficient management and administration of the education system. At Minin University, for students in the pedagogical direction of the 1st year, the discipline "Modern information technologies" is being developed with the inclusion of the section "End-to-end technologies" and the additional discipline "Introduction to artificial intelligence," within which students will get acquainted with the basic concepts and capabilities of artificial intelligence, study the principles of technology AI and create a project with elements of artificial intelligence.

As part of career guidance work with schoolchildren, Minin University conducts classes that increase interest in the field of artificial intelligence. In the first semester of the 2021–2022 academic years, we held an interactive lecture "What is artificial intelligence and how it works" and a master class "Artificial intelligence." Smart city: safe and convenient. In the classroom, students get acquainted with the main technologies of artificial intelligence (computer vision, natural language processing, and data analysis), work in artificial intelligence game applications, and examine how AI is used to ensure safety in a city.

The second direction of our work is the professional development of teachers in the field of artificial intelligence.

Advanced training programs "Artificial Intelligence Technologies for Everyone" have been developed: basic level (36 hours) and advanced level (72 hours). The programs are aimed at developing competencies in the field of artificial intelligence by acquiring the necessary skills, attitudes, and tools for their subsequent use in professional activities. The course introduces students to the main technologies of artificial intelligence and the possibility of using them to solve various socially significant problems.

The peculiarity of the program is that anyone can take part and study in it, regardless of the initial level of knowledge in the field of artificial intelligence. The program is built on top of the Intel® AI for Youth Program, AI for Everyone.

When studying the course at the stage of acquaintance with projects on artificial intelligence and the possibilities of AI, the goals of sustainable development are considered. Examples of real projects using artificial intelligence that solve the problems of sustainable development are given. As a task at this stage, it is proposed to think over what tasks of sustainable development could be solved using artificial intelligence. In addition to the positive effect that the use of artificial intelligence brings, the problems that arise when using it are also discussed, and ethical issues that arise when solving some problems, in particular, issues of trust and security when using artificial intelligence.

As a result of passing the advanced training program "Artificial Intelligence Technologies for Everyone," students acquire a correct understanding of artificial intelligence, skills in working with AI technologies and form the mindset necessary to use artificial intelligence in their professional activities.

4 Discussion

The result of our study was the actualization of the educational programs of the training areas: "Applied Informatics in Management," "Pedagogical Education with two profiles (Informatics and Technology)," which consists of the inclusion of artificial intelligence disciplines in the educational programs of work programs. We suggested that in these disciplines, in addition to the traditional study of artificial intelligence systems and technologies, attention should be paid to the issues of setting the task, the goals of using AI in each case and correlating the task with the goals of sustainable development. As one of the tasks, students independently formulate a problem that can be solved with the help of artificial intelligence and indicate which sustainable development goal this corresponds to. After filling in the table in the mode of joint work, there is a discussion of the identified problems and proposed solutions.

For students of the pedagogical direction of training with two profiles, the discipline of choice "Introduction to Artificial Intelligence" / "Introduction to Machine Learning" was added to the curriculum formed based on the "Core of Higher Pedagogical Education" in the 2nd year. The purpose of the discipline is to create conditions for the formation of a holistic view of the concept of artificial intelligence, modern technologies of artificial intelligence, and their application in the field of education.

In addition to studying the basic concepts in the discipline, the main directions of using AI in education and the role of artificial intelligence in ensuring the quality of education are considered. The experience of foreign countries on the use of intelligent systems to ensure the personalization of learning, the creation of intelligent teacher assistants, and data mining in education management systems are being studied.

Thus, we have presented the possibility of developing skills for sustainable development through the disciplines of the field of "Artificial Intelligence."

5 Conclusion

Modern approaches to sustainable development in Russia and the world are considered. The role of education in achieving sustainable development goals has been studied.

The possibilities of AI technologies for education for sustainable development are considered. It was found that strengthening training in the field of artificial intelligence within higher education is the most important condition for building up national experience in the field of artificial intelligence to solve the problems of sustainable development.

The possibility of forming skills for sustainable development through the disciplines of the field "Artificial Intelligence" within the framework of the Basic professional educational programs and additional education at Minin University is shown.

References

Presidential Executive Office (2019) *Decree "On the development of artificial intelligence in the Russian Federation"* (October 10, 2019 No. 490). Moscow, Russia. Available (consulted 20 February 2022) at: https://www.garant.ru/products/ipo/prime/doc/72738946/.

Business Portal TAdviser (2022, January 24) *Artificial intelligence in education.* Available (consulted 26 February 2022) at: https://tadviser.com/index.php/Article:Artificial_Intelligence_in_Education.

Draft document "Key directions of development of Russian education to achieve the Goals and objectives of sustainable development in the education system" until 2035. Available (consulted 16 January 2022) at: http://edu2035.firo-nir.ru/index.php/stati-opublikovannye-uchastnikami-soobshchestva/86-klyuchevye-napravleniya-2035.

Khlap AA (2022) Technogenic ideal in digital culture: building a research model. *Vestnik of Minin University* 10(1): 14. Available (consulted 20 February 2022) at: https://vestnik.mininuniver.ru/jour/article/view/1336/879.

Malinin VA, Povshednaya FV, and Pugachev AV (2022) Formation of the spiritual and moral qualities of the personality of students in the conditions of modern education. *Vestnik of Minin University* 10(1): 2. Available (consulted 20 February 2022) at: https://vestnik.mininuniver.ru/jour/article/view/1324/867.

Roscongress (2020, October 16) *Artificial intelligence in education: Challenges and Opportunities for sustainable development.* Available (consulted 26 February 2022) at: https://roscongress.org/en/materials/iskusstvennyy-intellekt-v-obrazovanii-problemy-i-vozmozhnosti-dlya-ustoychivogo-razvitiya/.

Samerkhanova EK, Bahtiyarova LN, Krupoderova EP, Krupoderova KR, Ponachugin AV (2022) The role of interactive technologies in the formation of professional competencies of students in the era of intelligent machinesn. In: Bogoviz AV, Suglobov AE, Maloletko AN, and Kaurova OV (eds) *Cooperation and sustainable development.* Cham, Switzerland: Springer, 507–514. https://doi.org/10.1007/978-3-030-77000-6_60.

Sedykh EP, Zhitkova VA, Lapshova AV, Paputkova GA, Khizhnyi AV (2022) Consolidation activities of universities in the digital economy. In: Bogoviz AV, Suglobov AE, Maloletko AN, and Kaurova OV (eds) *Cooperation and sustainable development.* Cham, Switzerland: Springer, 97–104. DOI: 10.1007/978-3-030-77000-6_12.

UN (n.d.) *Sustainable Development Goals.* Available (consulted 15 January 2022) at: https://www.un.org/sustainabledevelopment/ru/about/development-agenda/.

UN Documents (1987) Chapter 2: Towards sustainable development. In: *Our common future: Report of the World Commission on Environment and Development.* Available (consulted 15 January 2022) at: http://www.un-documents.net/ocf-02.htm.

UNECE (2005, March 23) *Strategy for Education for Sustainable Development.* Available (consulted 20 January 2022) at: https://unece.org/DAM/env/documents/2005/cep/ac.13/cep.ac.13.2005.3.rev.1.e.pdf.

Vinuesa R, Azizpour H, Leite I, Balaam M, Dignum V, Domisch S, ... Fuso Nerini, F (2020) The role of artificial intelligence in achieving the Sustainable Development Goals. *Nature Communications* 11: 233. Available (consulted 15 January 2022) at: https://www.nature.com/articles/s41467-019-14108-y.

PART 4

Educational Management to Reduce Social Inequality

CHAPTER 21

Progressive School as an Implementation of Current Trends in the Development of Education

Zhanna Y. Bakaeva, Ella N. Shchegoleva, Galina V. Kalinina, Ljudmila Yu. Alexandrova and Galina M. Lokhonova

Abstract

The paper aims to reveal the features of the implementation of the ideas of progressive pedagogy based on the identified trends in the development of the education system. Achieving this goal includes studying the world practice of implementing the philosophy of education on the example of Western European schools, as well as identifying current trends and prospects for the development of the education system. The methodological basis of the research is the main provisions of the philosophy of education. Such methods as analysis, synthesis, and systemic and structural-functional approaches have been applied during the analysis of the problem. The main principles of the philosophy of education are associated with three trends – existentialism (characterized by personal skills and knowledge), progressivism, and reconstructivism (associated with social change and relationships). These educational philosophies focus on such factors that the authors must teach as part of the curriculum. As the analysis showed, the optimal trends in teaching Western European schools are the variation of these three components. The research substantiates the relevance of implementing the ideas of progressive pedagogy based on the identified trends in the development of the education system for society as a whole and for the education sector. The authors substantiate the need for students to get a system of ideas about the great ideas of civilization that has the potential to solve problems in any era, including the digital one. This necessitates the search for enduring, permanent, and unchanging truths. In today's environment, it is crucial to teach these immutable principles.

Keywords

educational philosophy – development trends – reconstructivism – progressivism – existentialism – Western European school – social relations

1   Introduction

Nowadays, in connection with the implementation of a system-activity approach and competency-based model in education, the ideas and approaches that are aimed at the development of students' personalities and preparing them for their future life in society are in demand. Philosophical ideas about the structure of society lead to the emergence of ideas regarding the definition of the goals and content of education. The methodological foundations of pedagogy are the philosophical knowledge on which the study, design, and organization of the educational process are based.

Philosophical research contributed to the development of education, the formation of cultural, systemic, activity, and other approaches. As noted by Hessen, philosophy is the theoretical basis of pedagogy, and pedagogy is an applied philosophy (*Hessen*, 1995). Contemporary researchers of the philosophy of education continue to implement this idea. Thus, McInerney argues that philosophy is required to reflect on the significance of educational practice for a person (*McInerney*, 2021). Exploring constructivist pedagogy in the context of today's philosophy of education, Koptseva notes the need for a conceptual and methodological framework for updating educational practice in terms of the current problem of transition to e-learning (*Pring*, 2004). As practice shows, the implementation of the constructivist paradigm opens up wide opportunities for the effective construction of knowledge, allowing students to accumulate, constantly evaluate, and improve it (*Koptseva*, 2020; *Voon* et al., 2020). This is especially important in the aspect of the contemporary global problem of implementing an interdisciplinary approach to education (*Akanwa and Ovute*, 2014; *Arshinov* et al., 2016; *Kasavin*, 2014; *Knyazeva*, 2019; *Lubsky*, 2015; *Pozdneva*, 2016).

The progressive philosophy of education was founded in the 1920s in the USA. Its main supporter was Dewey (*Dewey*, 2008, 2020; *Robertson*, 1992; *Tomina*, 2011). One of the principles of the progressive philosophy of education was the fact that the school should improve the lifestyle of citizens by experiencing freedom and democracy in schools. Its main aspects are joint decision-making, planning the work of teachers with students, and topics chosen by students. Simultaneously, books take on the role of teaching tools and not something fundamental or dogmatic.

The word "education" comes from the Latin verb *educare*, which means "to bring out or draw out." The school's goal is to know each child well and, based on their interests and abilities, guide them to ever-expanding circles of knowledge, responsibility, understanding, social competence, and skill development.

Another key aspect of progressive education is what Dewey, a progressive educator at the turn of the last century, called "preparation for life in a democracy" (*Dewey*, 2020). This includes building on social justice, inclusion and diversity, community service, and global governance. Students must be accompanied by caring and compassion for others; they must learn to work collaboratively. Thus, a big part of the curriculum focuses on these key points. The main principles of the philosophy of education include: education of all qualities of the child; consideration of development needs; focus on understanding the problems and needs of the student; encouraging active participation; providing a safe environment for development; the predominance of the process over the result; training using integrated thematic blocks; training in cooperative groups; realization of diversity and creativity; community building; promotion of freedoms and responsibilities; offering a versatile curriculum; strengthening relationships; education of the heart and mind, etc.

2 Materials and Method

The methodological basis for studying the strategy of the philosophy of education of Western European schools is scientific works in the area of philosophy of education, as well as elements of a systemic approach that contribute to the development of an effective strategy for studying the aspects of this problem in their interconnection and interdependence. Systemic and structural-functional approaches allowed us to consider the current state and prospects for the practical application of the three trends in the philosophy of education – progressivism, existentialism, and reconstructivism.

3 Results

Today's education focuses on the content side of the learning process. In turn, the content determines the semantic component of the current worldview of the learning subject, which is reflected in the progressive philosophy of education. In the concept of Derrida, the meaning didactics is reflected in reconstructivism, which forms educational meanings from top to bottom and from bottom to top, i.e., they are interrelated (*Pozdneva*, 2016). The construction of meanings is represented by communicative processes that describe the reality of the external world. As was noted by Derrida and Locke, contradictions are formed in learning and perception of being from this (*Pozdneva*, 2016). The emphasis is on the internal understanding of the meaning of the individual in the process of education, the semiotic dimension.

The ideas of Bacon are reflected in the theory of the natural consonance of meaning in the pedagogy of Comenius (*Hessen*, 1995). The natural course of the cognitive activity of the subject presupposes the cognitive activity of the individual. The genetic characteristics of the personality are decisive in the training of the subject. The continuation of natural semantic conformity is the theory of Freud, which suggests that training and education give only the first level of the subject's activity, but the fundamental characteristic assumes the genetic essence of the individual (*Pring*, 2004). According to the concept of Rousseau, free education is the basis. Thus, the hierarchy of age education is determined by the force of nature of the learning subject (*McInerney*, 2021). The power of cognition and the development of the intellect are represented by the objective in the personality and by following the genetically inherent in the subject.

It follows that the methodology of semantic didactics is reconstructivism, progressivism, and existentialism in the context of natural methodological principles based on the elements of cultural conformity of today's life.

The development of the intellect is the highest priority in decent education. The demanding curriculum aims to achieve cultural literacy by emphasizing student growth in sustainable disciplines. The highest achievements of humans are emphasized – great works of literature and art, laws or principles of science. Supporters of this philosophy of education are Hutchins, who developed the Great Books program in 1963, and Adler, who developed a curriculum based on 100 great books of Western civilization. Essentialists believe that there is a common core of knowledge that needs to be passed on to students in a systemic and disciplined manner (*Bagley*, 1905; *Sahin*, 2019; *Wesley and William*, 2007). The emphasis in this conservative perspective is on the intellectual and moral standards that schools should teach. The basis of the curriculum is the necessary knowledge, skills, and academic rigor.

Although this educational philosophy has been similar for many years, essentialists agree with the idea that this core curriculum can change. Education must be practical, preparing students to become valuable members of society. It should be focused on facts – objective reality and "basics" – teaching students to read, write, speak, and calculate clearly and logically. Schools must not attempt to set or influence policy. Students must be taught diligence, respect for authority, and discipline. Teachers must help students control their unproductive instincts such as aggression or recklessness. This approach was a reaction to the progressive approaches that prevailed in the 1920s and 1930s. Bagley used progressive approaches to solving problems in the journal, which he founded in 1934 (*Bagley*, 1905). Other supporters of essentialism are Kerner, Rickover, Copperman, and Sizer (*Sahin*, 2019).

Progressives believe that education must be focused on the child as a whole and not on the content or the teacher. This educational philosophy emphasizes that students must test ideas through active experimentation. Learning lies in students' questions that arise in the process of learning about the world (*Campbell and Sherington*, 2006; *Labaree*, 2005;). The student is active. The teachers are problem solvers and thinkers; they make sense of their individual experiences in physical and cultural contexts. Effective teachers provide experiences so that students can learn through practical experience. The interests and questions of students determine the content of the curriculum. Progressive educators use the scientific method to enable students to systemically and firsthand study matters and events. The emphasis is on the process – it reflects how a student comes to knowledge.

Social reconstructivism is a philosophy that emphasizes the solution of social issues and the desire to create a better society and global democracy (*Richardson*, 2003; *Matthews*, 2002). Teachers-reenactors focus on a curriculum that emphasizes social reform as the goal of education. Brameld was the founder of social reconstructivism in response to the realities of World War II (*Richardson*, 2003). He recognized the potential to destroy humanity through technology and human cruelty or create a beneficent society using technology and human compassion. Critical theorists such as social reconstructionists believe that systems must be changed to overcome oppression and improve people's living conditions. Freire was a Brazilian scientist whose experience of living in poverty led him to become a proponent of education and literacy as a means of social change (*Matthews*, 2002). In his opinion, people must learn to resist oppression and not become its victims and not to oppress others. This requires dialogue and critical consciousness, the development of awareness to overcome domination and oppression. Instead of "teaching like banking," in which the teacher puts information into students' minds, Freire saw teaching and learning as a process of exploration in which children must invent and reinvent the world. For social reconstruction specialists and critical theorists, the curriculum focuses on student experiences and social action to address real-world issues such as violence, hunger, international terrorism, inflation, and inequality. The focus is on strategies for resolving contentious issues (especially in social studies and literature), research, dialogue, and multiple points of view. Community-based learning and bringing the world into the classroom are also strategies.

Eclecticism is a conceptual approach that does not strictly adhere to a single paradigm or set of assumptions. It draws on multiple theories, styles, and ideas to gain additional knowledge about the subject or applies different theories to particular cases. This cannot be elegant, and eclecticists are sometimes criticized for lack of consistency in their thinking. However, this situation is common in many areas of study. For example, most psychologists accept parts of behaviorism but do not attempt to use the theory to explain all aspects of human behavior.

A statistician may use frequency methods in one case and Bayesian methods in another. An example of eclecticism in economics is the eclectic theory of international production by Dunning (*Ananyev* et al., 2020). According to the theory of existentialism, "childhood is not adulthood; childhood is such a game, and no child ever gets enough play." Summerhill's theory lies in the fact that when a child has played enough, he will start working and encounter difficulties and the ability of students to perform well at work will remain (*Aizyatov and Bakaeva*, 2018).

The existentialist movement in education is based on an intellectual position that philosophers call existentialism. While the famous existentialists passionately disagreed with each other on many basic philosophical issues, they were united by a respect for individualism. In particular, they argued that traditional approaches to philosophy do not adequately consider the unique interests of each individual. The classic formulation of Sartre's existentialism – "existence precedes essence" means that there is no universal, innate human nature (*Sahin*, 2019). People are born and exist, and only after this do they freely determine our essence (i.e., our inner nature). Some philosophers associated with the existentialist tradition have never entirely accepted the principle that "existence precedes essence." However, this principle is fundamental to the educational existentialist movement.

Existentialism, like its namesake, arose out of a determined rejection of traditional philosophy. Educational existentialism arose from a determined rejection of the traditional essentialist approach to education. Existentialism rejects the existence of any source of objective and authoritative truth about metaphysics, epistemology, and ethics. Instead, people are responsible for determining what is "true" or "false," "right" or "wrong," "beautiful" or "ugly." For the existentialist, there is no universal form of human nature; every person has the free to develop as they want. In the existentialist class, the subject comes second, helping students understand and appreciate themselves as unique individuals who take full responsibility for their thoughts, feelings, and actions. The teacher's role is to determine their preferred ways. Because feeling is not separated from reason when making decisions, the existentialist demands the education of the whole person, not only his or her mind.

Although many existentialist educators offer specific curriculum structures, existentialism gives learners greater freedom in choosing a subject than other educational philosophies. In an existentialist curriculum, students are given a wide variety of options to choose from. As far as staff, rather than trainees, influences the curriculum, the liberal arts are usually given a huge amount of attention. They are explored to provide learners with mediated experiences that will help them discover their creativity and self-expression. For example, instead of focusing on historical events, existentialists pay special attention to the actions of historical figures, each of which provides possible models for student behavior. Unlike the humanities, mathematics and the natural sciences may be underestimated because their subject matter will be considered "cold," "dry," "objective," and, therefore, less productive for self-awareness. Moreover, vocational education is seen more as a tool for educating students about themselves and their potential than as a tool for earning a livelihood. In art education, existentialism encourages individual creativity and imagination more than copying and imitating the established models. Existentialist methods focus on the individual. Learning is self-paced and self-directed; it includes a lot of individual contact with a teacher who treats each student openly and honestly. While elements of existentialism occasionally appear in public schools, the philosophy has found wider acceptance in private schools and alternative public schools.

Let us turn to the experience of one of the schools that implement the principles of the progressive philosophy of education – Presidio Hill. This is a progressive school in San Francisco, teaching children since 1918. At Presidio Hill, classes are taught by highly trained and exceptionally dedicated and creative teaching staff. The *educare* principle, fundamental to Presidio Hill's educational philosophy, is that children come to school with pre-developed interests and skills. Presidio Hill students build and reinforce their knowledge through the learning process, and the teachers' experience and carefully organized guidance allow them to organize research and reflection while spending significant time in nature.

The teaching methodology at Presidio Hill is based on the tradition of progressive learning and includes the following provisions:
– Decisions are made considering the interests that are most favorable for the development of the child;
– Classes are planned in such a way that children learn scientific activity: put forward hypotheses, collect and generalize data, share information, experiment, etc., but not just get acquainted with it;
– Materials of interdisciplinary nature are used for research;
– Students are involved in joint learning;

- Authentic progressive learning strategies are used for assessment tools: portfolios, narrative reports, etc.;
- Training is carried out mostly without textbooks;
- Elements of empirical education are used: excursions, overnight stays, outdoor training, environmental education, etc.;
- Situations are modeled aimed at studying ethical values in the process of learning.

Presidio Hill teachers create an environment of inspiration for their students. Their activities aim to continue to learn outside of school when they communicate and develop with their students. The school team strives to get to know each other, learn from each other, and accept each other with all their strengths, talents, problems, and differences, reflecting the trends of progressive education philosophy.

4 Discussion

Thus, educational practices reflect contemporary philosophical trends – orientation towards realism and idealism, preservation of the past, reconstruction of the present, changing society, and shaping the future. The educational process focuses on learning and active self-learning. Its important components are intellectual orientation, training, the discipline of the mind, participation in problem-solving, and social tasks. When receiving knowledge, students are passively engaged in discoveries and construct knowledge. For this training, such concepts as freedom and democracy, compliance with authority, knowledge and discipline, creativity, self-actualization, and direct experience are important. Merit-based equality of education is equal to the change in the values of the disadvantaged group of society, the acceptance of norms, joint and coordinated behavior, individual growth, individual abilities, as well as the importance of the individual.

5 Conclusion

The research demonstrated that the philosophy of education in Western European schools is dominated by three main trends that have an experience of successful practical implementation. The first one is existentialism, which characterizes students with personal norms and ideas. The second is progressivism, which considers the social relations of students. Reconstructivism is associated with social change in the learning environment. These trends aim to promote active learning, which corresponds to the practical orientation of the processes of cognition and learning of the subject in current conditions. These trends must be given special attention in the organization and implementation of the educational process.

References

Aizyatov FA, and Bakaeva JYu (2018) Philosophical foundations of the nature of value relations of the personality of an information society. In: *Materials of the 2nd International scientific-practical conference "Scientific research in the socio-economic development of society."* Saransk, Russia: Print-Publishing, 16–18.

Akanwa UN, and Ovute AO (2014) The effect of constructivist teaching model on sss physics students' achievement and interest. *Journal of Research and Method in Education* 4: 35–38.

Ananyev MA, Bakaeva ZhYu, Matveeva OL, Steklova IV, and Shchegoleva EN (2020) Globalization of the transport system of the agro-industrial complex in the conditions of modern society. *E3S Web of Conferences* 176: 05020. DOI: 10.1051/e3sconf/202017605020.

Arshinov V, Budanov V, Gorokhov V, Kiseleva M, Kiyashchenko L, Kuznetsov V, … Yaroslavtseva E (2016) Science, technology, society: The problem of interdisciplinary in the context of reforms of Russian science. *Philosophy of Science and Technology* 21(1): 5–35. Available (consulted 18 February 2022) at: https://iphras.ru/uplfile/root/biblio/ps/ps_21_1.pdf.

Bagley WC (1905) *The educative process*. Norwood, MA: Norwood Press.

Campbell C, and Sherington GA (2006) Genealogy of an Australian system of comprehensive high schools: The contribution of educational progressivism to the one best form of universal secondary education (1900–1940). *Paedagogica Historica* 42(1–2): 191–210. DOI: 10.1080/00309230600552120.

Dewey J (2008) *The school and society*. New York, NY: Cosimo Classics. (Original work published 1899).

Dewey J (2020) *Democracy and education: An introduction to the philosophy of education* (Transl. from English). Moscow, Russia: Pedagogy-Press. (Original work published 1916).

Hessen SI (1995) *Fundamentals of pedagogy. Introduction to applied philosophy*. Moscow, Russia: School-Press.

Kasavin IT (2014) Interdisciplinary studies and the social picture of the world. *Philosophy of Science* 19(1): 9–26.

Knyazeva, E. N. (2019). *Philosophy of Science. Cross-disciplinary strategy of researches: A Textbook*. Moscow, Russia: Jurite.

Koptseva NP (2020) Constructivist pedagogy in the context of the modern philosophy of education. *Science and Education Perspectives* 6(48): 40–54. DOI: 10.32744/pse.2020.6.4.

Labaree D (2005) Progressivism, schools and schools of education: American romance. *Paedagogica Historica* 41(1–2): 275–288. DOI: 10.1080/00309230420000335583.

Lubsky AV (2015) Interdisciplinary scientific research: Cognitive "fashion" or social "challenge." *Sociological Research* 10: 3–11.

Matthews MR (2002) Constructivism and science education: A further appraisal. *Journal of Science Education and Technology* 11(2): 121–134. DOI: 10.1023/A:1014661312550.

McInerney R (2021) *Philosophy and the metaphysical achievements of education*. London, UK: Bloomsbury Publishing.

Pozdneva SP (2016) Universal principle of interdisciplinary: Ontognoseological grounds. *Journal of Higher School* 6: 18–25. DOI: 10.20339/AM.06-16.018.

Pring R (2004) *Philosophy of education: Aims, theory, common sense and research*. London, UK: Continuum.

Richardson V (2003) Constructivist pedagogy. *Teachers College Record* 105(9): 1623–1640. Available (consulted 18 February 2022) at: https://www.sfu.ca/~jcnesbit/EDUC 220/ThinkPaper/Richardson2003.pdf.

Robertson E (1992) Is Dewey's educational vision still viable? *Review of Research in Education* 18: 335–381.

Sahin M (2019) Essentialism in Philosophy, psychology, education, social and scientific scopes. *Journal of Innovation in Psychology, Education and Didactics* 22(2): 193–204.

Tomina EF (2011) Pedagogical ideas of John Dewey: History and modernity. *Bulletin of Orenburg State University* 2: 360–366. Available (consulted 18 February 2022) at: http://vestnik.osu.ru/2011_2/62.pdf.

Voon XP, Wong LH, Looi CK, and Chen W (2020) Constructivism-informed variation theory lesson designs in enriching and elevating science learning: Case studies of seamless learning design. *Journal of Research in Science Teaching* 57(10): 1531–1553. DOI: 10.1002/tea.21624.

Wesley J, and William C (2007) Bagley and the founding of essentialism: Untold story in American educational history. *Teachers College Record* 109(4): 1013–1055. DOI: 10.1177/016146810710900408.

CHAPTER 22

Inclusiveness and Competitiveness vs. Quality and Efficiency of Universities

Conflicts of Interest and Common Ground

Svetlana A. Lyausheva, Bella Kh. Khamukova, Zarema Kh. Kurmalieva and Fatima K. Tuguz

Abstract

The paper aims to investigate the conflict of interests in the implementation by universities of their internal (focused on the regional economy and local communities) and external (related to international activities) functions and identify common ground between these functions as prospects for their systemic implementation in the practice of university management in Russia. The authors use the methods of regression and correlation analysis to determine the relationship between the quality and efficiency of the top three Russian universities from the QS ranking in 2021 and their global competitiveness in 2013–2021. The paper contributes to the development of the theory of public and corporate governance of higher education through the justification of the key role of inclusiveness (international activities) in this governance. The authors conclude that inclusiveness is a unique and promising mechanism for balancing the management of the global competitiveness, quality, and efficiency of contemporary universities. The theoretical significance of the obtained results is that they have demonstrated the logical connection of university rankings and formed a theoretical vision of the prospects of the systemic implementation of both functions of universities based on balanced management of global competitiveness, quality, and efficiency through increased inclusiveness of universities. Based on the modeling results, the authors propose university management implications for the transition to a cyclical approach to university management, the most important tool of which is increasing inclusiveness.

Keywords

inclusiveness – competitiveness – quality – efficiency – universities – conflicts of interest – common ground – system management

1 Introduction

Today's universities perform two important functions in economic systems, holistically contributing to sustainable development and the Sustainable Development Goals (SDGs). The first function is related to meeting the internal needs of society and the economy in educational services and scientific products (innovations, technologies). In fulfilling this function, universities provide training (SDG 8) and support lifelong learning (SDG 4) on equal conditions for all (SDG 5 and SDG 10).

Universities support the sustainable development and economic growth of territories (SDG 11) through staffing and increasing mass literacy in various fields. Universities also provide innovation and technology for economic modernization and entrepreneurship (SDG 9), as well as responsible production and consumption (SDG 12). By increasing the level of public education, universities create and strengthen social elevators, contributing to the fight against poverty (SDG 1).

Universities support all other SDGs through the creation and diffusion of knowledge, innovations, and technologies of relevant specialization (e.g., agricultural innovations in support of SDG 2; health innovations in support of SDG 3; water innovations in support of SDG 6; energy innovations in support of SDG 7; environmental and climate change innovations in support of SDG 13–15; legal innovations in support of SDG 16).

The second function is to strengthen the external (on the world stage) status of the scientific and educational system. This function boils down to supporting a single sustainable development goal – SDG 17. In fulfilling this function, universities position themselves as world centers of science and higher education, ensuring the prestige of the national innovation economy and knowledge society, as well as integrate into world science and education (to prevent the stagnation of knowledge and technology and drawing of new ideas, exchange of experience).

Universities also expand markets for educational services, innovations, and technologies, and establish and develop international scientific and educational cooperation and partnerships (e.g., through forums, symposia, and conferences). Universities provide international diplomas, student exchanges, and faculty internships.

Each designated function is self-sufficient. Thus, until recently, most universities in Russia performed only one of these functions. That is, there was a division of labor between universities within the national system of education and science. Many regional (local) universities concentrated on the first function. For this purpose, they were enlarged (merged) to form regional flagship universities. Connection with the regions made it possible to meet their needs in the most effective way.

In contrast, the leading metropolitan universities (Moscow and St. Petersburg) and universities of federal importance (e.g., national research universities) performed the second function. At the beginning of the "Decade of Action" in 2020, the *Ministry of Science and Higher Education of the Russian Federation* (2022) launched the "Priority 2030" program, which set a strategic goal for Russian universities to provide strategic academic leadership in the country by 2030.

This required every university in Russia to successfully and simultaneously perform both functions described above. There is a solid foundation for this. For example, in 2021, the QS (2022) international university ranking included 32 Russian universities from various cities, many of which are regional flagship universities (e.g., Novosibirsk State Technical University and Voronezh State University).

The problem lies in the uncertainty of how to manage universities to fulfill both functions simultaneously, which are largely contradictory. For example, improving the position of a university on the world stage requires investment in its development, while the regional economy does not benefit from increased funding for universities. In building a university's international status, the greater the number of its faculty (in aggregate and in proportion to the number of students), the better. However, measures are taken at the regional level to reduce the staff of universities to optimize costs. Similarly, externally oriented international publications distract universities from the educational process.

This paper focuses on finding a solution to this problem. The paper aims to investigate the conflict of interests in the implementation by universities of their internal (focused on the regional economy and local communities) and external (related to international activities) functions and identify common ground between these functions as prospects for their systemic implementation in the practice of university management in Russia.

2 Literature Review

This research draws on the theory of public and corporate governance of higher education. This research focuses on the problem of conflicting university rankings. The success of universities in fulfilling the first function is evaluated by the government (the Ministry of Science and Higher Education) in terms of the quality of higher education services and the effectiveness of universities. The results of the assessment are reflected in national university rankings, in particular in the annual monitoring of higher education by the *Main Information and Computing Center of the MIREA* (2022a, 2022b, 2022c) in Russia.

The results of the second function are considered by international organizations in terms of the global competitiveness of universities and are reflected in international university rankings, in particular the QS (2022) ranking. In this regard, on the one hand, the global competitiveness of universities require them to be inclusive (gender and cultural inclusion, accessibility to learning for people with disabilities, international openness, etc.). On the other hand, quality assurance requires universities to select students rigorously; efficiency is achieved by cutting costs, while inclusiveness is resource-intensive.

Garcia-Alvarez-Coque et al. (2021), *Juříková* et al. (2021), *Kotchegura* et al. (2022), *Okanović* et al. (2021) note that the inclusiveness of universities enhances their global competitiveness. Simultaneously, inclusiveness contradicts and impedes the quality and effectiveness of universities. *Bratukhina* et al. (2020), *Cheglakova* et al. (2020), *Johnes* et al. (2022), *Kuklin* et al. (2021), *Nushi* et al. (2022), *Owusu* (2022), *Sibirskaya* et al. (2019) indicate that only external governance aimed at increasing the openness of universities is required for universities to be inclusive. Quality and efficiency management are separate and distinct from university competitiveness management.

This raises the research question (RQ) of how to manage universities to ensure that they simultaneously manage both functions and systematically improve their quality, efficiency, and global competitiveness. Based on the works of *Contini and Salza* (2020) and *Rodrigo and Ladrido* (2022), which provide separate evidence on the benefits of university inclusiveness for quality and efficiency, this research hypothesizes that inclusiveness allows universities to improve competitiveness, quality, and efficiency simultaneously. The authors examine the case experience of the higher education system in Russia to illuminate the existing problem, find an answer to the posed RQ, and test the hypothesis.

3   Materials and Methods

To test the hypothesis, the authors use the methods of regression and correlation analysis to determine the relationship between the quality and efficiency of the top three Russian universities in the QS ranking in 2021 – Lomonosov Moscow State University, Saint Petersburg State University, and Novosibirsk State University – and their global competitiveness. Table 22.1 provides statistics on the quality (educational and research activities), efficiency (financial and economic activities), and inclusiveness (international activities) of the universities selected for this research.

Table 22.2 shows the arithmetic mean of the quality, efficiency, and inclusiveness of the studied universities, as well as their global competitiveness as measured by the QS (2022).

As shown in Table 22.2, all indicators of the top three Russian universities have improved over the reviewed period. The quality of educational activities increased by 8.90% (from 77.89 points in 2013 to 84.82 points in 2021), and the quality of research activities increased by 84.66% (from 452.60 thousand rubles in 2013 to 835.76 thousand rubles in 2021). The efficiency (financial and economic activity) increased by 80.72% (from 2678.49 thousand rubles in 2013 to 4840.59 thousand rubles in 2021). The inclusiveness (international activities) of the selected universities increased by 147.53% (from 5.47% in 2013 to 13.54% in 2021). Global competitiveness (as measured by QS) increased by 5.45% (from 45.9 points in 2013 to 48.4 points in 2021).

4   Results

4.1   Modeling the Relationship of Inclusion to Quality and Efficiency in Top Three Russian Universities

To determine the impact of inclusiveness on the quality and efficiency of the top three Russian universities, the authors modeled it using the statistics in Table 22.2. The results are shown in Tables 22.3–22.5.

According to Table 22.3, if the inclusiveness (international activity) of the top three Russian universities increases by 1%, the quality of their educational activity increases by 0.6981 points. The correlation of the indicators is high (79.94%). Modeling results are reliable at a significance level of 0.01 (as significance F=0.0097).

According to Table 22.4, if the inclusiveness (international activity) of the top three Russian universities increases by 1%, the quality of their scientific activity increases by 56.2385 thousand rubles. The correlation of the indicators is high (91.44%). The modeling results are reliable at the significance level of 0.01 (as significance F=0.0005).

According to Table 22.5, if the inclusiveness (international activity) of the top three Russian universities increases by 1%, their efficiency increases by 246.9015 thousand rubles. The correlation of the indicators is high (87.72%). The modeling results are reliable at the significance level of 0.01 (as significance F=0.0019).

TABLE 22.1 Quality, efficiency, and inclusion of the top three Russian universities from QS Rankings 2013–2021: detailed statistics

Year	Lomonosov Moscow State University, Moscow, Russia (MSU)				Saint Petersburg State University, Saint Petersburg, Russia (SPbSU)				Novosibirsk State University, Novosibirsk, Russia (NSU)			
	EDUCATIONAL ACTIVITY, POINTS 1–100	RESEARCH ACTIVITY[a], THOUSAND RUBLES	INTERNATIONAL ACTIVITY[b], %	FINANCIAL AND ECONOMIC ACTIVITY[c], THOUSAND RUBLES	EDUCATIONAL ACTIVITY, POINTS 1–100	RESEARCH ACTIVITY[a], THOUSAND RUBLES	INTERNATIONAL ACTIVITY[b], %	FINANCIAL AND ECONOMIC ACTIVITY[c], THOUSAND RUBLES	EDUCATIONAL ACTIVITY, POINTS 1–100	RESEARCH ACTIVITY[a], THOUSAND RUBLES	INTERNATIONAL ACTIVITY[b], %	FINANCIAL AND ECONOMIC ACTIVITY[c], THOUSAND RUBLES
2013	83.25	414.81	3.77	1816.22	78.39	259.32	6.37	3291.53	72.02	683.67	6.28	2927.71
2014	85.89	523.62	5.06	2314.61	82.53	255.93	7.08	2690.44	79.38	597.00	6.24	4223.26
2015	81.57	582.83	5.70	2243.99	84.03	247.93	5.16	2794.71	77.34	685.73	6.52	5653.48
2016	82.55	687.52	6.35	2516.79	85.69	374.23	8.18	2783.94	77.51	595.63	7.06	4238.11
2017	82.68	749.77	6.57	2635.22	86.01	436.05	9.33	2881.85	78.00	487.01	7.31	3131.81
2018	81.97	688.32	7.31	2882.57	84.57	465.42	10.53	2919.54	78.84	514.60	5.73	3373.94
2019	83.81	979.35	7.50	3637.88	86.91	603.40	13.87	4236.28	81.00	586.81	5.72	3773.55
2020	85.85	919.70	8.88	3108.77	87.60	839.59	12.93	4984.45	82.82	857.61	9.40	4933.08
2021	84.19	726.42	12.25	4015.53	86.43	813.64	18.37	5552.71	83.84	967.23	10.00	4953.52

Note:
a   Volume of R&D per one member of academic staff, thousand rubles
b   Share of foreign students, %
c   Revenues from all sources per one member of academic staff, thousand rubles

SOURCE: COMPILED BY THE AUTHORS BASED ON (*MAIN INFORMATION AND COMPUTING CENTER OF THE MIREA*, 2022A; 2022B; 2022C)

TABLE 22.2 Quality, efficiency, inclusiveness, and competitiveness of the top three Russian universities from the QS rankings in 2013–2021: summary statistics

Year	Educational activity points 1–100	Scientific and research activity[a], thousand rubles	International activity[b], %	Financial and economic activity[c], thousand rubles	QS university ranking (top 3), score 0–100
2013	77.89	452.60	5.47	2678.49	45.9
2014	82.60	458.85	6.13	3076.10	49.3
2015	80.98	505.50	5.79	3564.06	52.1
2016	81.92	552.46	7.20	3179.61	51.5
2017	82.23	557.61	7.74	2882.96	46.5
2018	81.79	556.11	7.86	3058.68	49.6
2019	83.91	723.19	9.03	3882.57	46.7
2020	85.42	872.30	10.40	4342.10	47.5
2021	84.82	835.76	13.54	4840.59	48.4

Note:
a Volume of R&D per one member of academic staff, thousand rubles
b Share of foreign students, %
c Revenues from all sources per one member of academic staff, thousand rubles
SOURCE: CALCULATED AND COMPILED BY THE AUTHORS BASED ON (GLOBAL INNOVATION INDEX, 2021; MAIN INFORMATION AND COMPUTING CENTER OF THE MIREA, 2022A; 2022B; 2022C)

To determine the impact of quality and efficiency on the inclusiveness of Russian universities, the authors also modeled it using the statistics from Table 22.2. The results are shown in Table 22.6.

According to Table 22.6, if the quality of educational activity increases by one point, the inclusiveness of the top three Russian universities increases by 0.0981 thousand rubles; when the quality of scientific activity increases by 1 thousand rubles, the inclusiveness increases by 0.0137 thousand rubles. The correlation of the indicators is high (91.55%). Modeling results are reliable at a significance level of 0.01 (as significance F=0.0042).

TABLE 22.3 Regression statistics on the dependence of the quality of educational activity on the inclusiveness of the top three Russian universities

Regression statistics						
Multiple R	0.7994					
R-square	0.6390					
Normalized R-square	0.5875					
Standard error	1.4420					
Observations	9					
Variance analysis						
	df	SS	MS	F	Significance of F	
Regression	1	25.7680	25.7680	12.3919	0.009725	
Balance	7	14.5560	2.0794			
Total	8	40.3239				
	Coefficients	Standard error	t-statistics	P-value	Lower 95%	Upper 95%
Y-intersection	76.7209	1.6821	45.6110	0.0000	72.7434	80.6983
International activity, %	0.6981	0.1983	3.5202	0.0097	0.2292	1.1670

SOURCE: CALCULATED AND COMPILED BY THE AUTHORS

5 Discussion

The research contributes to the development of the theory of public and corporate governance of higher education by substantiating the key role of inclusiveness (international activities) in this governance. In contrast to *Garcia-Alvarez-Coque* et al. (2021), *Juříková* et al. (2021), *Kotchegura* et al. (2022), *Okanović* et al. (2021), the authors argue that increasing the inclusiveness of universities enhances not only their global competitiveness but also the quality and efficiency of their activities. In contrast to *Bratukhina* et al. (2020), *Cheglakova* et al. (2020), *Johnes* et al. (2022), *Kuklin* et al. (2021), *Nushi* et al. (2022), *Owusu* (2022), *Sibirskaya* et al. (2019), the authors prove that managing the inclusiveness of universities can and should be external (international activities) and internal (educational and scientific activities – quality management).

TABLE 22.4 Regression statistics on the dependence of the quality of scientific activity on the inclusiveness of the top three Russian universities

Regression statistics

Multiple R	0.9144
R-square	0.8361
Normalized R-square	0.8127
Standard error	68.4278
Observations	9

Variance analysis

	df	SS	MS	F	Significance of F
Regression	1	167240.3435	167240.3435	35.7170	0.000555
Balance	7	32776.5737	4682.3677		
Total	8	200016.9172			

	Coefficients	Standard error	t-statistics	P-value	Lower 95%	Upper 95%
Y-intersection	155.5735	79.8188	1.9491	0.0923	-33.1681	344.3151
International activity, %	56.2385	9.4101	5.9764	0.0006	33.9870	78.4899

SOURCE: CALCULATED AND COMPILED BY THE AUTHORS

This points to the limitations of the current linear (increasing inclusivity to increase competitiveness) approach to university management – this approach holds back their development. This approach should be replaced by a cyclical approach, the advantage of which is the systemic accrual of university outcomes – greater inclusivity promotes competitiveness, quality, and efficiency, which, in turn, increases inclusiveness, and so on. In the recommended approach, all university indicators are comprehensively improved with each new cycle, and balanced development of university competitiveness, quality, and efficiency is achieved.

TABLE 22.5 Regression statistics on the dependence of efficiency on the inclusiveness of the top three Russian universities

Regression statistics

Multiple R	0.8772
R-square	0.7694
Normalized R-square	0.7365
Standard error	371.4891
Observations	9

Variance analysis

	df	SS	MS	F	Significance of F		
Regression	1	3223455.2354	3223455.2354	23.3577	0.001893		
Balance	7	966029.2307	138004.1758				
Total	8	4189484.4660					
	Coefficients	Standard error	t-statistics	P-value	Lower 95%	Upper 95%	
Y-intersection	1493.6302	433.3301	3.4469	0.0107	468.9674	2518.2929	
International activity, %	246.9015	51.0868	4.8330	0.0019	126.1003	367.7027	

SOURCE: CALCULATED AND COMPILED BY THE AUTHORS

6 Conclusion

Thus, the obtained results have proved the hypothesis put forward and allow the authors to conclude that inclusiveness is a unique and promising mechanism for balancing the management of global competitiveness, quality, and efficiency of today's universities. The contribution of the research to the literature lies in the justification of the centrality of inclusion to state and corporate governance of higher education.

The theoretical significance of the results is that they demonstrate the logical connection of university rankings and form a theoretical vision of the prospects of the systemic implementation of both functions of universities based

TABLE 22.6 Regression statistics of the dependence of inclusiveness on the quality and efficiency of the top three Russian universities

Regression statistics

Multiple R	0.9155
R-square	0.8382
Normalized R-square	0.7843
Standard error	1.1942
Observations	9

Variance analysis

	df	SS	MS	F	Significance of F
Regression	2	44.3219	22.1609	15.5406	0.004236
Balance	6	8.5560	1.4260		
Total	8	52.8779			

	Coefficients	Standard error	t-statistics	P-value	Lower 95%	Upper 95%
Y-intersection	-8.3394	26.6625	-0.3128	0.7650	-73.5802	56.9014
Educational activities, points 1–100	0.0981	0.3547	0.2765	0.7914	-0.7698	0.9660
Research and development, thousand rubles	0.0137	0.0050	2.7176	0.0348	0.0014	0.0260

SOURCE: CALCULATED AND COMPILED BY THE AUTHORS

on balanced management of global competitiveness, quality, and efficiency through increased inclusiveness of universities. Based on these modeling results, the authors propose university management implications for the transition to a cyclical approach to university management, the most important tool of which is increasing inclusiveness.

References

Bratukhina EA, Lysova EA, Lapteva IP, and Malysheva NV (2020) Marketing management of education quality in the process of university reorganization in industry 4.0: Goals of application and new tools. *International Journal for Quality Research* 14(2): 369–386. DOI: 10.24874/ijqr14.02-03.

Cheglakova LS, Devetyarova IP, Agalakova OS, and Kolesova YA (2020) Marketing strategy of quality management during reorganization of regional universities in the process of modernization of education in the conditions of region's transition to industry 4.0. *International Journal for Quality Research* 14(1): 33–50. DOI: 10.24874/IJQR14.01-03.

Contini D, and Salza G (2020) Too few university graduates. Inclusiveness and effectiveness of the Italian higher education system. *Socio-Economic Planning Sciences* 71: 100803. DOI: 10.1016/j.seps.2020.100803.

Garcia-Alvarez-Coque J-M, Mas-Verdú F, and Roig-Tierno N (2021) Life below excellence: Exploring the links between top-ranked universities and regional competitiveness. *Studies in Higher Education* 46(2): 369–384. DOI: 10.1080/03075079.2019.1637843.

Global Innovation Index (2021) *Explore the interactive database of the GII 2021 indicators.* Available (consulted 22 May 2022) at: https://www.globalinnovationindex.org/analysis-indicator.

Johnes G, Johnes J, and Virmani, S (2022) Performance and efficiency in Indian universities. *Socio-Economic Planning Sciences* 81: 100834. DOI: 10.1016/j.seps.2020.100834.

Juříková M, Kocourek J, andLižbetinová L (2021) Building the prestige of a university as a tool to achieve competitiveness. *Communication Today* 12(2): 128–145. Available (consulted 22 May 2022) at: https://communicationtoday.sk/wp-content/uploads/10_JURIKOVA-et-al_CT-2-2021.pdf.

Kotchegura A, De Martino M, and Farazmand A (2022) Enhancing competitiveness of the Russian higher education: The 5–100 University Excellence Program through the lens of efficiency and performance. *International Journal of Public Administration* 45(2): 185–197. DOI: 10.1080/01900692.2021.2025071.

Kuklin AV, Bratukhina EA, and Gorokhovitskaya YO (2021) Quality as the key landmark of education management in the regional economy. *International Journal for Quality Research* 15(2): 451–468. DOI: 10.24874/IJQR15.02-06.

Main Information and Computing Center of the MIREA (2022a) *Information and analytical materials on the results of monitoring the effectiveness of educational institutions of higher education in 2021: Federal State Budget Educational Institution of Higher Education "Lomonosov Moscow State University."* Available (consulted 22 May 2022) at: https://monitoring.miccedu.ru/iam/2021/_vpo/inst.php?id=1725.

Main Information and Computing Center of the MIREA (2022b) *Information and analytical materials on the results of monitoring the effectiveness of educational institutions of higher education in 2021: Federal State Budgetary Educational Institution of Higher Education "St. Petersburg State University."* Available (consulted 22 May 2022) at: https://monitoring.miccedu.ru/iam/2021/_vpo/inst.php?id=1771.

Main Information and Computing Center of the MIREA (2022c) *Information and analytical materials on the results of monitoring the effectiveness of educational institutions of higher education in 2021: Federal State Autonomous Educational Institution of Higher Education "Novosibirsk National Research State University."* Available (consulted 22 May 2022) at: https://monitoring.miccedu.ru/iam/2021/_vpo/inst.php?id=178.

Ministry of Science and Higher Education of the Russian Federation (2022) *Priority 2030.* Available (consulted 22 May 2022) at: https://priority2030.ru/en.

Nushi M, Momeni A, and Roshanbin M (2022) Characteristics of an effective university professor from students' perspective: Are the qualities changing? *Frontiers in Education* 7: 842640. DOI: 10.3389/feduc.2022.842640.

Okanović A, Ješić J, Đaković V, Vukadinović S, and Panić AA (2021) Increasing university competitiveness through assessment of green content in curriculum and eco-labeling in higher education. *Sustainability* 13(2): 712. DOI: 10.3390/su13020712.

Owusu AA (2022) Determinants of quality education delivery in selected public universities in Ghana: Students' perceptions. *International Journal of Learning, Teaching and Educational Research* 21(2): 133–154. DOI: 10.26803/ijlter.21.2.8.

QS (2022) *World University Rankings 2021.* Available (consulted 22 May 2022) at: https://www.topuniversities.com/university-rankings/world-university-rankings/2021.

Rodrigo MMT, and Ladrido EMM (2022) Promoting equity and assuring teaching and learning quality: Magisterial lectures in a Philippine university during the COVID-19 pandemic. *Education Sciences* 12(2): 146. DOI: 10.3390/educsci12020146.

Sibirskaya E, Popkova E, Oveshnikova L, and Tarasova I (2019) Remote education vs traditional education based on effectiveness at the micro level and its connection to the level of development of macro-economic systems. *International Journal of Educational Management* 33(3): 533–543. DOI: 10.1108/IJEM-08-2018-0248.

CHAPTER 23

The Dilemma of Choice in the Direction of Development of the National Education System
An Educated or Professionally Trained Person

Eugenia A. Neretina, Natalya S. Komleva, Evgeniy A. Leonenko and Elena G. Shcherbakova

Abstract

The research of the future indicates that NBIC technologies (in English, the terms Nano, Bio, Inform, and Cognitive) are the core of the sixth technological structure, which includes developed countries. According to the representatives of the US National Science Foundation governing the funding of scientific projects, NBIC technologies will determine the development of civilization in the next 50 years.

Russia's entry into the new sixth technological way is impossible without profound changes in the national education system. The article considers the emerging negative trends in the education system development of the Russian Federation in connection with the transition to a market economy, political and institutional changes and integration into the global educational space. The conversion in this situation requires the solution of the fundamentally important tasks: what should be the result of the development in the national system of education: educational or professionally trained people. This dilemma is considered in the article from the perspective of the interests of a person, employer, society, and the state.

The problem supplied in the issue is debatable. Its solution is relevant for all countries and their citizens. The article's content not only meets the scope of the journal "Integration of education" and its target audience but also represents the interests of employers, public authorities, and the general public.

Keywords

NBIC technologies – education – national educational system – educated person – professionally trained people – consumer society

1 Introduction

Russia's entry into the new technological order is the most important strategic task. Its solution requires the formation of a state target program, within which one of the priorities should be the development of the education system based on the development of qualitatively new educational programs.

In the United States, since 2003, the National Science Foundation began to implement the research program "Human and Social Dynamics" within the scenario of technology convergence (*Kazantsev* et al., 2012, p. 104). The US was followed by many EU countries (Great Britain, Germany, France, Spain, etc.). Scientific research in the EU has covered the most complex and controversial area of human brain research and medical and cognitive technologies. Meanwhile, it is the cognitive technologies associated with the study of the human brain, its cognitive abilities, according to scientists, that will most actively stimulate the development of an innovative economy.

Russia has also entered a new technological wave. Innovative transformations require a deep rethinking of the current state of the domestic education system and justification of the strategic vectors of its development. It should be largely reoriented to the training of highly qualified specialists for science-intensive industries. Meanwhile, large-scale and profound changes in the education system of the Russian Federation due to economic, political, and institutional transformations have led to the loss of leading positions in the global educational space.

According to A. Mechanik, "Soviet power was in the nature of a grandiose educational project" (*Mehanik*, 2016a, p. 59). The USSR occupied one of the leading places in terms of the number of students per 10 thousand inhabitants, as well as in terms of the quality of training specialists in natural science areas, which was confirmed by international experts. However, by the end of the 1980s, according to UNESCO, the country ranked only 39th in the world in terms of the number of students per 10,000 inhabitants. The proportion of students studying at universities in the evening and part-time departments, where the quality of specialist training was significantly lower, reached 56% (*Mehanik*, 2016b, p. 64). Since the early 2000s, there have been other negative trends in the development of the national education system: education began to turn from a social good into an educational service; the growth of commercialization in the education system has led to a violation of the principle of public access to education; rapid and unjustified growth in the number of non-state educational institutions, which do not always provide quality education, etc.

TABLE 23.1 Ideas about education and an educated person

Author	Statements about education and an educated person
Halifax J. (XVIII century) (*Kazantsev* et al., 2012)	Education is what remains when we have forgotten everything we have been taught.
Skinner B.F. (XX century) (*Samonova*, 2016)	Education is what remains when everything learned is forgotten.
Kovus K. (*Samonova*, 2016)	Education is the face of the mind
Rubakin N.A. (*Rubakin*, 1962, p. 125)	An educated person is a person who has his own worldview, his own opinions about all aspects and areas of life around him.
Valentinova V. (*Baudrillard*, 2006)	An educated person is an individual who has received the knowledge offered by civilization itself. He has cultural and life experience, historically accumulated in the process of development and formation of culture, industry, industry.
Tolstoy L.N. (*Tolstoy*, 1936)	If a student at school does not learn to create anything himself, then in life he will always only imitate, copy
Nietzsche F. (*Nietzsche*, 1990)	The man of the future is the one with the longest memory

SOURCE: COMPILED BY AUTHORS BASED ON (BAUDRILLARD, 2006; KAZANTSEV ET AL., 2012; NIETZSCHE, 1990; RUBAKIN, 1962; SAMONOVA, 2016; TOLSTOY, 1936)

2 Materials and Method

A retrospective analysis of scientific views and approaches to the problems of education and the formation of an educated person showed that they have always excited and aroused interest among scientists, representatives of business structures, the state, and society. This is evidenced by the statements of scientists, writers, and public figures, some of which are presented in Table 23.1.

The problem of the significance of choosing a profession for further self-determination and personal development is given special attention to Gorbacheva S.M., Strishko I.I. According to Gorbacheva should be understood as "a part of human ontogenesis from the beginning of the formation of professional intentions to the end of active professional activity" (*Gorbacheva and Strizhko*, 2015).

Most modern researchers believe that it is necessary to be educated, and not just a professionally trained person, that is, to have an idea of the diversity of the world. Characteristic features of an educated and professionally trained person are shown in Figure 23.1.

To become an educated person, one must have general and special education. General education gives a person a broad, holistic worldview, which allows them not only to understand the phenomena and processes of social life, to comprehend them critically, but also to participate in the transformation of the world around them actively. Consequently, general education allows one to have their own ideas of the ongoing processes and phenomena; a person can distinguish real events from empty rhetoric, lies, and chatter and determine the direction of his or her actions and behavior.

Special education provides a person with a certain range of professional knowledge and skills. The desire to penetrate more deeply into one's specialty

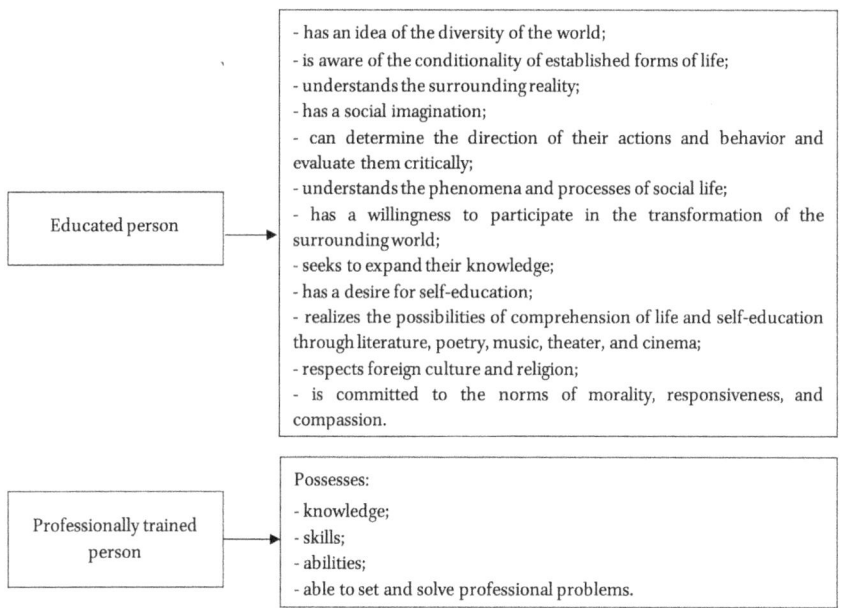

FIGURE 23.1 Characteristics of an educated and professionally trained person

inevitably leads a person beyond the limits of professional knowledge and leads him or her to realize the need to expand general knowledge. Consequently, the contours of education itself must be diverse. Education is both enlightenment, historical thinking, the ability to navigate the phenomena and processes taking place in the world, and awareness of the forms of life and patterns of behavior chosen by people (*Rubakin*, 1975). In order to realize all this and act accordingly, a person must "form" himself. Others can also learn it, but only he can "educate" himself since education requires fortitude, self-knowledge, and self-organization.

The material for the preparation of the article was the statements of foreign and domestic scientists, writers, and public figures about education and an educated person; studies of the future of the countries included in the sixth technological order and their followers, and developing strategies for the convergence of NBIC technologies into the socio-economic sphere; national research programs in the areas of human and social dynamics, education and training of citizens; normative-legal and program documents of the Government of the Russian Federation in the field of education; results of sociological research and rating assessments of the quality of education.

The methodological basis of the study was the methods of scientific abstraction, analysis and synthesis, retrospective analysis, comparison, generalization, and peer review.

3   Results and Discussion

Untimely and inadequate response of state authorities and public institutions and structures to a new technological wave and other challenges of the external environment led to a crisis situation in the economy, as well as in the field of education of the Russian Federation, as evidenced by the results of numerous studies presented in the domestic and foreign scientific literature (*Komleva and Shcherbakova*, 2014; *Paulsen*, 1900; *Privalov*, 2016; *Senge* et al., 2004).

First, when assessing the current state of the national education system, there is a decrease in the quality of school education. "In the latest ranking of the quality of school education in the twenty leading countries of the world, we are not only far behind the leaders, we are not even in the golden mean. The place of Russia turned out to be the last, 20th" (*Nietzsche*, 1990). In school curricula, due attention is not paid to the fundamental academic disciplines: mathematics, physics, chemistry, biology, Russian language, and literature. In the article "It is painfully ashamed. But not to the authorities," Olga Kitova notes: "According to the results of the Unified State Examination in the Russian language, out of every four graduates of this year, three speak Russian with difficulty (100 points for 1% of graduates and "good" for 25%). Many schoolchildren not only do not know how to think logically and build sentences properly, they do not even have a vocabulary to express their scanty thoughts" (*Kitova*, 2016).

There are many other examples that testify to the degradation of school education. Children do not want to learn, and most importantly, they do not want to think and "be educated." Knowledge ceases to be a value in a consumer society, into which, along with developed countries, Russia "stepped" in the 1980s–1990s. The consumer society is characterized by the accumulation of vast consumer resources and a culture centered on consumption as a key value. By changing the values and goals of young people, the consumer society makes them dependent on material goods and, at the same time, spiritually and morally poor, susceptible to manipulation by certain social groups that impose their worldview on them (*Baudrillard*, 2006).

The moral values of the consumer society deny the need for a comprehensive mental and spiritual development of a person. Gadget mania, which has formed in recent years, not only negatively affects mental activity and leads young people into virtual reality, but also worsens their health and mental state. The "button" generation is not motivated to obtain high-quality knowledge and its reasonable practical use. Many schoolchildren have "blurred" historical thinking.

The consumer society is characterized by two types of education: playbes and elite. For the first, the training of specialists with a narrow profile is typical, who should not think about complex things and social processes. At the same time, the elite wants to be a highly educated, privileged part of society. Accordingly, she does not socially identify herself with the majority of the country's citizens. Its values and patterns of behavior have already been drawn into the orbit of the consumer society of the most developed countries (*Chuykov*, 2016).

The materials of sociological research indicate that in the Russian Federation, the proportion of school graduates, and especially their parents, oriented towards obtaining higher education by their children remains high (80%). Meanwhile, in 1954, 60% of schoolchildren went to colleges and technical schools to receive working professions and become leaders of the lower management level at enterprises. There were 2200 vocational schools operating in the country. In the 60s, 30% of school graduates studied at vocational schools and technical schools, and in 1976 – only 3% (*Mehanik*, 2016a, p. 59). At the same time, by the beginning of the 21st century, the number of university students increased from 2790 thousand to 4741 thousand people compared to 1995 and continued to grow until 2008 (up to 7513 thousand people).

The measures taken in recent years by the country's government for structural reforms in the field of education led to a reduction in the number of universities from 1134 in 2008 to 896. However, this did not solve the main problems either in higher education or in the system of training workers.

The reforms of higher education carried out in Russia in recent decades, according to A. Mekhanik, are, in many ways, a copy of Western models (*Mehanik*, 2016a, p. 58). V. P. Tretyakov, the dean of the Higher School of Television of Lomonosov Moscow State University, also drew attention to this issue in his interview with the newspaper "Arguments of the Week." He noted that the beneficiaries of the Russian reforms are the leading European and American universities, which do not use the Bologna system but use classical national systems (*Chuykov*, 2016).

The conducted research indicates that the Russian education system is poorly included in the system of genuine social exchange, primarily between business entities and society. Meanwhile, it is education that is the basis of tomorrow's innovative reality and the level of economic development. According to Joe Jaworski, the former head of the planning team at Royal Dutch/Shell, the competitive advantage is on the side of those who learn faster from the experience of change, mobilizing intellectual energy and activity, and mastering new knowledge (*Senge* et al., 2004, p. 504).

Joining the Bologna process destroyed the foundations of the national education system of the Russian Federation but also had a negative impact on the provision of the country's economy with highly qualified personnel. With the help of the Bologna system, the best of the professionally trained specialists in Russia leave for developed countries. The "brain drain" is facilitated not only by higher living standards and favorable conditions for creative and entrepreneurial activity in these countries, but also by the civic position that has not been formed among graduates of Russian universities. "Our universities graduate not educated, but professionally trained people. Their graduates may be good biologists, historians, or mathematicians, but one cannot call them educated people because they do not even know the basics of disciplines unrelated to their professions" (*Privalov*, 2016, p. 51).

4 Conclusion

Education is an active, reforming force. It motivates a person to action. In this regard, knowledge should not be mechanical, it should lead to a change in the individual and her behavior in society. A person himself chooses the sphere of professional activity, guided by his interests, abilities, and ideas about professional and life careers. The implementation of the goals largely depends on his motivation for self-education and continuous development.

The most important element of self-education is art. Education opens up bright opportunities for a person to comprehend life through literature, poetry, music, theater, and cinema. It also develops a subtle social imagination in a person and forms a sense of justice, adherence to moral standards, responsiveness, and compassion.

Educated people ensure social progress and the growth of the welfare of humankind. It is no coincidence that in Singapore, under Lee Kwan Yew, increasing IQ was officially declared a national idea. At the same time, the deputy prime minister of the Russian Federation, O. Golodets, stated in July 2016 that 65% of Russians would not need higher education (*Mehanik*, 2016b). The Chairman of the Government of the Russian Federation, D. A. Medvedev, noted that Russia needs workers and that there are too many people with higher education in the country. Such ideas are in tune with the attitudes characteristic of a consumer society, where education is increasingly losing its former importance. In many countries, including modern Russia, it is being replaced by vocational training. However, education, as discussed above, is not only a profession but also a culture, a person's spiritual, moral and civic position, and the desire for a better transformation of life.

The foreign concepts adopted in the Russian Federation, educational models and standards focused on the applied training of people, in contrast to the formation of a comprehensively developed personality, which was the target setting in the Soviet education system, are already bearing fruit. Having turned education from a social good, the most important intangible value, into an educational service, that is, increasingly commercializing the education sector, Russia not only reduces the quality of education, it wastes and does not reproduce the intellectual capital that supports the moral and cultural foundations of society. Russian society is characterized by the growth of asociality and passivity of citizens. In this regard, it should also be noted that the national education system has not yet been able to solve the problem of forming a new type of person – a free person. This is due primarily to the contradictory actions of existing social institutions. They still mainly use the mechanisms of reproduction of human resources inherited from the old totalitarian system, despite certain modernization transformations. The liberal ideas of changing Russian society did not justify themselves, since they did not provide stability and decent standards for the level and quality of life of citizens.

Realizing the current situation in the national education system, the country's government is taking certain actions to reform the education system. The law "On Education," adopted in 1992, declares the need to change the priorities of education, according to which the interests of the individual should be put in the first place in the process of education, the second – society, the third – the interests of the state (*Russian Federation*, 1992).

In order to integrate science and education and build up the intellectual and innovative potential of the regions of the Russian Federation, 29 national research and 10 federal universities were created, for the development of which significant funds were allocated from the state budget (*Vidyakina and Dmitrieva*, 2014). In 2013, the 5–100 Project was launched, within which the country's leading universities were tasked with increasing their competitiveness and entering the TOP 100 of the world's best universities (*Lindt*, 2016). Such participants of the 5–100 Project as Tomsk Polytechnic University, Tomsk State University, HSE, St. Petersburg Polytechnic University, ITMO University, Siberian Federal University, National Research Technological University MISiS, and other leading universities of the country determined the strategic directions of their development, models of behavior and mechanisms for increasing sustainability in the global scientific and educational space.

Transformations at the level of school education began as part of the National Education Initiative "Our New School." In order to improve the quality of education and its competitiveness in the global educational space, new formats of schools are being created, and their integration with universities is increasing. An example is the one created in 2013 at the National Research Nizhny Novgorod State University. N.I. Lobachevsky "University Education Cluster." Along with the university, it presents 10 leading schools in Nizhny Novgorod and the region, which are regularly included in the "TOP-50" of the best schools in Russia. In these schools, already from the middle grades (5th–9th), the preparation of students is carried out according to complicated programs. An important role for the future of Russia is played by schools for gifted children, the number of which is increasing every year. Their students demonstrate high results at international olympiads and competitions in mathematics, physics, and chemistry.

In recent decades, positive changes have been outlined in the system of training workers and managers of middle and lower levels of management. The need for training and development of not only managers, managers of middle and lower levels of management, but also the working staff was recognized by many Russian manufacturing companies. However, not many of them are ready to invest in education and fundamentally change the forms and technologies of training to increase employee involvement in achieving the organization's goals. According to the research of the American company Aon Hewit, the level of staff involvement directly affects the company's business indicators (revenue, total income of shareholders). According to this indicator, all companies are usually divided into three groups: risk zone (less than 50%), neutral (50%–70%), and high-performance zone (above 70%). The average level of personnel involvement in the industry of the Russian Federation is 54% (*Nietzsche*, 1990, p. 29). A few Russian industrial companies belong to the zone of high performance. Among them is the "Technonikol" corporation, which is one of the largest manufacturers and suppliers of roofing, waterproofing, and heat-insulating materials. It produces 2000 types of products and, has a turnover of 60 billion rubles and labor productivity of 14 million rubles per year per employee, exports products to 79 countries. This company pays considerable attention to the education and development of its employees. Since 2015, the "Technonikol" corporation has been gradually introducing a methodology for training workers in the self-testing mode, which has demonstrated high performance due to the involvement of employees both in the learning process and in the self-assessment of its results. According to Ekaterina Sorokina, HR director of the Mineral Isolation direction of the "Technonikol" corporation, the use of this technique destroyed the myth that workers are "grimy locksmiths." Many employees of the "Technonikol" company are developed people with higher education, with a broad outlook, who, within the framework of the production system, get acquainted with the enterprise's strategy and know their place in the value chain (*Krasnova*, 2017, p. 30).

 The accumulated positive experience in the domestic education system, of course, affects the renewal of the vectors and contours of its further development. However, the successes of several dozens of higher educational institutions, schools, and enterprises discussed above only slightly change the overall picture of the current unstable, contradictory state of the national education system. A change of paradigm and architectural construction of the national educational system of Russia is required. In our opinion, when solving these problems, it is necessary, from the existing dilemma for the Russian Federation: an educated or professionally trained person, of course, one should choose an educated person. It is on the basis of this value orientation that harmoniously combines the interests of a person, society, and the state that a concept, strategy, and program for the development of the education system of the Russian Federation should be developed.

References

Russian Federation. (1992) *Federal Law "On education"* (July 10, 1992 No. 3266–1). Moscow, Russia. Available (consulted 20 June 2022) at: https://www.consultant.ru/document/cons_doc_LAW_1888/.

Baudrillard J (2006) *Consumer society, its myths and structure* (EA Samarskaya Transl. from French). Moscow, Russia: Republic Publishing House. (Original work published 1970).

Chuykov A (2016) The brain column of the Bologna system. *Arguments of the Week*, 34(525), 4–5.

Gorbacheva SM, and Strizhko II (2015) Professional orientation of students. *Young Scientist* 21(101): 778–781.

Kazantsev AK, Kiselyov VN, Rubvalter DA, and Rudenskiy OV (2012) NBIC technologies: Innovative civilization of the XXI century. Moscow, Russia: INFRA-M.

Kitova O (2016) Excruciatingly embarrassing. But not power. *World of News* 22(1002), 4–7.

Komleva NS, and Shcherbakova EG (2014) The modern system of education in European countries: Problems and prospects. *Bulletin of the Volga University after V.N. Tatischev* 4(32): 69–77.

Krasnova V (2017) How to train guys who always play. *Expert* 4(1014): 29–31.

Lindt M (2016) Five out of a hundred. *Expert* 8(997): 71–77.

Mehanik A (2016a) Reforms that ruin education. *Expert* 27(994): 58–59.

Mehanik A (2016b) What awaits higher education in Russia. *Expert* 8(976): 64–67.

Nietzsche FW (1990) *Human, all too human. Works in 2 Volumes* (Volume 1) (SL Frank Transl. from German). Moscow, USSR: Mysl Publishing House. (Original work published 1878).

Paulsen F (1900) *Education.* Moscow, Russian Empire: Sabashnikov Publishing House.

Privalov A (2016) Fifteen chances for a miracle. *Expert* 28–29(995): 50–53.

Rubakin NA (1975) *Selected works in 2 Volumes.* Moscow, USSR: Publishing House "Kniga".

Rubakin NA (1962) *How to educate yourself.* Moscow, USSR: Soviet Russia.

Samonova A (2016) Five dozen shades of medium. *Arguments of the Week* 43(534): 3–4.

Senge P, Kleiner A, Roberts S, and Roth G (2004) *The dance of change: The challenges to sustaining momentum in learning organizations* (B. Pinsker Transl. from English). Moscow, Russia: JSC "Olimp-Business." (Original work published 1999).

Tolstoy LN (1936) *On the importance of public education.* Moscow, USSR: State Publishing House "Khudozhestvennaya literatura".

Vidyakina OV, and Dmitrieva, EM (2014) *Personnel training system for innovative training in Russia.* Moscow, Russia: Prospect.

CHAPTER 24

Trends in the Development of the State Educational Standard of Higher Professional Education of the Kyrgyz Republic

Elvira E. Samatova, Baktyyar M. Asanov and Diloram I. Khasanova

Abstract

The chapter aims to evaluate and present the results of the historical study of three generations of standards, the organization and technical equipment of the educational process, teaching classes, and the organization of feedback to students in the relevant areas. Moreover, the chapter assesses the documentation of the process and the quality of educational services in the university and describes the prospects and approaches to addressing the quality of higher education. The chapter presents the results of assessing the state educational standards of higher professional education in the Kyrgyz Republic (the standard) from 2012 to 2021. A comparative analysis and study results on three generations of standards are presented. The chapter is based on the analysis of the results of the questionnaire survey of full-time students of the 1st–4th years at the Department of "Business and Management" of the Osh State University, which was obtained from December 2021 to January 2022. The proposed research methods can be used to achieve long-term practical results in supporting universities, their managers, teachers, students, and all stakeholders in the organization and conduct of the educational process. Moreover, these methods can be applied to overcome barriers to teachers' access to information on using digital tools and technical equipment in the educational process. The authors made recommendations for the implementation of the third-generation standard (2021) in the educational process of the direction 580 100 "Economics" at the Osh State University. It is recommended to bring the results of the survey to the management of the faculty and use the obtained results during the organization and conduct of the educational process and overcoming barriers to the use of technical equipment in the educational process to improve the quality of education in the university. The novelty of the conducted research lies in the study and evaluation of the standards of three generations, the search for the ways to solve the difficulties of students and teaching staff of the Osh State University in the organization and technical equipment of the educational process and quality of education in the university, and the description of the prospects and approaches to addressing the quality of education in the university.

Keywords

higher education institution – questionnaire – survey – standard – technical equipment – educational process

1   Introduction

The problem of education has been at the forefront of the world for centuries. Combating staff shortages, training of personnel and their professional development are aimed at the development of society and particular enterprises, industries, and the national economy.

However, to prepare personnel for the national economy of the Kyrgyz Republic, it is necessary to consider the issue of legislative norms, requirements, educational standards, etc.

The relevance of the research topic lies in the fact that various legislative and regulatory documents (e.g., the Law of the Kyrgyz Republic "On education," state educational standards, etc.) have been adopted in the Kyrgyz Republic and are in force, contributing to the organization and the conduct of the educational process, its monitoring, and control. Thus, the training of future personnel in higher education institutions, a historical study of the standards of three generations, a sociological study of the organization, technical equipment of the educational process, the study of the quality of educational services in higher education, the description of prospects and approaches to addressing the quality of education in higher education currently play an important role and require a comprehensive study.

The chapter aims to study, review, and compare the state educational standards of higher professional education in the Kyrgyz Republic. The study is conducted from a historical perspective. The authors surveyed full-time students on the quality of educational services and analyzed the results. According to the survey results, the authors developed a table, conducted a comparative analysis of the data, and gave recommendations to the university on improving the quality of educational services.

Research objectives are as follows:
1. To review the state educational standards of higher professional education of the Kyrgyz Republic (the standard) from 2012 to 2021;
2. To conduct a comparative analysis of the standards;
3. To survey full-time students of the 1st–4th years at the Department of "Business and Management" of the Osh State University in December 2021 and January 2022;

4. To prepare recommendations for the implementation of the third-generation standard (2021) in the educational process of the direction 580 100 "Economics" at the Osh State University;
5. To inform the management of the faculty of the survey results and implement these results in the organization and conduct of the educational process;
6. To describe perspectives and approaches to solving the problem of quality of education in higher education.

2   Materials and Methods

Trends in the development of the state educational standard of higher professional education of the Kyrgyz Republic are studied, considered, and researched in the legislative and regulatory documents of the Kyrgyz Republic, including the following:

a. State educational standards of higher professional education, direction 580 100 "Economics," Academic degree: Bachelor (approved by the Decree of the Government of the Kyrgyz Republic of July 4, 2012, No. 472, pp. 1–33) (*Ministry of Education and Science of the Kyrgyz Republic*, 2012);
b. State educational standards of higher professional education, direction 580 100 "Economics," Academic degree: Bachelor (approved by the Decree of the Government of the Kyrgyz Republic of September 15, 2015, No. 1179/1, pp. 1–19) (*Ministry of Education and Science of the Kyrgyz Republic*, 2015);
c. State educational standards of higher professional education, direction 580 100 "Economics," Academic degree: Bachelor (approved by the Decree of the Government of the Kyrgyz Republic of September 21, 2021, No. 1578, pp. 1–13) (*Ministry of Education and Science of the Kyrgyz Republic*, 2021);
d. State standard of the French Republic on the competences of the holder of a diploma (degree) "Licence: Law" (LICENCE: MENTION DROIT) – the analog of the Russian Bachelor of Jurisprudence, (Decree "On the license" of August 1, 2011) (*Official Website of the French Government "Légifrance"* [Légifrance], 2011), etc.

The term "education" is defined by V. Dal (1979).

The main task of the higher education institution – the formation of academic knowledge and skills in students is studied in the works of E. E. Samatova, D. I. Khasanova, S. N. Yakubov, and Zh. R. Raimzhanov (*Samatova* et al., 2021), as well as in the work by E. E. Samatova, G. K. Tashkulova, and N. Zhanbolotova (*Samatova* et al., 2019).

The state of the quality of education, educational process, its organization, technical equipment, etc. are considered, studied, and analyzed in the materials of the questionnaire (list of questions in the questionnaire) of the sociological survey "Teacher in the eyes of students" (*Sociological Survey Questionnaire*, 2021) and questionnaire (questionnaire data) of the sociological survey among full-times students of the 1st–4th years, conducted at the Department of "Business and Management" of the Osh State University on January 3, 2022 (*Sociological Survey Questionnaire*, 2022).

The Bologna system and its implementation (introduction) in the Osh State University and other universities of the Kyrgyz Republic are studied according to data and sources of Internet resources (*Adylbek kyzyi and Dzholdosheva*, 2012).

During the research, we applied the method of sociological survey, framed it in questionnaires, collected, processed, and analyzed the data on the quality of education at the Department of "Business and Management" of the Osh State University, and compiled a summary table on them (*Sociological Survey Questionnaire*, 2022).

The purpose of the survey is to collect data on the attitudes of students and problems emerging during the organization and conduct of lectures and seminars (study sessions). The survey questionnaire will help us to better know and understand how the training session is organized, technically equipped, and conducted, what problems arise, what should be changed or improved, and what the priorities for institutional development are. The survey of students was conducted within the framework of teaching the discipline "Quality Management" due to the need and importance of showing, teaching, and involving students in the process of developing the survey questionnaire, conducting the survey, collecting and processing questionnaire data, and bringing (summary and grouping) them into tables on various attributes. During the survey, students learned how to conduct a survey, fill out questionnaires, collect answers to questions and summarize them in tables, make charts and write interpretations to tables, and much more. Simultaneously, we pursued the goal of collecting information on the posed problem and communicating the results of the survey to the administration of the faculty, as well as drawing up a study and sending it to print. The survey was conducted in accordance with national scientific approaches, including the following:

– Novelty and relevance;
– Practical usefulness, the possibility of implementing these recommendations and conclusions;

– Availability of previous experience and experience of researchers in conducting scientific research.

We collected, analyzed, and conducted a graphical comparison of the data obtained.

The survey was conducted offline and was based on the principles of anonymity and confidentiality. It should be noted that respondents (students) have repeatedly participated in surveys, have been familiar with the essence of the raised problem of the quality of education, and have answered the questionnaire based on their own experience.

Students who, for various reasons, were absent from class on January 3, 2022, or were unable or unwilling to participate in the designated event did not participate in the survey.

The survey involved students from four courses of the Department of "Business and Management" at the Osh State University, studying in the direction of training 580 100 "Economics." The survey was anonymous. There was no special selection of students for the questionnaire.

A survey among full-time students from the first to the fourth courses was conducted by students and teachers on January 3, 2022, at the Department of "Business and Management" at the Osh State University. A total of 201 people participated in the survey. There were 11 questions in the questionnaire, of which eight questions were on the survey topic, and three were demographic questions. The survey results are presented in Table 24.1 (*Sociological Survey Questionnaire*, 2022).

The Bologna system came to the Kyrgyz Republic from Europe and was first implemented (introduced) at the Osh State University (OSU) in 2004. It should be noted that medical specialties remained unchanged. In other words, medical students continue to receive an education according to the six-year plan (according to the old Soviet system) with a specialty in the corresponding direction.

On July 13, 2012, most universities in the Kyrgyz Republic received the right to transition to a two-tier education system. This change came into force from the 2012–2013 school year. The change provided for the introduction of two levels of training. The first level involves four years of study. Upon completion, the student received a bachelor's degree. After two more years of study, the student received a master's degree.

As noted by E. E. Samatova, G. K. Tashkulova, and N. Zhanbolotova, "contemporary education is represented by a two-level system of education, which is based on state educational standards, oriented to the criteria proposed by accreditation agencies (e.g., Association of Educational Institutions "EdNet")" (*Samatova* et al., 2019).

TABLE 24.1 Data on the conducted sociological survey among full-time students in the 1st–4th years at the Department of "Business and Management" of the Osh State University conducted on January 3, 2022

No.	Questions of the questionnaire (survey)	Year of study	Yes	No	Do not know	Insufficiently	Very little	Sometimes	Not always	Depending on the topic of the class	Total
1	Are you satisfied with the quality of education?	1	21	4	6	-	-	-	-	-	31
		2	44	2	6	-	-	-	-	-	52
		3	61	18	12	-	-	-	-	-	91
		4	18	7	2	-	-	-	-	-	27
2	Does the department have sufficient office equipment for all types of classes?	1	18	3	-	4	1	3	-	-	29
		2	35	0	-	10	0	7	-	-	52
		3	37	4	-	36	7	8	-	-	92
		4	16	2	-	9	-	-	-	-	27
3	Do teachers use office equipment in all types of classes?	1	15	1	-	4	5	5	-	-	30
		2	31	0	-	6	4	11	-	-	52
		3	33	3	-	20	13	23	-	-	92
		4	11	2	-	6	2	6	-	-	27
4	Do teachers use interactive methods in all types of classes?	1	16	2	-	-	-	10	3	-	31
		2	32	2	-	-	-	10	8	-	52
		3	24	5	-	-	-	31	12	-	72
		4	15	4	-	-	-	7	1	-	27

TRENDS IN THE DEVELOPMENT OF THE STATE EDUCATIONAL STANDARD   335

No.	Questions of the questionnaire (survey)	Year of study	Yes	No	Do not know	Insufficiently	Very little	Sometimes	Not always	Depending on the topic of the class	Total
5	Do you solve tasks during practical classes?	1	16	3	-	-	-	7	1	7	34
		2	30	1	-	-	-	5	3	11	50
		3	39	6	-	-	-	7	6	16	74
		4	19	0	-	-	-	4	1	6	30
6	Do you take notes during lecture classes?	1	25	0	-	-	-	4	2	-	31
		2	45	1	-	-	-	4	2	-	52
		3	76	6	-	-	-	5	4	-	91
		4	23	0	-	-	-	2	2	-	27
7	Do you get homework?	1	28	1	-	-	-	1	1	-	31
		2	46	1	-	-	-	4	1	-	50
		3	78	1	-	-	-	4	6	-	89
		4	26	0	-	-	-	1	1	-	28
8	Have you received a syllabus, savings card, and other documents from the teacher to organize and conduct the study session?	1	26	0	-	-	-	2	3	-	31
		2	35	5	-	-	-	8	4	-	52
		3	65	1	-	-	-	8	10	-	84
		4	19	2	-	-	-	2	4	-	27

SOURCE: (*SOCIOLOGICAL SURVEY QUESTIONNAIRE, 2022*)

According to the explanatory dictionary of V. Dal (1979), "to form – to give an image to something, to give an appearance to something, to make something whole, to create, to bring together into one whole," which clearly presents the model of a future graduate.

E. E. Samatova (*Samatova* et al., 2021) emphasizes that "the main task of a higher education institution becomes the formation of students' academic knowledge and, above all, the ability to work, live, and adapt in a rapidly changing world. If we look into the history of formation and definitions of the term education, we see that it has very broad meanings, such as create, form, cultivate, and create something new whole." Thus, we can conclude that a future specialist in the relevant direction can and must have certain knowledge, skills, and abilities defined in the state educational standard of higher professional education of the Kyrgyz Republic.

The Bologna system uses a credit system for evaluating a student's education. The curriculum set down to universities by the Ministry of Education and Science of the Kyrgyz Republic includes three sections:
1. Compulsory disciplines (state component);
2. Variative disciplines (university component);
3. Courses that students can choose for themselves (elective courses) (*Ministry of Education and Science of the Kyrgyz Republic*, 2012).

The most important thing about the Bologna system is that students can choose not only the discipline but also the instructors.

In the context of the global financial crisis, reducing costs and improving the efficiency of education has become one of the most important tasks of educational institutions. Therefore, the issue of improving the state educational standards of higher professional education in the system of higher education in the Kyrgyz Republic is currently of particular relevance.

The cumulative total is 240 semester credits, with 30 credits each semester and a total of eight semesters of learning. How to assess and check the process of organization and technical support of the educational process and its progress and identify the training results? There are many questions, but the market now demands a trained, fast-talking, and communicative workforce. Today's workforce must know, be able, and possess the skills for their future profession. Thus, the leadership of the Kyrgyz Republic, the Ministry of Education, the Educational and Methodological Association, universities, faculties, departments, and all interested structures are faced with the urgent question of developing and implementing the "third generation" standards.

Each department compiles a self-assessment report and prepares material for the major educational program to prepare students in their respective majors. Simultaneously, each teacher participates in the learning process and creates the educational-methodical complex, work program, syllabus, and other instructional documents to help and methodologically provide (design) lecture and seminar classes.

The student evaluates the instructor's work at the end of the semester and the academic year. A sociological survey (questionnaire) "Teacher in the eyes of students" is conducted (*Sociological Survey Questionnaire*, 2021). The proposed survey is conducted twice an academic year at the Osh State University. The first time it is carried out is at the end of the winter session. The results of the questionnaire make it possible to assess the attitude of students to the learning process and students' evaluation of the teacher (through the suggestions at the end of the questionnaire; in question No. 13, students can make suggestions and comments to a particular teacher and express their points of view, attitude towards a particular teacher, and dissatisfaction or satisfaction with the quality of educational services offered). In general, the survey "Teacher in the eyes of students" aims to monitor the satisfaction of consumers of educational services (students) with the educational process in the winter semester and the quality of services received. Using the AVN program, upon completion of the survey, each teacher can track the results, suggestions, and comments made, either eliminating or taking them into account. For the second time, the survey is conducted on the results of the summer session (*Sociological Survey Questionnaire*, 2021). The questionnaire contains a question that touches on elements and facts of corruption (question No. 12). The results of the questionnaire will be further applied (used) by the dean's office and the rectorate in the competitive election for the appropriate position: senior lecturer, associate professor, and professor. When passing the competition to fill the appropriate position, the teachers must include in the package of documents a certificate of the results of the survey "Teacher in the eyes of students." The survey results are necessarily considered when deciding to fill the appropriate position.

Theoretically, the survey results can and should become one of the criteria for evaluating, charging, and applying the appropriate coefficients in differentiated pay. However, this approach to payroll has not yet been applied at the Osh State University. In 2021, the first assessment rating of teachers' performance at the Osh State University was conducted. A rating was developed based on the monitoring results, which identified about 300 applicants for a bonus for scientific, methodological, and other activities. The first attempt of evaluation has been made, and the staff of the Osh State University has focused on high achievements in pedagogy, science, and other areas of activity because they will receive allowances for this. That is, the elements of differentiated wages started to be applied.

Considering the historical development of education in Kyrgyzstan, we can note that the 2005–2006 academic year was crucial in the activities of many universities in Kyrgyzstan because the Ministry of Education revoked the licenses of many universities. The Ministry of Education decided to make the universities of Kyrgyzstan profile. For example, humanitarian universities were recommended to prepare specialists in the humanities; technical universities were recommended to prepare technical specialists, etc.

Thus, universities can train specialists only in a specific leading profile. The years show that the decision was timely and correct. The universities of the Kyrgyz Republic became profile.

Currently, universities in the post-Soviet space are deciding to join the Bologna process and harmonize educational systems. This is a complex and long process. The work in this direction has been going on for many years in all higher education institutions in Kyrgyzstan. Certain experience has been accumulated, their own opinion has been formed, and the graduates successfully work for the country's benefit in various areas of activity, including small and medium-sized businesses.

The work of entering and strengthening the Bologna system in the Kyrgyz Republic is a painstaking and complex process. The country's universities are improving their efforts to implement the Bologna system.

Over the past 18 years, the Osh State University has done much to introduce, strengthen, and implement the Bologna system. In particular, to improve the activities of universities, the government repeatedly improved the state educational standards of higher professional education in the Kyrgyz Republic (the standard). The M. Ryskulbekov Kyrgyz Economic University (KEU) plays an important role in improving the standards, in which the educational and methodological association of the relevant areas, such as 580 100 "Economics" (Bachelor of Economics), is working fruitfully.

The 2012 standard was a rather lengthy document, consisting of the following sections:
1. General provisions;
2. Area of application;
3. General characteristics of the training area;
4. General requirements for the conditions for the implementation of the basic educational program (BEP);
5. Requirements for the BEP of Bachelor's degree program (*Ministry of Education and Science of the Kyrgyz Republic*, 2012).

The 2015 and 2021 standards are similar to the 2012 standard in the composition of the sections. However, their internal content has significant differences, changes, and additions. Let us consider them in more detail.

The first section of the 2012 and 2015 standards are similar, and no changes have been made (*Ministry of Education and Science of the Kyrgyz Republic*, 2015). The first section provides information that the standard was developed by the Ministry of Education of the Kyrgyz Republic, the Law "On education," and other legislative and regulatory documents in the field of education. This section clearly defines that the adopted and the approved standard is mandatory for all universities in the country. The section also contains all terms, definitions, designations, and abbreviations (they also remain unchanged). The 2021 standard added terms such as credit, general academic competencies, instrumental competencies, socio-personal and general cultural competencies, and professional standards; such terms as discipline cycles and module are removed from the standard (*Ministry of Education and Science of the Kyrgyz Republic*, 2021).

The most interesting and important thing is that the wording "academic degree" is changed to a "bachelor's degree" on the title page of the 2021 standard. Such innovation is a significant change. Accordingly, the concepts of bachelor's and master's have changed their wording and have become more precise, correct, and short. However, terms such as credit, general scientific competence, instrumental competence, socio-personal and general cultural competence, and professional standard have been added, which clearly define the knowledge, skills, and abilities of students (*Ministry of Education and Science of the Kyrgyz Republic*, 2021).

The second section of the standard clearly states who can base and use the standard. No changes were made to this section in the 2012 and 2015 standards. However, the 2021 standard no longer indicates that the standard could be used by university applicants. This change is correct because the applicant, with all the desire, can not see and understand such a complex normative document as the educational standard (*Ministry of Education and Science of the Kyrgyz Republic*, 2021).

For many years, the standard indicated that applicants in the arts and physical education take entrance exams and are not subject to nationwide testing (ORT). In the 2021 standard, the above statement has been removed. Thus, applicants in the above areas are also admitted to the university on a general basis on the ORT results (*Ministry of Education and Science of the Kyrgyz Republic*, 2021).

The third section of the 2012 and 2015 standards has no deep changes. However, the 2021 standard indicates that the implementation of programs can be carried out on an accelerated program and, in special cases, adopted and introduced by the university itself. The section on types of professional activities of graduates now includes entrepreneurial activity; pedagogical activity was removed. Accordingly, the tasks of professional activity are changed in accordance with the set types of professional activity.

The fourth section of the 2012, 2015, and 2021 standards have no profound changes (*Ministry of Education and Science of the Kyrgyz Republic*, 2012, 2015, 2021). The 2012 and 2015 standards clearly defined that universities are obliged to annually update with the development of science, culture, economy, engineering, technology, and social sphere, adhering to the recommendations to ensure the quality of education in the university. The 2021 standard adds that universities are required to update the educational program at least every five years, considering developments in science, culture, economy, engineering, technology, and social sphere, adhering to the recommendations to ensure the quality of education in the university (*Ministry of Education and Science of the Kyrgyz Republic*, 2021).

The fifth section of the 2012 standard indicates that the requirements for the bachelor's degree program include the following universal and professional competencies (*Ministry of Education and Science of the Kyrgyz Republic*, 2012). Universal competencies include the following:

1. General scientific competencies – 16 competencies;
2. Instrumental competencies – 12 competencies;
3. Socio-personal and general cultural competencies – 12 competencies.

Professional competencies include the following:

1. Calculation and economic competencies – 3 competencies;
2. Analytical and research competencies – 10 competencies;
3. Pedagogical competencies – 2 competencies.

In total, the 2012 standard for higher professional education in the direction 580 100 "Economics" (Bachelor of Economics) indicates 55 competencies (*Ministry of Education and Science of the Kyrgyz Republic*, 2012). When this standard was implemented, time showed that it was very difficult and time-consuming to implement these competencies.

The fifth section of the 2015 standard indicates that the requirements for the bachelor's degree program include universal and professional competencies (*Ministry of Education and Science of the Kyrgyz Republic*, 2015). Universal competencies include the following:

1. General scientific competencies – 6 competencies;
2. Instrumental competencies – 6 competencies;
3. Socio-personal and general cultural competencies – 5 competencies.

Professional competencies include the following:

1. Calculation and economic competencies – 3 competencies;
2. Analytical and research competencies – 7 competencies;
3. Organizational and managerial competencies – 3 competencies

4. Pedagogical competencies – 2 competencies.

In total, the 2015 standard for higher professional education in the direction 580 100 "Economics" (Bachelor of Economics) indicates 32 competencies (*Ministry of Education and Science of the Kyrgyz Republic*, 2015).

A comparative analysis of the 2012 and 2015 standards revealed that the general scientific competencies were reduced from 16 to 6 competencies. The instrumental competencies were reduced from 12 to 6 competencies. The socio-personal and general cultural competencies were reduced from 12 to 5 competencies. The professional competencies remained unchanged (17 competencies). In total, in the 2012 and 2015 standards for higher professional education in the direction 580 100 "Economics" (Bachelor of Economics), the number of planned competencies was reduced to 23 competencies (*Ministry of Education and Science of the Kyrgyz Republic*, 2015).

A comparative analysis of the 2015 and 2021 standards revealed that the general scientific competencies were reduced from 6 to 1. The instrumental competencies were reduced from 6 to 3. The socio-personal and general cultural competencies were reduced from 5 to 1. The professional competencies were reduced from 15 to 12 competencies. Simultaneously, the new standard introduced the new professional competence PC-9 "Able to apply normative and legal documents in professional activities and comply with their requirements" (*Ministry of Education and Science of the Kyrgyz Republic*, 2021). However, the most important thing is that the 2021 standard notes that the profile is determined by additional special professional competencies, not more than five items; it is independently determined by the university (*Ministry of Education and Science of the Kyrgyz Republic*, 2021).

The 2012 and 2015 standards allocated six study cycles. In turn, the 2021 standard allocated three blocks:
1. Block 1 – disciplines (modules);
2. Block 2 – Practice;
3. Block 3 – State final attestation.

The 2015 standard changes the core of Block 1, which means 28 credits are reduced to 26 credits. Thus, the variable part in the 2012 standard was defined in the amount of 10 credits and was reduced to 8 credits in the 2015 standard. The changes did not affect the total labor intensity of the BEP – 240 credits (*Ministry of Education and Science of the Kyrgyz Republic*, 2015).

In the 2021 standard, the structure of the bachelor's degree program in the direction 580 100 "Economics" is presented simply enough and summarized in the table. The changes simplified the procedure for determining the volume of the program and did not affect the total labor intensity of the program – 240 credits (*Ministry of Education and Science of the Kyrgyz Republic*, 2021).

We can conclude that the 2012 standard is professionally and competently drafted. This document clearly identifies the requirements for the mandatory minimum content of the educational professional training program 580 100 "Economics." For all courses offered, there is a clearly defined minimum of topics and questions that the instructor must deliver to students.

The standard has Appendix 2, which provides a list of disciplines offered by the educational and methodological association on the profile, which highlights the names of disciplines, workload, and the competencies formed in specific disciplines. The faculty member who teaches a particular discipline had no qualms about not fully presenting and covering the subject (discipline). The structure of the bachelor's degree program in the direction 580 100 "Economics" is formed in the table, which highlights the subjects, competencies that students should master, and learning outcomes (*Ministry of Education and Science of the Kyrgyz Republic*, 2012).

The 2015 standard has been improved over 2–3 years. Nevertheless, it is similar to the 2012 standard. The number of competencies was reduced from 55 (in 2012) to 35 (in 2015) and then to 17 (in 2021). From year to year, the educational standard is improved and adjusted; the work of teachers is becoming easier. Comparing the state educational standards of higher professional education in the direction 580 100 "Economics" (Bachelor of Economics) for the years 2012, 2015, and 2021, we can conclude that the 2012 standard is 33 pages, the 2015 standard is 19 pages, and the 2021 standard is 12 pages. The number of pages in the standards decreases from year to year, but their value increases. The third-generation standard (*Ministry of Education and Science of the Kyrgyz Republic*, 2021) is specified and improved; competencies are staffed. The latest standard provides an opportunity to improve the quality of education and the provision of educational services.

3 Results and Discussion

A 2022 survey of full-time students of the 1st-4th years yielded the following results.

The survey involved 204 participants. The distribution of respondents by gender is as follows:
– Men – 73 people (35.78%);
– Women – 131 people (64.22%).

Although it is widely believed that consumers of educational services are not satisfied with the quality of education at universities in the southern region of Kyrgyzstan, 70.58% of surveyed students responded that they are satisfied with the quality of education in their university (Chart 24.1).

During the survey, it was important to determine the following:
- Are students satisfied with the quality of education at the Department of "Business and Management" at the Osh State University?
- Does the department have sufficient office equipment for all types of classes?
- Do teachers use office equipment in all types of classes?
- Do teachers use interactive methods in all types of classes?
- Do they solve tasks during practical classes?
- Do students take notes during lecture classes?
- Do students get homework?
- Have students received a syllabus, savings card, and other documents from the teacher to organize and conduct the study session?

Answering whether the department has sufficient office equipment for all types of classes, 106 (51.96%) respondents answered that the department has all the necessary office equipment.

According to 90 (44.12%) respondents, teachers use office equipment in all types of classes.

According to 84 (42.65%) out of 204 respondents, teachers use interactive methods in all types of classes.

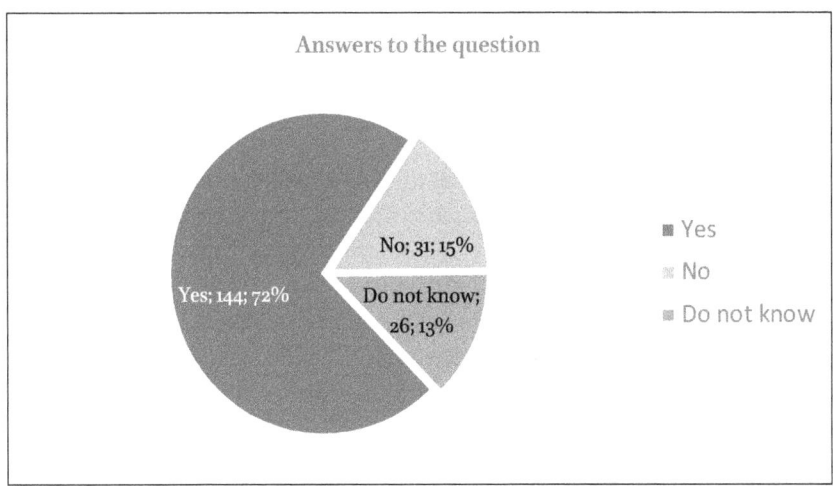

CHART 24.1   Answers to the question: "Are you satisfied with the quality of education at the Department of "Business and Management" at the Osh State University?"
SOURCE: COMPILED BY THE AUTHORS BASED ON TABLE 24.1

More than half of the respondents (104 respondents (50.98%)) indicated that they solved tasks during practical classes.

Out of 204 respondents, 169 (82.84%) students indicated that they took notes during lecture classes.

A total of 178 (87.25%) respondents indicated that they got homework.

Out of 204 respondents, 145 (71.08%) students indicated that they received a syllabus, savings card, and other documents from the teacher to organize and conduct the study session.

Thus, the survey to assess the quality of education at the Department of "Business and Management" at the Osh State University took place. The results of the survey and the analysis are recommended for use in compiling a self-assessment report on the direction 580 100 "Economics" for national and program accreditation.

However, not all students positively responded to the posed questions:
- 31 (12.92%) students said that they were dissatisfied with the quality of education at the Osh State University;
- 9 (4.4%) students responded that the department had insufficient office equipment for conducting all types of classes;
- 6 (2.9%) respondents said that not all teachers use office equipment in all types of classes. However, this is because not all classrooms of the university are equipped with a computer, projector, electronic whiteboard, etc. for the training session;
- 13 (6.4%) students responded that not all teachers use interactive methods in all types of classes;
- 10 (4.9%) students responded that they do not always solve tasks during practical classes;
- 7 (3.4%) respondents answered that they do not always take notes during lecture classes;
- 3 (1.5%) respondents answered that they do not always get homework;
- 8 (3.9%) respondents answered that they had not received a syllabus, a savings card, and other documents from the instructor that they needed to organize and conduct the class.

About 13% of respondents are dissatisfied with the quality of education at the Department of "Business and Management." This fact should be considered by the administration of the faculty and departments and take appropriate measures to eliminate it.

We also recommend that the administration and all interested parties pay attention to the "no" answers in the questionnaire, which show disadvantages in the educational process to which special attention should be paid.

4 Conclusion

The results allow us to conclude that teachers, like students, are the main participants in the learning process:
- Administration of the department organizes the learning process, makes all kinds of schedules, distributes the classroom fund, controls the progress of lectures and seminars, etc.;
- Teachers deliver their disciplines in accordance with the state educational standard of higher professional education in the Kyrgyz Republic.

One of the ways to solve the problem of quality education in the university is a technical configuration of classroom stock of the department, the control of the educational process, and the provision of its educational and methodological support. It is primarily necessary to create all necessary conditions for the teacher to be able to implement and conduct lectures and seminars fully. Each classroom should be equipped with a computer, projector, electronic whiteboard, and access to the Internet so that the teacher can easily start and conduct a lecture or seminar class. Students want quality Internet access, that is, the Internet availability in each classroom via Wi-Fi.

Using interactive methods, information resources, communication technologies, pedagogical skills, and experience, teachers promote and help the young specialist in obtaining knowledge, skills, and abilities inherent in the state educational standard of higher professional education of the Kyrgyz Republic in the direction 580 100 "Economics" (Bachelor of Economics).

All subjects (courses) are available electronically at the website of the Osh State University (avn.oshsu.kg). Students can view and monitor class schedules, contract payments, etc., online via the avn-student app.

Over the past five years, the practice has shown that the standards approved and applied in the Kyrgyz Republic are very cumbersome. Although they reduced the number of competencies from 55 to 35, their practical implementation was difficult. There were many questions about it. However, the practical application of the 2015 standards provided an opportunity to identify inaccuracies and obscure areas and take note of them. The 2021 standards are being implemented, and time will show how advanced and easy they have become in practice. In the 2021 standards, the number of competencies is reduced to 17, and the main emphasis is placed on professional competencies. The 2011 National Standard of the French Republic states that "competence is the ability to put into practice an organized body of knowledge, skills, and abilities to accomplish a number of tasks. Competence can never be viewed as the result of a single course of study or a short course of education" (*Légifrance*, 2011).

Requirements for the results of mastering the basic educational program at the direction 580 100 "Economics" (Bachelor of Economics) allocate universal competence, highlighting the main requirements for the values of life, patriotism, compulsory knowledge of languages and computer skills, entrepreneurial abilities, etc. In terms of universal competencies, considering the global experience of Russia, Kazakhstan, and other countries, the standard has become clear and now clearly defines the main universal requirements presented to students. The professional competencies clearly define the wording of the requirements for students. The profile is determined by additional special professional competencies in the number of no more than five competencies; it is determined by the university independently (*Ministry of Education and Science of the Kyrgyz Republic*, 2021). The higher educational institutions of the Kyrgyz Republic are currently working diligently to master and implement the new third-generation standards. Time will show how applicable and relevant these standards are.

Educational standards in Kyrgyzstan have changed three times in the last decade. The changes made to them were due to the experience gained and the need to improve the standards. As full members of the Bologna system, working in accordance with relevant legislation and regulations, universities in the Kyrgyz Republic must comply with the requirements of the state educational standard of higher professional education of Kyrgyz Republic. The experience gained, comments, inaccuracies, ambiguities, and shortcomings need to be eliminated, which is a prerequisite for making changes and additions to the standards. The 2021 standard is currently the main regulatory document, the requirements of which universities are obliged to fulfill (implement). All ongoing activities aim to improve the quality of educational services of the Osh State University of the Kyrgyz Republic.

However, there has been a lot of controversy surrounding the Bologna system and its existence in the Russian Federation. Russia is currently developing a new education model and has already officially rejected the Bologna system because it does not reflect the demands of the labor market. Perhaps, Russia will create a hybrid of the Bologna system. The achievements of past years show that the specialist's degree provides an opportunity for in-depth study of the specialty (especially technical and medical specialties). Nevertheless, the Bologna system should theoretically give the graduate the possibility of mutual recognition of education abroad, which is not the case in practice. Having created a global European system of education and implementing it for more than 20 years, we currently see that it does not meet the requirements. However, the Bologna system has positive aspects, such as the Unified School Examination (USE). Neither Kyrgyzstan nor Russia has adopted 12 years of schooling. However, the issue of introducing 12-year education in school is currently being discussed in the Kyrgyz Republic at all levels. Time will show if the Bologna system remains in Kyrgyzstan and 12 years of schooling are introduced. Given the interests of the economy of Kyrgyzstan and opportunities for students, we can conclude that Kyrgyz education will create its own (unique) model, considering the gained experience for the further development of education.

Acknowledgments

The authors would like to express their gratitude to the third-year students and all teachers who helped to develop and implement the questionnaire.

References

Ministry of Education and Science of the Kyrgyz Republic (2012) *State educational standard of higher professional education, direction 580 100 "Economics," Academic degree: Bachelor* (approved by the Decree of the Government of the Kyrgyz Republic of July 4, 2012, No. 472). Bishkek, Kyrgyzstan. Available (consulted 13 July 2022) at: https://bafe.edu.kg/wp-content/uploads/2015/01/ГОС-ВПО-580100-Экономика.pdf.

Ministry of Education and Science of the Kyrgyz Republic (2015) *State educational standard of higher professional education, direction 580 100 "Economics," Academic degree: Bachelor* (approved by the Decree of the Government of the Kyrgyz Republic of September 15, 2015, No. 1179/1). Bishkek, Kyrgyzstan. Available (consulted 13 July 2022) at: https://mnu.kg/wp-content/uploads/2018/03/ГОСТ-ВПО-580100-Экономика-Бакалавриат-2015-г..pdf.

Ministry of Education and Science of the Kyrgyz Republic (2021) *State educational standard of higher professional education, direction 580 100 "Economics," Academic degree: Bachelor* (approved by the Decree of the Government of the Kyrgyz Republic of September 21, 2021, No. 1578). Bishkek, Kyrgyzstan. Available (consulted 13 July 2022) at: https://muk.iuk.kg/wp-content/uploads/2022/02/580100-Ekonomika.pdf.

Official Website of the French Government "Légifrance" (2011) *State standards of the French Republic in relation to the competencies of the holder of a diploma (degree) "Licence: Law"* (LICENCE: MENTION DROIT) – *Analogous to the Russian Bachelor of Jurisprudence* (Resolution "On the licence" of August 1, 2011, NOR: ESRS1119411A). Available (consulted 13 July 2022) at: https://www.legifrance.gouv.fr/loda/id/JORFTEXT000024457754/.

Adylbek kyzyi A, and Dzholdosheva K (2012, July 13) *Ministry of Education: All universities have received licenses for the transition to the Bologna system*. Available (consulted 13 July 2022) at: https://kloop.kg/blog/2012/07/13/minobrazovaniya-vse-vuzy-poluchili-litsenzii-dlya-perehoda-na-bolonskuyu-sistemu/.

Dal V (1979). *Explanatory Dictionary of the Living Great Russian Language* (Vol. 2). Moscow, USSR, p. 613.

Samatova EE, Khasanova DI, Yakubov SN, and Raimzhanov ZhR (2021) Problems of formation of the graduate model in modern conditions. *Science and Innovative Technologies* 4(21): 185–196.

Samatova EE, Tashkulova GK, and Zhanbolotova N. (2019) Innovative development of science and education. In: *Problems and areas of educational institution in the formation of personnel policy and human resource management strategy*. Penza, Russia: Science and Enlightenment, 28–35.

Sociological Survey Questionnaire (2021) *Teacher in the eyes of students*. Available (consulted 13 July 2022) at: http://oshtu.kg/wp-content/uploads/2018/02/anketirovanie.pdf.

Sociological Survey Questionnaire (2022) *Data from a questionnaire survey among full-time students in the 1st-4th years of the Department of "Business and Management" at the Osh State University* (the survey was conducted on January 3, 2022).

CHAPTER 25

Professional Training of a Contemporary Teacher of Mathematics

Designing an Educational Program for a Bachelor's Degree in the Direction of "Physics and Mathematics Education" on a Modular-Competency Basis

Anarkan Dj. Attokurova

Abstract

This chapter focuses on designing an educational program for the bachelor's degree in the direction of training "physics and mathematics education" based on the methodology of learning outcomes. The methodological foundations for designing and evaluating the learning outcomes of an educational program based on the competencies of graduates have not been sufficiently studied in the higher education of Kyrgyzstan. The relevance of this chapter lies in the design of the learning outcomes for the educational program for bachelors of physics and mathematics education training (the profile "Mathematics") at the Osh State University based on the criteria of the EdNet Agency for quality assurance of educational field in Kyrgyzstan with the state educational standard in the pedagogical direction and international requirements. As a result of studying and analyzing the universal and professional competencies presented in the state educational standard and researching the opinions of the educational stakeholders, additional competencies were developed which consider the local demand of the labor market related to future mathematics teachers. To develop the learning outcomes of the educational program, we combined and grouped relevant universal, professional, and additional competencies into clusters of related competencies. This empirical work is important because it represents the first attempt to determine the main types of professional tasks of a mathematics teacher because a professional standard for a teacher has not yet been developed in Kyrgyzstan. This chapter defines clusters of related competencies as competently significant qualities. Based on the learning outcomes of the educational program, the content of the modular curriculum has been developed.

Keywords

learning outcomes – physics and mathematics education – modular-competency basis – cluster of competencies – competently significant qualities

1 Introduction

One of the main strategic objectives for the development of Osh State University is the organization of high-quality professional training of teachers for general educational institutions within the Kyrgyz Republic, which combines teachers in humanities, socio-economic, mathematical, and natural science and professional education in general. Under the globalization process, a rapid information flow and changes affecting spheres and conditions of human activity and life, a timely change in the system of training teachers is especially relevant. The need for transformation of contemporary teachers has been mentioned in the literature: "The teacher of the 21st century should have a number of new qualities and competencies that are not typical for specialists of previous generations, namely, professional competence; methodological culture, creativity and research abilities; intelligence, formation of humane qualities; knowledge, practical skills from sciences related to pedagogy such as philosophy, psychology, medicine, cybernetics, ethics, economics, law, etc.; continuous self-education; mastering progressive technologies of training and education, new achievements of domestic and foreign experience" (*Andreev*, 1994, pp. 12–13). This is certainly a global tendency and a challenge. The issue of training and educating teachers in undergraduate and graduate programs is especially important in developing countries such as Kyrgyzstan. In accordance with the Kyrgyz state education regulations for the professional training of mathematics teachers, the Faculty of Mathematics and Information Technology of Osh State University annually recruits applicants for the specialization "Physics and Mathematics Education" (an undergraduate level).

The chapter aims to examine the issues in the process of designing the learning outcomes of the educational program in the specialization "Physics and Mathematics Education" (with the training profile "Mathematics") based on the criteria of the Agency for Quality Assurance in Education EdNet (EdNet) – a local organization responsible for ensuring compliance of the educational program with the Kyrgyz state educational standard and the requirements of stakeholders, as well as the development of educational modules of the educational program based on the learning outcomes of the educational program. Before discussing the process of development of learning outcomes at the Osh

State University, we briefly refer to the Bologna process, turn to key literature (definitions) on learning outcomes, and mention important international and local frameworks in the field of higher education.

2 Literature Review

In 2012, almost all universities in Kyrgyzstan had switched to a two-level training of professional personnel as a result of joining the Bologna process. Likewise, in 2012, a draft and, three years later, the final version of the State Educational Standard of Higher Professional Education in the specialization "Physics and Mathematics Education" (State standard) on a competency basis was released. According to this document, the educational process at the Osh State University ensured the formation of universal and professional competencies of the future teachers of mathematics, computer science, and physics. The document defines the educational program as "a set of educational and methodological documentation that regulates the goals, expected results, content, and implementation of the educational process in the relevant area of training" (*Ministry of Education and Science of the Kyrgyz Republic*, 2015, p. 49).

According to the Bologna process, the description of graduates' qualifications and development of educational programs and modules need to be implemented using the methodology of learning outcomes.

We agree with D. Kennedy that learning outcomes describe what students can demonstrate in terms of knowledge, skills, and attitudes upon completion of a program (*Kennedy*, 2006, p. 19).

The ECTS User's Guide provides the following definition: "Learning outcomes are verifiable statements of what learners who have obtained a particular qualification, or completed a program or its components, are expected to know, understand, and be able to do. ... Learning outcomes statements are typically characterized by the use of active verbs expressing knowledge, comprehension, application, analysis, synthesis, evaluation, etc." (*European Communities*, 2009, p. 13).

The learning outcomes of an educational program represent the most important aspects of what students will be able to demonstrate upon graduation. While developing the learning outcomes of the educational program, the previously described learning outcomes classifications and the levels of Bloom's taxonomy (*Bloom* et al., 1956) could be used. Thus, we can presume that learning outcomes of the educational program are formed with the help of active verbs from Bloom's taxonomy; they indicate what the student will need to know, understand, and be able to demonstrate at the end of the educational program. "It is recommended to use one active verb for one learning outcome, followed by a transition to a contextual description. Terms that are unclear from an assessment point of view, such as know, understand, be informed, etc., should be avoided. Learning outcomes should include different levels of Bloom's taxonomy, usually raising the bar to high levels of hierarchy" (*Rebrin*, 2012, p. 17). As the literature review section noted, despite the presence of various definitions, the methodological foundations for designing the learning outcomes of the educational program, represented by the universal and professional competencies of the prospective mathematics teacher, have not been sufficiently studied.

3 Methodology

This chapter suggests the integration of the provisions and principles of the system-activity and competence-based approaches as a conceptual basis for designing learning outcomes of an educational program.

The EdNet developed criteria for formulating the aims and learning outcomes of an educational program. In this case, the aims of an educational program are to be defined in accordance with a demand of all stakeholders within the framework of the university's mission, the State standard (*Agency for Quality Assurance in Education "EdNet"*, 2017, pp. 10–11).

As some researchers in the field of pedagogical education note, "the current stage of the socio-economic development of countries such as Russia and Kazakhstan is characterized by the situation when the labor market becomes the most significant indicator that determines the targets in the education system" (*Abylkasymova* et al., 2018, pp. 30–31). A similar situation directly relates to the higher professional education of the Kyrgyz Republic in terms of integration into the global educational space.

The results of the analysis of universal and professional competencies formed as a result of the implementation of the State standard and the study of the opinions of stakeholders and the opinion of experts are included in the educational program in the direction "Physics and Mathematics Education" with the training profile "Mathematics" as additional competencies (AC), considering the regional demand of the labor market for a future mathematics teacher:

– Owns professionally important qualities (pedagogical motivation, enthusiasm, professional responsibility, and independence) and soft skills (customer focus, communication skills, analytical and critical thinking, teamwork, and leadership skills) (AC-1);

- Owns the methodology of using digital technologies in teaching mathematics (AC-2);
- Knows and understands mathematics and the scientific fundamentals of the school course of mathematics, solves mathematical problems (AC-3);
- Knows and understands computer science and programming languages, composes programs of varying complexity (AC-4);
- Owns approaches to the assessment and monitoring of learning outcomes (AC-5).

Thus, the Osh State University has developed a competency model for graduates of the educational program in the direction "Physics and Mathematics Education" with the training profile "Mathematics," as a set of interrelated knowledge, skills, abilities, and values necessary for a future specialist to work effectively in educational organizations of Kyrgyzstan.

Based on the State standard, the training profile "Mathematics" (*Ministry of Education and Science of the Kyrgyz Republic*, 2015), Bloom's taxonomy, and our research (*Attokurova*, 2019; *Baisalov and Attokurova*, 2020), the author developed the following learning outcomes of an educational program in this direction (Table 25.1):

As some researchers point out, the disciplinary approach used in the system of training specialists no longer meets the contemporary requirements. The disciplinary approach is replaced by a modular or, more precisely, a credit-modular approach to the organization of the educational process. In the future, there will be other principles for establishing the status of disciplines, for example, the modular principle of curriculum formation (*Sosnin*, 2007; *Wilandeberk and Shubina*, 2008).

Some researchers of innovations in the area of pedagogical education, in the context of the requirements of the Russian Federal State Educational Standard of Higher Education 3++, highlight the role of the module approach to the development of educational programs (*Bermus*, 2015; *Buyanova*, 2015; *Pilipenko* et al., 2016).

The author believes that in the modular-competence-based approach to the design of the educational program of higher education, it is advisable to designate modules as competent-significant. In our opinion, a given set of competencies (cluster) can become a didactic mechanism for designating a competently significant module, the combination of which acts as a way to achieve some kind of complex learning outcomes. It should be noted that a competently significant module sets a fragment of the content of the educational program education and is also determined by the technologies for mastering this content. It is important to emphasize that to diagnose the achievement of the learning outcomes of a competently significant module based on the results of its

TABLE 25.1 Learning outcomes (LO) of educational program (EP) training of bachelors of Physics and Mathematics education, training profile "Mathematics"

Code LO EP	Upon successful completion of the program, the graduate:	Competences
LO-1	Demonstrates oral and written speech in the state and official languages and social communication in English	IC-2, IC-3.
LO-2	Demonstrates orientation in the values of life and culture, active civic position	GSC-1, SPC-5.
LO-3	Demonstrates psychological and pedagogical competence in solving professional problems	IC-4, SPC-1, PC-1, PC-9.
LO-4	Designs an outline of a lesson in mathematics in accordance with the specifics of the topic and sections of the program and the curriculum	PC-2, PC-3, PC-6, PC-14.
LO-5	Demonstrates the use of advanced information and communication technologies to improve professional knowledge and skills in teaching mathematics	IC-1, PC-12, AC-2.
LO-6	Solves problems of varying complexity in fundamental areas of mathematics and develops programs in one of the programming languages	AC-3, AC-4.
LO-7	Demonstrates professionally important qualities, soft skills, and readiness for personal and professional development	GSC-6, SPC-4, PC-7, GSC-5, IC-5, AC-1.
LO-8	Designs learning outcomes and develops test materials to evaluate learning outcomes	GSC-3, PC-5.
LO-9	Designs the educational process using advanced, evidence-based learning technologies and approaches to assessing and monitoring learning outcomes that correspond to general and specific patterns and features of the age development of the individual	GSC-2, PC-8, AC-5.
LO-10	Develops a research plan using the main methods of scientific research in the field of physics and mathematics education	GSC-4, PC-10, PC-11.
LO-11	Demonstrates the creation of a safe educational environment	SPC-2, SPC-3, IC-6.

TABLE 25.1 Learning outcomes (LO) of educational program (EP) (cont.)

Code LO EP	Upon successful completion of the program, the graduate:	Competences
LO-12	Solves actual problems of teaching mathematics	PC-15, PC-4, PC-13, PC-16.

Note: IC – instrumental competencies, GSC – general scientific competencies, SPC – social and personal competencies, PC – professional competencies, AD – additional competencies
SOURCE: DEVELOPED BY THE AUTHOR BASED ON THE COMPETENCIES DATA FROM THE STATE STANDARD (MINISTRY OF EDUCATION AND SCIENCE OF THE KYRGYZ REPUBLIC, 2015, PP. 56–58)

completion (mastering by students), it is necessary to use a single (complex) assessment tool.

4 Results

The learning outcomes we designed for the undergraduate educational program in the direction of physics and mathematics education determined the modular structure as follows:

Module 1. Worldview and position is aimed at developing students' ability to navigate the values of life and culture and take an active civic position.

Module 2. Speech communication is designed to develop the abilities of students to correctly build their oral and written speech in the state and official languages, communicate in one of the foreign languages and produce effective speech communication in the field of pedagogical communication.

Module 3. Basics of education is devoted to developing psychological and pedagogical competencies for solving professional problems.

Module 4. Methodological training of the teacher sets the task of developing the ability to design lessons in mathematics.

Module 5. Digital technologies in pedagogical activity is aimed at developing the skills to use advanced information educational technologies in pedagogical activity.

Module 6. Mathematics and Computer Science is designed to improve the level of subject training in mathematics and computer science.

Module 7. Personal and professional development sets tasks for personal development and further education and forms professionally important qualities and soft skills of students.

Module 8. Designing educational programs is designed to form the ability to predict learning outcomes and evaluate them, choose educational programs.

Module 9. Modern learning technologies is built to prepare students for applying advanced learning technologies in teaching mathematics.

Module 10. Educational research aims to develop the ability to develop and correct a research plan and analyze and interpret the collected data under supervision.

Module 11. Safe educational environment is to form the ability to create a safe educational environment and instill healthy lifestyle skills in students.

Module 12. Actual problems of teaching mathematics is aimed at forming the readiness of future teachers to create conditions for professional self-determination, solve educational problems of a cultural and educational nature, and conduct individual work with students of a corrective or developmental nature based on the content of the school mathematics course.

5   Conclusion

The expediency of the variability of the educational program modules is due to the need to reflect the profile of the educational program in their content. Thus, the methodological features of the current educational program in the direction of "Physics and Mathematics Education," the training profile "Mathematics" of Osh State University can be summarized in the following way:

– Modular "architecture": each module ensures the formation of a competent-significant quality in a future mathematics teacher (e.g., worldview and position), including a theoretical block, a block of practical training, and practice;
– Specially organized ways of developing individual skills, abilities, and types of activities; unified assessment tools and predetermined reflective diagnostic procedures for assessing the formation of the competent-significant quality that should be developed by the module;
– "Cluster principle" of learning outcomes planning of competently significant modules: the formation of the competent-significant quality is set by a set (cluster) of competencies, while this set of module competencies can be formed using the following "formula": "universal competencies (UC) +

professional competencies (PC)" (other "formulas" are also possible if appropriate).

Competency-relevant modules specified in the educational program, being in inter-dependent relations, to a certain extent form universal, professional, and additional competencies, constituting one entity in the making of the future mathematics teacher.

References

Ministry of Education and Science of the Kyrgyz Republic (2015) State educational standard of higher professional education in the direction of "Pedagogical education" (for bachelor's and master's programs) (approved by the order "On approval of state educational standards of higher professional education" No. 1179/1 of September 15, 2015). Bishkek, Kyrgyzstan. Available (consulted 17 June 2022) at: https://mnu.kg/wp-content/uploads/2018/03/ГОСТ-ВПО-по-направле нию-Педагогическое-образование-Бакалавриат-и-Магистратура.pdf.

Abylkasymova AE, Kalney VA, and Shishov SE (2018) International trends in the formation of continuous pedagogical education for the training of personnel relevant to the digital economy. *Pedagogical Sciences* 3: 28–39. Available (consulted 17 June 2022) at: https://cyberleninka.ru/article/n/mezhdunarodnye-tendentsii-formir ovaniya-nepreryvnogo-pedagogicheskogo-obrazovaniya-dlya-podgotovki-kad rov-relevantnyh-tsifrovoy.

Agency for Quality Assurance in Education "EdNet" (2017). *A guide to conducting a self-assessment of a first cycle educational program.* Bishkek, Kyrgyzstan. Available (consulted 17 June 2022) at: https://www.asmi.kg/wp-content/document/PDF -ednet.pdf.

Andreev VI (1994) Model of the creative self-developing personality of a teacher of the 21st century. In: *Materials of the international scientific and practical conference: Pedagogical education for the 21st century.* Moscow, Russia: Moscow State V. I. Lenin Pedagogical Institute.

Attokurova ADj (2019) Preparation of modern teacher: Results of analysis of the system of views by academic I. Bekboev and professor M. Nazarov about the professional qualities of teachers of mathematics. *Bulletin of Jalal-Abad State University* 2(41): 33–38.

Baisalov DjU, and Attokurova ADj (2020) Goals and learning outcomes of the main educational program for the preparation of bachelors of physical and mathematical education, profile "Mathematics." *Science and Life of Kazakhstan: International Scientific Journal* 5(5): 95–103.

Bermus AG (2015) cluster-modular approach to designing educational programs in continuing education system. *Lifelong Education: The XXI Century* 4(12): 1–15.

Bloom BS, Engelhart MD, Furst EJ, Hill WH, and Krathwohl DR (1956). Taxonomy of educational objectives: The classification of educational goals (Handbook I: Cognitive domain). New York, NY: David McKay Company, Inc. Available (consulted 17 June 2022) at: https://www.ifeet.org/files/-Benjamin_S._Bloom-_Taxonomy_of_Educational_Object.pdf.

Buyanova IB (2015) Modular approach to construction of basic professional educational programs of teacher training in accordance with the professional standard of the teacher. *Humanitarian Sciences and Education* 3(23): 81–84.

European Communities (2009) *ECTS users' guide*. Luxembourg: Office for Official Publications of the European Communities. Available (consulted 17 June 2022) at: http://www.gzgu.ru/doc/bolon/new/ECTS2009_engl.pdf.

Kennedy D. (2006) *Writing and using learning outcomes: A practical guide*. Cork, Ireland: University College Cork. Available (consulted 17 June 2022) at: https://cora.ucc.ie/handle/10468/1613.

Pilipenko SA, Zhidkov AA, Karavaeva EV, and Serova AV (2016) Conjugation of GEF and professional standards: Identified problems, possible approaches, recommendations for updating. *Higher Education in Russia* 6: 5–15.

Rebrin OI (2012) Use of learning outcomes in the design of Ural Federal University educational programs. Yekaterinburg, Russia: Ural Publishing House. Available (consulted 17 June 2022) at: https://fgosvo.ru/uploadfiles/npo/20121229180040.pdf.

Sosnin N. (2007). Competence-based approach: Development problems. *Higher Education in Russia* 6: 42–45.

Wilandeberk AA, and Shubina NL (2008) *New technologies for evaluating learning outcomes (level education): Methodological guide for teachers*. St. Petersburg, Russia: Publishing House of the Herzen State Pedagogical University of Russia.

CHAPTER 26

Russian Education in the Pandemic

Challenges and Responses

Anna A. Arinushkina, Olga A. Mashkina and Valentina V. Kuznetsova

Abstract

The paper examines the functioning and change of educational technology in the COVID-19 pandemic in Russia at the level of general and higher education. The authors provide examples of cases from different regions of Russia. Additionally, the authors consider different aspects of the readiness of Russian education to the challenges of online learning, the macro challenge of school education, educational problems of educational organizations, and the complexity of constructing a psychological and motivational atmosphere in the virtual classroom. Thus, the authors consider the readiness of Russian education for the challenges of online learning, including the situation when schools had to move classes from a face-to-face format to distance learning. The unexpected transition to distance learning occurred differently in various subjects of Russia. The authors consider several groups of problems evident in the sudden change of the school regime: macro problems, problems of educational organizations, and problems of families and students. The authors studied pedagogical problems of educational organizations, including appropriate psychological and motivational climate for the successful absorption of knowledge by students. Moreover, the authors analyzed objective and subjective problems in the organization of distance learning in the conditions of general and higher education system.

Keywords

pandemic – Russian education – distance learning – education management in the pandemic – education in extreme conditions – new challenges for learning – education management – educational community – educational information technology – higher education – general education

1 Introduction

COVID-19 interrupted the school year of hundreds of millions of students worldwide (*UNESCO*, 2020). Russia was no exception. The closure of full-time education at all levels was a part of a government strategy to prevent the spread of COVID-19 in the affected countries. The transition to distance learning exacerbated many issues that were previously discussed or partially resolved. In the rhythm of ordinary life, educational authorities, the teaching community, and suppliers of educational information technology developed no coherent solutions.

All at once, there appeared a wave of publications by scholars, teachers, parents, and students discussing online learning problems (*Anderson*, 2020; *Frsa*, 2020; *Nicolás*, 2020; *Rieley*, 2020; *Tam and El-Azar*, 2020). The vivid reactions to the extreme circumstances revealed a wide range of opinions and assessments from extremely pessimistic to extremely optimistic, as reflected in this research.

The mass practice of using various distance learning methods allows us to summarize the first empirical data on the advantages, limitations, and problems of their further use in educational processes after the COVID-19 pandemic. Without attempting to provide a detailed review of responses to the challenges of the pandemic, this research highlights, on the one hand, the problems faced by all national education systems during the COVID-19 pandemic and, on the other hand, the problems currently being solved in the education system of Russia.

2 Methods

The research considered and structured the issues of readiness of Russian education to the challenges associated with online learning in a pandemic. For this purpose, the authors analyzed the indicators of the national project "Education." The authors summarized the results of the discussion and expert statements from the discussion "New higher education: What it will be like after the forced period of distance learning" held at the Moscow International Salon of Education (MMSE-2020) and the results of 45 experts' presentations at regular scientific-methodical seminars of the Faculty of Pedagogical Education and the Institute of Asian and African Studies of Lomonosov Moscow State University. The authors conducted a chronological analysis of the practice of changing the education forms in the constituent entities of Russia.

3 Research

3.1 Readiness of Russian Education for the Challenges of Online Learning

One of the most critical areas of modernization of Russian education was the provision of a stable and fast Internet to all educational organizations in the country as part of the national project "Education" (2019–2024). The following was envisaged for the development of a digital learning environment:
- Creation of a target model of the digital educational environment across the country;
- Introduction of advanced digital technology into the educational programs of 25% of general educational organizations in 75 regions of Russia for at least 500,000 children;
- Provision of 100% of educational institutions in urban areas with Internet access at a speed of at least 100 Mbps, in rural areas – 50 Mbps;
- Creation of a network of digital education centers covering at least 136 thousand children per year.

The Russian government allocated 79.8 billion rubles to implement these tasks (*Ministry of Education of the Russian Federation*, 2018).

By the beginning of the mass transition to distance learning, the implementation of the national project was still in its early stages. The situation in the country was highly diverse. The provision of educational organizations with high-speed Internet in different regions ranged from almost 100% (large cities) to a minimal level (settlements in remote mountainous and forest areas).

The Russian education system switched to distance learning literally overnight. Thus, on March 14, 2020 (Saturday), the Ministry of Education of the Russian Federation published an appeal to regional authorities recommending that they act according to the circumstances and, if necessary, transfer educational organizations to distance learning. On Monday, educational organizations in many Russian regions were required to conduct classes using various electronic platforms. All levels of the educational system faced various problems.

3.2 School Education: Challenges and Answers

Within several days, schools had to move classes from a face-to-face format to distance learning. Russia is a large, multinational, and diverse country in terms of geographical, socio-economic, cultural, and historical development. For these reasons, the unexpected transition to distance learning occurred differently in various subjects of Russia; for example, all schools in Moscow switched to distance learning.

The Russian school system faced many diverse challenges. We can distinguish several groups of problems evident in the sudden change of the school regime. In general, these problems can be grouped into three groups:
- Macro problems;
- Problems of educational organizations;
- Problems of families and students.

Macro problems. In the transition to distance learning, most schools were not ready for the change in format within the time frame set by the government. According to the Minister of Education of the Russian Federation Sergei Kravtsov, even Moscow schools, well-equipped with e-learning modalities, did not establish a proper learning process in the first days (*Kolesnikova*, 2020b).

The analysis of the infrastructure provision of schools conducted by the Ministry of Education of the Russian Federation and the Ministry of Digital Development of the Russian Federation shows that, at that time, no more than 25% of students had the resources necessary for distance learning (*Vasilyeva et al.*, 2020). Inaccessible or weak Internet connections in disadvantaged and remote areas prevented children from full participation in digital learning. E. Yamburg (the honored teacher of Russia, author of the adaptive school model, director of Moscow school No. 109) described the situation in one of the rural schools as follows, "Children are taken in cars to a pole on the hill where they can get at least some Internet. There they get assignments, go home, and solve them. In the evening, they go back to the pole to pass their homework and report to the teachers" (*Kolesnikova*, 2020a).

The electronic platforms were not ready for the high loads and often went down during the morning *school peak* hours. Online platforms that would be suitable for simultaneous multi-million classes in all educational institutions proved extremely scarce. The online services, selected by the Ministry of Education and school administrations for conducting lessons, could not cope with the workload. As a result, many teachers were forced to increase the amount of homework that students had to prepare and email for review. The teachers posted information about homework on the official school portals. First, this format of teaching interrupted direct teacher-student contact and group communication. According to the established practice, teachers and students need real-time feedback rather than waiting for work to be completed. Second, distance learning significantly increased the workload of all participants in the educational process, which, in addition to teachers and students, involved parents, many of whom were also on forced leave and home isolation mode.

In the conditions of crisis, the Ministry of Education of the Russian Federation recommended regions to independently solve the issue of early termination of the academic year. On April 10, 2020, Deputy Minister V. Basyuk gave the following explanations, "Schools have the autonomy in making decisions about the organization of the educational process. Thus, we gave them a variety of options for the way to end the school year. ... Early and full completion of the school year is out of the question" (*"Education in Moscow,"* 2020a).

In fact, the decision to end the school year early involved elementary and basic school (i.e., grades 1–8). Thus, the Khabarovsk Territory announced the beginning of summer vacations for students in grades 1–3 from April 13, for grades 4–6 from April 20, and for students in grades 7–8 from April 27 (*"Education in Moscow,"* 2020a). The Moscow government decided that summer vacations for all grades should start by May 15. The last two weeks of May were free to attend in a distance format (*"Education in Moscow,"* 2020a). Thus, teaching continued at the request of students who felt that they had not mastered the learning material. However, classes were held without homework or grades.

As for high school (grades 9–11), the main challenge that needed to be urgently solved was the date and method of holding the Unified State Exam (USE). V. Basyuk said, "The final decision has not yet been made, but more than 99.5% of 11th graders have already successfully completed the final essay, which is considered a required condition for admission to the State Final Examination" (*"Education in Moscow,"* 2020b).

This period of struggle of educational organizations against the COVID-19 can be considered a time of bold, successful, or not very successful experiments with new forms of training, administration, and organization of education. Many experts also believe that now is the right time to accelerate reforms and expand the space for cooperation and mutual exchange of experience. Support for distance learning and homeschooling are provided free of charge by educational platforms and online services of universities, major Internet holdings, social networks, and TV channels (*Shestoperov and Chernykh*, 2020). The service Uchi.ru has opened free access to its courses, indicating that the existing online projects have been in great demand due to the mass transition of all schools and universities to distance learning, so the service has had to mobilize and engage all the resources. The number of visitors to the platform has doubled in the last month, and a fivefold increase in activity is expected in the future (*Mironova*, 2020).

Pedagogical problems of educational organizations. Few teachers in the country were ready for remote teaching using Internet technology. The unpreparedness of teachers revealed the following most important manifestations:
– Lack of necessary computer literacy skills;
– Undeveloped methods of distance learning;

- Failure to create an appropriate psychological and motivational climate for the successful absorption of knowledge by students.

The Presidential Decree "On National Goals and Strategic Development Goals of the Russian Federation for the Period to 2024" instructed to establish a national system of teacher growth (NSDS), which would, among other things, create a "mentoring system" between teachers and promote their "continuous development" (*Presidential Executive Office*, 2018). Nevertheless, during the recent forced introduction of distance learning, it became apparent that teachers, primarily older teachers, could not cope with the transfer of classes to an online format since targeted training for teachers to work with advanced information technology was not conducted and was left to the discretion and initiative of the teachers themselves.

The problems encountered are both *objective and subjective*. Subjective problems reveal the most common complaints of the two most active groups – educators and parents. For example, one of the popular closed Facebook groups, with more than 7,000 parents and education officials, has had dozens of messages every day regarding problems with distance learning. The most common complaints have been as follows:

- "Freezing" electronic journal, which has not allowed either students or parents to receive and post homework on time;
- Difficulties of working on electronic platforms for teachers;
- Cancellation of a class because the teacher fails to conduct the class online;
- Lack of a computer, laptop, or smartphone for a child to work;
- Inability of graduate students to fully prepare for the USE;
- Lack of specialized online lessons for children with disabilities (*Mironova*, 2020).

The problems of an objective nature are more complex and profound. They can be grouped into several groups.

The difficulties of constructing a psychological and motivational atmosphere in a virtual classroom. In practice, every teacher has had to find their own approaches to engage and retain students' attention in the absence of live contact, achieve the development of students' cognitive abilities, and maintain a healthy mental atmosphere for children finding themselves in a confined space. Similar to doctors, teachers found themselves mobilized for life. While doctors have been fighting for the physical health of sick people, teachers have been responsible for developing the cognitive abilities and the mental and emotional intelligence of adolescents and young adults who have found themselves in an unfamiliar environment. When the pandemic is over, society should appreciate the selfless work of teachers who have put aside their personal and household duties and lived for the interests of those whose educational rights and interests have been threatened by extreme external circumstances.

Lack of necessary computer literacy skills. Teachers are learning new teaching technologies, and students are learning new ways to learn quickly. Although both face technical challenges, students often show better technical management skills than teachers. According to Honored Teacher of the Russian Federation E. Yamburg, children are the natives in the virtual world, and the teachers are aliens. In the absence of trusting and mutually respectful relations between the two subjects of education (teacher and student), this can lead to an erosion of the teacher's authority.

A shortage of online learning methods. Before the COVID-19, Russia has had considerable educational experience in 34 hospital schools (*Kolesnikova*, 2020a). Teachers working in hospital schools with ill children have been well versed in e-learning technology and have understood how to keep learning motivated. The experience of teaching children in long-term hospital care is different from working with healthy children. Still, there are similarities due to forced isolation. Unfortunately, this experience has not yet been widely popularized in the Russian and international teaching communities.

Changing working conditions for educators. Teachers have had a tremendous burden of preparing lessons and checking homework. Pandemic has taught teachers to be creative and patient, to communicate, and to collaborate. E. Yamburg described the situation as follows, "To prepare an online lesson or video conference, it is necessary to sit at the computer day and night. Believe me, it really is a very challenging job. Teachers fall off their feet. Offline lessons are one thing – hand out the material and explain it; you see the child's reaction. It is different online. It is necessary to take the most important ideas, hold the class's attention, and meet the deadline in a matter of minutes. An online lesson can last no more than 20 minutes in elementary school, with older children – no more than 30 minutes. Otherwise, we strain their eyes. The teacher develops a beautiful scenario for them. We say, *lesson design*. Moreover, it is necessary to create a new design for each topic and each class. There are plenty of them. Additionally, children are very different – some are developmentally impaired, some are advanced. It is necessary to chat and talk with everyone. It is a frantic job. Nevertheless, these are the people the kids need. If we do not do it, children will go nuts" (*Kolesnikova*, 2020a).

Even a short period of online learning revealed *several important limitations of distance learning.*

1. Self-isolation causes stress in a person of any age, especially in children deprived of the usual routine and communication with friends and teachers at school. Distance communication cannot provide them with

full-fledged communication, disrupting socialization. School is not only an individual learning process, which, with the proper motivation, can be independently built by students in a virtual space. It is also a place of socialization where young people build relationships with peers and elders, acquire cooperation skills, leadership, tolerance, or intolerance. Moreover, school is a social institution designed to provide security and a minimum of necessities of life, especially for children from dysfunctional families. There is a great deal of truth in the jocular definition of school as a safe in which parents keep their children during office hours.

2. The boundaries of learning can be extended. In turn, digital education has limits. In particular, it cannot fill the entire spectrum of the teacher-student relationship. Teachers are the most important key that opens the door to the world of learning; they must also become trusted figures in the life of a young person. Professor Shalva Amonashvili, the famous Soviet and Russian educator, psychologist, researcher, and innovator in the field of educational psychology, rightly noted, "There is only one pillar for the educational process to be alive, joyful, and upward-looking. This is a teacher." Asked how self-isolation would affect the learning and education at school and in the family, the 89-year-old teacher S. Amonashvili said, "After the coronavirus and isolation, we will have to change our approaches, change ourselves. We are no longer coming to the children of yesterday. Can teachers come out of isolation the same way they were before? New children do not fit in the old pedagogy" (*Bakal*, 2020).

3. The dramatic shift to distance learning has made more pronounced the inequalities previously smoothed out by the full-time compulsory school. These inequalities are as follows:
   - Material inequality. Children whose families cannot provide them with a variety of advanced electronic devices are cut off from *universally accessible compulsory education*. Loss of jobs and reduced earnings of parents can marginalize children. The economic crisis (recession) resulting from a forced halt in economic activity of the population may increase inequality in children's access to education;
   - Not all parents have the necessary level of digital literacy to help their children learn online. Other family constraints may also manifest themselves. For example, a lack of parental skills to provide children with the help they need to learn during difficult times;
   - Inequality of self-learning and information retrieval abilities. "If you do not know how to learn on your own, if you do not know how to plan your time, if you are not intrinsically motivated, you will not

succeed in a new environment" (*Anderson*, 2020). In this context, one has to ponder the question of how an adult incapable of self-learning (a teacher or parent) can teach children how to become successful in the new rapidly changing conditions of life and work. Despite the many challenges, Russian teachers remain optimistic and humorous. This is how a school teacher and mother of two assessed the situation, "History knows many examples of children and adults who have been isolated due to external circumstances of insurmountable force. These circumstances were often many times worse than ours. However, there was time left in them for the important things: sunshine, laughter, arguments, reading, diaries, love, and a stubborn look into the future, where everything is sure to work out. We are already a bit of a hero, and we also have kids, jobs, love, stubbornness, and food delivery, so things will get better" (*Naumova*, 2020).

3.3 *Higher School: Problems and Prospects*

During the pandemic, Russian universities switched to distance learning from March 16, 2020. First, distance learning was introduced by the largest universities of the country: Lomonosov Moscow State University (MSU) (*RIA News*, 2020), Moscow Institute of Physics and Technology (MIPT), St. Petersburg University (SPBU), MGIMO University, Bauman Moscow State Technical University, Ural Federal University (UFU), Novosibirsk State University, Plekhanov Russian University of Economics, and National University of Science and Technology MISIS (NUST MISIS). In the second half of April, more than 90% of universities in Russia switched to distance learning.

Higher education moved to online learning more easily because many universities have actively implemented various distance learning courses and created their own educational platforms even before the lockdown. In 2015, the Higher School of Economics and eight leading Russian universities (MSU, Higher School of Economics, MIPT, UFU, NUST MISIS, ITMO University, SPBU, and Peter the Great St. Petersburg Polytechnic University) initiated a project to create a National Platform for Open Education. Currently, this platform hosts 564 courses in various training areas (*"Open Education,"* n.d.). Among the most actively visited online platforms of universities, we should note the multifunctional learning platform "University Without Borders." This platform allows one to master distance courses by leading MSU professors (*Center for the Development of Electronic Educational Resources at MSU*, n.d.). The organization of the learning space on the "University Without Borders" platform provides a variety of opportunities, such as:
– Organizing students into streams and groups in an online course;
– Posting text documents for tasks;

- Organization of tests as training and testing materials (with the possibility of limiting the start and execution time);
- Accepting homework from students;
- Tracking and assessing student activities;
- Communication with students in synchronous and asynchronous formats (chat/forum);
- Organizing a conference for remote webinars and consultations (*Center for the Development of Electronic Educational Resources at MSU*, 2020).

The "EDCRUNCH UNIVERSITY" based at the NUST MISIS (*EdCrunch University*, n.d.), the platform "Online Education at the Higher School of Economics" (*HSE Online*, n.d.), and online resources of many other Russian universities have been successfully operating under lockdown conditions. Currently, the Ministry of Science and Higher Education of the Russian Federation forms a common base of online courses provided by Russian universities to their students, students from other universities, students of secondary schools, and everyone who wants to improve their erudition and qualifications. We can argue that the contemporary educational products created jointly by teachers of leading Russian universities and edu-business allow organizing a full-fledged educational process, taking into account the requirements of individualization of educational paths and learning personalization.

Teachers' reactions to distance learning. According to teachers' statements on social media, the shift to online learning has revealed several advantages and disadvantages. The *advantages* include the following:

1. *Psychological emancipation of students.* A. Fokin, associate professor of national history at Tyumen State University, wrote, "The main advantage is that the gadget screen removes the psychological block of many students. They are more willing to participate in the discussion. Those who would have preferred to remain silent in the classroom are now active" (*Mironova*, 2020).
2. *Development of new pedagogical methods.* There has been a surge in teacher activity to create online courses and e-learning materials. The crisis has forced teachers to do things that previously seemed unnecessary. Teachers have started to urgently change the established courses, looking for new methods of presenting instructional material and check the degree of its assimilation.
3. *Possibilities of combining the visual and verbal presentation of information.*
4. *Exchange of experience.* Strong players, especially leading universities, have started to actively share their experience, information capacities, and all possible resources in the field of online learning.

5. *Development of network cooperation between universities in different countries* in the field of online learning. Staying at home, students will be able to study theoretical material from an online course developed by different universities. This will accelerate the dissemination of new knowledge and make education more open (*Erokhina*, 2020).

Simultaneously, on social media, university professors, discussing the challenges faced, point to *several considerable shortcomings*:

1. Online classes require students to be highly self-disciplined and diligent. Not every student can study all subjects of the curriculum with the same intensity.
2. The effectiveness of continuous online learning is questionable. The teacher's personality largely determines students' interest in a subject. Through personal contact with faculty members, students often get a better sense of what they are interested in and what they would like to do in the future.
3. The format of online classes with live streaming, which allows for instant collective discussion of the subject and dialogue between the teacher and students, is still underdeveloped. Nevertheless, this format of teacher-student interaction is the most demanded by the current generation of students.
4. Not every teacher can fully master the different possibilities of working on digital educational platforms without methodological assistance and technical support from universities. With the instant transition to online learning, most educators have opted for the easiest means of communication, moving seminar sessions to Zoom or Skype rather than specifically designed education platforms.
5. Even within one department, the decision to choose specific technology of distance learning is left to the professor and the faculty. Professors keep in touch with students through convenient social networks and messengers. Thus, students often have to switch from one portal to another.
6. There are no computer simulators and laboratories for some of the studied disciplines of the natural sciences cycle. The available solutions do not fully correspond to the complexity of the curriculum. This puts students in engineering and science programs at risk of failing to meet the curriculum. Moreover, some experts do not believe that "the virtual laboratory can replace the real one. It is a game world, and if you break something in it, you can go back to the beginning, which is impossible in the real world. Additionally, creating virtual labs is a very expensive process, and technology is advancing rapidly. There may occur situations where what is digitalized today will be irrelevant tomorrow" (*Erokhina*, 2020).

7. Failure to protect teachers' copyrights. Many courses for senior university students are copyrighted. The transition to open online learning raises the issue of faculty and university copyright protection. Additionally, there are no publicly available test materials for many courses. Thus, it is necessary to spend much time developing and then checking them, especially if many students attend the course.

It seems reasonable to create an official and publicly available online catalog of teachers' ideas, samples, techniques, and programs for organizing lessons. The exposure to established experience and new practices will minimize psychological stress, give an impetus to the growth of professional skills, and allow authors to protect their pedagogical and scientific achievements.

3.4 Results of the Student Survey

In 2019, the Higher School of Economics surveyed 21,000 students to identify their learning activity within a course using the online learning platform Coursera. The survey results have shown the following:
– Students prefer to watch video lectures rather than read them;
– 65% of students have zero activity as early as the second week of study;
– Only 10% of students remain active for the whole duration of the online course;
– Only about 5% increase their learning activity during the course (*Mironova*, 2019).

The results of this survey also confirm students' statements about distance learning during the COVID-19 pandemic. They are skeptical about their readiness and the readiness of their teachers for a full transition to online learning. Full-time students are dissatisfied with the cancellation of offline lectures because university professors send "template presentations without explanations" instead. Although students enjoy doing seminars on Zoom, Skype, or other platforms, they are not willing to do the dramatically increased amount of homework in writing. Moreover, according to the students, it is extremely challenging to perform some assignments on their own at the proper level because it is impossible to get free access to specialized literature from home (*Mironova*, 2020).

3.5 Reactions of International Students Studying at Russian Universities

In recent years, the number of Chinese students in Russian universities has been growing steadily. The positive trend is reflected in the statistics of the Russian Ministry of Internal Affairs: 47,895 Chinese citizens were registered to study in Russia in 2016, 58,352 Chinese citizens in 2017, and 76,470 Chinese citizens in 2018, of which about 20,000 are students enrolled in the main educational programs of Bachelor's and Master's degrees (*Kuznetsova*, 2019). According to the International Department of MSU, 4,500 Chinese students were enrolled in the MSU educational programs of all levels in the 2019–2020 academic year.

An earlier survey of Chinese students studying at MSU has shown that most of them choose to study at Russian universities not only because of the high quality of education and low financial costs but also because of the attraction to the Russian culture, visiting museums, theaters, and enjoying the natural beauty of Russia (*Mashkina*, 2010).

This year, however, the expectations of many Chinese students have not been met due to restrictions and quarantine measures on both sides. Some students were unable to return to Russia after the winter break. Some of them, being in China, are currently continuing their studies according to individual curricula. Others, together with Russian students, are attending online classes using various communication channels. The main problems faced by the latter group of Chinese students are as follows:
– Inaccessibility of certain digital platforms and social networks;
– Insufficient quality of Internet communication;
– Difference in time zones between Russian and Chinese regions, which causes problems with schedules.

The Chinese students who returned to Russia after the winter break were immediately placed under a two-week quarantine. Isolation for students without the support of family and friends was a certain challenge. Immediately after the start of the spring semester, almost all Russian universities were switched to distance learning. Unlike Russian students, who mostly live at home with their families, international students have very limited opportunities to leave the dormitories. As a result, various inconveniences of life (from the ban on going out for walks and shopping to the lack of the usual Chinese food in the student canteens) were added to the academic stresses.

Nevertheless, most Chinese students are optimistic about the future. According to the results of the express survey, many Chinese students use their time free from other classes to read Russian literature and improve their Russian speaking skills. They like that they can record lectures and repeatedly listen to them. Chinese students are also happy to have their professors send them materials to study beforehand since this makes it easier to understand the video lectures. Chinese students see listening to Russian speech as one of the most difficult aspects of communication. Now that communication with professors and other students is not face-to-face, but through audiovisual means of communication, these difficulties have increased.

Along with the realities positively perceived by Chinese students, there are several shortcomings making Chinese students feel insecure and dissatisfied. Although pre-writing for a class is a common practice for Chinese students, they have noticed that homework increased significantly. Additionally, there are more individual assignments difficult to do correctly on their own. When professors ask during a video lesson if there are any questions, many Chinese students are too shy to ask a question for fear of losing face in front of the other chat participants. Due to the uncertainty surrounding the effects of COVID-19 on personal and academic life, some students are stressed and want to return to China, where the epidemic situation has now improved. Nevertheless, it should be noted that there have been only isolated cases of COVID-19 infection of students in Russia, which can be a serious argument for foreign applicants to plan their studies at Russian universities.

3.6 Perspectives on the Future through the Eyes of Educators

Teachers and administrators at Russian universities, as well as students, understand that education will not return to the old ways once the epidemic is over. Nevertheless, the extent to which the traditional model of classroom education will change and the timing of this process remain unclear. There are opposed assessments and forecasts – from the idea of the complete disappearance of full-time education and universities to the categorical denial of the effectiveness of distance learning.

Several university professors rate their online experience as low-impacting. They come from the tradition of Russian education, which is built on the principle "from master to master, the transfer of knowledge and experience occurs with direct contact between student and teacher" (*Erokhina*, 2020). Additionally, students, especially those in their junior year, often have no experience with independent study. Thus, their motivation needs to be maintained more intensively by the teacher than is possible in online courses. For these reasons, they expect the learning process to return to the familiar, traditional classroom format after the lockdown is over. At the same time, such a conservative approach is characteristic of a minority of teachers.

Nowadays, the prevailing view among Russian university administrators and teachers is that the educational system will certainly change after the end of the pandemic. However, they highlight that the face-to-face form of teacher-student interaction will retain its importance. For example, rector of Lomonosov Moscow State University, Academician Viktor Sadovnichy, responding to the question, "Will there be no need for universities in their traditional form after the pandemic?" replied, "I spoke on this topic three or four years ago, when representatives of the educational platform Coursera came to visit us. The idea is not new; it is suggested by some foreign experts: in time, there will be just one distance university, and it will handle all the training. I believe this idea is unrealizable and unlikely to happen because, by its nature, university education is more than the absorption of some information and knowledge. It is also a process of personality formation; there are a lot of emotions and spiritual forces involved. Above all, it is communication with colleagues and teachers, it is also work with books, and in-depth self-reflection" (*Boriskin*, 2020).

Most Russian university professors agree with this assessment of the rector of Lomonosov Moscow State University. They write that although educational organizations, especially universities, "are tempted to stay in this system at the end of the quarantine since everything went so easily online," it is still necessary to "keep up working with a live audience" (*Boriskin*, 2020).

University professors and researchers emphasize that "it is one thing to use online formats on demand; it is another thing to have virtually no alternative" (*Erokhina*, 2020). With the dramatic shift to online learning, the educational process without the support of appropriate methodologies has become a chaotic combination of online meetings, webinars, and self-paced courses on international and national online educational platforms. In the sudden transition to distance learning, both teachers and students have not been properly motivated to learn techniques for effectively using educational platforms. Based on the belief that the situation is temporary and short-term, they have chosen the easiest ways to interact. This has allowed continuing the educational process but not selecting technological capabilities that will allow education to make a qualitative leap forward.

Simultaneously, the pedagogical community believes there will be a natural selection of information educational technologies – "useful ideas will be fixed, unsuccessful options will be discarded" (*Mironova*, 2020).

According to practitioners, four options for online education will be in demand:
- Full online courses;
- Mixed forms (an online course replaces only lectures, and the rest takes place in the traditional format);
- Online conferences;
- Digital libraries and training simulators (*HSE University*, 2020).

4   Conclusion

The transition of the Russian educational system to a distant format has solved the main task of protecting students, teachers, and other employees of educational institutions from possible infection by COVID-19.

A great achievement of online learning is the expansion of individual choice of means, forms, and methods of teaching and learning. By the end of the pandemic, all courses will be available simultaneously in offline and online formats. This can be a major challenge for teachers and universities. It is essential to think about this situation in advance and understand what factors will prevail in students' choices – should they go to the classroom in person or listen remotely? How will this choice affect the organization and structure of higher education? Should full-time universities take strict directive action on students or use flexible methods of testing and assessing mastery of the material? How to assess the formation of universal competencies (e.g., scientific thinking, teamwork, leadership, communication, and intercultural interaction) prescribed in the educational standards?

Equally important positive results of the transition to distance learning formats are as follows:
- Accelerated equipment of the country's schools with fast Internet;
- Provision of free services by most educational platforms;
- Providing free use of various technical means of education (e.g., computers, tablets, etc.) to disadvantaged schools and students from needy families.

On April 27, the Moscow International Salon of Education (MMCO-2020) held a discussion "New higher education: What it will be like after the forced period of distance work." Opening the Salon's program dedicated to the higher school, the Minister of Science and Higher Education of the Russian Federation V. Falkov said, "Our task is to take the best that we accumulate in these difficult times, the best ideas and the best models, and make Russian higher education more attractive in the world" (*HSE University*, 2020).

We share the opinion of Academician V. Sadovnichy, rector of Lomonosov Moscow State University, that Russian universities have coped with the transition to online learning (*Boriskin*, 2020). The accumulated experience will contribute to the greater use of information technology in educational processes. It will be a catalyst for developing a blended learning format, which will make higher education publicly available and provide a more individualized creative process.

Acknowledgments

The research was prepared within the framework of the state assignment of the Ministry of Education of the Russian Federation to the Federal State Budgetary Scientific Institution "Institute of Management of Education of Russian Academy of Education."

References

Ministry of Education of the Russian Federation (2018) *National Project "Education": Passport of the Federal Project "Digital Educational Environment"* (accepted December 7, 2018 Protocol No. 3). Available (consulted 25 July 2021) at: https://goo.su/8DDF.

Presidential Executive Office (2018) *Decree "On the national goals and strategic objectives of the development of the Russian Federation for the period up to 2024"* (accepted May 7, 2018 No. 204.). Moscow, Russia. Available (consulted 25 July 2021) at: http://static.kremlin.ru/media/acts/files/0001201805070038.pdf.

All-Russian Educational Portal "Education in Moscow" (2020a, Aprll 10). *Do children go on summer vacation or not? The Ministry of Education is "troubling the water" again.* Available (consulted 23 July 2021) at: https://obrmos.ru/go/go_scool/news/go_go_scool_news_dosr_reg_y_n.html.

All-Russian Educational Portal "Education in Moscow" (2020b, April 8). *There will be no State Final Examination in schools in 2020! Students will be graded based on the results of the first three quarters!* Available (consulted 23 July 2021) at: https://obrmos.ru/go/go_scool/news/go_go_scool_news_oz.html.

Anderson J (2020, March 30). The coronavirus pandemic is reshaping education. *Quartz Media.* Available (consulted 23 July 2021) at: https://qz.com/1826369/how-coronavirus-is-changing-education/.

Bakal L (2020, April 21) "We have to change. New children do not fit into the old pedagogy." Shalva Amonashvili on how self-isolation will affect us all. *Mel.* Available (consulted 23 July 2021) at: https://mel.fm/istorii/3254791-shalva_amonashvili?utm_source=newsletter&utm_medium=email&utm_campaign=April.

Boriskin K (2020, April 28) "It is not a front line, but the situation is tough, too": MSU Rector on the University in the Age of the Pandemic. *Russian News Agency TASS.* Available (consulted 26 July 2021) at: https://www.msu.ru/press/smiaboutmsu/seychas-ne-front-no-situatsiya-tozhe-tyazhelaya-rektor-mgu-o-vuze-v-epokhu-pandemii.html?sphrase_id=3720126.

Center for the Development of Electronic Educational Resources at MSU (n.d.) *University without borders: Open courses of MSU*. Available (consulted 26 July 2021) at: https://distant.msu.ru/course/index.php?categoryid=70.

Center for the Development of Electronic Educational Resources at MSU (2020, November 5). *Information about the center*. Available (consulted 26 July 2021) at: https://distant.msu.ru/mod/page/view.php?id=10156.

EdCrunch University (n.d.) *Center of Excellence in online education and digital corporate training*. Available (consulted 29 July 2021) at: https://university.edcrunch.ru/.

Erokhina E (2020, March 16) Universities keep their distance. How the coronavirus will affect Russian higher education. *Indicator*. Available (consulted 25 July 2021) at: https://indicator.ru/humanitarian-science/vuzy-derzhat-distanciyu.htm.

Frsa PM (2020, March 23) Higher education in the time of corona. *The RSA*. Available (consulted 25 July 2021) at: https://www.thersa.org/discover/publications-and-articles/rsa-comment/2020/03/higher-education-in-the-time-of-corona.

HSE Online (n.d.) *Platform for online learning in HSE University*. Available (consulted 25 July 2021) at: https://online.hse.ru/.

HSE University (2020, April 28) Higher education is not going back to the old format. Available (consulted 25 July 2021) at: https://www.hse.ru/news/edu/360910425.html.

Kolesnikova K (2020a, April 27) The doctor prescribed the lesson. Yevgeny Yamburg: 34 hospital schools were ready for distance learning before anyone else in the country. *Rossiyskaya Gazeta*. Available (consulted 25 July 2021) at: https://rg.ru/2020/04/27/iamburg-34-gospitalnye-shkoly-okazalis-gotovy-k-udalenke-ranshe-vseh.html.

Kolesnikova K (2020b, April 27) The Minister of Education admitted that schools are not ready for online learning. *Rossiyskaya Gazeta*. Available (consulted 25 July 2021) at: https://rg.ru/2020/04/27/ministr-prosveshcheniia-priznal-negotovnost-shkol-k-onlajn-obucheniiu.html.

Kuznetsova P (2019, September 2) They study with extreme diligence and respect. The number of Chinese students studying at Russian universities is growing year by year. *Rossiyskaya Gazeta*. Available (consulted 25 July 2021) at: https://rg.ru/2019/09/02/chislo-kitajcev-studentov-rossijskih-vuzov-rastet-s-kazhdym-godom.html.

Mashkina OA (2010) Chinese students and Master's students in Russian universities: Problems of social, cultural, and linguistic adaptation. In: *Proceedings of the 11th International Scientific Conference: Knowledge Civilization. Problems of Russia's Modernization*. Moscow, Russia: Russian New University, 208–215.

Mironova K (2019, July 18) Students were tested for online adherence. Researchers at the Higher School of Economics have developed a mathematical model for evaluating distance learning programs. *Kommersant*. Available (consulted 25 July 2021) at: https://www.kommersant.ru/doc/4033814.

Mironova K (2020, March 28) Difficulties at a distance. Was the Russian education system ready to go online because of the coronavirus. *Kommersant*. Available (consulted 25 July 2021) at: https://www.kommersant.ru/doc/4307297?from=doc_vrez.

Naumova T (2020, March 23) Self-isolation and me: How to survive if you are a school teacher and mom of two. *Mel*. Available (consulted 25 July 2021) at: https://mel.fm/lichny_opyt/8936402- self_isolation?utm_source=newsletter&utm_medium=email&utm_campaign=March.

Nicolás ES (2020, April 15) *Education in coronavirus times: Trial and error*. Available (consulted 25 July 2021) at: https://euobserver.com/coronavirus/148063.

RIA News (2020, March 16) *MSU has allowed students to switch to distance learning*. Available (consulted 25 July 2021) at: https://ria.ru/20200316/1568668548.html.

Rieley JB (2020, March 12) *Corona Virus and its impact on higher education*. Available (consulted 25 July 2021) at: https://www.researchgate.net/post/Corona_Virus_and_its_impact_on_higher_education.

Russian Educational Platform "Open Education" (n.d.) *Courses from Russia's leading universities for everyone without restriction*. Available (consulted 25 July 2021) at: https://openedu.ru/.

Shestoperov D, and Chernykh A (2020, April 23) "VKontakte with the school. The social network will be involved in the creation of a state platform for digital learning." *Kommersant*. Available (consulted 25 July 2021) at: https://www.kommersant.ru/doc/4328391?utm_source=newspaper&utm_.

Tam G, and El-Azar D (2020, April 13) 3 ways the coronavirus pandemic could reshape education. *World Economic Forum*. Available (consulted 25 July 2021) at: https://www.weforum.org/agenda/2020/03/3-ways-coronavirus-is-reshaping-education-and-what-changes-might-be-here-to-stay/.

UNESCO (2020, March 24) *COVID-19 educational disruption and response*. Available (consulted 25 July 2021) at: https://en.unesco.org/news/covid-19-educational-disruption-and-response.

Vasilyeva A, Bolshakova E, Prakh A, and Nikiforov V (2020, April 9) Schooling is left for a second year. The Ministry of Education allowed the junior and middle classes to rest early. *Kommersant*. Available (consulted 25 July 2021) at: https://www.kommersant.ru/doc/4317285.

CHAPTER 27

Socio-economic Development of Educational Activities in the Context of the Modernization of Lifelong Education

Zhanna V. Smirnova, Igor E. Mizikovsky, Michael N. Pavlenkov, Elena V. Romanovskaya and Lyubov I. Kutepova

Abstract

Researched the issue of development educational activities in the context of the modernization of continuing education, in the 1930s. The theoretical substantiation of the development pedagogical process at the present stage. The purpose of the study is to analyze the development of lifelong education at the present stage of socio-economic changes. The process of changing the qualitative indicators of innovative technologies for the organization of the educational process is considered. An example of continuous education in the educational environment of the university through the creation of a technopark as an innovative platform for educational activities is given. The main feature of the development of vocational education is highlighted, which is that it is directly related to the economic development of our country. In this regard, the question arises of the development of vocational education aimed at improving the quality of all levels of education.

Keywords

educational activities – continuous education – socio-economic development – modernization

1 Introduction

The historical development of the modernization process today is defined as the development of society, aimed at more competitive and efficient systems of social and economic relations through the use of innovative development technologies in general.

At the moment, the stage of modernization in the economic development of the country is associated with an innovative transition to a new type of society, which is determined by the socio-economic development of educational activities. Modern educational activity forms one of the most intellectually intensive branches of the modern economy.

When studying the education system, it is necessary to focus on the problems of educating children and youth in kindergartens, schools and universities. Such a system of educational institutions in the formation of a post-industrial society is determined by the continuity of educational activities.

Thus, the development of continuous education in our country has become the subject of scientific research, defining the education system as the production and accumulation of human capital with knowledge, skills and abilities at any age of the socio-economic society (*Artemyeva* et al., 2022).

2   Materials and Method

The study of the significance of the issue of the development of lifelong education as a socio-economic development of society interested scientific researchers who reflected this problem in their scientific works. This issue is reflected in the works of Jan Amos Comenius. In the works of Russian researchers, the problem of continuous education is determined by the prerequisites for the need to develop a system of continuous education in the socio-economic development of society.

The main purpose of the study of this problem is to analyze the development of lifelong education at the present stage of socio-economic changes in the technologies for mastering knowledge, skills and abilities.

In the course of the study, we considered the basic principles of lifelong education and the technology of applying them to practices in educational institutions in the structure: kindergarten – school – university.

The considered system of continuity of educational activity will allow us to ensure the development of socio-economic society through the modernization of educational technologies in general.

The organization of the application of the system of continuous education was considered at a number of events organized by Minin University at the educational site of the technopark and quantorium, the opening of which provided for educational activities at different stages of the context of the modernization of continuous education (*Biryukov*, 2006).

3 Results

With regard to the modernization of educational activities, the process of changing qualitative indicators, the use of innovative technologies for organizing the educational process is considered.

The main priorities of the organization in educational institutions of continuous education include:
- application of new innovative teaching methods, new teaching methods in the system of continuous education;
- free access to information about educational opportunities;
- creation of educational innovation centers.

The main idea of the new approach to continuous education is to develop new basic knowledge, skills and abilities (*Chaykina* et al., 2022).

The modern system of continuous education includes several levels:
Pre-professional training (children's preschool institutions, pedagogical classes, courses, initial preparatory courses in secondary schools, etc.)
Primary, secondary and higher vocational education (vocational schools, colleges, technical schools, colleges, universities, universities, academies).
The system of continuous education contains the following levels: First level. Pre-vocational training, e.g. preschool Second level. Primary, secondary and higher vocational education. Third level. Postgraduate education, for example, postgraduate studies, doctoral studies (*Gromkova*, 2005).
Lifelong education at certain stages of knowledge formation is understood as an integral process of creative development of the individual. The main role in this process is played by the person himself, his personality and his interests in cognition.
Today, continuous education has become one of the most relevant systems of educational activities in general. Educational institutions are faced with the task of consistent, continuous professional training of the individual. Starting from pre-vocational training and ending with postgraduate forms of education. Such a system allows developing from the simplest to the most complex in the chosen direction of the professional activity of the individual, with the acquisition of a qualitative level of knowledge.
The socio-economic development of the country is also understood as the professional development of society, and professional education itself is an important context for the modernization of lifelong education.
Socio-economic development in the framework of the modernization of the educational activities include the process of diversifying the education of the Quantorium pedagogical technopark, created on base of the Minin University (*Kuznetsov* et al., 2021).

4 Discussion

At the end of 2021, technopark and quantorium were put into operation on the basis of Mini University. One of the important tasks of these platforms is the use of educational space to improve the quality of education, the possibility of using end-to-end technologies for teaching schoolchildren and students of digital laboratories in chemistry lessons, digital microscopy of genetic objects and modeling of genetic processes in biology lessons, and the use of robotics in technology lessons.

The technopark of Minin University is equipped with all new equipment. There are eleven laboratories, three prototyping centers, three modern lecture halls, four terminal classes and a resource center for preschool education. At the technopark site, areas related to analytical chemistry, fundamental physics, radiography, genetics, physiology, alternative energy, robotic systems, competitive robotics, virtual and augmented reality, artificial intelligence, computer graphics and computer-aided design will be developed. In June, Minin University launched a summer school for children of primary school age from educational institutions of the Avtozavodsky district of Nizhny Novgorod (*Kuznetsova* et al., 2022b).

The summer school is a joint project of the Institute of Continuing Education and the Pedagogical "Quantorium" with the support of the Department of Education of the city administration. The children took part in 6 thematic classes "Mysteries of DNA", "In the lens of a microscope: the world of plants", "Space of virtual reality: let's start with a game!", "How to make a friend of a person out of a robot (entertaining robotics: first steps)", "School of design: decorative toy", "Satin Ribbon and Braid Jewelry Workshop".

For younger students, these are the first "pre-professional" tests that will help identify talents in scientific and technical creativity.

The summer school will last until the end of June; it will be attended by more than 170 children from various educational organizations (MBEI "School No. 6", MBEI "School No. 130", MBEI "School No. 169"). As a result of the additional general development program, the children will receive certificates from Minin University (*Kuznetsova* et al., 2022a).

On the basis of the technopark, educational interactive events "Mastering practical competencies by students at the sites of the Interfaculty technopark of Universal Pedagogical Competences and the quantorium pedagogical technopark" were held at Minin University in Educational Building No.

Schoolchildren get acquainted with the equipment of lecture halls, an artificial intelligence laboratory and a physical laboratory, a resource center for preschool education, a laboratory for computer graphics and computer-aided design. Technopark laboratory assistants showed how the sewing and embroidery equipment of the textile workshop, 3D printer and prototyping center machines work.

The guys saw in action digital laboratories for the study of human life support systems, laboratories for alternative energy, and also got acquainted with robotic kits and held machine competitions.

It should be noted that the organization of continuous education within the framework of the quantorium Pedagogical technopark is an innovative platform in the educational activities of Minin University. The contingent of participants has a wide range, ranging from younger children, children from preschool institutions and ending with university students (*Pavlova*, 2017).

In the process of sociological research, it was revealed that the population in the current socio-economic conditions is increasingly turning to educational needs, including the most diverse groups of the population in educational life. From this we can conclude that self-education is one of the important forms of continuous education.

In our sociological study, more than 72% of positive attitudes relate to the organization of educational activities at the innovative sites of Minin University. Especially with great interest is the demand for the organization of master classes for children of preschool age. They have the opportunity to see the reality of innovative educational technologies: new equipment, new programs and an interesting educational environment increase interest in a particular professional activity, which in the future may affect the choice of their future profession.

For schoolchildren, such an innovative platform is useful in solving practice-oriented tasks. The opportunity to conduct lessons in the technopark allows nearby schools to make changes to the schedule and conduct classes in the technopark of Minin University.

University students are given a tremendous opportunity to conduct their scientific research on the latest equipment, the opportunity to learn new forms and methods of teaching disciplines.

Thus, the creation of new high-tech educational spaces, like the technopark, creates a unified educational environment that allows you to train teachers, and also develops professional skills (*Romanovskaya* et al., 2022).

5   Conclusion

Thus, the modernization of continuous education is the most important factor in the socio-economic development of society. The creation of modern educational spaces makes it possible to open up opportunities for the population to form professional competencies through organized events. The opening of a technopark at Minin University is a clear example of the organization of continuous education in the context of modernizing the educational environment of the university. The events held and the educational process at this site open up opportunities for children, schoolchildren and students to express themselves in their professional activities (*Smirnova* et al., 2022).

References

Artemyeva MV, Garina EP, Kuznetsova SN, Potashnik YS, and Bezrukova NA (2022) Ecommerce surge as an element of a modern economy integration mechanism development. In: Popkova EG (ed) Imitation market modeling in digital economy: Game theoretic approaches. Cham, Switzerland: Springer, 492–500. DOI: 10.1007/978-3-030-93244-2_54.

Biryukov A (2006) Internationalization of Russian higher education. *World Economy and International Relations* 10: 76–83.

Chaykina ZV, Mukhina MV, Gruzdeva ML, Smirnova ZV, and Golubeva OV (2022) Integration of information, communication, and pedagogical technologies in the framework of blended learning in classes with students of pedagogical university. In: Popkova EG, and Sergi BS (eds) *Digital education in Russia and Central Asia*. Singapore: Springer, 383–389. DOI: 10.1007/978-981-16-9069-3_42.

Gromkova MT (2005) *Andragogy: Theory and practice of adult education: Textbook*. Moscow: UNITY-DANA.

Kuznetsov VP, Kuznetsova SN, Tsymbalov SD, Romanovskaya EV, and Andryashina NS (2021) Investment attractiveness of artificial intelligence technologies in industrial parks. In: Popkova EG, and Ostrovskaya VN (eds) *Meta-scientific study of artificial intelligence*. Charlotte, NC: Information Age Publishing, 625–631.

Kuznetsova SN, Romanovskaya EV, Andryashina NS, Kozlova EP, and Kutepov MM (2022a) Integration mechanism for improving planning for innovative engineering enterprises. In: Popkova EG (ed) *Imitation market modeling in digital economy: Game theoretic approaches*. Cham, Switzerland: Springer, 275–282. DOI: 10.1007/978-3-030-93244-2_31.

Kuznetsova SN, Romanovskaya EV, Andryashina NS, Kozlova EP, and Lebedeva TE (2022b) Application of lean construction management innovation economy development technology in industrial parks. In: Popkova EG (ed) *Imitation market modeling in digital economy: Game theoretic approaches*. Cham, Switzerland: Springer, 465–471. DOI: 10.1007/978-3-030-93244-2_51.

Pavlova SM (2017) Problems of development of continuous education in Russia. *Scientific Review. Pedagogical Sciences* 1: 144–148.

Romanovskaya EV, Smirnova ZV, Andryashina NS, Artemyeva MV, and Kuznetsova SN (2022). Economic integration as a mechanism for managing service activities. In: Popkova EG, Polukhin AA, and Ragulina JV (eds) *Towards an increased security: Green innovations, intellectual property protection and information security.* Cham, Switzerland: Springer, 515–520. DOI: 10.1007/978-3-030-93155-1_56.

Smirnova ZV, Chaykina ZV, Kutepova LI, Andryashina NS, and Smetanina OM (2022) Game Teaching Methods as a Means of Integration in Educational Activities. In: Popkova EG, and Sergi BS (eds) *Digital education in Russia and Central Asia.* Singapore: Springer, 415–422. DOI: 10.1007/978-981-16-9069-3_46.

Conclusion

∴

Worsening of Social Inequalities in the Fifth Industrial Revolution

The New Role of Higher Education in Social Mobility

Elena G. Popkova, Bruno S. Sergi and Konstantin V. Vodenko

Social inequality is a historical and serious social problem that is deeply rooted in tradition. The new institutional perspective on social inequality presented in this book shows that the way for its solution is based on the modernization of institutions, that is, overcoming "institutional traps." A significant contribution to solving this problem was made by the emergence of the knowledge society, which contributed to the formation of a progressive – inclusive culture.

Society became open to all people, regardless of their characteristics. Open universities have made higher education massively accessible, supporting social mobility. We should also note the significant contribution of the Fourth Industrial Revolution, which, through the spread of digital technologies in society and, in particular, in higher education, has supported an inclusive culture of the knowledge society. For example, distance learning has contributed to the objective assessment of students' knowledge and given people with disabilities the opportunity to receive higher education on an equal basis with other students.

However, everything is changing with the advent of the Fifth Industrial Revolution, the first manifestations of which are already visible. Ubiquitous automation, covering entire value chains, is causing a new form of social inequality: the digital divide. One of the examples is robotic production in smart industrial plants, followed by automated marketing of finished products using smart chatbots and intelligent logistics controlled by artificial intelligence.

Under the influence of the Fifth Industrial Revolution, a new model of social structure is taking shape, in which "smart" machines become new participants in conditional-social (quasi-social) relations. In this context, two new forms of contingent social relations arise simultaneously. The first form is machine-to-machine communications via the Internet of Things. The second form is man-machine communications through artificial intelligence with a friendly user interface.

A feature of the digital divide in Industry 5.0 is that, for the first time, social communication barriers have emerged not for individual social groups but for people as a general social group. This transforms the nature of social mobility, which, in the Industry 5.0 conditions, aims not to create social elevators in society but to erase the boundaries between people and smart machines, make man-machine society open to all participants and ensure their effective, barrier-free, and sustainable communication – to form inclusive cyber-social systems.

In this context, higher education is given a new role in supporting social mobility: machine learning, on the one hand, and teaching people digital competencies, on the other. This actualizes a new scientific and practical problem related to the aggravation of social inequalities in Industry 4.0. This problem is just emerging but will become increasingly acute with each new stage of the Fifth Industrial Revolution. In this regard, it is recommended that further scholarly work in the sequel to this book pay attention to elaborating on the new role of higher education in social mobility.

Index

Cultural Differences   191, 192, 193, 194, 195, 198, 201

Digital Technology   4, 34, 147, 361
Distance Learning   13, 250, 251, 253, 254, 255, 256, 271, 277, 359, 360, 361, 362, 363, 364, 365, 366, 367, 368, 369, 370, 371, 372, 373, 374, 387

Efficiency (University Efficiency)   282, 305, 308, 309, 311, 313, 314, 315, 336
e-learning   183, 184, 185, 248, 249, 250, 254, 257, 296, 362, 365, 368

Global Competitiveness   194, 198, 200, 201, 305, 308, 309, 312, 314, 315

Higher Education   1, 2, 3, 4, 7, 8, 9, 10, 11, 12, 13, 15, 16, 32, 46, 47, 48, 49, 50, 53, 55, 56, 57, 58, 59, 62, 63, 64, 65, 71, 87, 89, 91, 93, 100, 107, 108, 110, 114, 115, 120, 121, 122, 123, 124, 125, 127, 128, 131, 132, 133, 134, 135, 136, 137, 138, 139, 140, 144, 145, 146, 147, 148, 150, 153, 154, 155, 156, 157, 158, 159, 160, 161, 162, 163, 164, 165, 169, 171, 172, 176, 177, 181, 183, 184, 185, 186, 187, 188, 191, 192, 193, 194, 196, 197, 202, 205, 206, 207, 208, 211, 212, 214, 215, 218, 219, 220, 221, 222, 223, 224, 225, 226, 227, 228, 229, 240, 249, 250, 251, 263, 266, 269, 271, 277, 286, 290, 305, 306, 307, 308, 312, 314, 323, 324, 325, 327, 329, 330, 331, 336, 338, 346, 349, 351, 359, 360, 367, 368, 374, 387, 388

Inclusive Universities   12, 13, 46, 58, 115
Innovative   286, 319, 324, 326, 378, 379, 380, 382
International Education   13, 14, 15, 70, 192, 261

Knowledge Economy   4, 75, 76, 77, 78, 82, 84, 120, 121

Lifelong Education   378, 379, 380

Openness   2, 3, 4, 7, 8, 13, 215, 308

Pandemic   237, 239, 241, 243, 244, 249, 251, 253, 257, 266, 267, 269, 270, 359, 360, 364, 365, 367, 370, 372, 373, 374
Persons with Disabilities   169, 170, 171, 172, 173, 174, 175, 176, 181, 183, 186, 218, 219
Professional Training   342, 350, 380

Quality (Education Quality)   259, 260, 261, 263, 271, 274, 337, 340, 342, 343, 344, 345, 346, 349, 350, 352, 356, 366, 371, 378, 381

Regional Universities   114, 205, 206, 207, 208, 209, 210, 211, 212, 213, 214

Social Development   21, 85, 87, 227, 258, 259, 260
Social Inequality   1, 3, 4, 273, 387
Social Mobility   1, 2, 3, 4, 387, 388
Sustainable Development   64, 82, 192, 238, 281, 283, 284, 286, 287, 288, 289, 290, 306

University Management   13, 64, 65, 71, 72, 109, 169, 177, 305, 307, 313, 315
University Rankings   176, 183, 184, 191, 192, 193, 194, 195, 201, 206, 305, 307, 308, 314
University   8, 9, 11, 15, 21, 24, 27, 28, 32, 35, 36, 43, 47, 48, 49, 51, 52, 63, 64, 65, 66, 67, 69, 71, 72, 94, 95, 99, 108, 109, 110, 111, 112, 113, 114, 115, 122, 124, 145, 146, 148, 149, 157, 162, 164, 165, 169, 170, 171, 172, 173, 174, 175, 176, 183, 184, 185, 186, 187, 191, 192, 193, 194, 195, 196, 197, 200, 201, 206, 207, 208, 210, 212, 213, 238, 239, 249, 250, 251, 256, 260, 263, 266, 277, 281, 282, 286, 288, 290, 305, 307, 308, 310, 311, 313, 314, 315, 323, 324, 326, 329, 330, 331, 332, 334, 336, 337, 338, 339, 340, 341, 343, 344, 345, 346, 349, 350, 351, 352, 353, 356, 366, 367, 368, 369, 370, 372, 373, 374, 378, 379, 380, 381, 382, 383

Milton Keynes UK
Ingram Content Group UK Ltd.
UKHW010148110624
444001UK00013B/46